Annual Editions: State and
Local Government, 16/e

by Bruce Stinebrickner

http://create.mcgraw-hill.com

ISBN-10: 1259175448   ISBN-13: 9781259175442

Contents

Preface

T his book is the sixteenth edition of a reader on state and local government. Beginning with the first edition in 1984, the book has been designed for use in courses on state and local government and in state and local government segments of courses on American government. The educational goal is to provide a collection of up-to-date articles that are informative and interesting to students who are learning about subnational governments in the United States.

The 50 state governments and more than 80,000 local governments in the United States have a great deal in common. They also exhibit remarkable diversity. Inevitably, the contents of the book reflect both this commonality and diversity. Some selections treat individual states or localities in considerable detail. Other articles focus on particular dimensions of more than one state or local government. Still other articles explicitly compare and contrast regions, states, or localities. Taken together, the selections provide an overview of similarities and differences among state and local governments in the United States.

When Newt Gingrich became Speaker of the House of Representatives in 1995, he and his fellow Republican members of Congress said that they would shift significant government responsibilities from the national government in Washington to the 50 states. Two prominent bills signed into law by President Clinton, one restricting unfunded mandates and the other reforming the welfare system, were aimed at making the states more important and autonomous actors in the American federal system. Taking their turn in this process of devolution, some state governments shifted selected responsibilities to their local governments.

The events of September 11, 2001, partly reversed these trends, as national, state, and local responsibilities for public safety and what came to be known as "homeland security" were reconsidered and modified. The Great Recession of 2007–2009 introduced a new chapter in national-state-local relations. Soon after President Obama assumed office in January 2009, the national government enacted an unprecedentedly large economic stimulus law that channeled billions of dollars to state and local governments. Even though they were reeling from the Great Recession, subnational governments were typically not allowed to engage in the sort of deficit spending that has consistently characterized national government financing for more than the past half-century. In turn, the stimulus funds saved many state and local governments from wholesale lay-offs of teachers, police officers, firefighters, and the like. While state and local governments certainly had to tighten their belts, the stimulus money enabled them to avoid even more draconian measures to balance their budgets. When the two-year duration of most stimulus funding drew to a close in 2011, there were concerns about whether the sluggish recovery would produce enough revenues for state and local governments to prevent further layoffs and reductions in services. Since that time, state and local governments have continued to struggle as the sluggish economic recovery has continued.

In the fall of 2013, Americans' attention was inevitably drawn to the 16-day shutdown of the national government and the probably even more serious national debt ceiling crisis. Accompanying those fiscal dramas was the scheduled October 1 opening of the national government's Affordable Care Act's website, whose high-profile malfunctioning quickly led to widespread consternation and controversy. Obamacare (the commonly used term for the Affordable Care Act of 2010) mandated a wide-ranging set of changes to health insurance and health-care delivery in the United States. Not surprisingly, state governments, especially governors and state health commissioners, had important decisions to make in connection with those changes. As this book goes to press in November 2013, President Obama and his administration continue to struggle with "fixes" to various Obamacare problems (including, but not only, the website), and state health commissioners and governors, among others, continue to be importantly involved.

Every selection in this book can be read in the context of the overall mosaic of national, state, and local governments in the United States. Indeed, the American political system seems to be characterized by continuing—probably never-ending—attempts to achieve an appropriate division of powers and responsibilities among national, state, and local governments.

The book is divided into seven units. Unit 1 is devoted to eighteenth- and nineteenth-century historic commentaries on American federalism and state and local governments. Unit 2 addresses relations among national, state, and local governments and provides a mixed assessment of recent shifts in power and responsibilities. Unit 3 covers elections, political parties, interest groups, referenda, news media, and related matters and pays special attention to unusual features of state and local "linkages." Unit 4 turns to government institutions. Local politics and policy issues—in metropolitan areas, cities, and suburbs, as well as in counties and small towns—provide the subject matter for Unit 5, while Unit 6 is devoted to revenues, expenditures, and economic development. Unit 7 concludes the book with an examination of selected policy opportunities and challenges facing state and local governments.

The book generally groups articles that treat particular aspects of state and local governments in the same units and sections. For example, Unit 4 covers government institutions at both the state and local levels, with individual sections devoted to state *and* local legislatures, executives, and courts, respectively. Unit 5, which addresses governance in localities and metropolitan areas, is an exception to this general rule in that it focuses on issues involving local governments and mostly ignores state governments.

Deciding what articles to include when preparing this edition of *Annual Editions: State and Local Government* was not easy. I assessed articles according to significance and relevance of the subject matter, readability for students, and usefulness for stimulating students' interest in state and local government. Potential selections were evaluated not only as they stood alone, but also as complements to other likely selections.

As always, I solicit responses to this edition as well as suggestions of articles for use in the next edition.

Editor

Bruce Stinebrickner is Professor of Political Science at DePauw University in Greencastle, Indiana, and has taught American politics at DePauw since 1987. He has also taught at Lehman College of the City University of New York (1974–1976), at the University of Queensland in Brisbane, Australia (1976–1987), and in DePauw programs in Argentina (1990) and Germany (1993). He served fourteen years as chair of his department at DePauw after heading his department at the University of Queensland for two years. He earned his BA *magna cum laude* from Georgetown University in 1968, his MPhil from Yale University in 1972, and his PhD from Yale in 1974.

Professor Stinebrickner is the co-author (with Robert A. Dahl) of *Modern Political Analysis,* sixth edition (Prentice Hall, 2003) and has published articles on the American presidential selection process, American local governments, the career patterns of Australian politicians, and freedom of the press. He has served as editor of the fifteen earlier editions of this book as well as thirty-seven editions of its American Government counterpart in the McGraw-Hill Annual Editions series. His current research interests focus on government policies involving children (e.g., schooling, child custody, and foster care). In both his teaching and his writing, Professor Stinebrickner applies insights on politics gained from living, teaching, and lecturing abroad. He served four years (2008–2012) on the Greencastle, Indiana, school board and on the City of Greencastle's Redevelopment Commission, both of which provided him with firsthand experience in the workings of state and local governments.

Academic Advisory Board

Members of the Academic Advisory Board are instrumental in the final selection of articles for each edition of ANNUAL EDITIONS. Their review of articles for content, level, and appropriateness provides critical direction to the editors and staff. We think that you will find their careful consideration well reflected in this volume.

Correlation Guide

The *Annual Editions* series provides students with convenient, inexpensive access to current, carefully selected articles from the public press. **Annual Editions: State and Local Government, 16/e** is an easy-to-use reader that presents articles on important topics such as *economic development, federalism, policymaking,* and many more. For more information on *Annual Editions* and other *McGraw-Hill Create™* titles, visit www.mcgrawhillcreate.com.

This convenient guide matches the articles in **Annual Editions: State and Local Government, 16/e** with **State and Local Government, 9/e** by Saffell/Basehart.

State and Local Government, 9/e by Saffell/Basehart	Annual Editions: State and Local Government, 16/e
Chapter 1: The Setting of State and Local Government	The American System of Townships . . . Federalist No. 17 (Hamilton) Federalist No. 45 (Madison) Local Government: Observations Nature of the American State
Chapter 2: Intergovernmental Relations	Devolution and Arrogance Merger Inertia States *vs.* Feds Taking Stock The Untied States of America
Chapter 3: Political Parties and Interest Groups	Altered States Caperton's Coal: The Battle over an Appalachian Mine Exposes a Nasty Vein in Bench Politics The Last Democrat in Dixie License to Kill States of Conservatism
Chapter 4: Political Participation and Elections	5 Trends Shaping Redistricting Portland Fluoride: For the Fourth Time since 1956, Portland Voters Reject Fluoridation The Progressive Tax Rebellion States of Conservatism Voting Matters
Chapter 5: State and Local Legislatures	267 Years and Counting: The Town Hall Meeting Is Alive and Well in Pelham, Mass Are City Councils a Relic of the Past? The Legislature as Sausage Factory: It's about Time We Examine This Metaphor Legislatures: All Over the Map Should School Boards Be Expelled?
Chapter 6: Governors, Bureaucrats, and Mayors	Altered States The Badgered State: Wisconsin Governor Scott Walker Is the Left's Public Enemy No. 1 The Last Democrat in Dixie The Life of the Mayor-for-Life The Millennials in the Mayor's Seat
Chapter 7: Courts, Police, and Corrections	The Conservative War on Prisons Cross Examination Justice by Numbers Under the Gaydar
Chapter 8: Suburbs, Metropolitan Areas, and Rural Communities	267 Years and Counting: The Town Hall Meeting Is Alive and Well in Pelham, Mass The Life of the Mayor-for-Life Merger Inertia Rebel Towns The Sentient City
Chapter 9: Financing State and Local Government	The 'B' Word The (New) Rules of the Road The Secret Tax Explosion Snookered Two Cheers for the Property Tax

State and Local Government, 9/e by Saffell/Basehart	Annual Editions: State and Local Government, 16/e
Chapter 10: State and Local Policy Making: Conflict and Accommodation	Fixing the Rotten Corporate Barrel Gagging on the Ag-Gag Laws License to Kill One Size Doesn't Fit All Raising Children: It Takes State and Local Governments, Too

Topic Guide

This topic guide suggests how the selections in this book relate to the subjects covered in your course.

All the articles that relate to each topic are listed below the bold-faced term.

Attorneys general

The Last Democrat in Dixie

Child custody

Raising Children: It Takes State and Local Governments, Too
Under the Gaydar

Cities

Are City Councils a Relic of the Past?
The 'B' Word
Devolution and Arrogance
The Enticement Window
The Life of the Mayor-for-Life
Merger Inertia
The Millennials in the Mayor's Seat
Portland Fluoride: For the Fourth Time since 1956, Portland Voters
   Reject Fluoridation
Public Meetings and the Democratic Process
The Sentient City
Taking Stock

Corporations and state and local governments

Caperton's Coal: The Battle over an Appalachian Mine Exposes a
   Nasty Vein in Bench Politics
Counter Cultures
Fixing the Rotten Corporate Barrel
Gagging on the Ag-Gag laws
The (New) Rules of the Road
Rebel Towns
Snookered

Counties

Cross Examination
Local Government: Observations

Courts

Caperton's Coal: The Battle over an Appalachian Mine Exposes a
   Nasty Vein in Bench Politics
Justice by Numbers
Under the Gaydar

Criminal justice system

The Conservative War on Prisons
Cross Examination
Justice by Numbers
License to Kill
Raising Children: It Takes State and Local Governments, Too

Devolution

Devolution and Arrogance

Economic development

The Enticement Window
The (New) Rules of the Road
Snookered

Education

One Size Doesn't Fit All
Raising Children: It Takes State and Local Governments, Too
Should School Boards Be Expelled?

Elections and electoral systems

5 Trends Shaping Redistricting
Caperton's Coal: The Battle over an Appalachian Mine Exposes a
   Nasty Vein in Bench Politics
The No-Tax Pledge
States of Conservatism
Voting Matters

Federalism

Altered States
Devolution and Arrogance
Federalist No. 17 (Hamilton)
Federalist No. 45 (Madison)
Nature of the American State
States *vs.* Feds
The Untied States of America

Governors

Altered States
The Badgered State: Wisconsin Governor Scott Walker Is the Left's
   Public Enemy No. 1

Interest groups

Caperton's Coal: The Battle over an Appalachian Mine Exposes a
   Nasty Vein in Bench Politics
Gagging on the Ag-Gag Laws
License to Kill
Portland Fluoride: For the Fourth Time since 1956, Portland Voters
   Reject Fluoridation

Internet and technology

Ready, Set, PAN
The Sentient City

Legislatures, state

5 Trends Shaping Redistricting
Fixing the Rotten Corporate Barrel
The Legislature as Sausage Factory: It's about Time We Examine This
   Metaphor
Legislatures: All Over the Map
License to Kill
Newbies
Voting Matters
What Legislatures Need Now

Mayors

The Life of the Mayor-for-Life
The Millennials in the Mayor's Seat

Millennials

The Enticement Window
The Millennials in the Mayor's Seat

News media

Cross Examination
Embracing the Future
Ready, Set, PAN

Political Parties

Altered States
The Last Democrat in Dixie
States of Conservatism

Unit 1

UNIT

Prepared by: Bruce Stinebrickner, *DePauw University*

Early Commentaries

The American political system includes three levels of government—national, state, and local. Although not unique among nations today, this arrangement was unusual in the late eighteenth century when the United States won its independence from England. Early commentaries on the American political system paid considerable attention to each of these levels of government, as well as to interactions among the three levels. Such writings suggest the important roles that state and local governments have always played in the United States.

Debate about the desirability of the proposed new Constitution of 1787—the Constitution that remains in force to this day—often focused on the relationship between the national government and the states. Some people thought that the states were going to be too strong in the proposed new union, and others worried that the national government would have too much power. Three prominent supporters of the new Constitution—Alexander Hamilton, James Madison, and John Jay—wrote a series of articles in 1787–1788 explaining and defending it. Many of these articles, which came to be known as *The Federalist Papers*, discussed the federal relationship between the national government and the states. So did many of the writings of other early and perceptive observers, including what came to be called the *Anti-Federalist Papers*, which were authored by adversaries of the proposed Constitution who opposed the new national government that would co-exist with the states. All these commentaries reflect the importance that was attached to the new federal relationship and the states right from the start.

State and local governments were also the subject of considerable attention in early commentaries, especially by distinguished and perceptive European observers of the American political system. Alexis de Tocqueville, a French nobleman visiting the United States early in the nineteenth century, recorded his observations in a book entitled *Democracy in America* (1835). Tocqueville remarked on the extraordinary vitality of American local government institutions, comparing what he saw in the United States with European institutions at that time. Today American local government still plays a prominent role in the country's overall governing process, probably more so than in any other nation in the world.

Later in the nineteenth century, an Englishman, James Bryce, published another influential commentary on the United States, *The American Commonwealth* (1888). Bryce discussed American federalism and American state and local governments. He described and explained differences among local government structures in three different regions of the country, the considerable similarities among the states that existed at the time of his visit, and what he saw as the lamentable performance of city governments. Like Tocqueville, Bryce was able to identify and analyze distinctive elements of the American system of government and make a lasting contribution to the study of the American political system.

Early commentaries on American federalism and state and local governments such as those mentioned here can enrich our understanding of the contemporary political system in several respects. They can provide a baseline from which to understand the way(s) in which federalism and American subnational governments have changed over time and standards with which to assess the contemporary functioning of American federalism as well as of state and local governments.

Article

Prepared by: Bruce Stinebrickner, *DePauw University*

Federalist No. 17 (Hamilton)

Learning Outcomes

After reading this article, you will be able to:

- Evaluate Alexander Hamilton's contention, in light of more than 200 years of history, that "it will always be far more easy for the State governments to encroach upon the national authorities" than for the opposite to occur.

- Assess Hamilton's contention, again in light of more than 200 years of experience, that Americans will feel (and do feel) greater affection ("bias") toward their state governments than to the national government.

To the People of the State of New York:

An objection, of a nature different from that which has been stated and answered, in my last address, may perhaps be likewise urged against the principle of legislation for the individual citizens of America. It may be said that it would tend to render the government of the Union too powerful, and to enable it to absorb those residuary authorities, which it might be judged proper to leave with the States for local purposes. Allowing the utmost latitude to the love of power which any reasonable man can require, I confess I am at a loss to discover what temptation the persons intrusted with the administration of the general government could ever feel to divest the States of the authorities of that description. The regulation of the mere domestic police of a State appears to me to hold out slender allurements to ambition. Commerce, finance, negotiation, and war seem to comprehend all the objects which have charms for minds governed by that passion; and all the powers necessary to those objects ought, in the first instance, to be lodged in the national depository. The administration of private justice between the citizens of the same State, the supervision of agriculture and of other concerns of a similar nature, all those things, in short, which are proper to be provided for by local legislation, can never be desirable cares of a general jurisdiction. It is therefore improbable that there should exist a disposition in the federal councils to usurp the powers with which they are connected; because the attempt to exercise those powers would be as troublesome as it would be nugatory; and the possession of them, for that reason, would contribute nothing to the dignity, to the importance, or to the splendor of the national government.

But let it be admitted, for argument's sake, that mere wantonness and lust of domination would be sufficient to beget that disposition; still it may be safely affirmed, that the sense of the constituent body of the national representatives, or, in other words, the people of the several States, would control the indulgence of so extravagant an appetite. It will always be far more easy for the State governments to encroach upon the national authorities, than for the national government to encroach upon the State authorities. The proof of this proposition turns upon the greater degree of influence which the State governments, if they administer their affairs with uprightness and prudence, will generally possess over the people; a circumstance which at the same time teaches us that there is an inherent and intrinsic weakness in all federal constitutions; and that too much pains cannot be taken in their organization, to give them all the force which is compatible with the principles of liberty.

The superiority of influence in favor of the particular governments would result partly from the diffusive construction of the national government, but chiefly from the nature of the objects to which the attention of the State administrations would be directed.

It is a known fact in human nature, that its affections are commonly weak in proportion to the distance or diffusiveness of the object. Upon the same principle that a man is more attached to his family than to his neighborhood, to his neighborhood than to the community at large, the people of each State would be apt to feel a stronger bias towards their local governments than towards the government of the Union; unless the force of that principle should be destroyed by a much better administration of the latter.

This strong propensity of the human heart would find powerful auxiliaries in the objects of State regulation.

The variety of more minute interests, which will necessarily fall under the superintendence of the local administrations, and which will form so many rivulets of influence, running through every part of the society, cannot be particularized, without involving a detail too tedious and uninteresting to compensate for the instruction it might afford.

There is one transcendent advantage belonging to the province of the State governments, which alone suffices to place the matter in a clear and satisfactory light,—I mean the ordinary administration of criminal and civil justice. This, of all others, is the most powerful, most universal, and most attractive source of popular obedience and attachment. It is that which, being the immediate and visible guardian of life and property, having its benefits and its terrors in constant activity before the public eye, regulating all those personal interests and familiar concerns in which the sensibility of individuals is more immediately awake, contributes, more than any other circumstance, to impressing upon the minds of the people, affection, esteem, and reverence towards the government. This great cement of society, which will diffuse itself almost wholly through the channels of the particular governments, independent of all other causes of influence, would insure them so decided an empire over their respective citizens as to render them at all times a complete counterpoise, and, not unfrequently, dangerous rivals to the power of the Union.

The operations of the national government, on the other hand, falling less immediately under the observation of the mass of the citizens, the benefits derived from it will chiefly be perceived and attended to by speculative men. Relating to more general interests, they will be less apt to come home to the feelings of the people; and, in proportion, less likely to inspire an habitual sense of obligation, and an active sentiment of attachment.

The reasoning on this head has been abundantly exemplified by the experience of all federal constitutions with which we are acquainted, and of all others which have borne the least analogy to them.

Though the ancient feudal systems were not, strictly speaking, confederacies, yet they partook of the nature of that species of association. There was a common head, chieftain, or sovereign, whose authority extended over the whole nation; and a number of subordinate vassals, or feudatories, who had large portions of land allotted to them, and numerous trains of inferior vassals or retainers, who occupied and cultivated that land upon the tenure of fealty or obedience to the persons of whom they held it. Each principal vassal was a kind of sovereign within his particular demesnes. The consequences of this situation were a continual opposition to authority of the sovereign, and frequent wars between the great barons or chief feudatories themselves. The power of the head of the nation was commonly too weak, either to preserve the public peace, or to protect the people against the oppressions of their immediate lords. This period of European affairs is emphatically styled by historians, the times of feudal anarchy.

When the sovereign happened to be a man of vigorous and warlike temper and of superior abilities, he would acquire a personal weight and influence, which answered, for the time, the purposes of a more regular authority. But in general, the power of the barons triumphed over that of the prince; and in many instances his dominion was entirely thrown off, and the great fiefs were erected into independent principalities of States. In those instances in which the monarch finally prevailed over his vassals, his success was chiefly owing to the tyranny of those vassals over their dependents. The barons, or nobles, equally the enemies of the sovereign and the oppressors of the common people, were dreaded and detested by both; till mutual danger and mutual interest effected a union between them fatal to the power of the aristocracy. Had the nobles, by a conduct of clemency and justice, preserved the fidelity and devotion of their retainers and followers, the contests between them and the prince must almost always have ended in their favor, and in the abridgment or subversion of the royal authority.

This is not an assertion founded merely in speculation or conjecture. Among other illustrations of its truth which might be cited, Scotland will furnish a cogent example. The spirit of clanship which was, at an early day, introduced into that

kingdom, uniting the nobles and their dependents by ties equivalent to those of kindred, rendered the aristocracy a constant overmatch for the power of the monarch, till the incorporation with England subdued its fierce and ungovernable spirit, and reduced it within those rules of subordination which a more rational and more energetic system of civil polity had previously established in the latter kingdom.

The separate governments in a confederacy may aptly be compared with the feudal baronies; with this advantage in their favor, that from the reasons already explained, they will generally possess the confidence and good-will of the people, and with so important a support, will be able effectually to oppose all encroachments of the national government. It will be well if they are not able to counteract its legitimate and necessary authority. The points of similitude consist in the rivalship of power, applicable to both, and in the concentration of large portions of the strength of the community into particular deposits, in one case at the disposal of individuals, in the other case at the disposal of political bodies.

A concise review of the events that have attended confederate governments will further illustrate this important doctrine; an inattention to which has been the great source of our political mistakes, and has given our jealousy a direction to the wrong side. This review shall form the subject of some ensuing papers.

PUBLIUS

Critical Thinking

1. What powers of state governments does Hamilton think will be fundamentally unattractive to those running the new national government, even if they do have a "love of power"?

2. Why will it always be far easier for state governments to "encroach" upon the national government than vice versa?

3. What is the one "transcendent advantage" that state governments have in any rivalry with national government authorities?

4. Are state or national governments more likely to inspire citizens' feelings of loyalty, sense of obligation, and the like? Why?

5. Given concerns that the new national government in the United States will become too powerful, what has experience in other countries with powers divided between a central authority and other smaller units shown?

Create Central

www.mhhe.com/createcentral

Internet References

The Federalist Papers.org
www.thefederalistpapers.org

PBS: The American Experience—Alexander Hamilton
www.pbs.org/wgbh/amex/hamilton

Teaching American History.org: Introduction to the Antifederalists
http://teachingamericanhistory.org/fed-antifed/antifederalis

From *The Federalist Papers*, 1787.

Article   Prepared by: Bruce Stinebrickner, *DePauw University*

Federalist No. 45 (Madison) (How we are getting along)

Learning Outcomes

After reading this article, you will be able to:

- Determine the accuracy of Madison's predictions about whether the new federal government would be "dangerous" to the continuing power and authority of the states.

- Note and assess Madison's predictions about the relative number of employees of the new federal government and of the state government.

- Evaluate Madison's contention that the Constitution mostly "invigorates" original powers of the national government and gives only one new power to the national government.

To the People of the State of New York:

Having shown that no one of the powers transferred to the federal government is unnecessary or improper, the next question to be considered is, whether the whole mass of them will be dangerous to the portion of authority left in the several States.

The adversaries to the plan of the convention, instead of considering in the first place what degree of power was absolutely necessary for the purposes of the federal government, have exhausted themselves in a secondary inquiry into the possible consequences of the proposed degree of power to the governments of the particular States. But if the Union, as has been shown, be essential to the security of the people of America against foreign danger; if it be essential to their security against contentions and wars among the different States; if it be essential to guard them against those violent and oppressive factions which embitter the blessings of liberty, and against those military establishments which must gradually poison its very fountain; if, in a word, the Union be essential to the happiness of the people of America, is it not preposterous, to urge as an objection to a government, without which the objects of the Union cannot be attained, that such a government may derogate from the importance of the governments of the individual States? Was, then, the American Revolution effected, was the American Confederacy formed, was the precious blood of thousands spilt, and the hard-earned substance of millions lavished, not that the people of America should enjoy peace, liberty, and safety, but that the government of the individual States, that particular municipal establishments, might enjoy a certain extent of power, and be arrayed with certain dignities and attributes of sovereignty? We have heard of the impious doctrine in the Old World, that the people were made for kings, not kings for the people. Is the same doctrine to be revived in the New, in another shape—that the solid happiness of the people is to be sacrificed to the views of political institutions of a different form? It is too early for politicians to presume on our forgetting that the public good, the real welfare of the great body of the people, is the supreme object to be pursued; and that no form of government whatever has any other value than as it may be fitted for the attainment of this object. Were the plan of the convention adverse to the public happiness, my voice would be, Reject the plan. Were the Union itself inconsistent with the public happiness, it would be, Abolish the Union. In like manner, as far as the sovereignty of the States cannot be reconciled to the happiness of the people, the voice of every good citizen must be, Let the former be sacrificed to the latter. How far the sacrifice is necessary, has been shown. How far the unsacrificed residue will be endangered, is the question before us.

Several important considerations have been touched in the course of these papers, which discountenance the supposition that the operation of the federal government will by degrees prove fatal to the State governments. The more I revolve the subject, the more fully I am persuaded that the balance is much more likely to be disturbed by the preponderancy of the last than of the first scale.

We have seen, in all the examples of ancient and modern confederacies, the strongest tendency continually betraying itself in the members, to despoil the general government of its authorities, with a very ineffectual capacity in the latter to defend itself against the encroachments. Although, in most of these examples, the system has been so dissimilar from that under consideration as greatly to weaken any inference concerning the latter from the fate of the former, yet, as the States will retain, under the proposed Constitution, a very extensive portion of active sovereignty, the inference ought not to be wholly disregarded. In the Achæan league it is probable that the federal head had a degree and species of power, which gave it a considerable likeness to the government framed by the convention. The Lycian Confederacy, as far as its principles and form and transmitted, must have borne a still greater analogy to it. Yet history does not inform us that either of them ever degenerated, or tended to degenerate, into one consolidated government. On the contrary, we know that the ruin of one of them proceeded from the incapacity of the federal authority to prevent the dissensions, and finally the disunion, of the subordinate authorities. These cases are the more worthy of our attention, as the external causes by which the component parts were pressed together were much more numerous and powerful than in our case; and consequently less powerful ligaments within would be sufficient to bind the members to the head, and to each other.

In the feudal system, we have seen a similar propensity exemplified. Notwithstanding the want of proper sympathy in every instance between the local sovereigns and the people, and the sympathy in some instances between the general sovereign and the latter, it usually happened that the local sovereigns prevailed in the rivalship for encroachments. Had no external dangers enforced internal harmony and subordination, and particularly, had the local sovereigns possessed the affections of the people, the great kingdoms in Europe would at this time consist of as many independent princes as there were formerly feudatory barons.

The State governments will have the advantage of the Federal government, whether we compare them in respect to the immediate dependence of the one on the other; to the weight of personal influence which each side will possess; to the powers respectively vested in them; to the predilection and probable support of the people; to the disposition and faculty of resisting and frustrating the measures of each other.

The State governments may be regarded as constituent and essential parts of the federal government; whilst the latter is nowise essential to the operation or organization of the former. Without the intervention of the State legislatures, the President of the United States cannot be elected at all. They must in all cases have a great share in his appointment, and will, perhaps, in most cases, of themselves determine it. The Senate will be elected absolutely and exclusively by the State legislatures. Even the House of Representatives, though drawn immediately from the people, will be chosen very much under the influence of that class of men, whose influence over the people obtains for themselves an election into the State legislatures. Thus, each of the principal branches of the federal government will owe its existence more or less to the favor of the State governments, and must consequently feel a dependence, which is much more likely to beget a disposition too obsequious than too overbearing towards them. On the other side, the component parts of the State governments will in no instance be indebted for their appointment to the direct agency of the federal government, and very little, if at all, to the local influence of its members.

The number of individuals employed under the Constitution of the United States will be much smaller than the number employed under the particular States. There will consequently be less of personal influence on the side of the former than of the latter. The members of the legislative, executive, and judiciary departments of thirteen and more States, the justices of peace, officers of militia, ministerial officers of justice, with all the country, corporation, and town officers, for three millions and more of people, intermixed, and having particular acquaintance with every class and circle of people, must exceed, beyond all proportion, both in number and influence, those of every description who will be employed in the administration of the federal system. Compare the members of the three great departments of the thirteen States, excluding from the judiciary department the justices of peace, with the members of the corresponding departments of the single government of the Union; compare the militia officers of three millions of people with the military and marine officers of any establishment which is within the compass of probability, or, I may add, of possibility, and in this view alone, we may pronounce the advantage of the States to be decisive. If the federal government is to have collectors of revenue, the State governments will have theirs also. And as those of the former will be principally on the sea-coast, and not very numerous, whilst those of the latter will be spread over the face of the country, and will be very numerous, the advantage in this view also lies on the same side. It is true, that the Confederacy is to possess, and may exercise, the power of collecting internal as well as external taxes throughout the States; but it is probable that this power will not be resorted to, except for supplemental purposes of revenue; that an option will then be given to the States to supply their quotas by previous collections of their own; and that the eventual collection, under the immediate authority of the Union, will generally be made by the officers, and according to the rules, appointed by the several States. Indeed it is extremely probable, that in other instances, particularly in the organization of the judicial power, the officers of the States will be clothed with the correspondent authority of the Union. Should it happen, however, that separate collectors of internal revenue should be appointed under the federal government, the influence of the whole number would not bear a comparison with that of the multitude of State officers in the opposite scale. Within every district to which a federal collector would be allotted, there would not be less than thirty or forty, or even more, officers of different descriptions, and many of them persons of character and weight, whose influence would lie on the side of the State.

The powers delegated by the proposed Constitution to the federal government are few and defined. Those which are to remain in the State governments are numerous and indefinite. The former will be exercised principally on external objects, as war, peace, negotiation, and foreign commerce; with which last the power of taxation will, for the most part, be connected. The powers reserved to the several States will extend to all the objects which, in the ordinary course of affairs, concern the lives, liberties, and properties of the people, and the internal order, improvement, and prosperity of the State.

The operations of the federal government will be most extensive and important in times of war and danger; those of the State governments in times of peace and security. As the former periods will probably bear a small proportion to the latter, the State governments will here enjoy another advantage over the federal government. The more adequate, indeed, the federal powers may be rendered to the national defence, the less frequent will be those scenes of danger which might favor their ascendancy over the governments of the particular States.

If the new Constitution be examined with accuracy and candor, it will be found that the change which it proposes consists much less in the addition of new powers to the Union, than in the invigoration of its original powers. The regulation of commerce, it is true, is a new power; but that seems to be an addition which few oppose, and from which no apprehensions are entertained. The powers relating to war and peace, armies and fleets, treaties and finance, with the other more considerable powers, are all vested in the existing Congress by the articles of Confederation. The proposed change does not enlarge these powers; it only substitutes a more effectual mode of administering them. The change relating to taxation may be regarded as the most important; and yet the present Congress have as complete authority to require of the States indefinite supplies of money for the common defense and general welfare, as the future Congress will have to require them of individual citizens; and the latter will be no more bound than the States themselves have been, to pay the quotas respectively taxed on them. Had the States complied punctually with the articles of Confederation, or could their compliance have been enforced by as peaceable means as may be used with success towards single persons, our past experience is very far from countenancing an opinion, that the State governments would have lost their constitutional powers, and have gradually undergone an entire consolidation. To maintain that such an event would have ensued, would be to say at once, that the existence of the State governments is incompatible with any system whatever that accomplishes the essential purposes of the Union.

PUBLIUS

Critical Thinking

1. According to Madison, what has experience in all past and present confederacies shown about whether the central government or the smaller units have prevailed in rivalries between them?
2. In what ways will the new central (national or federal) government be dependent on state governments?
3. Which level of government, national or state, will have more employees?
4. Which level of government, national or state, will have "few and defined" powers, and which will have "numerous and indefinite" ones?
5. What new or "invigorated" powers will the new Constitution give to the new national government?

Create Central

www.mhhe.com/createcentral

Internet References

The Federalist Papers.org
www.thefederalistpapers.org
James Madison's Montpelier
www.montpelier.org
Teaching American History.org: Introduction to the Antifederalists
http://teachingamericanhistory.org/fed-antifed/antifederalist

From *The Federalist No.* 45, 1788.

Article   Prepared by: Bruce Stinebrickner, *DePauw University*

Nature of the American State

JAMES BRYCE

Learning Outcomes

After reading this article, you will be able to:

- Assess Bryce's contention that the American states are more similar than one might reasonably expect.

- Evaluate the only three limitations, according to Bryce, on the rights and powers of a state.

- Weigh the validity of Bryce's assertion that the national government "touches the direct interests of the citizen less" than state governments do, but "touches his sentiment more."

As the dissimilarity of population and of external conditions seems to make for a diversity of constitutional and political arrangements between the States, so also does the large measure of legal independence which each of them enjoys under the Federal Constitution. No State can, as a commonwealth, politically deal with or act upon any other State. No diplomatic relations can exist nor treaties be made between States, no coercion can be exercised by one upon another. And although the government of the Union can act on a State, it rarely does act, and then only in certain strictly limited directions, which do not touch the inner political life of the commonwealth.

Let us pass on to consider the circumstances which work for uniformity among the States, and work more powerfully as time goes on.

He who looks at a map of the Union will be struck by the fact that so many of the boundary lines of the States are straight lines. Those lines tell the same tale as the geometrical plans of cities like St. Petersburg or Washington, where every street runs at the same angle to every other. The States are not natural growths. Their boundaries are for the most part not natural boundaries fixed by mountain ranges, nor even historical boundaries due to a series of events, but purely artificial boundaries, determined by an authority which carved the national territory into strips of convenient size, as a building company lays out its suburban lots. Of the States subsequent to the original thirteen, California is the only one with a genuine natural boundary, finding it in the chain of the Sierra Nevada on the east and the Pacific ocean on the west. No one of these later

States can be regarded as a naturally developed political organism. They are trees planted by the forester, not self-sown with the help of the seed-scattering wind. This absence of physical lines of demarcation has tended and must tend to prevent the growth of local distinctions. Nature herself seems to have designed the Mississippi basin, as she has designed the unbroken levels of Russia, to be the dwelling-place of one people.

Each State makes its own Constitution; that is, the people agree on their form of government for themselves, with no interference from the other States or from the Union. This form is subject to one condition only: it must be republican.[1] But in each State the people who make the constitution have lately come from other States, where they have lived and worked under constitutions which are to their eyes the natural and almost necessary model for their new State to follow; and in the absence of an inventive spirit among the citizens, it was the obvious course for the newer States to copy the organizations of the older States, especially as these agreed with certain familiar features of the Federal Constitution. Hence the outlines, and even the phrases of the elder constitutions reappear in those of the more recently formed States. The precedents set by Virginia, for instance, had much influence on Tennessee, Alabama, Mississippi, and Florida, when they were engaged in making or amending their constitutions during the early part of this century.

Nowhere is population in such constant movement as in America. In some of the newer States only one-fourth or one-fifth of the inhabitants are natives of the United States. Many of the townsfolk, not a few even of the farmers, have been till lately citizens of some other State, and will, perhaps, soon move on farther west. These Western States are like a chain of lakes through which there flows a stream which mingles the waters of the higher with those of the lower. In such a constant flux of population local peculiarities are not readily developed, or if they have grown up when the district was still isolated, they disappear as the country becomes filled. Each State takes from its neighbours and gives to its neighbours, so that the process of assimilation is always going on over the whole wide area.

Still more important is the influence of railway communication, of newspapers, of the telegraph. A Greek city like Samos or Mitylene, holding her own island, preserved a distinctive character in spite of commercial intercourse and the sway of Athens. A Swiss canton like Uri or Appenzell, entrenched behind its mountain ramparts, remains, even now under the strengthened central government of the Swiss nation, unlike its neighbours of the lower country. But an American State traversed by great trunk lines of railway, and depending on the markets of the Atlantic cities and of Europe for the sale of its grain, cattle, bacon, and minerals, is attached by a hundred always tightening ties to other States, and touched by their weal or woe as nearly as by what befalls within its own limits. The leading newspapers are read over a vast area. The inhabitants of each State know every morning the events of yesterday over the whole Union.

Finally the political parties are the same in all the States. The tenets (if any) of each party are the same everywhere, their methods the same, their leaders the same, although of course a prominent man enjoys especial influence in his own State. Hence, State politics are largely swayed by forces and motives external to the particular State, and common to the whole country, or to great sections of it; and the growth of local parties, the emergence of local issues and development of local political schemes, are correspondingly restrained.

These considerations explain why the States, notwithstanding the original diversities between some of them, and the wide scope for political divergence which they all enjoy under the Federal Constitution, are so much less dissimilar and less peculiar than might have been expected. European statesmen have of late years been accustomed to think of federalism and local autonomy as convenient methods either for recognizing and giving free scope to the sentiment of nationality which may exist in any part of an empire, or for meeting the need for local institutions and distinct legislation which may arise from differences between such a part and the rest of the empire. It is one or other or both of these reasons that have moved statesmen in such cases as those of Finland in her relations to Russia, Hungary in her relations to German Austria, Iceland in her relations to Denmark, Bulgaria in her relations to the Turkish Sultan, Ireland in her relations to the United Kingdom. But the final causes, so to speak, of the recognition of the States of the American Union as autonomous commonwealths, have been different. Their self-government is not the consequence of differences which can be made harmless to the whole body politic only by being allowed free course. It has been due primarily to the historical fact that they existed as commonwealths before the Union came into being; secondarily, to the belief that localized government is the best guarantee for civic freedom, and to a sense of the difficulty of administering a vast territory and population from one centre and by one government.

I return to indicate the points in which the legal independence and right of self-government of the several States appears. Each of the forty-two has its own—

Constitution (whereof more anon).

Executive, consisting of a governor, and various other officials.

Legislature of two Houses.

System of local government in counties, cities, townships, and school districts.

System of State and local taxation.

Debts, which it may (and sometimes does) repudiate at its own pleasure.

Body of private law, including the whole law of real and personal property, of contracts, of torts, and of family relations.

Courts, from which no appeal lies (except in cases touching Federal legislation or the Federal constitution) to any Federal court.

System of procedure, civil and criminal.

Citizenship, which may admit persons (e.g. recent immigrants) to be citizens at times, or on conditions, wholly different from those prescribed by other States.

Three points deserve to be noted as illustrating what these attributes include.

I. A man gains active citizenship of the United States (*i.e.* a share in the government of the Union) only by becoming a citizen of some particular State. Being such citizen, he is forthwith entitled to the national franchise. That is to say, voting power in the State carries voting power in Federal elections, and however lax a State may be in its grant of such power, *e.g.* to foreigners just landed or to persons convicted of crime, these State voters will have the right of voting in congressional and presidential elections.[2] The only restriction on the States in this matter is that of the fourteenth and fifteenth Constitutional amendments, . . . They were intended to secure equal treatment to the negroes, and incidentally they declare the protection given to all citizens of the United States.[3] Whether they really enlarge it, that is to say, whether it did not exist by implication before, is a legal question, which I need not discuss.

II. The power of a State over all communities within its limits is absolute. It may grant or refuse local government as it pleases. The population of the city of Providence is more than one-third of that of the State of Rhode Island, the population of New York city more than one-fifth that of the State of New York. But the State might in either case extinguish the municipality, and govern the city by a single State commissioner appointed for the purpose, or leave it without any government whatever. The city would have no right of complaint to the Federal President or Congress against such a measure. Massachusetts has lately remodelled the city government of Boston just as the British Parliament might remodel that of Birmingham. Let an Englishman imagine a county council for Warwickshire suppressing the muncipality of Birmingham, or a Frenchman imagine the department of the Rhone extinguishing the municipality of Lyons, with no possibility of intervention by the central authority, and he will measure the difference between the American States and the local governments of Western Europe.

III. A State commands the allegiance of its citizens, and may punish them for treason against it. The power has rarely been exercised, but its undoubted legal existence had much to do with inducing the citizens of the Southern States to follow their governments into secession in 1861. They conceived themselves to owe allegiance to the State as well as to the Union, and when it became impossible to preserve both, because the State had declared its secession from the Union, they might hold the earlier and nearer authority to be paramount. Allegiance to the State must now, since the war, be taken to be subordinate to the Union. But allegiance to the State still exists; treason against the State is still possible. One cannot think of treason against Warwickshire or the department of the Rhone.

These are illustrations of the doctrine which Europeans often fail to grasp, that the American States were originally in a certain sense, and still for certain purposes remain, sovereign States. Each of the original thirteen became sovereign when it revolted from the mother country in 1776. By entering the Confederation of 1781–88 it parted with one or two of the attributes of sovereignty, by accepting the Federal Constitution in 1788 it subjected itself for certain specified purposes to a central government, but claimed to retain its sovereignty for all other purposes. That is to say, the authority of a State is an inherent, not a delegated, authority. It has all the powers which any independent government can have, except such as it can be affirmatively shown to have stripped itself of, while the Federal Government has only such powers as it can be affirmatively shown to have received. To use the legal expression, the presumption is always for a State, and the burden of proof lies upon any one who denies its authority in a particular matter.[4]

What State sovereignty means and includes is a question which incessantly engaged the most active legal and political minds of the nation, from 1789 down to 1870. Some thought it paramount to the rights of the Union. Some considered it as held in suspense by the Constitution, but capable of reviving as soon as a State should desire to separate from the Union. Some maintained that each State had in accepting the Constitution finally renounced its sovereignty, which thereafter existed only in the sense of such an undefined domestic legislative and administrative authority as had not been conferred upon Congress. The conflict of these views, which became acute in 1830 when South Carolina claimed the right of nullification, produced Secession and the war of 1861–65. Since the defeat of the Secessionists, the last of these views may be deemed to have been established, and the term "State sovereignty" is now but seldom heard. Even "States rights" have a different meaning from that which they had thirty years ago.[5] . . .

The Constitution, which had rendered many services to the American people, did them an inevitable disservice when it fixed their minds on the legal aspects of the question. Law was meant to be the servant of politics, and must not be suffered to become the master. A case had arisen which its formulae were unfit to deal with, a case which had to be settled on large moral and historical grounds. It was not merely the superior physical force of the North that prevailed; it was the moral forces which rule the world, forces which had long worked against slavery, and were ordained to save North America from the curse of hostile nations established side by side.

The word "sovereignty," which has in many ways clouded the domain of public law and jurisprudence, confused men's minds by making them assume that there must in every country exist, and be discoverable by legal inquiry, either one body invested legally with supreme power over all minor bodies, or several bodies which, though they had consented to form part of a larger body, were each in the last resort independent of it, and responsible to none but themselves.[6] They forgot that

a Constitution may not have determined where legal supremacy shall dwell. Where the Constitution of the United States placed it was at any rate doubtful, so doubtful that it would have been better to drop technicalities, and recognize the broad fact that the legal claims of the States had become incompatible with the historical as well as legal claims of the nation. In the uncertainty as to where legal right resided, it would have been prudent to consider where physical force resided. The South however thought herself able to resist any physical force which the rest of the nation might bring against her. Thus encouraged, she took her stand on the doctrine of States Rights: and then followed a pouring out of blood and treasure such as was never spent on determining a point of law before, not even when Edward III and his successors waged war for a hundred years to establish the claim of females to inherit the crown of France.

What, then, do the rights of a State now include? Every right or power of a Government except:—

> The right of secession (not abrogated in terms, but admitted since the war to be no longer claimable. It is expressly negatived in the recent Constitutions of several Southern States).
>
> Powers which the Constitution withholds from the States (including that of intercourse with foreign governments).
>
> Powers which the Constitution expressly confers on the Federal Government.

As respects some powers of the last class, however, the States may act concurrently with, or in default of action by, the Federal Government. It is only from contravention of its action that they must abstain. And where contravention is alleged to exist, whether legislative or executive, it is by a court of law, and, in case the decision is in the first instance favourable to the pretensions of the State, ultimately by a Federal court, that the question falls to be decided.[7]

A reference to the preceding list of what each State may create in the way of distinct institutions will show that these rights practically cover nearly all the ordinary relations of citizens to one another and to their Government.[8] An American may, through a long life, never be reminded of the Federal Government, except when he votes at presidential and congressional elections, lodges a complaint against the post-office, and opens his trunks for a custom-house officer on the pier at New York when he returns from a tour in Europe. His direct taxes are paid to officials acting under State laws. The State, or a local authority constituted by State statutes, registers his birth, appoints his guardian, pays for his schooling, gives him a share in the estate of his father deceased, licenses him when he enters a trade (if it be one needing a licence), marries him, divorces him, entertains civil actions against him, declares him a bankrupt, hangs him for murder. The police that guard his house, the local boards which look after the poor, control highways, impose water rates, manage schools—all these derive their legal powers from his State alone. Looking at this immense compass of State functions, Jefferson would seem to have been not far wrong when he said that the Federal government was nothing more than the American department of foreign affairs. But although the National government touches the direct interests of the citizen less than does the State government, it touches his sentiment more. Hence the strength of his attachment to the former and his interest in it must not be measured by the frequency of his dealings with it. In the partitionment of governmental functions between nation and State, the State gets the most but the nation the highest, so the balance between the two is preserved.

Thus every American citizen lives in a duality of which Europeans, always excepting the Swiss, and to some extent the Germans, have no experience. He lives under two governments and two sets of laws; he is animated by two patriotisms and owes two allegiances. That these should both be strong and rarely be in conflict is most fortunate. It is the result of skilful adjustment and long habit, of the fact that those whose votes control the two sets of governments are the same persons, but above all of that harmony of each set of institutions with the other set, a harmony due to the identity of the principles whereon both are founded, which makes each appear necessary to the stability of the other, the States to the nation as its basis, the National Government to the States as their protector.

Notes

1. The case of Kansas immediately before the War of Secession, and the cases of the rebel States, which were not readmitted after the war till they had accepted the constitutional amendments forbidding slavery and protecting the freedmen, are quite exceptional cases.

2. Congress has power to pass a uniform rule of naturalization (Const. Art. §. 8).

   Under the present naturalization laws a foreigner must have resided in the United States for five years, and for one year in the State or Territory where he seeks admission to United States citizenship, and must declare two years before he is admitted that he renounces allegiance to any foreign prince or state. Naturalization makes him a citizen not only of the United States, but of the State or Territory where he is admitted, but does not necessarily confer the electoral franchise, for that depends on State laws.

   In more than a third of the States the electoral franchise is now enjoyed by persons not naturalized as United States citizens.

3. "The line of distinction between the privileges and immunities of citizens of the United States, and those of citizens of the several States, must be traced along the boundary of their respective spheres of action, and the two classes must be as different in their nature as are the functions of their respective governments. A citizen of the United States as such has a right to participate in foreign and interstate commerce, to have the benefit of the postal laws, to make use in common with others of the navigable waters of the United States, and to pass from State to State, and into foreign countries, because over all these subjects the jurisdiction of the United States extends, and they are covered by its laws. The privileges suggest the immunities. Wherever it is the duty of the United States to give protection to a citizen against any harm, inconvenience, or deprivation, the citizen is entitled to an immunity which pertains to Federal citizenship. One very plain immunity is exemption from any tax, burden, or imposition under State laws as a condition to the enjoyment of any right or privilege under the laws of the United States. . . . Whatever one may claim as of right under the Constitution and laws of the United States by virtue of his citizenship, is a privilege of a citizen of the United States. Whatever the Constitution and laws of the United States entitle him to exemption from, he may claim an exemption in respect to. And such a right or privilege is abridged whenever the State law interferes with any legitimate operation of Federal authority which concerns his interest, whether it be an authority actively exerted, or resting only in the express or implied command or assurance of the Federal Constitution or law. But the United States can neither grant nor secure to its citizens rights or privileges which are not expressly or by reasonable implication placed under its jurisdiction, and all not so placed are left to the exclusive protection of the States."—Cooley, *Principles*, pp. 245–247.

4. It may of course be said that as the colonies associated themselves into a league, at the very time at which they revolted from the British Crown, and as their foreign relations were always managed by the authority and organs of this league, no one of them ever was for international purposes a free and independent sovereign State. This is true, and Abraham Lincoln was in this sense justified in saying that the Union was older than the States. But what are we to say of North Carolina and Rhode Island, after the acceptance of the Constitution of 1787–89 by the other eleven States? They were out of the old Confederation, for it had expired. They were not in the new Union, for they refused during many months to enter it. What else can they have been during these months except sovereign commonwealths?

5. States rights was a watchword in the South for many years. In 1851 there was a student at Harvard College from South Carolina who bore the name of States Rights Gist, baptized, so to speak, into Calhounism. He rose to be a brigadier-general in the Confederate army, and fell in the Civil War.

6. A further confusion arises from the fact that men are apt in talking of sovereignty to mix up legal supremacy with practical predominance. They ought to go together, and law seeks to make them go together. But it may happen that the person or body in whom law vests supreme authority is unable to enforce that authority: so the legal sovereign and the actual sovereign—that is to say, the force which will prevail in physical conflict—are different. There is always a strongest force; but the force recognized by law may not be really the strongest; and of several forces it may be impossible to tell, till they have come into actual physical conflict, which is the strongest.

7. See Chapter XXII. *ante*.

8. A recent American writer well observes that nearly all the great questions which have agitated England during the last sixty years would, had they arisen in America, have fallen within the sphere of State legislation. —Jameson, "Introduction to the Constitutional and Political History of the States," in *Johns Hopkins University Studies*.

Critical Thinking

1. What five circumstances, according to Bryce, contribute to making the American states more similar to one another than might be reasonably expected?

2. What does it mean to say that most state boundaries are "artificial," and not "natural growths"?

3. Which existed first, the states or the national government? How does this historical fact relate to considering why states are more similar to one another than might be expected?

4. How much power does a state have over local governments within that state?

5. What does it mean to say that every American citizen "lives in a duality"?

Create Central

www.mhhe.com/createcentral

Internet References

Encyclopedia Brittanica: James Bryce, Viscount Bryce

www.britannica.com/EBchecked/topic/82530/James-Bryce-Viscount-Bryce

Online Library of Liberty: James Bryce, The American Commonwealth

http://oll.libertyfund.org/?option=com_staticxt&staticfile=show.php%3Ftitle=1850

From *The American Commonwealth*, 1888.

Article

Prepared by: Bruce Stinebrickner, *DePauw University*

The American System of Townships . . .

Why the writer begins his examination of political institutions with the township. There are townships in every nation. Difficulty of establishing and maintaining their communal freedom. Its importance. Why the writer has chosen the organization of the New England township as the main subject to examine.

ALEXIS DE TOCQUEVILLE

Learning Outcomes

After reading this article, you will be able to:

- Assess Toqueville's assertions about the different origins of kingdoms and republics, on one hand, and townships, on the other.

- Evaluate Tocqueville's reason for focusing on New England townships and the ways that they differ from townships and counties elsewhere in the United States.

It is not by chance that I consider the township first. The township is the only association so well rooted in nature that wherever men assemble it forms itself.

Communal society therefore exists among all peoples, whatever be their customs and their laws; man creates kingdoms and republics, but townships seem to spring directly from the hand of God. But though townships are coeval with humanity, local freedom is a rare and fragile thing. A nation can always establish great political assemblies, because it always contains a certain number of individuals whose understanding will, to some extent, take the place of experience in handling affairs. But the local community is composed of coarser elements, often recalcitrant to the lawgiver's activity. The difficulty of establishing a township's independence rather augments than diminishes with the increase of enlightenment of nations. A very civilized society finds it hard to tolerate attempts at freedom in a local community; it is disgusted by its numerous blunders and is apt to despair of success before the experiment is finished.

Of all forms of liberty, that of a local community, which is so hard to establish, is the most prone to the encroachments of authority. Left to themselves, the institutions of a local community can hardly struggle against a strong and enterprising government; they cannot defend themselves with success unless they have reached full development and have come to form part of national ideas and habits. Hence, until communal freedom has come to form part of mores, it can easily be destroyed, and it cannot enter into mores without a long-recognized legal existence.

So communal freedom is not, one may almost say, the fruit of human effort. It is seldom created, but rather springs up of its own accord. It grows, almost in secret, amid a semibarbarous society. The continual action of laws, mores, circumstances, and above all time may succeed in consolidating it. Among all the nations of continental Europe, one may say that there is not one that understands communal liberty.

However, the strength of free peoples resides in the local community. Local institutions are to liberty what primary schools are to science; they put it within the people's reach; they teach people to appreciate its peaceful enjoyment and accustom them to make use of it. Without local institutions a nation may give itself a free government, but it has not got the spirit of liberty. Passing passions, momentary interest, or chance circumstances may give it the external shape of independence, but the despotic tendencies which have been driven into the interior of the body social will sooner or later break out on the surface.

To help the reader understand the general principles on which the political organization of townships and counties in the United States depends, I thought it would be useful to take one particular state as an example and examine in detail what happens there, subsequently taking a quick look at the rest of the country.

I have chosen one of the states of New England.

Townships and counties are not organized in the same way in all parts of the Union; nevertheless, one can easily see that throughout the Union more or less the same principles have guided the formation of both township and county.

Now, I thought that in New England these principles had been carried further with more far-reaching results than elsewhere. Consequently they stand out there in higher relief and are easier for a foreigner to observe.

The local institutions of New England form a complete and regular whole; they are ancient; law and, even more, mores make them strong; and they exercise immense influence over the whole of society.

For all these reasons they deserve our attention.

Limits of the Township

The New England township is halfway between a *canton* and a *commune* in France. It generally has from two to three thousand inhabitants;[1] it is therefore not too large for all the inhabitants to have roughly the same interests, but is big enough to be sure of finding the elements of a good administration within itself.

Powers of the New England Township

In the township, as everywhere else, the people are the source of power, but nowhere else do they exercise their power so directly. In America the people are a master who must be indulged to the utmost possible limits.

In New England the majority works through representatives when it is dealing with the general affairs of the state. It was necessary that that should be so; but in the township, where both law and administration are closer to the governed, the representative system has not been adopted. There is no municipal council; the body of the electors, when it has chosen the officials, gives them directions in everything beyond the simple, ordinary execution of the laws of the state.[2]

Such a state of affairs is so contrary to our ideas and opposed to our habits that some examples are needed to make it understandable.

Public duties in the township are extremely numerous and minutely divided, as we shall see later on, but most of the administrative power is concentrated in the hands of a few yearly elected individuals called "selectmen."[3]

The general laws of the state impose certain duties on the selectmen. In administering these they do not require the authorization of the governed, and it is their personal responsibility if they neglect them. For example, the state law charges them to draw up the municipal voting lists, and if they fail to do so, they are guilty of an offense. But in all matters within the township's control the selectmen carry out the popular will, just as our mayors execute the decisions of the municipal council. Usually they act on their own responsibility, merely putting into practice principles already approved by the majority. But if they want to make any change in the established order to start some new undertaking, they must go back to the source of their power. Suppose they want to start a school; the selectmen summon all the voters to a meeting on a fixed day and place; they there explain the need felt; they state the means available for the purpose, how much it will cost, and the site suggested. The meeting, consulted on all these points, accepts the principle, decides the site, votes the tax, and leaves the selectmen to carry out its orders.

Only the selectmen have the right to call a town meeting, but they may be required to do so. If ten owners of property conceive some new project and wish to submit it to the approval of the township, they demand a general meeting of the inhabitants; the selectmen are bound to agree to this and preserve only the right to preside over the meeting.[4]

The people as the origin of power in the township as elsewhere. They handle their principal affairs themselves. No municipal council. The greater part of municipal authority concentrated in the hands of the "selectmen." How the selectmen function. Town meeting. List of all municipal officials. Obligatory and paid functions.

Such political mores and social customs are certainly far removed from ours. I do not, at this moment, want to pass judgment on them or to reveal the hidden reasons causing them and giving them life; it is enough to describe them.

The selectmen are elected every year in April or May. At the same time, the town meeting also elects many other municipal officials[5] to take charge of important administrative details. There are assessors to rate the township and collectors to bring the taxes in. The constable must organize the police, take care of public places, and take a hand in the physical execution of the laws. The town clerk must record all resolutions; he keeps a record of the proceedings of the civil administration. The treasurer looks after the funds of the township. There are also overseers of the poor whose difficult task it is to execute the provisions of the Poor Laws; school commissioners in charge of public education; and surveyors of highways, who look after roads both large and small, to complete the list of the main administrative officials of the township. But the division of functions does not stop there; among municipal officials one also finds parish commissioners responsible for the expenses of public worship, fire wardens to direct the citizens' efforts in case of fire, tithing men, hog reeves, fence viewers, timber measurers, and sealers of weights and measures.[6]

Altogether there are nineteen main officials in a township. Every inhabitant is bound, on pain of fine, to accept these various duties; but most of them also carry some remuneration so that poorer citizens can devote their time to them without loss. Furthermore, it is not the American system to give any fixed salary to officials. In general, each official act has a price, and men are paid in accordance with what they have done.

Life in the Township

I have said before that the principle of the sovereignty of the people hovers over the whole political system of the Anglo-Americans. Every page of this book will point out new applications of this doctrine.

In nations where the dogma of the sovereignty of the people prevails, each individual forms an equal part of that sovereignty and shares equally the government of the state.

Each individual is assumed to be as educated, virtuous, and powerful as any of his fellows.

Why, then, should he obey society, and what are the natural limits of such obedience?

He obeys society not because he is inferior to those who direct it, nor because he is incapable of ruling himself, but because union with his fellows seems useful to him and he knows that that union is impossible without a regulating authority.

Therefore, in all matters concerning the duties of citizens toward each other he is subordinate. In all matters that concern himself alone he remains the master, he is free and owes an account of his actions to God alone. From this derives the maxim that the individual is the best and only judge of his own interest and that society has no right to direct his behavior unless it feels harmed by him or unless it needs his concurrence.

This doctrine is universally accepted in the United States. Elsewhere I will examine its general influence on the ordinary actions of life; here and now I am concerned only with townships.

The township, taken as a whole in relation to the central government, resembles any other individual to whom the theory just mentioned applies.

So in the United States municipal liberty derives straight from the dogma of the sovereignty of the people; all the American republics have recognized this independence more or less, but there were circumstances particularly favorable to its growth among the people of New England.

In that part of the Union political life was born in the very heart of the townships; one might almost say that in origin each of them was a little independent nation. Later, when the kings of England claimed their share of sovereignty, they limited themselves to taking over the central power. They left the townships as they had found them. Now the New England townships are subordinate, but in the beginning this was not so, or hardly so. Therefore they have not received their powers; on the contrary, it would seem that they have surrendered a portion of their powers for the benefit of the state; that is an important distinction which the reader should always bear in mind.

In general the townships are subordinate to the state only where some interest that I shall call *social* is concerned, that is to say, some interest shared with others.

In all that concerns themselves alone the townships remain independent bodies, and I do not think one could find a single inhabitant of New England who would recognize the right of the government of the state to control matters of purely municipal interest.

Hence one finds the New England townships buying and selling, suing and being sued, increasing or reducing their budgets, and no administrative authority whatsoever thinks of standing in their way.[7]

But there are social duties which they are bound to perform. Thus, if the state needs money, the township is not free to grant or refuse its help.[8] If the state wants to open a road, the township cannot bar its territory. If there is a police regulation, the township must carry it out. If the government wants to organize education on a uniform plan throughout the country, the township must establish the schools required by the law.[9] We shall see, when we come to speak of the administration of the

United States, how and by whom, in these various cases, the townships are constrained to obedience. Here I only wish to establish the fact of the obligation. Strict as this obligation is, the government of the state imposes it in principle only, and in its performance the township resumes all its independent rights. Thus taxes are, it is true, voted by the legislature, but they are assessed and collected by the township; the establishment of a school is obligatory, but the township builds it, pays for it, and controls it.

In France the state tax collector receives the communal taxes; in America the township tax collector collects state taxes.

So, whereas with us the central government lends its agents to the commune, in America the township lends its agents to the government. That fact alone shows how far the two societies differ.

Each man the best judge of his own interest. Corollary of the principle of the sovereignty of the people. How American townships apply these doctrines. The New England township sovereign in all that concerns itself alone, subordinate in all else. Duties of the township toward the state. In France the government lends officials to the commune. In America the township lends its officials to the government.

Spirit of the Township in New England

In America not only do municipal institutions exist, but there is also a municipal spirit which sustains and gives them life.

The New England township combines two advantages which, wherever they are found, keenly excite men's interest; they are independence and power. It acts, it is true, within a sphere beyond which it cannot pass, but within that domain its movements are free. This independence alone would give a real importance not warranted by size or population.

It is important to appreciate that, in general, men's affections are drawn only in directions where power exists. Patriotism does not long prevail in a conquered country. The New Englander is attached to his township not so much because he was born there as because he sees the township as a free, strong corporation of which he is part and which is worth the trouble of trying to direct.

It often happens in Europe that governments themselves regret the absence of municipal spirit, for everyone agrees that municipal spirit is an important element in order and public tranquillity, but they do not know how to produce it. In making municipalities strong and independent, they fear sharing their social power and exposing the state to risks of anarchy. However, if you take power and independence from a municipality, you may have docile subjects but you will not have citizens.

Why the New England township wins the affection of the inhabitants. Difficulty of creating municipal spirit in Europe. In America municipal rights and duties concur in forming that spirit. The homeland has more characteristic features in America than elsewhere. How municipal spirit manifests itself in New England. What happy results it produces there.

Another important fact must be noted. The New England township is shaped to form the nucleus of strong attachments, and there is meanwhile no rival center close by to attract the hot hearts of ambitious men.

County officials are not elected and their authority is limited. Even a state is only of secondary importance, being an obscure and placid entity. Few men are willing to leave the center of their interests and take trouble to win the right to help administer it.

The federal government does confer power and renown on those who direct it, but only a few can exercise influence there. The high office of President is hardly to be reached until a man is well on in years; as for other high federal offices, there is a large element of chance about attaining to them, and they go only to those who have reached eminence in some other walk of life. No ambitious man would make them the fixed aim of his endeavors. It is in the township, the center of the ordinary business of life, that the desire for esteem, the pursuit of substantial interests, and the taste for power and self-advertisement are concentrated; these passions, so often troublesome elements in society, take on a different character when exercised so close to home and, in a sense, within the family circle.

With much care and skill power has been broken into fragments in the American township, so that the maximum possible number of people have some concern with public affairs. Apart from the voters, who from time to time are called on to act as the government, there are many and various officials who all, within their sphere, represent the powerful body in whose name they act. Thus a vast number of people make a good thing for themselves out of the power of the community and are interested in administration for selfish reasons.

The American system, which distributes local power among so many citizens, is also not afraid to multiply municipal duties. Americans rightly think that patriotism is a sort of religion strengthened by practical service.

Thus daily duties performed or rights exercised keep municipal life constantly alive. There is a continual gentle political activity which keeps society on the move without turmoil.

Americans love their towns for much the same reasons that highlanders love their mountains. In both cases the native land has emphatic and peculiar features; it has a more pronounced physiognomy than is found elsewhere.

In general, New England townships lead a happy life. Their government is to their taste as well as of their choice. With profound peace and material prosperity prevailing in America, there are few storms in municipal life. The township's interests are easy to manage. Moreover, the people's political education has been completed long ago, or rather they were already educated when they settled there. In New England there is not even a memory of distinctions in rank, so there is no part of the community tempted to oppress the rest, and injustices which affect only isolated individuals are forgotten in the general contentment. The government may have defects, and indeed they are easy to point out, but they do not catch the eye because the government really does emanate from the governed, and so long as it gets along somehow or other, a sort of parental pride protects it. Besides, there is no basis of comparison. Formerly England ruled the colonies as a group, but the people always looked after municipal affairs. So the sovereignty of the people in the township is not ancient only, but primordial.

The New Englander is attached to his township because it is strong and independent; he has an interest in it because he shares in its management; he loves it because he has no reason to complain of his lot; he invests his ambition and his future in it; in the restricted sphere within his scope, he learns to rule society; he gets to know those formalities without which freedom can advance only through revolutions, and becoming imbued with their spirit, develops a taste for order, understands the harmony of powers, and in the end accumulates clear, practical ideas about the nature of his duties and the extent of his rights.

Notes

1. In 1830 there were 305 townships in Massachusetts; the population was 610,014; that gives an average of about 2,000 for each township.

2. The same rules do not apply to the large townships. Those generally have a mayor and a municipal body divided into two branches, but a law is needed to authorize such an exception. See the law of February 23,1822, regulating the powers of the city of Boston. *Laws of Massachusetts,* Vol. II, p. 588. [*The General Laws of Massachusetts,* Vol. II, Boston, 1823, p. 588 ff.] That applies to the large towns. Small towns also often have a particular administration. In 1832 104 such municipal administrations were counted in the state of New York. (*Williams's New York Annual Register.*) [*The New York Annual Register for the Year of Our Lord 1832,* by Edwin Williams, New York, 1832.]

3. There are three selectmen in the smallest townships and nine in the largest. See *The Town Officer,* p. 186. [Tocqueville refers here to a book by Isaac Goodwin, *Town Officer or Law of Massachusetts* (Worcester, 1829), which incidentally is to be found among the volumes of his library at the Château de Tocqueville.] See also the main laws of Massachusetts concerning selectmen:

    Law of February 20, 1786, Vol. I, p. 219; February 24, 1796, Vol. I, p. 488; March 7, 1801, Vol. II, p. 45; June 16, 1795, Vol. I, p. 475; March 12,1808, Vol. II, p. 186; February 28, 1787, Vol. I, p. 302; June 22, 1797, Vol. I, p. 539.

4. See *Laws of Massachusetts,* Vol. I, p. 150; law of March 25, 1786.

5. *Ibid.*

6. All these officials really do exist. To find out the details

of all their duties see *The Town Officer,* by Isaac Goodwin (Worcester, 1829), and the *General Laws of Massachusetts* in 3 vols. (Boston, 1823).

7. See *Laws of Massachusetts,* law of March 23, 1786, Vol. I, p. 250.

8. *Ibid.,* law of February 20, 1786, Vol. I, p. 217.

9. See the same collection, law of June 25, 1789, Vol. I, p. 367, and March 10, 1827, Vol III, p. 179.

Critical Thinking

1. According to Tocqueville, who creates kingdoms and republics? In contrast, what seems to be the origin of townships?

2. What is the connection between local government institutions and liberty?

3. What is special about the New England town(ship)?

4. What roles do town meetings and selectmen play in New England towns?

5. What is the difference between tax collection processes in France and the United States, especially as they relate to local governments?

Create Central

www.mhhe.com/createcentral

Internet References

Alexis de Tocqueville: Democracy in America
http://xroads.virginia.edu/~HYPER/DETOC

In Search of Tocqueville's Democracy in America
www.tocqueville.org

From *Democracy in America* by Alexis de Tocqueville, 1835.

Article   Prepared by: Bruce Stinebrickner, *DePauw University*

Local Government: Observations

JAMES BRYCE

Learning Outcomes

After reading this article, you will be able to:

- Explain how different historical circumstances led to the development of different local government structures in different regions of the United States.

- Compare the chief functions of late nineteenth-century local governments in the United States identified by James Bryce with the chief functions of contemporary local governments.

This is the place for an account of local government in the United States, because it is a matter regulated not by Federal law but by the several States and Territories, each of which establishes such local authorities, rural and urban, as the people of the State or Territory desire, and invests them with the requisite powers. But this very fact indicates the immensity of the subject. Each State has its own system of local areas and authorities, created and worked under its own laws; and though these systems agree in many points, they differ in so many others, that a whole volume would be needed to give even a summary view of their peculiarities. All I can here attempt is to distinguish the leading types of local government to be found in the United States, to describe the prominent features of each type, and to explain the influence which the large scope and popular character of local administration exercise upon the general life and well-being of the American people.

Three types of rural local government are discernible in America. The first is characterized by its unit, the Town or Township, and exists in the six New England States. The second is characterized by a much larger unit, the county, and prevails in the southern States. The third combines some features of the first with some of the second, and may be called the mixed system. It is found, under a considerable variety of forms, in the middle and north-western States. The differences of these three types are interesting, not only because of the practical instruction they afford, but also because they spring from original differences in the character of the colonist who settled along the American coast, and in the conditions under which the communities there founded were developed.

The first New England settlers were Puritans in religion, and sometimes inclined to republicanism in politics. They were largely townsfolk, accustomed to municipal life and to vestry meetings. They planted their tiny communities along the seashore and the banks of rivers, enclosing them with stockades for protection against the warlike Indians. Each was obliged to be self-sufficing, because divided by rocks and woods from the others. Each had its common pasture on which the inhabitants turned out their cattle, and which officers were elected to manage. Each was a religious as well as a civil body politic, gathered round the church as its centre; and the equality which prevailed in the congregation prevailed also in civil affairs, the whole community meeting under a president or moderator to discuss affairs of common interest. Each such settlement was called a Town, or Township, and was in fact a miniature commonwealth, exercising a practical sovereignty over the property and persons of its members—for there was as yet no State, and the distant home government scarcely cared to interfere—but exercising it on thoroughly democratic principles. Its centre was a group of dwellings, often surrounded by a fence or wall, but it included a rural area of several square miles, over which farmhouses and clusters of houses began to spring up when the Indians retired. The name "town" covered the whole of this area, which was never too large for all the inhabitants to come together to a central place of meeting. This town organization remained strong and close, the colonists being men of narrow means, and held together in each settlement by the needs of defence. And though presently the towns became aggregated into counties, and the legislature and governor, first of the whole colony, and, after 1776, of the State, began to exert their superior authority, the towns (which, be it remembered, remained rural communities, making up the whole area of the State) held their ground, and are to this day the true units of political life in New England, the solid foundation of that well-compacted structure of self-government which European philosophers have admired and the new States of the West have sought to reproduce. Till 1821[1] the towns were the only political corporate bodies in Massachusetts, and till 1857 they formed, as they still form in Connecticut, the basis of representation in her Assembly, each town, however small, returning at least one member. Much of that robust, if somewhat narrow, localism which characterizes the representative system of America is due to this originally distinct and self-sufficing corporate life of the seventeenth century towns. Nor is it without interest to observe that although they owed much to the conditions which surrounded the early colonists, forcing them to develop a civic patriotism resembling that of the republics of ancient Greece and Italy, they owed something also to those Teutonic traditions of semi-independent local communities, owning common property, and governing themselves by a primary assembly of all free inhabitants, which the English had brought with them from the Elbe and the Weser, and which had been perpetuated in the practice of many parts of England down till the days of the Stuart kings.

Very different were the circumstances of the Southern colonies. The men who went to Virginia and the Carolinas were not Puritans, nor did they mostly go in families and groups of families from the same neighbourhood. Many were casual adventurers, often belonging to the upper class, Episcopalians in religion, and with no such experience of, or attachment to, local self-government as the men of Massachusetts or Connecticut. They settled in a region where the Indian tribes were comparatively peaceable, and where therefore there was little need of concentration for the purposes of defence. The climate along the coast was somewhat too hot for European labour, so slaves were imported to cultivate the land. Population was thinly scattered; estates were large; the soil was fertile and soon enriched its owners. Thus a semi-feudal society grew up, in which authority naturally fell to the land-owners, each of whom was the centre of a group of free dependants as well as the master of an increasing crowd of slaves. There were therefore comparatively few urban communities, and the life of the colony took a rural type. The houses of the planters lay miles apart from one another; and when local divisions had to be created, these were made large enough to include a considerable area of territory and number of land-owning gentlemen. They were therefore rural divisions, counties framed on the model of English counties. Smaller circumscriptions there were, such as hundreds and parishes, but the hundred died out,[2] the parish ultimately became a purely ecclesiastical division, and the parish vestry was restricted to ecclesiastical functions, while the county remained the practically important unit of local administration, the unit to which the various functions of government were aggregated, and which, itself controlling minor authorities, was controlled by the State government alone. The affairs of the county were usually managed by a board of elective commissioners, and not, like those of the New England towns, by a primary assembly; and in an aristocratic society the leading planters had of course a predominating influence. Hence this form of local government was not only less democratic, but less stimulating and educative than that which prevailed in the New England States. Nor was the Virginian county, though so much larger than the New England town, ever as important an organism over against the State. It may almost be said, that while a New England State is a combination of towns, a Southern State is from the first an administrative as well as political whole, whose subdivisions, the counties, had never any truly independent life, but were and are mere subdivisions for the convenient dispatch of judicial and financial business.

In the middle States of the Union, Pennsylvania, New Jersey, and New York, settled or conquered by Englishmen some time later than New England, the town and town meeting did not as a rule exist, and the county was the original basis of organization. But as there grew up no planting aristocracy like that of Virginia or the Carolinas, the course of events took in the middle States a different direction. As trade and manufactures grew, population became denser than in the South. New England influenced them, and influenced still more the newer commonwealths which arose in the North-west, such as Ohio and Michigan, into which the surplus population of the East poured. And the result of this influence is seen in the growth through the middle and western States of a mixed system, which presents a sort of compromise between the County system of the South and the Town system of the North-east. There are great differences between the arrangements in one or other of these middle and western States. But it may be said, speaking generally, that in them the county is relatively less important than in the southern States, the township less important than in New England. The county is perhaps to be regarded, at least in New York, Pennsylvania, and Ohio, as the true unit, and the townships (for so they are usually called) as its subdivisions. But the townships are vigorous organisms, which largely restrict the functions of the county authority, and give to local government, especially in the North-west, a character generally similar to that which it wears in New England. . . .

It is noteworthy that the Americans, who are supposed to be especially fond of representative assemblies, have made little use of representation in their local government. The township is usually governed either by a primary assembly of all citizens or else, as in such States as Ohio and Iowa, by a very small board, not exceeding three, with, in both sets of cases, several purely executive officers.[3] In the county there is seldom or never a county board possessing legislative functions;[4] usually only three commissioners or supervisors with some few executive or judicial officers. Local legislation (except as it appears in the bye-laws of the Town meeting or selectmen) is discouraged. The people seem jealous of their county officials, electing them for short terms, and restricting each to a special range of duties. This is perhaps only another way of saying that the county, even in the South, has continued to be an artificial entity, and has drawn to itself no great part of the interest and affections of the citizens. Over five-sixths of the Union each county presents a square figure on the map, with nothing distinctive about it, nothing "natural" about it, in the sense in which such English counties as Kent or Cornwall are natural entities. It is too large for the personal interest of the citizens: that goes to the township. It is too small to have traditions which command the respect or touch the affections of its inhabitants: these belong to the State.[5]

The chief functions local government has to discharge in the United States are the following:—

Making and repairing roads and bridges. —These prime necessities of rural life are provided for by the township, county, or State, according to the class to which a road or bridge belongs. That the roads of America are proverbially ill-built and ill-kept is due partly to the climate, with its alternations of severe frost, occasional torrential rains (in the middle and southern States), and long droughts; partly to the hasty habits of the people, who are too busy with other things, and too eager to use their capital in private enterprises to be willing to spend freely on highways; partly also to the thinness of population, which is, except in a few manufacturing districts, much less dense than in western Europe. In many districts railways have come before roads, so roads have been the less used and cared for.

The administration of justice was one of the first needs which caused the formation of the county: and matters connected with it still form a large part of county business. The voters elect a judge or judges, and the local prosecuting officer, called the district attorney, and the chief executive officer, the sheriff.[6] Prisons are a matter of county concern. Police is always locally regulated, but in the northern States more usually by the township than by the county. However, this branch of government, so momentous in continental Europe, is in America comparatively unimportant outside the cities. The rural districts get on nearly everywhere with no guardians of the peace, beyond the township constable;[7] nor does the State government, except, of course, through statutes, exercise any control over local police administration.[8] In the rural parts of the eastern and middle States property is as safe as anywhere in the world. In such parts of the West as are disturbed by dacoits, or by solitary highwaymen, travellers defend themselves, and, if the sheriff is distant or slack, lynch law may usefully be invoked. The care of the poor is thrown almost everywhere upon local and not upon State authorities,[9] and defrayed out of local funds, sometimes by the county, sometimes by the township. The poor laws of the several States differ in so many particulars that it is impossible to give even an outline of them here. Little out-door relief is given, though in most States the relieving authority may, at his or their discretion, bestow it; and pauperism is not, and has never been, a serious malady, except in some five or six great cities, where it is now vigorously combated by volunteer organizations largely composed of ladies. The total number of persons returned as paupers in the whole Union in 1880 was 88,665, of whom 67,067 were inmates of alms-houses, and 21,598 in receipt of out-door relief. This was only 1 to 565 of the whole population.[10] In England and Wales in 1881 there were 803,126 paupers, to a population of 25,974,439, or 1 to 32 of population.

Sanitation, which has become so important a department of English local administration, plays a small part in the rural districts of America, because their population is so much more thinly spread over the surface that the need for drainage and the removal of nuisances is less pressing; moreover, as the humbler classes are better off, unhealthy dwellings are far less common. Public health officers and sanitary inspectors would, over the larger part of the county, have little occupation.[11]

Education, on the other hand, has hitherto been not only a more distinctively local matter, but one relatively far more important than in England, France, or Italy. And there is usually a special administrative body, often a special administrative area, created for its purposes—the school committee and the school district.[12] The vast sum expended on public instruction has been already mentioned. Though primarily dealt with by the smallest local circumscription, there is a growing tendency for both the county and the State to

interest themselves in the work of instruction by way of inspection, and to some extent of pecuniary subventions. Not only does the county often appoint a county superintendent, but there are in some States county high schools and (in most) county boards of education, besides a State Board of Commissioners.[13] I need hardly add that the schools of all grades are more numerous and efficient in the northern and western than in the southern States.[14] In old colonial days, when the English Commissioners for Foreign Plantations asked for information on the subject of education from the governors of Virginia and Connecticut, the former replied, "I thank God there are no free schools or printing presses, and I hope we shall not have any these hundred years;"[15] and the latter, "One-fourth of the annual revenue of the colony is laid out in maintaining free schools for the education of our children." The disparity was prolonged and intensified in the South by the existence of slavery. Now that slavery has gone, the South makes rapid advances; but the proportion of illiteracy, especially of course among the negroes, is still high.[16]

It will be observed that of the general functions of local government above described, three, viz. police, sanitation, and poor relief, are simpler and less costly than in England, and indeed in most parts of western and central Europe. It has therefore proved easier to vest the management of all in the same local authority, and to get on with a smaller number of special executive officers. Education is indeed almost the only matter which has been deemed to demand a special body to handle it. Nevertheless, even in America the increasing complexity of civilization, and the growing tendency to invoke governmental aid for the satisfaction of wants which were not previously felt, or if felt, were met by voluntary action, tend to enlarge the sphere and multiply the functions of local government.

How far has the spirit of political party permeated rural local government? I have myself asked this question a hundred times in travelling through America, yet I find it hard to give any general answer, because there are great diversities in this regard not only between different States, but between different parts of the same State, diversities due sometimes to the character of the population, sometimes to the varying intensity of party feeling, sometimes to the greater or less degree in which the areas of local government coincide with the election districts for the election of State senators or representatives. On the whole it would seem that county officials are apt to be chosen on political lines, not so much because any political questions come before them, or because they can exert much influence on State or Federal elections, as because these paid offices afford a means of rewarding political services and securing political adhesions. Each of the great parties usually holds its county convention and runs its "county ticket," with the unfortunate result of intruding national politics into matters with which they have nothing to do, and of making it more difficult for good citizens outside the class of professional politicians to find their way into county administration. However, the party candidates are seldom bad men, and the ordinary voter is less apt to vote blindly for the party nominee than he would be in Federal or State elections. In the township and rural school district party spirit is much less active. The offices are often unpaid, and the personal merits of the candidates are better known to the voters than are those of the politicians who seek for county office.[17] Rings and Bosses are not unknown even in rural New England. School committee elections are often influenced by party affiliations. But on the whole, the township and its government keep themselves pretty generally out of the political whirlpool: their posts are filled by honest and reasonably competent men.

Notes

1. Boston continued to be a town governed by a primary assembly of all citizens till 1822; and even then the town-meeting was not quite abolished, for a provision was introduced, intended to satisfy conservative democratic feeling, into the city charter granted by statute in that year, empowering the mayor and aldermen to call general meetings of the citizens qualified to vote in city affairs "to consult upon the common good, to give instructions to their representatives, and to take all lawful means to obtain a redress of any grievances." Such primary assemblies are, however, never now convoked.

2. In Maryland hundreds, which still exist in Delaware, were for a long time the chief administrative divisions. We hear there also of "baronies" and "townlands," as in Ireland; and Maryland is usually called a "province," while the other settlements are colonies. Among its judicial establishments there were courts of pypowdry (*piè poudré*) and "hustings." See the interesting paper on "Local Institutions in Maryland," by Dr. Wilhelm, in *Johns Hopkins University Studies,* Third Series.

   The hundred is a division of small consequence in southern England, but in Lancashire it has some important duties. It repairs the bridges; it is liable for damage done in a riot; and it had its high constable.

3. In a few Western States the Town board has (like the New England selectmen) a limited taxing power, as well as administrative duties.

4. In New York, however, there is a marked tendency in this direction.

5. In Virginia there used to be a county feeling resembling that of England, but this has vanished in the social revolution that has transformed the South.

6. The American sheriff remains something like what the English sheriff was before his wings were clipped by legislation some seventy years ago. Even then he mostly acted by deputy. The justices and the county police have since that legislation largely superseded his action.

7. Or, in States where there are no townships, some corresponding officer.

8. Michigan is now (1888) said to be instituting a sort of State police for the enforcement of her anti-liquor legislation.

9. In some States there are State poor-law superintendents, and frequently certain State institutions for the benefit of particular classes of paupers, *e.g.* pauper lunatics.

10. New York had 15,217 paupers (of whom 2810 were out-door), Colorado 47 (1 out-door), Arizona 4. Louisiana makes no return of indoor paupers, because the parishes (= counties) provide for the maintenance of their poor in private institutions. (The accuracy of these returns has been questioned.)

11. Sanitation, however, has occupied much attention in the cities. Cleveland on Lake Erie claims to have the lowest death rate of any large city in the world.

12. Though the school district frequently coincides with the township, it has generally (outside of New England) administrative officers distinct from those of the township, and when it coincides it is often subdivided into lesser districts.

13. In some States provision is made for the combination of several school districts to maintain a superior school at a central spot.

14. The differences between the school arrangements of different States are so numerous that I cannot attempt to describe them.

15. Governor Sir William Berkeley, however, was among the Virginians who in 1660 subscribed for the erection in Virginia of "a colledge of students of the liberal arts and sciences." As to elementary instruction he said that Virginia pursued "the same course that is taken in England out of towns, every man according to his ability instructing his children. We have forty-eight parishes, and our ministry are well paid, and, by consent, should be better if they would pray oftener and preach less." —*The College of William and Mary,* by Dr. H. B. Adams.

16. The percentage of persons unable to read to the whole population of the United States was, in 1880,13.4; it was lowest in Iowa (2.4), highest in South Carolina (48.2) and Louisiana (45.8). The percentage of persons unable to write was in the whole United States 17; lowest in Nebraska (3.6), highest in South Carolina (55.4) and Alabama (50.9).

    It has recently been proposed in Congress to reduce the surplus in the U.S. treasury by distributing sums among the States in aid of education, in proportion to the need which exists for schools, *i.e.* to their illiteracy. The objections on the score of economic policy, as well as of constitutional law, are so obvious as to have stimulated a warm resistance to the bill.

17. Sometimes the party "ticket" leaves a blank space for the voter to insert the name of the candidates for whom he votes for township offices.

Critical Thinking

1. According to Bryce, what are the three different systems of rural local government in the United States?

2. What factors led to the establishment of the system of local government in New England that is anchored by towns (or townships)?

3. How did religion, differences in the European origins of the first settlers, and relations with "Indians" (now called "Native Americans") contribute to differences between the local government systems established in New England and in the South?

4. What features characterize local government in the "middle" states of New York, Pennsylvania, and New Jersey?

5. What are the chief functions of local government in the United States?

Create Central

www.mhhe.com/createcentral

Internet References

Encyclopedia Britannica: James Bryce, Viscount Bryce
www.britannica.com/EBchecked/topic/82530/James-Bryce-Viscount-Bryce

The Imaginative Conservative: "A Masterpiece of Conservative Thought: Bryce's The American Commonwealth"
www.theimaginativeconservative.org/2013/07/political-thought-bryce-american-commonwealth.html

From *Local Government: Observations*, 1888.

Unit 2

UNIT

Prepared by: Bruce Stinebrickner, *DePauw University*

Intergovernmental Relations

Three levels of government—national, state, and local— coexist in the American political system. They not only operate alongside one another, but they also cooperate and conflict with each other in carrying out their functions. The legal bases for relationships among governments in the American political system include the United States Constitution, 50 state constitutions, decisions by both state and federal courts, and state and national legislation. But legal guidelines do not prevent complications from arising in a three-tier system of government. These three levels of American government have been likened to a layer cake: three layers in one overarching system of government. Still using the cake analogy, political scientist Morton Grodzins has argued that a marble cake better represents the interactions of local, state, and national governments in the American political system.

According to Grodzins, these interactions are far less tidy than the model of a layer cake suggests. Governments closest to the scene seem best able to handle certain kinds of problems, but at the same time, higher, more "distant" levels of government often have access to better sources of revenue to finance government activities. Citizens give different degrees of loyalty and support to different levels of government, and the competing ambitions of politicians at different levels of government can obstruct much needed cooperation.

The formal relationship between the national government and the states is quite different from that between the states and their local governments. The national–state relationship is formally "federal" in character, which means that, in theory, the states and the national government each have autonomous spheres of responsibility. In contrast, the state–local relationship is not a formally federal one. Local governments are mere "creatures" of the states and are not on equal footing with their creators. In practical terms, however, the national government has generally gained the upper hand in most dealings with the states, and in some circumstances, localities operate on almost equal footing with state governments.

Public school governance illustrates some of the complexities of intergovernmental relations in the American political system. Public schooling is usually viewed as primarily a local government function. But, as Grodzins pointed out, state governments play powerful roles by providing financial aid, certifying teachers, prescribing curriculum requirements, and regulating measures concerning school safety and students' health. The national government is also involved in public schooling. In the last 50 years, the United States Supreme Court and lower federal courts have made numerous decisions aimed at ending racial segregation

in public schools. In addition, for several decades national government grants have helped finance various activities such as school breakfasts and lunches, and special education programs. In 2001, the "No Child Left Behind" Act was enacted with President Bush's strong support, and it introduced what some observers have seen as a historic new level of national government involvement in public schooling. The increasing involvement of state governments and especially the national government in educational governance has led to the increasing importance of standardized testing in the evaluation of students, teachers, principals, schools, and school districts as a whole. Even this brief review of local, state, and national involvement in one area, schooling, should show why Grodzins believed that a marble cake better reflects the reality of the American three-tier system of government than a layer cake does.

Intergovernmental transfers of money are an important form of interaction among local, state, and national governments. "Strings" are almost always attached to money that one level of government transfers to another level. For example, when the national government provides grants to states and localities, requirements concerning the use of that money accompany the funds, although the extensiveness and specificity of the requirements vary greatly in different programs. Similarly, financial aid from state governments to local governments also involve strings of one kind or another.

Presidents and other government leaders often make proposals about how to structure relations and divide responsibilities among the national, state, and local governments. In the 1980s, President Reagan's "new federalism" was aimed at shifting greater responsibility back to the states and localities. The change in direction that began under Reagan continued under the first President Bush, and state and local governments had to operate in the context of what has been called "fend-for-yourself federalism."

Whatever changes the Clinton administration tried to make in intergovernmental relations faded into obscurity after Republicans took control of the House of Representatives and Senate in January 1995. Newt Gingrich, the first Republican Speaker of the House of Representatives in 40 years, made shrinking the role of the national government and giving increased responsibilities to the states an important part of his campaign promises in the November 1994 congressional elections. In turn, the House of Representatives initiated a number of bills fulfilling Gingrich's campaign promises. One bill was designed to make it very difficult for Congress to mandate that state and local governments do something without providing the necessary funding. The welfare reform bill of 1996 rewrote the welfare system that had begun in the 1930s as part of the New Deal. At the core of the reform was the devolution to state governments of more responsibilities in the provision of government assistance to the needy. While the national government remained mostly responsible for funding the welfare system, state governments were given increased responsibility for determining and implementing welfare policies. In sum, during the last two decades of the twentieth century, the United States seemed to have entered a new era of intergovernmental relations that involved substantial increases in the power and autonomy of state and local governments.

Then came the terrorist attacks of September 11, 2001. The resulting preoccupation with the war on terror produced an increase in national government power and activity in the sphere of homeland security, with a corresponding change in state and local responsibilities. U.S. military campaigns in Afghanistan and Iraq also distracted attention from intergovernmental relations on the domestic scene. By 2011, however, the national government's long-term debt and annual deficits had become the focus of heated debate in Washington and around the country, and there were proposals to have states assume

even more responsibility for administering and funding Medicaid, the program established in the 1960s to give poor Americans better access to medical care.

The enactment in 2010 of what came to be known as "Obamacare" promised to introduce new complexities into national–state relations in the health care sector. States had to choose among various options in providing their residents with access to health care insurance, and hospitals, some of which are associated with state or local governments, were affected as well. The high-profile malfunctioning of the Obamacare website after it opened on October 1, 2013, and other Obamacare problems led to widespread consternation and controversy and soon involved state health commissioners and state governments more generally. What the future of Medicaid and Obamacare holds in store for intergovernmental relations is unknown, but it seems almost certain that those relationships will remain an ever-changing and, at least some of the time, problematic phenomenon in the American political system.

Selections in this unit address various dimensions of the relationships among national, state, and local governments in the American political system.

Article   Prepared by: Bruce Stinebrickner, *DePauw University*

Taking Stock

Recalling 22 years of assessing the ebb and flow of states and localities.

ALAN EHRENHALT

Learning Outcomes

After reading this article, you will be able to:

- Assess whether the balance between states and cities described by Ehrenhalt in his 2010 article seems to have continued until today. In other words, has the "ebb and flow" that Ehrenhalt mentions led to apparent changes in the states-cities "balance" in the early decades of the 21st century?

- Consider what effect, if any, 9/11 had on state-cities "balance" and on national/state/local "balance" in the American political system.

When the first issue of *Governing* appeared 22 years ago, the editors made clear that this was a magazine about states and localities—their strengths, weaknesses, accomplishments and challenges—not a publication focused on one level of government or the other.

At the same time, it was clear which one was the senior partner in the American federal system. States were in good fiscal shape and more innovative than they had been in years. Governors of both parties, led by Jim Blanchard in Michigan and Dick Thornburgh in Pennsylvania, were dreaming up all sorts of economic development schemes to keep their states healthy in a post-industrial world. Bill Clinton in Arkansas and Tommy Thompson in Wisconsin were experimenting with changes in welfare law that paved the way for federal welfare reform enacted a decade later.

In 1988, journalist David Osborne wrote a book detailing the many varieties of state entrepreneurship and called it *Laboratories of Democracy,* echoing the phrase coined by Justice Louis Brandeis more than 50 years earlier. President Ronald Reagan's promise to devolve power to the states may have gone largely unrealized during his two terms in office, but states treated it as a license for seeking solutions to the myriad domestic policy problems that weren't being addressed at the federal level. As anybody who was around state government in those days will recall, it was a heady time.

And it lasted quite a while. Notwithstanding a pair of moderately severe recessions, states remained the fulcrum of public policy experiment in America for the better part of two decades. When it came to health, energy policy and a wide variety of other subjects, there was far more innovation at the state level in the 1990s and 2000s than in the federal government.

The contrast between the vitality of states and cities circa 1987 couldn't have been greater. Urban America was experiencing the twin ravages of AIDS and crack cocaine. Rates of violent crime were reaching levels never before seen in the nation's history.

There were more than 2,000 homicides in New York City in 1987, nearly three times as many as a quarter-century before, and the rate was continuing to increase. Whole city sections had become bywords for physical and social degradation; Paul Newman's movie, *Fort Apache, the Bronx,* characterized one of New York's boroughs as a hellhole more reminiscent of Third World chaos than of the largest metropolis in the United States.

While crime was shooting up, urban population was plunging. Cities such as Cleveland, Detroit and St. Louis were half the size they had been a generation earlier, and their downtowns were pockmarked with empty storefronts and underused office buildings, the streets lonely and dangerous anytime after dark. New York's psyche was still damaged by the painful memory of the near-bankruptcy of the previous decade; Cleveland still had not recovered from the humiliating bond default of 1978.

This was the balance that prevailed between states and localities when *Governing* published its first issue. To call it a balance at all is to underestimate what things were like. Many states were feisty and eager to take on new challenges. Cities were struggling just to survive.

To say that the balance has shifted in 22 years would be to make an even greater understatement. In 2010, the states aren't laboratories of democracy; they aren't laboratories of anything, unless it's insolvency. The numbers are familiar enough that there's no need to spend whole paragraphs repeating them: Suffice it to say that states as a whole are facing, by reliable estimates, a combined fiscal shortfall of up to $170 billion this year and $120 billion next year; that some are looking at budget holes equal to a quarter of their general fund or even more; that they are laying off thousands of workers and furloughing many thousands more; and that this still leaves them far short of the revenue they need to meet constitutional balanced-budget requirements.

The recession may be about over, but the fiscal crisis is not. The majority of states are looking at long-term pension and retiree health-care costs that must be addressed before they can be fiscally comfortable again. So far, none of the states with the most serious long-term problems has shown much resolve in addressing them.

The bottom line is that it may be unrealistic to consider states major innovators in public policy anytime in this decade. There are creative things they can do that don't cost a lot—they can pass new laws dealing with highway safety or cable TV regulation—but since most genuine innovation requires spending, it's fair to say that the laboratories of democracy will be closed, or at least inactive, for quite a while.

I f life has changed dramatically in the state capitols over the past two decades, it has changed just as much in the cities. And on the whole, it has changed for the better. To start with, there is safety. The number of homicides in New York City last year was 466, a level reached in 1987 before the end of March. Population is growing again as well, not just in New York, but also in Chicago, Washington, D.C., and numerous other cities that used to dread each decade's census for its inevitable documentation of continuing decline.

To say cities are doing better is not to minimize the perilous fiscal shape that many of them are in right now. Even as it becomes safer and more attractive to new residents, New York is having to raise taxes, lay off workers and cut back on social programs. That is a common predicament. But on the whole, urban fiscal problems are more recession-based and less structural than those of the states. Cities don't have Medicaid to worry about. Some have locked themselves into dangerous long-term pension commitments—Vallejo, Calif., went bankrupt over pension costs and San Diego nearly did a few years ago—but on the whole, cities have done better than states at avoiding this trap. And they have been more creative at finding ways to raise the revenues they need to render the services citizens demand of them. Raising taxes and fees hasn't always been the best economic development strategy, but it has helped keep budgets under control.

In any case, the renewal of cities is not primarily a fiscal matter. It is shown more clearly in the revival of residential life and street vitality all across the country; in the light rail systems taking shape in places one would never even associate with public transportation, such as Phoenix, Dallas and Charlotte, N.C.; and in the nodes of urban density that have begun to spring up along the transit lines once they are built. Most of all, urban revival is linked with changing demographics, as increasing numbers of people in their teens, 20s and early 30s, the vast majority of them singles or childless couples, express a preference for some form of urbanized life as a change from the cul-de-sac suburbia in which many of them grew up.

The urban comeback has stalled in the recession, as lending for central-city residential and commercial development has dried up. Some experts insist the comeback hasn't only stalled but ended: They believe once the economy recovers, suburban sprawl will simply resume. I think the evidence, from demographics, surveys and simple on-the-ground realities of the past few years, is clearly against them.

Whatever the future of urban revival may be, its recent past reflects a record of impressive innovation by many mayors. From the downtown development strategies of Richard M. Daley in Chicago, to the environmental activism of Greg Nickels in Seattle, the transportation planning initiatives of Michael Bloomberg in New York, and the housing reforms under Shirley Franklin in Atlanta, the past decade has seen a budding of new ideas in urban policy far more interesting than anything that preceded it for a long time.

Some may be tempted to say that the laboratories of democracy haven't closed; they simply have moved from state capitols to city halls. But I would be wary of taking the argument too far. If we have learned anything at *Governing* over the past 22 years, it is that power and creativity in the American federal system ebb and flow in cycles. The states have a huge task of restructuring ahead of them in the next decade. It will be excruciating, but once they accomplish it—and they really have no choice but to accomplish it, if they want to survive as legitimate political entities—there is reason to hope that they can eventually regain the spirit of optimism and innovation they displayed two decades ago.

I f my arithmetic is right, this is the 215th Assessments column I have written as editor of *Governing*. It is also the last. I'm moving on to try my hand at some new research on the states and to finish a book I'm writing on the future of American cities. I've heard from many of you personally in the past 19 years, and have appreciated every letter and e-mail, even (or perhaps especially) the many that took issue with things I've said. I expect to pop up in print in quite a few places in the coming months and years; I hope you'll continue to let me know what you think.

Critical Thinking

1. What, according to Ehrenhalt, was the balance between the vitality of states and the vitality of cities in the late 1980s?

2. What is the balance today?

3. What are some of the changes that have occurred in cities since the late 1980s? In states?

Create Central

www.mhhe.com/createcentral

Internet References

Council of State Governments
    www.csg.org
Advisory Commission on Intergovernmental Relations
    www.library.unt.edu/gpo/acir/Default.html
National League of Cities
    www.nlc.org/build-skills-and-networks/resources/cities-101/city-structures/local-us-governments

Article   Prepared by: Bruce Stinebrickner, *DePauw University*

The Untied States of America

The power is with the states

D. Scott
Dylan Scott

Learning Outcomes

After reading this article, you will be able to:

- Assess whether the phenomenon of growing differences in policies in the states is good or bad for the United States and its people.

- Weigh the impact of demographic "sorting" on politics and policymaking at all levels of American government.

- Evaluate the likelihood that "sorting" will continue to increase in the United States and how the continuing dispersion of Hispanics may play a role in your evaluation.

Less than five months after the massacre at Sandy Hook Elementary School, Connecticut enacted comprehensive gun control legislation. At the same time, 1,300 miles south and an ideological world away, Mississippi lawmakers considered a bill that would explicitly prohibit state officials from enforcing any new federal gun regulations. That last measure proved unnecessary. After months of controversy and extensive debate, Congress did not muster the votes to pass any federal law at all.

The same kind of split prevails on gay marriage. Last year, North Carolina joined more than 30 other states that have explicitly outlawed same-sex marriage. In just the past three months, Rhode Island, Delaware and Minnesota have legalized it, joining nine other states and the District of Columbia. The Supreme Court is currently deciding how far to wade into the gay marriage dispute—or whether it should wade in at all.

A third case: Voters in Colorado and Washington state chose to fully legalize marijuana in last November's election. On the same day, voters in Arkansas handily defeated a proposal to allow the drug even for medicinal purposes. The use of marijuana remains illegal under federal law; the Obama administration hasn't taken a position on last fall's actions but has made it clear that federal regulations will not be enforced.

This is more than just party polarization. It is part of a tectonic shift away from federal authority and toward power in the states. While the divided Congresses that have followed the 2010 Tea Party insurgency have been among the least productive in U.S. history, rife with partisan bickering and a chronic inability to compromise, robust action is common at the state

level. Connecticut's quick and seamless movement from tragedy to statute is one of countless examples. In turn, ideologues and interest groups increasingly view states as the most promising venues for policymaking. Why waste your time in Washington—where you might pass a watered-down, largely impotent bill if you're lucky—when you can head to Austin or Sacramento and advance your agenda intact and with relative ease?

And while states pass legislation with an almost industrial efficiency, America, as is often noted these days, is becoming a more and more splintered nation. Red states are redder; blue states are bluer.

Take a look at a U.S. map colored by state party control. In the upper right-hand corner down to the Mid-Atlantic, it's all blue. In the South and across the Great Plains, you see a blanket of red. That crimson sea begins to break at the Rocky Mountains until you reach a stretch of blue along the West Coast. In a way, we are returning to our roots as a loose confederation of culturally and geographically distinct governments.

States led by Democrats are moving toward broader Medicaid coverage, stricter gun laws and a liberalized drug policy. They've legalized gay marriage, abolished the death penalty and extended new rights to undocumented immigrants. Republican strongholds are working quickly to remove government from the business sphere—reducing taxes, pushing anti-union right-to-work laws and rebelling against the Affordable Care Act (ACA). They're also pressing forward on some of their most valued social issues, promoting pro-life abortion policies and protecting the rights of gun owners.

The divisions generate fundamental questions about the nature of federalism. The sweeping national interventions of the New Deal and the comprehensive federal social legislation of the 1960s have been replaced by a more decentralized approach to governance. States are openly defying federal law and resurrecting the concept of nullification.

These are not merely legal or rhetorical exercises. They are fostering real change and real consequences for average Americans. If one bill that's currently pending in the Mississippi legislature is upheld by higher courts, the state will have effectively outlawed abortion altogether. In New York, meanwhile, Gov. Andrew Cuomo has introduced legislation that would make abortions easier for women in his state to obtain. Income taxes may go up this year in California and Massachusetts; several Republican governors say they want to abolish income taxes completely. Illinois will insure nearly 1 million additional people next year by expanding its Medicaid program under the federal health law, while Texas is expected to leave up to 2 million people without coverage because Gov. Rick Perry has steadfastly refused to do the same.

"Polarization has resulted in this changing relationship between the states and the federal government. There's a clear connection," says Alan Abramowitz, a political scientist at Emory University. "It's leading to gridlock at the federal level, which in turn is leading to many issues being decided at the state level because the federal government seems to be incapable of deciding anything."

"That's the hydraulics of political power. Power always seeks an outlet," agrees Heather Gerken, a law professor at Yale University. "When Congress is no longer doing anything, people are going to go to the states and localities."

This rebalancing of the federalist system has permeated almost every corner of public policy, taking center stage in the most controversial debates of the last few years. Last summer, Chief Justice John Roberts made the unexpected decision to join with his liberal colleagues and uphold the bulk of Obamacare and its individual mandate to purchase health insurance. But on the less publicized question of the law's Medicaid expansion, which was supposed to require states to extend eligibility for the program to those earning up to 138 percent of the federal poverty level, Roberts took a startling turn. He ruled, for the first time in the court's history, that the federal government had gone beyond its constitutional powers when it threatened to withhold all of a state's federal Medicaid funding if it refused to comply with the expansion.

The immediate implication was a dramatic reassertion of individual states' sovereignty. In the year since the court's decision, a Southern wall of conservative states, which fought against the ACA in the first place and have been encouraged by national Republican leaders, have decided to take this new option that Roberts legitimized and have refused to expand Medicaid.

On other issues, states have rebuffed federal policy or preempted it. The Real ID Act of 2005, mandating state adoption of what is effectively a national identification card, has been foiled in the last decade by states refusing to comply with its federal requirements. More than 40 states have agreed to adopt the Common Core State Standards for K-12 education, which involve new curricula and assessments developed by state policymakers, in part because they didn't want another federal education regime after the failure of No Child Left Behind. The distribution of medical marijuana in 17 states, paired with outright legalization in Colorado and Washington, is a clear flouting of the federal Controlled Substances Act.

Such assertiveness or outright defiance by the states is a dramatic shift from the assumptions of federal preeminence that have prevailed during most of the years since the enactment of comprehensive social legislation during the 1960s, which included the passage of the Civil Rights Act, the Voting Rights Act and Medicare. Some would place the beginning of the erosion of the federal model in the Reagan administration, which introduced the waiver concept to state-federal programs such as Medicaid.

But it is also a reflection of changing public opinion: The Pew Research Center found this April that people's trust in state and local government had settled comfortably above 50 percent. Trust in the federal government, meanwhile, sat at a dismal 28 percent in 2012. That's a far cry from the early 1960s, when public confidence in Washington approached 80 percent.

"People had lost confidence that states were really up to the task of dealing with problems of modern society, so the federal government filled that vacuum," says Ernest Young, a constitutional law scholar at Duke University. "We're living in a new era now where the opposite is true. People have more trust in their state and local governments than the federal government."

Coinciding with this movement toward more state-centric governance has been the ideological polarization of the two political parties. Conservative Southern Democrats and moderate Northeast Republicans have slowly disappeared both from Congress and from state legislatures in the last generation. The Democratic Party is more uniformly liberal, and the Republican Party more uniformly conservative, than either has ever been. They therefore command certain regions of the country more consistently; the turnover of conservative Southerners to the Republican Party has turned the Deep South impenetrably red. Republicans have become a weak minority in much of the Northeast and West Coast.

This natural political sorting has led to two very different outcomes. With the GOP controlling the U.S. House and the Democrats controlling the Senate and the White House, productivity in Washington is at a historic low. Multiple analyses ranked the 112th Congress, which met in 2011 and 2012, at or near the bottom in terms of legislation passed and signed by the president. There was some optimism that the 113th Congress would see an uptick in action, due to the supposed mandates of the 2012 presidential election, but there is little to support that thesis so far.

While Capitol Hill trudges through political molasses, the states are as prolific as they have ever been—and the primary reason is the prevalence of single-party rule in the nation's statehouses. One party or the other is in full charge of both chambers of the legislative branch in 43 states. This is the highest concentration of partisan power since the 1940s. Half the legislatures have veto-proof supermajorities.

So when anti-abortion advocates want to roll back Roe v. Wade, they turn to conservative-controlled states. Arkansas and North Dakota are two of the most recent single-party legislatures to pass abortion restrictions, outlawing abortions after 12 and six weeks of pregnancy, respectively. Arkansas' Republican senate and house passed this legislation over the veto of Democratic Gov. Mike Beebe, one of only two Democratic governors left in the South.

On the other end of the spectrum, California, tired of waiting for federal action on climate change, established its own cap-and-trade system last year; the nation's largest and arguably most liberal state had little trouble charting its own course on legislation that's essentially been a pipe dream in Washington since the 2010 midterms.

Individual states or coalitions of states can increasingly be viewed as proxies for what their ruling party's elites would like to accomplish at the national level, but currently cannot. Take Washington state as the liberal example. The Democratic legislature and governor have legalized gay marriage, taken an active role in implementing Obamacare and begun work this year to meet the goal of reducing the state's greenhouse gas emissions to 1990 levels by 2020.

Conservative counterparts are plentiful: Texas has become the flagship opponent of the federal health law, leading a coalition that includes nearly every state below the Mason-Dixon Line. Its legislature voted to defund Planned Parenthood because of its ties to abortion providers. Kansas, Nebraska and Louisiana have weighed the elimination of their state income taxes this year. Republicans in Indiana and Michigan last year joined the anti-union right-to-work movement that conservatives have been promoting since the 1940s. At least 10 GOP-controlled states have passed laws this year loosening their gun regulations.

"As the parties become more distinct from each other, they're generating a lot of ideas. They've become very programmatic parties, and they've been doing a lot of policy implementation in the states," says Seth Masket, a political scientist at the University of Denver. "If you want to change the ways things are, you're almost invariably going to be frustrated at the federal level. If you're going to get anything done, a unified state government is the place to do it."

So where are we headed? Is this movement toward decentralization and polarization a momentary lapse in what once seemed an unavoidable march toward federal control? Or are we seeing a permanent revival of the 10th Amendment to the U.S. Constitution, under which most governmental power is reserved to the states and regional fracture is assumed to be the norm?

There is a good deal of evidence to suggest that political polarization across states and regions will solidify. One argument is that people seem to be choosing, consciously or unconsciously, to live in communities that share their ideological beliefs. This is known in sociological circles as "sorting." It offers a powerful explanation for the growing homogeneity within states and regions, and some statistical analysis backs the theory.

In 1976, 26 percent of Americans lived in "landslide counties,'" defined as those that voted for one presidential candidate by at least a 20-percentage-point margin over the other, according to an analysis by social commentator Bill Bishop and University of Texas sociologist Robert Cushing. By 2012, that number doubled to 52 percent. In the 1976 election, 20 states were decided by five percentage points or less in the race between Jimmy Carter and Gerald Ford; only four were that close in 2012 with Barack Obama and Mitt Romney on the ballot.

Some doubt the sorting thesis, both as a reason for polarization and as a predictor of future trends. They instead attribute the widening political gap to simple ideological reshuffling—conservatives coalescing in the Republican Party, and liberals on the Democratic side. Gerrymandering is sometimes blamed for appearing to sort like-minded people into the same jurisdictions.

Several variables could determine whether this movement persists in the coming years. In particular, the dispersion of Hispanics and other minority populations into new communities where they haven't historically lived could upset the political balance in those places. The Democratic goal of turning Texas blue within the next two decades is the most noteworthy endorsement of this belief. Or perhaps the millennial generation won't remain as thoroughly liberal as it seems to be right now.

But many prominent thinkers give credence to the sorting thesis, and if it does hold some truth, then ideological and geographic divisions should harden in the coming decades. New England would continue on its path toward liberalized social democracy; the South would move further toward laissez-faire or libertarian capitalism.

If the sorting rule bears out, and states and regions continue to drift further and further apart on public policy, people might increasingly decide where to live based on these differences. That would create a self-perpetuating cycle that would continue to decentralize political power and destabilize our concept of a national identity.

"The trouble is within these places, there's less diversity where you live, but there's more diversity from place to place. As a result, there's less of a sense of a country as a whole," says social commentator Bishop, who drew national attention to the idea in his 2008 book, "The Big Sort: Why the Clustering of Like-Minded America Is Tearing Us Apart." "So you have this phenomenon where like-minded people get together and they become more extreme in the way they're like-minded."

In this future as a sectarian nation, which some say has already arrived, states emerge as the best forum for meaningful policymaking. The federal government will always have a dominant role on some subjects—foreign relations and international trade being the most obvious—but as long as Washington is politically divided, the number of issues on which it can effectively act is likely to shrink.

"When states become very homogeneous inside, and more heterogeneous across state lines," says Michael Greve, a law professor at George Mason University and director of the Federalism Project at the American Enterprise Institute, "it becomes much, much harder to write federal legislation that wraps all of them under one federal cartel."

The Affordable Care Act, which might stand as the last significant legislative achievement of a single-party Congress and White House for the foreseeable future, has become a testament to how difficult it is to institute national initiatives when some states actively resist federal prescriptions.

The refusal of conservative states to expand Medicaid has undercut the law's ability to insure low-income Americans. More than 30 states have refused to set up health-care marketplaces, which has left the Obama administration scrambling to pick up the slack. Questions are mounting about what will happen in these conservative states in 2014, when the law's major changes are supposed to take effect. On the other hand, the liberal states that have embraced the law's policies will fundamentally overhaul their insurance markets next year, as was originally intended. But the law's goal of universal health coverage will be stifled by the dissenting states.

Supporters of a revised immigration law remain hopeful for federal action during the 113th Congress. But the resulting legislation, if it passes, will likely be an undesirable compromise for both parties, a vanilla law that really pleases no one. If you want ideological purity, look a few miles away to Democratic Maryland, where Gov. Martin O'Malley and his legislature have in the past year legalized gay marriage, cracked down on guns, passed a DREAM Act that eases access to education for undocumented immigrants and eliminated the death penalty. Or go to Republican Mississippi, where the Second Amendment is sacrosanct, abortion is being made extremely difficult and residents have one of the lowest tax burdens in the nation. It's still possible to achieve philosophical cohesion within a single-party state, and there are more of them than ever. If you want to change policy, look to the states. That's where the action is these days.

Critical Thinking

1. What are some recent examples of a significant re-assertion of individual states' sovereignty?

2. What, according to Dylan Scott, is the primary reason that state governments have been significant and even prolific policymakers during a period when the national government is seen to be grid-locked and unproductive?

3. What is "sorting" and how it does help explain growing homogeneity within states and regions of the United States?

Create Central

www.mhhe.com/createcentral

Internet References

Same Sex Marriage Laws (National Council of State Legislators)
www.ncsl.org/research/human-services/same-sex-marriage-laws.aspx

State Gun Laws (Brady campaign)
http://bradycampaign.org/?q=programs/million-mom-march/state-gun-laws

State Medical Marijuana Laws (National Council of State Legislators)
www.ncsl.org/research/health/state-medical-marijuana-laws.aspx

Scott, Dylan. From *Governing*, June 2013, pp. 44–47. Copyright © 2013 by e.Republic Inc. Reprinted by permission via Wright's Media.

polarization will be the downfall of America

States vs. Feds

The growing schism between states and the federal government makes for a difficult and deteriorating relationship, with a few exceptions.

CARL TUBBESING

Learning Outcomes

After reading this article, you will be able to:

- Evaluate the relative seriousness of the five "cracks" or problem areas in national-state relations today.

- Weigh several "bright spots" against the "cracks" in national-state relations and assess whether the "bright spots" are enough to counterbalance the "cracks" in an overall assessment.

The challenges facing state officials as they deal with the federal government are enough to make them nostalgic for the good old days of unfunded mandates and preemption. As pernicious as these phenomena were—and still are—they were easily explained, and their effects on state flexibility and innovation were easily understood.

Cracks in the Federal System

The current tensions in the federal system are more nuanced and resistant to solution than they were only a decade or so ago. And the prospects for any long-term improvement in the states' relations with the federal government are downright discouraging. That's the gloomy assessment offered by all four federalism experts interviewed for this article.

The bright spot in their analyses is that states continue to be policy activists and innovators, sometimes even in defiance of federal law, demonstrating the resilience and vitality of the federal system, even in a time of great tension.

Five recent developments present significant challenges for state officials in achieving a healthy partnership with the national government.

1. Reauthorization of Federal Laws

Historically, most federal laws have come with an expiration date. In order for them to remain in place, they must receive congressional reauthorization, or at least be amended or extended for the short term. The reauthorization process, however, has been one of the casualties of the near-paralysis that characterizes much of the activity in Washington, D.C., these days. In fact, some major laws have never been reauthorized and others haven't been for decades. The Clean Air Act was last amended in 1990, the Safe Drinking Water Act in 1996. The Temporary Assistance for Needy Families was reauthorized in 2005, but has existed on a series of short-term extensions ever since. Both the Workforce Investment Act of 1998 and the No Child Left Behind education act of 2001, have never been reauthorized. This failure to act places uncertainty on the laws' futures that not only inhibits states' abilities to plan ahead and implement the laws, but also to improve them.

George Mason University's Paul Posner notes that when the reauthorization process works, states' experiences with implementing the law can provide important insight into how to improve it. But the current breakdown in the reauthorization process, says Michael Bird, former senior federal affairs counsel for NCSL, prevents state legislators from working with Congress to fix problems in the laws.

John Kincaid from Lafayette College and Florida State's Carol Weissert point out a sobering reality: Even when Congress does reauthorize a law, it seldom listens to state officials. "Years ago," Weissert says, "there was much more deference to state legislators and governors." She points to a study by political scientist Kevin Esterling that showed during Medicaid hearings in the U.S. House, members of Congress were more likely to favor the testimony of industry, trade associations and think tanks over that of state officials.

2. Waiver Authority

States may apply for waivers from certain provisions in many federal laws. One theory behind the concept is that it saves Congress from writing even more detail into legislation, and it allows the executive branch to accommodate differences among states. Waivers can also be used to encourage a specific state action. In fact, waivers have become a prominent focal point in state-federal relations. President George W. Bush and his Education Department, for example, used waivers to encourage states to comply with the No Child Left Behind law. Likewise, waivers have been an essential tool in negotiations between the

Obama administration and state governors over the Affordable Care Act.

Posner views the increased use of waivers as a presidential reaction to congressional inaction. By making accommodations and improvements to laws on a state-by-state basis, "waivers have become the functional equivalent of reauthorizations," he says. The word Weissert likes to use to describe today's waiver-filled federal system is "bargaining."

"Things are negotiable," she says. And although waivers provide legislators and governors with a certain degree of flexibility, Weissert questions whether there is enough transparency in the granting of waivers and whether states are treated equitably.

3. Competitive Grants

First used by the national government as long ago as the mid-1960s, competitive grants are awarded to states at the discretion of federal agencies based on criteria or standards established by law or regulation. The Obama administration has been particularly enamored with them. The president used competitive grants in the American Recovery and Reinvestment Act for high-speed rail and other transportation projects as well as broadband deployment. And the president's most recent budget offering includes several new competitive grants, including ones to encourage energy efficiency and preschool improvements.

But by almost any measure, Obama's Race to the Top initiative, also included in the economic stimulus law approved in 2009, has been the most successful ever at achieving dramatic state policy changes. What has set Race to the Top apart is the huge pot of money—$4.35 billion—available for the grants and the way it has brought about reforms in state education laws, among both the states that won and those that didn't.

Posner believes competitive grants represent "a resurgence of creative federalism" that began in the Lyndon Johnson years. His argument is that they "drive a lot of change," while accommodating differences among the states. Besides, he says, they're voluntary, states don't have to participate.

Critics argue there's something wrong with this picture. They say the motivation behind competitive grants is upside down. Traditionally, states have served as the "laboratories of democracy," experimenting with solutions to difficult challenges, refining and shaping them to differing circumstances, state by state. Often this process results in action by the federal government, argues Posner, but not until a significant number of states have acted—not until the issue is "finally ripe for solution" at the national level, he says.

Competitive grants represent top-down—and often coercive—federalism, which Kincaid argues has been the dominant feature of state-federal relations since the late 1960s. Although states may not have to apply for the grants, Kincaid says the amount of money involved, especially when states are so strapped for funds, makes them very hard to resist.

4. Institutional Connections

Michael Bird's Washington career began in the latter half of Ronald Reagan's presidency, when the Advisory Commission on Intergovernmental Relations (ACIR) was a vital forum for discussion and research among state, federal and local officials. At that time, the U.S. House and Senate had full, standing committees devoted to intergovernmental issues. The White House intergovernmental staffs had clout in administration policy deliberations. Several federal agencies, including the Census Bureau and the Office of Management and Budget, produced

Federalism

John Kincaid is director of the Meyner Center for the Study of State and Local Government and professor of government and public service at Lafayette College in Pennsylvania. Kincaid served on the staff of the U.S. Advisory Commission on Intergovernmental Relations for eight years and was the executive director from 1988 to 1994. He has written numerous books and articles on federalism and federal systems, and was the editor of *Publius: The Journal of Federalism* for 25 years.

Paul Posner is director of the public administration program at George Mason University and a former president of the American Society of Public Administration. He led the budget and public finance work at the U.S. Government Accountability Office for 14 years, wrote "The Politics of Unfunded Mandates" and many articles on public budgeting and federalism, and has worked with senior budget leaders of advanced nations through the Organization for Economic Cooperation and Development.

Carol Weissert is professor of political science and director of the LeRoy Collins Institute for Public Policy at Florida State University and is the editor of *Publius*. Her early career

included three years at the National Legislative Conference (one of the organizations that merged to form NCSL) and positions at the U.S. Advisory Commission on Intergovernmental Relations and the National Governors Association. She has been a professor of political science and director of the Institute for Public Policy and Social Research at Michigan State University and has written many books and articles on federalism and public policy, particularly health policy.

Michael Bird began his service to state legislatures in 1970 as an intern in the Illinois General Assembly, followed by a stint with the Program for Legislative Improvement, working on projects to modernize the Colorado and Arizona legislatures. After working on a similar project with the U.S. Virgin Islands Legislature, he directed the fiscal staff of the Oklahoma Senate. He joined NCSL in 1985 as a member of the state-federal relations team in Washington, D.C. As NCSL's senior federal affairs counsel, Bird coordinated lobbying activities and was the liaison to congressional leadership offices and the White House. Bird retired from NCSL in May 2013.

invaluable information and analysis on state and federal fiscal matters.

When Bird retired in May, the advisory commission had long since been dismantled, the congressional committees were gone, the role of White House intergovernmental staff had been diminished and intergovernmental fiscal reports were no longer produced.

For Bird, the demise of these forums is symbolic of the cracks in the federal system. Cracks that affect how state, local and federal officials communicate and work with one another to craft solutions to common problems.

Weissert, whose early career included seven years at ACIR, maintains that the disappearance of these kinds of institutions is "one of the really bad things" that has happened over the past several years and particularly laments the loss of intergovernmental research.

"ACIR was created and was successful at a unique time, when political parties were not so polarized and could work together in settings like that," says Kincaid, who directed the commission for eight years. He says he has no expectation that it or any of these forums will ever be revived.

5. A Political Disconnect

About half the members of Congress once served in their state legislatures, making them obvious potential state cheerleaders. For more than three decades, NCSL staff have cultivated relationships with these lawmakers in their work for states. They have sought them out to sponsor key amendments. They have encouraged state legislators to bring these former colleagues back to the state capitol to remind them of their roots. They have heard them say, "You don't have to worry about me on this. I came from a legislature, you know."

That connection, though still a factor, may be disintegrating. Weissert has studied the bills that former state legislators introduce in Congress and has concluded that while federal lawmakers may recognize the role of states in the legislation they introduce, the bills are not necessarily "state-friendly." Similarly, Posner's analysis of votes on unfunded mandates showed that having served in state or local office had no effect on how members voted.

Bird recalls a prime example of that. The first vote cast by a former NCSL president was against an NCSL policy position. Posner relates an analogous story involving a former chairman of the National Governors Association. "Federalism isn't animating discussions any longer," Posner argues. "Even states' champions aren't necessarily their champions anymore."

How has this happened? Weissert and Posner point to partisanship and private interests. "There is just so much more partisanship at both levels," Weissert says. That, along with "private interests," have eclipsed the states' role, says Posner.

Kincaid argues that so much of this has to do with elections. The way congressional districts are drawn, the kind of candidates who win primary elections and the need to raise large amounts of money all work to devalue state experience and interests as influences over congressional behavior. It is also very difficult for polarized state officials to come to consensus on federal matters. Posner, for example, points out that the National Governors Association, once a power in negotiations over almost all domestic policy matters, has had to sit out the work on such major recent legislation as health care, immigration reform and No Child Left Behind, because its members have been unable to find common ground on the issues.

The Bright Spots

Despite these cracks in the federal system, experts believe state officials are, and will continue to be, effective players in shaping public policy. Here are three reasons why.

States Have Great Influence in Implementing Federal Laws

A popular belief is that states have become nothing more than branch managers for the federal government, implying that they do little more than administer laws passed by Congress. Not so, Weissert says. It's when state and federal officials get down to the business of making federal laws work that they have their greatest influence, she says.

Kincaid concurs. He believes the level of cooperation required at the implementation stage, when state and federal officials must work together, is a positive contrast from the coercive way the federal government usually treats the states.

Posner and Bird say the partnership works well when the federal government needs the states—a phenomenon Posner describes as an "episodic attachment to federalism" and Bird characterizes as "convenient federalism." Posner notes, for example, that the federal government had to rely on the states when it did not have sufficient resources to administer the 2009 recovery act, thereby giving states leverage over how many of the law's many elements to carry out.

Although states are weaker than they once were in shaping legislation as it moves through Congress, Posner argues they have plenty of influence through the back-door—through the waiver process and other state-by-state negotiations—and their influence is greatest during the early stages of implementing a new law. Weissert points to the separate deals that governors are making over Medicaid expansions as part of the health reform act as a prime example of this back-door influence.

States Are as Innovative as Ever

A willingness to tackle tough issues is the stuff of New York Times headlines: "Connecticut Deal on Gun Control May Be Nation's Most Sweeping." "Arkansas Adopts Restrictive Abortion Law." "States Shifting Aid for Schools to the Families." Gun control, abortion, charter schools, immigration, elections, climate change and marijuana are among the nation's most intransigent and controversial issues. Yet, state legislatures and governors take them on session after session. Posner asserts "state policymaking is as fertile as ever."

Many of the areas in states' current policy activism are "morality issues" the federal government finds almost impossible to handle, Weissert says. Current state action has been facilitated by the fact that, in an unprecedented number of states, one party controls both the legislature and the governorship, making controversial issues easier to resolve.

Sometimes States Take the Ball and Go Home

State legislators are finding leverage, too, by refusing to abide by federal directives. Passage of the REAL ID Act in 2005 provoked large scale "civil disobedience" among state legislators and governors. The result? Only 19 states have been deemed in compliance with the law. When states refuse to comply with REAL ID, carve out exceptions to No Child Left Behind, reject high speed rail funds or refuse to expand Medicaid, Posner says they are demonstrating a "resistance impulse."

Other state legislatures are engaging in "de facto nullification," Kincaid believes, by passing state laws in defiance of federal law. Nullification is a legal theory that says state lawmakers have the right to invalidate any federal law they view as unconstitutional. In some areas, such as restricting abortions and legalizing marijuana, Kincaid says states are nullifying federal law, state by state.

Systemic Challenges

The resiliency and vitality that states have demonstrated in the federal system for more than two centuries are undergoing an especially critical test. In the recent past, when unfunded mandates and preemption placed strains on the system, state legislators looked for solutions in legislation—the Unfunded Mandate Reform Act—and in presidential directive—the Federalism Executive Order.

The causes of the current tensions, experts agree, are systemic: namely, extreme partisanship and polarization and the federal government's structural fiscal woes. These challenges are not susceptible to legislative or regulatory fixes.

The cracks in the federal system, in other words, are deep and may be widening for quite some time.

Critical Thinking

1. What are five "cracks" or problem areas that are working to obstruct good national-state relations today?
2. What are several "bright spots" that may make it likely that state government officials will continue to be important participants in shaping public policy in the United States?
3. How does the high level of partisanship in Congress today affect certain elements in state-national government relations and make optimism for better state-national relations seem unwarranted?

Create Central

www.mhhe.com/createcentral

Internet References

Advisory Commission on Intergovernmental Relations
www.library.unt.edu/gpo/acir/Default.html
Council of State Governments
www.csg.org
History Learning Site: Federalism
www.historylearningsite.co.uk/fed.htm

CARL TUBBESING, a frequent contributor to State Legislatures throughout his 35-year career with NCSL, continues writing in retirement. He joined NCSL shortly after its formation in 1975 and served 11 years in its Denver office before becoming director of NCSL's Washington, D.C., office where he managed state-federal activities. He was deputy executive director of NCSL when he retired in 2010. Tubbesing holds a Ph.D. in political science from Washington University in St. Louis and now lives in Maine, where he serves on several volunteer boards and enjoys the "prototypical retirement activities" of gardening, golf, and bird watching.

Article

Prepared by: Bruce Stinebrickner, *DePauw University*

Devolution and Arrogance

States can't resist the temptation to boss their localities around.

ALAN EHRENHALT

Learning Outcomes

After reading this article, you will be able to:

- Explore why national and state government officials often put into practice the Golden Rule in reverse—Do Unto Others as Somebody One Rung Above Has Just Done Unto You?

- Evaluate the desirability of the principle of "subsidiarity" in national-state-local relations.

Shortly before it adjourned this spring, the West Virginia Legislature approved a bill to expand the home rule power of many of the state's cities. Among other things, cities were given more freedom to impose a sales tax, clear blighted properties and streamline the granting of development permits.

Sounds like a good deal for the cities. And it would have been, had the lawmakers not slipped a couple of extra provisions into the legislation shortly before passing it. One stipulated that in order to qualify for the new home rule status, cities had to repeal most laws on their books limiting the sale or use of handguns. Another required them to stay out of the business of same-sex marriage. Pass a gay marriage law, the state told the cities, and you can forget about that new sales tax.

Now, states are notorious for passing preemptive laws that bar cities from acting as autonomous political entities. But as far as I know, only West Virginia has been brazen enough to put preemption right in the middle of legislation supposedly advancing the cause of devolution.

Even state officials who ended up supporting the whole package sounded embarrassed about it. West Virginia Gov. Earl Ray Tomblin, who signed the bill, allowed that it seemed to him "a little bit of a contradiction." Tomblin added that "when you think of home rule . . . , it's giving them more flexibility, and this does tie their hands somewhat." More than somewhat, as a matter of fact. Charleston, which has had a gun background check law since the early 1990s, was told to get rid of it or drop out of the home rule project altogether.

This wasn't a matter of partisanship. Tomblin and the legislative leaders are Democrats, but both parties supported the clumsy intrusion of the state into what are fundamentally local affairs.

It would be one thing if West Virginia were an aberration in the politics of 2013. But it's more like the extreme example of local preemption that's seized state legislatures nationwide this year. States are stumbling their way from their own bitter complaints about federal meddling—and even outright defiance of federal authority—to imposing dictatorial mandates on the local governments with whom they're supposed to work cooperatively.

Georgia's a good example. In the legislative session that concluded this spring, the Republican legislature redrew the election lines of the state's largest local jurisdiction, Fulton County, to create more Republican voting power in the county's Republican-held north and fewer seats in the mostly black southern portion. Two black Democratic commissioners in the county's south were forced into the same district, which will eliminate one seat. The legislature seized control of the largely Democratic county election commission and gave Republican Gov. Nathan Deal the power to appoint the county's top election official.

Meanwhile, in neighboring and mostly black DeKalb County, Deal suspended six members of the local school board and replaced them with his own appointees. Several of the members displaced are seeking reinstatement, and the law under which Deal acted is being challenged in court as unconstitutional. For next year, GOP legislators are readying plans to privatize many of the functions of the Atlanta-run MARTA public transit agency. Why are they doing these things? The standard explanation is that the agencies were being mismanaged and obstructing political and administrative reform.

"We're not trying to run the day-to-day operations," one proponent of the changes insisted to a reporter. "If it became a permanent meddling, I think that you would see some discontent." But a Democratic legislator from Atlanta reacted to the DeKalb intervention by telling an *Atlanta Journal-Constitution* reporter

sounds like a monarchy

that "this is setting a precedent of the state doing major power grabs on city councils and school boards as well as county commissions."

North Carolina is another interesting case. As the state's financial, commercial and cultural center, Charlotte has always played an outsized role in state politics. It has alternated between Democratic and Republican rule at city hall. But in the past few years, Charlotte has been trending increasingly Democratic. The city and surrounding Mecklenburg County were among the few jurisdictions in North Carolina to support President Obama for re-election in 2012. Charlotte's former Democratic mayor, Anthony Foxx, is now the federal transportation secretary.

Still, conflict between Charlotte and the Republicans who dominate state politics seemed unlikely since the state's new governor, elected in 2012, was Pat McCrory, himself a former Republican mayor of Charlotte. McCrory came into office this year with an ambitious agenda focused on economic development and education. And the legislators devoted attention to those issues. But what they spent much of their session arguing about was how to take power away from Charlotte, the state's largest city, and give it to state and regional boards responsive to the state's GOP leadership. Among the bills considered this year in Raleigh were ones to deny Charlotte taxing authority to support a new sports stadium; to regionalize control of a local social services agency; to limit the city's annexation and environmental enforcement powers; and to deny previously committed funds for expansion of the city's light rail transit line.

These moves generated an incredulous reaction even from some of the state's most experienced and nonpartisan observers. "For years we heard conservatives say that the government closest to the people governs best," the veteran columnist Rob Christensen wrote recently. "But they were talking about Washington. When it comes to Raleigh, they haven't hesitated to use state power to advance their own agenda—even if it means disregarding local sentiment."

And disregard local sentiment is just what they've done. The most egregious example in North Carolina this year was a legislative effort to take control of the Charlotte airport out of city hands and put it in the control of yet another regional commission. There were no significant allegations that the airport was being mismanaged, nor were there a large number of citizen complaints about service quality. The best that supporters of this blatant power grab could muster was the argument that a regional governing body can better prepare local aviation for 21st-century demands. No solid evidence for this proposition has been produced.

The airport coup was too much even for McCrory. He brokered a compromise under which the airport's future would be determined by a blue-ribbon panel dominated by members of the legislature. Not surprisingly, city officials turned this down. Until it was demonstrated that they had done something wrong, they argued, compromise was inappropriate. But shortly before the legislative session ended in late July, both the House and the Senate approved a bill to strip the city of airport control.

I sometimes advertise myself as a believer in devolution, but that's not precisely correct. What I believe in is decision-making at the least exalted level possible. Except in extreme cases of constitutional defiance, Congress should defer to the judgment of the states. And states should defer to the judgment of cities and counties on matters that relate strictly to local affairs. I realize that what constitutes a state or local issue in this country is a subject of unending debate. But I find it distasteful for higher levels of government to throw their weight around, especially when they are making judgments based more on ideology than on the expressed wishes of the people affected.

It could be that I believe these things so strongly because I've never been elected to any office above the neighborhood level. If I had, I might have been unable to resist sticking my nose into the prerogatives of the unfortunate government underneath me.

Just about every public official I know of has been unable to resist it. I used to admire the late Chief Justice William Rehnquist as an advocate of both devolution and the rights of lower-level government institutions. Then Rehnquist joined in the decision overriding the judgment of Florida's elected Supreme Court and deciding the 2000 presidential election dispute.

Of all the significant concepts of democratic government, devolution may be the one with the greatest gap between theory and practice. It's a concept that goes back far beyond the founding of the American republic, to the medieval Roman Catholic Church, which held that doctrinal disputes should whenever possible be settled at the level closest to that of the individual worshipers. That was called subsidiarity. It still is. A secular form of subsidiarity remains a fundamental legal tenet of the European Union, which honors it more in the breach than in the observance.

Perhaps, given the events of this legislative year, the time has come to stop mourning the hypocrisies of federalism and to start laughing at them. I was tempted to do this when I first read of the West Virginia home rule law. I had a similar reaction when I noticed that Missouri's Legislature was simultaneously considering a bill that would nullify federal gun laws and another that would impose financial penalties on local governments that banned smoking. That was happening while Mississippi enacted a law forbidding the state's localities from restricting the consumption of sugary soft drinks.

In the end, there's no simple way—perhaps there's no way at all—to prevent governments from treating those below them as unruly children. Few of us like being ordered around; most of us very much enjoy ordering others around. When we hold political office, we have an opportunity to behave inconsistently in highly visible fashion. In a complex political system like the one that operates in this country, the key players practice a sort of Golden Rule in reverse: Do Unto Others as Somebody One Rung Above Has Just Done Unto You.

Critical Thinking

1. How does the Golden Rule in reverse—Do Unto Others as Somebody One Rung Above Has Just Done Unto You—seem to describe the way that state governments often seem to treat their local governments?

2. What is "subsidiarity" in the context of national-state-local government relations?

Create Central

www.mhhe.com/createcentral

Internet References

Alan Ehrenhalt profile (Governing)
www.governing.com/authors/Alan-Ehrenhalt.html

Devolution (Enclopedia Brittanica)
www.britannica.com/EBchecked/topic/155042/devolution

Unit 3

UNIT

Prepared by: Bruce Stinebrickner, *DePauw University*

Linkages between Citizens and Governments

The American political system is typically classified as a representative democracy. Top government officials are elected by the people and, as a result, government is supposed to be responsive and accountable to citizens. Both the theory and the practice of representative democracy are of interest to students of American politics. Political scientists study various political elements that seem essential to the healthy functioning of a representative democracy: political parties, interest groups, election laws, campaign techniques, and so forth. Attention is not limited to the national government; state and local governments are also examined in order to assess their responsiveness and accountability.

State and local governments operate under somewhat different institutional arrangements and circumstances than the national government. In many states and some localities, voters can participate directly in the policy process through mechanisms known as initiatives and referenda. In addition, some state and local voters can participate in removing elected officials from office by a procedure known as "recall." In many localities in the New England states, an annual open meeting of all local citizens, which is called a town meeting, functions as the local government legislature. These mechanisms provide direct avenues for citizens to determine state and local government policies, avenues that are not available to them with respect to the national government.

Generally speaking, party organization has historically been strongest at the local level and weakest at the national level, but this historic pattern has been eroding in recent decades. Party "machines" have been a well-known feature of the local political landscape in the United States, and colorful and powerful "bosses" have left their mark on local political history. While the heyday of bosses and machines is past, examples of contemporary political machines still exist. National elections, especially for the presidency, are usually contested vigorously by the two major parties and, over the long haul, the two parties tend to be reasonably competitive with each other. This is less true in states and localities, because a large majority of voters in some states and many localities are decidedly oriented toward one party or the other. Thus, in some states and localities, more significant competition can occur within the nominating process of the dominant party than between the two parties in general elections.

Party labels do not appear on the ballot in many localities, and this may or may not affect the way elections are conducted. In "nonpartisan" elections, candidates of different parties may, in fact, openly oppose one another as partisans, just as they do when party labels appear on the ballot. Another possibility is that parties field opposing candidates in a less-than-open fashion. As yet another alternative, elective offices may actually be contested without parties or political affiliations of candidates playing any role. One should not assume that formally nonpartisan elections in state and local governments bring genuine nonpartisanship, nor should one assume the opposite.

One last feature of the political processes at the state and local level deserves mention here. While members of the U.S. Senate and the U.S. House of Representatives hold well-paid, prestigious positions, the vast bulk of their state and local counterparts do not. Many state legislators are only part-time politicians who earn the bulk of their livelihoods pursuing other occupations. This is also true of most general-purpose local government officials. In addition, most local school board members are unpaid, even though many devote long hours to their responsibilities. That so many elected state and local officeholders do not earn their primary incomes from their positions in government may well affect the way they respond to constituents. After all, while they and their families typically live in the community that they are representing, their livelihoods do not depend on being re-elected.

Article   Prepared by: Bruce Stinebrickner, *DePauw University*

Voting Matters

A group of experts has some advice on how to improve elections.

WENDY UNDERHILL

Learning Outcomes

After reading this article, you will be able to:

- Identify a number of elements in the way American state governments run elections that could stand improvement.
- Explain the parallel between land grant colleges applying science and engineering to the agriculture of a state and applying them to elections.
- Evaluate each of the eight recommendations presented in terms of their importance, desirability, and feasibility.

In the year after a presidential election, legislators get busy trying to address any voting snafus that occurred in their own state. The result: a flurry of bills introduced to improve the system, usually double the number of other sessions. This year is shaping up to be no different.

In Hawaii, where not enough ballots were on hand in some polling places, a bill has been introduced to fix that. In Florida, where early voting was an issue, a bill has been introduced to permit a wider variety of buildings to serve as early voting sites. And in states hit by Hurricane Sandy (and some that were not) 2013 may well be the year when bills focus on solid contingency planning for elections.

Added to those are a host of bills dealing with national "hot potato" issues that surfaced in the run-up to the presidential election: early voting, absentee voting and voter ID.

Responding quickly to election imperfections makes a great deal of sense, but there are other ways to craft good election policy that might take a little more time. One is to consider the advice of experts.

But which experts? Advocates of every political stripe are ready, willing and even anxious to offer their perspectives. Instead of presenting a "one side says this, and the other side says that" overview, we'll examine the advice from the nonpartisan Caltech/MIT Voting Technology Project. It was formed in 2000 right after that exceedingly close presidential race, to investigate various kinds of voting technology. Quickly the group realized that technology is related to policy and policy is

related to administration and administration is related to reality. So the group's mission widened, with an eye toward gathering the evidence needed for good decision making.

In October 2012 the project released a report, "Voting: What Has Changed, What Hasn't, & What Needs Improvement." It opens by comparing the electoral landscape in 2000 to the one in 2012. The results are encouraging. In 2000, between 4 million and 6 million votes were lost, more than half due to voter registration problems, and others to faulty voting equipment and polling place problems. Changes made in the aftermath of *Bush vs. Gore,* however, have roughly cut the number of lost votes in half.

Good news, but there's still room for improvement, the report suggests. It presents 17 recommendations on how the nation can move closer to running elections in which every legal vote counts. Charles Stewart III, MIT professor and the Voting Technology Project's co-director, narrowed the recommendations to the following eight that fall within the bailiwick of state legislators.

1. Update Voting Technology

Stewart describes today's voting equipment in graphic terms: "like a rat going through a snake." He says that in most states, "the digested rat is about to come out the other end." In plain terms, most states' voting equipment is at the end of its useful life. This will require spending "money just to keep things going," says Stewart, in the neighborhood of $7 to $10 per voter.

Traditionally, local election officials have bought equipment with local funds, but that changed with the passage of the Help America Vote Act of 2002. It provided federal funding for replacing outdated machines, which most states did, some in one fell swoop. Virtually all of Mississippi's 82 counties, for example, switched to new electronic equipment at the same time.

With election soothsayers seeing no more federal funding on the horizon, state lawmakers will have to consider whose job it is both to choose the next generation of equipment and to pay for it: local communities, states or some combination.

2. Conduct Post-Election Audits

With or without shiny new equipment, CalTech/MIT's experts encourage legislatures to collect more data and conduct post-election audits. Audits count a small sample of ballots, extrapolating the final result. Although only a full recount can prove the winner "beyond the shadow of a doubt" (and that's a hugely expensive and time-consuming process), an audit can satisfy a statistician.

More than half the states require post-election audits to verify equipment and procedures operated as expected, often using a sample taken from 1 percent of precincts or 1 percent of voting machines. Now, a new creature, the "risk-limiting audit," is being tested in California. Its appeal is that it will likely be cheaper than traditional fixed-percentage audits because it reduces the number of ballots that have to be examined to verify the results statistically.

If audits can be teamed up with automatic ways to capture data about the election (waiting times, numbers of provisional ballots used and counted, voter experiences, etc.), so much the better. More and better data are what scientists crave and policymakers rely on.

3. Upgrade Voter Registration

Accurate voter registration rolls can be the first defense against fraudulent voting. Throughout the 2000s, states have replaced local-only voter registration databases with statewide ones that have reduced the number of inaccurately registered voters, primarily by identifying individuals who have moved within the state.

The "next level" helps states maintain even more accurate lists by using data from outside the state, making it easier to trace voters who move but fail to cancel previous voter registrations, who lose their eligibility due to felony convictions, or who die. Stewart encourages states to check their voter registrations against various federal and state lists. The Electronic Registration Information Center, for example, provides data matching for the seven participating states, but all states are welcome to join.

One caveat: Data obtained through any matching effort cannot be assumed to be perfect and should not be used to automatically remove voters from the rolls. Any discrepancies detected merely give local election officials a chance to investigate further to clear up any questionable registrations.

The CalTech/MIT Voting Technology Project was formed in December 2000 to study voting technology in order to prevent the kinds of problems that plagued the 2000 U.S. presidential election.

The project consists of a wide variety of academics: political scientists, statisticians and computer scientists. With no particular political agenda driving it, the group has expanded its scope of study to much more than just the technology used for voting and has researched all aspects of the election process. It's goal: to collect evidence and data about various election options to help policymakers make informed decisions. Participants in the group come from CalTech, MIT, Harvard and the University of Utah.

4. Rethink Polling Places and Poll Workers

State law dictates how polling places are run, from how many voting machines to have available to how many election workers to have on hand. These standards, says Stewart, were often set in the days when virtually all voting occurred on Election Day. Now, with around a third of votes cast before Election Day, through absentee ballots or in-person early voting, these old standards may no longer make sense.

Replacing paper poll books with electronic ones—a database of registered voters—can speed up voter check-in times. To move in that direction, state laws may need to be amended. And for a successful launch, electronic prototypes need to be tested, re-tested and tested again to ensure they are intuitive and easy to use, and therefore, actually faster for poll workers to use.

Voters, too, can do their "duty" more effectively if voter information—where to vote, what to bring and when the lines are likely to be the shortest—gets distributed on a timely basis.

5. Work with Universities

"It is the mission of land grant colleges to apply scientific advances in science and engineering to the problems of a state," says Stewart. Most people think of that function in terms of agriculture, but Stewart asks, "Why not voting also?" Since managing elections is becoming so complicated, smaller jurisdictions could consult with logistics and management experts in state universities. And, who better to research policies, procedures and equipment options than professional researchers?

The Center for Election Systems at Georgia's Kennesaw State University functions in much this way. University partnerships won't be a quick fix to any election-related problems, however. Partnerships can take time to set up, and they can take even more time to produce results. Keeping the focus on "real world" applications would be a must.

6. Reconsider Internet Voting

Although everyone seems to believe that someday we'll vote securely via the Internet, the CalTech/MIT Voting Technology Project says that "someday" is still years away. It's just too tricky to provide excellent security for Internet voting and ensure the secrecy of ballots.

Several states are piloting programs to permit voters to transmit completed ballots from overseas by scanning them and attaching them to emails. Even though this is different than voting online, it can still be problematic from a security perspective. So much so, in fact, that the National Institute of Standards and Technology advises against it for now. And yet, for some voters—those who can't get to a mailbox because of a hurricane, a war zone or any other reason—this may be a better-than-nothing choice. In these cases, voters must sign that they understand that the secrecy of their vote cannot be guaranteed.

7. Resist No-Excuse Absentee and All-Mail Voting

No-excuse absentee voting grew in popularity in the 2000s, and is now available in 27 states and the District of Columbia. With this option, any registered voter can request a ballot in advance, fill it out at leisure, and return it by mail or in person. And two states—Oregon and Washington—conduct all elections almost entirely by mail. Both ways are convenient for voters and often less expensive for election administrators.

The CalTech/MIT report advises against these practices, however, except for people with disabilities and overseas voters. It recommends expanding opportunities for in-person early voting instead. The concerns center on the inconsistent identification requirements among the different ways to vote; the surprising numbers of ballots received after the cut-off date and therefore rejected; and the greater possibilities of coercion or malfeasance since ballots are out of the hands of officials.

It's worth noting that citizens in states that have adopted no-excuse absentee voting and all-mail voting are very happy with these choices. In fact, more and more states are considering these convenient voting options.

8. Limit Provisional Balloting

Across the nation, everyone who shows up on Election Day can vote using a provisional ballot. If there is any doubt about their eligibility or registration, it is sorted out later. This can be time-consuming and expensive, and the criteria for counting these ballots vary greatly from state to state, or even from jurisdiction to jurisdiction. Anything states can do to limit the use of provisional ballots will reduce headaches, expenses and lost votes, advises the Voting Technology Project.

2016 and Everything Before

The next presidential election may seem far away. But with a plethora of suggestions on how to improve voting, there's plenty to study, debate and consider before 2016—not to mention all the state and local elections in the meantime. Working to make our nation's elections as fair, honest, reliable and convenient as possible is a worthy pursuit, because, after all, voting matters.

Critical Thinking

1. What are eight recommendations from the Voting Technology Project that fall within the jurisdiction of state legislators?
2. Which of the eight seem most important? Most easily implemented? Why?
3. What are some reasons for not allowing no-excuse and all-mail voting? Do you agree with those reasons?

Create Central

www.mhhe.com/createcentral

Internet References

Caltech/MIT Voter Technology Project
www.vote.caltech.edu
Center for Election Studies, Kennesaw State University
http://elections.kennesaw.edu

WENDY UNDERHILL tracks election issues for NCSL.

Underhill, Wendy. From *State Legislatures*, March 2013, pp. 31, 33–34. Copyright © 2013 by National Conference of State Legislatures. Reprinted by permission.

Article   Prepared by: Bruce Stinebrickner, *DePauw University*

5 Trends Shaping Redistricting

New dynamics are transforming the once-a-decade exercise of drawing political boundaries.

MORGAN CULLEN AND MICHELLE DAVIS

Learning Outcomes

After reading this article, you will be able to:

- Understand and assess five trends that significantly changed the redistricting process that occurred in the 50 states after the 2010 Census.

- Weigh the importance of redistricting for the practice of American democracy at both the state and national level.

In just a few weeks, candidates across the country will be elected to newly redrawn state legislative and congressional districts. Over the past two years, state legislatures have painstakingly redrawn district boundaries to reflect the population shifts identified in the 2010 Census.

It's not an easy task, but extremely important. How lines are drawn shape a state's partisan landscape for years. If maps are drawn improperly, the process can mire a state in legal challenges, fuel public cynicism toward government and add to partisan acrimony.

Many traditional geographic, legal and political constraints govern how states go about redrawing districts. But there are some new factors transforming the process. Here are five that had a significant impact on the latest redistricting cycle.

1. Shifting South by Southwest

What the decennial Census discovers about population changes is the basis for how maps are redrawn. It came as no surprise to most Americans when the 2010 Census revealed the U.S. population continues to migrate south and west. Between 2000 and 2010 the nation's population as a whole grew at a slower rate than in previous decades, averaging just 9.7 percent. But not everywhere. Nevada's population grew a whopping 35.2 percent in those 10 years. And Texas gained 4.3 million people, more than the total population of half the states.

This demographic shift had a huge impact on congressional reapportionment: Southern and Western states picked up 10 new congressional seats from states in the Northeast and Midwest.

Another notable trend from the last Census was the large growth in minority populations. Every major ethnic or racial minority group gained in proportion to the total U.S. population, and as a whole grew 29 percent. The Hispanic population grew four times faster (43 percent) than the population as a whole, mostly in the South and West, and now comprises 16 percent of the total population. Nearly half of the population in the West (47 percent) is now from a minority group.

The Census also revealed that Texas now has a "majority-minority" population, and joins California, Hawaii, New Mexico and Washington, D.C., in having non-Hispanic whites make up less than 50 percent of all residents, according to the Census Bureau.

This shift had a big effect on how congressional and state legislative maps were drawn in many states. Several states added new majority-minority statehouse and congressional districts to ensure fair representation of minority groups.

For example, with more than 80 percent of the population growth in Texas attributed to Latinos, a court-drawn interim plan added 13 new majority-minority districts to the House, for a total of 64 out of 150 seats. It also added two new majority-minority congressional districts—one Latino and the other a combined Latino/African-American.

Redistricting by the Numbers

9 and parts of 7
States required to get federal approval for redrawn maps

185
Court cases filed challenging redrawn district boundaries since 2010

3 to 18
The range of members on redistricting commissions in the 13 states that use them

1
State legislative districts added nationwide during redistricting

7,383
Total state legislative seats after redistricting

7,838
Total state legislative seats in 1963

8
States that gained congressional seats after reapportionment

10
States that lost congressional seats

"Over my 20 years plus in the Legislature, I have seen the Hispanic population in Texas surge at a rapid pace," says Senator Leticia Van De Putte (D) of San Antonio. "It is time for our representatives in state government to truly reflect the makeup of our state."

That's often easier said than done. The Texas Legislature finished drawing new congressional and state legislative lines in early 2011. But this August, a U.S. District Court found that both the congressional and legislative plans violated the Voting Rights Act of 1965, depriving minorities of adequate representation. The Texas attorney general wasted no time in saying the state would continue elections based on the interim plan and would appeal the case to the U.S. Supreme Court.

2. Tapping Into High-Tech Tools

Ten years is a long time in the world of technology. Rapidly changing redistricting software, databases and computer systems challenge legislatures—and their budgets—to keep up-to-date. But legislatures have little choice not to, considering the growing needs and expectations of lawmakers, staff and the general public, as well as the many benefits new high-tech tools offer.

The Internet took communication and collaboration this cycle to a whole new level. Legislators made proposals, received feedback and offered alternative plans electronically. New features and data were distributed to those redrawing boundaries in real time, greatly increasing uniformity and accuracy. New Web applications allowed the public to examine proposed plans and follow the process.

Florida citizens were among those able to track and react to the process through a Web application. "With the tools we had at our disposal, redistricting in 2010 certainly offered broader access and transparency for anyone who wanted to be involved in the process," says John Guthrie, a software engineer with the Florida Senate. "With the combination of our online mapping software and our public hearings, the public played a major role in all levels of Florida redistricting," he says.

The Brookings Institution, the American Enterprise Institute and Azavea offered redistricting software that allowed users to draw their own plans and compare them to maps produced by legislatures.

Michael McDonald, a professor at George Mason University, and Micah Altman, a research librarian at MIT, played a key role in designing the new software. "Providing this software to the general public really pulled back the curtain on the redistricting process in a way that had never been done before," says McDonald. Citizens obtained the same demographic and political data as legislatures through a database created by the Harvard Precinct Election Archive.

Another new tool, created by Nate Persily of Columbia Law School, offered nonpartisan congressional redistricting plans for all 50 states. The maps were produced by his law students using Caliper Corporation's Maptitude software, and were available through their website, DrawCongress.org. The students' maps received a lot of news coverage, and during a hearing on Connecticut's new maps were referred to by the state supreme court as fine examples of what "good" government plans should look like.

3. A Boost for Citizen Commissions

Every state is constitutionally required to undergo redistricting, but they aren't required to do it in the same way. In 37 states, the authority lies with the legislature. In the rest, the job now goes to a board or commission. Independent commissions, used in Alaska, Arizona, Idaho, Washington and most recently California, prohibit government officials from participating in order to insulate the process from partisan politics.

California citizens approved ballot initiatives in 2008 and 2010 directing the Legislature to transfer responsibility for redistricting to an independent, nonpartisan commission of 14 members to be appointed by the state auditor from a pool of qualified applicants.

The move was significant, affecting a large number of congressional and legislative districts. It took the commission's five Democrats, five Republicans and four unaffiliated citizens eight months to redraw the lines. They attended 23 public hearings and received more than 30,000 public comments. "Many people thought it would be impossible for us to pass a final plan with a supermajority," says Maria Blanco, a commission member from Los Angeles. "But everyone who sat on the commission, regardless of their political persuasion, wanted to reach consensus and draw a plan that truly reflected the diverse geography and demographic makeup of our state."

They finished the maps in August 2011, but the state Republican Party challenged the state Senate map as unfairly favoring Democrats. Tony Quinn, a former legislative staffer turned political commentator, was a vocal opponent of what he called a "clearly partisan plan" drawn by the commission. He argued that it will "obviously give the Democrats a two-thirds majority in the state Senate." The GOP filed a lawsuit and gathered enough signatures for a ballot measure to overturn the commission's map. They withdrew their support for the ballot measure after losing the court battle, although it remains on the ballot.

Plans drawn by commissions in Arizona and Colorado faced intense partisan opposition as well. Washington's four-member commission, made up of two Republicans and two Democrats, however, met with success. The group's unanimously approved maps faced little opposition from either party.

States have adopted commissions to insulate the redistricting process from politics. But the process is never entirely immune from it, and commissions don't necessarily produce better plans, according to research conducted by Seth Masket, a professor of political science at the University of Denver.

"From my own research, commissions don't seem to draw any more balanced districts or competitive elections than partisan legislatures do. Redistricting mostly tinkers around the edges of the huge historic trend toward greater polarization."

4. Tackling the Preclearance Test

Since 1965, Section 5 of the Voting Rights Act has required federal approval—preclearance—of any changes to voting laws or procedures in nine states and portions of seven others that have had a history of discrimination. Thousands of local jurisdictions with elected governing bodies fall under Section 5's provisions, from the local school board to the state legislature.

States have the option of requesting preclearance from the U.S. District Court for the District of Columbia or the U.S. Department of Justice, which is cheaper and simpler. Redistricting always brings an onslaught of preclearance requests, and states or jurisdictions usually opt for approval from the Department of Justice. But during this cycle, "an unprecedented trend occurred," according to Justin Levitt with Loyola Law School. States filed for preclearance through both avenues, or with the court exclusively, at a much higher rate.

One legal development may explain the noticeable change. The 2009 U.S. Supreme Court decision in Northwest Austin Municipal Utility District No. 1 v. Holder cast some doubt on the continuing need for preclearance and whether the Voting Rights Act's requirements were still applicable to the same group of states identified decades ago. The court decision suggested that questioning the continuation of preclearance was a legitimate pursuit.

"Section 5 is no longer corrective—it is now punitive," says Texas Senator Kel Seliger (R). He argues preclearance is no longer needed because "there will always be recourse through the court system."

Texas, along with Alabama, Florida and Georgia have disputed the continuing need for preclearance in their filings with the court. And while Florida and Georgia received preclearance of their redrawn districts, the rejection of Texas' plans puts the state on the fast track to challenge the constitutionality of Section 5 before the U.S. Supreme Court.

5. Putting Prisoners in Their Place

More and more jurisdictions are deciding to count prisoners at their "home" addresses instead of their prison locations. Maryland was the first to reallocate prisoners during this round of redistricting. California, Delaware and New York quickly followed suit, passing similar laws. This practice counters what critics claim is "prison gerrymandering"—the distorted political representation that results in areas with large prison populations.

In New York, for example, critics claimed the upstate region had an inflated representation in the Legislature because of the more than 58,000 inmates located in the area. Reallocating the prisoners in the most recent population count resulted in a loss of a state Senate district in that region.

Those against reallocation argue towns that have prisons incur costs and have unique concerns from housing inmates nearby, justifying the increase in political representation.

Adjusting the prisoner data is no small feat. Searching records and interviewing prisoners to obtain their last home addresses—if they had one—can be time-consuming and expensive.

Delaware, after passing a reallocation law for the 2010 redistricting cycle, found the costs to be too high. Lawmakers decided to postpone the practice until 2020. Maryland faced a different challenge. The state successfully reallocated its state prisoners to their home addresses, but the federal government, citing privacy concerns, refused to provide home addresses for the federal prisoners.

Despite these obstacles, lawmakers in Connecticut, Illinois and Massachusetts are considering similar laws, according to the Massachusetts-based Prison Policy Initiative. They are supported by recent court actions. A U.S. District Court upheld Maryland's prisoner reallocation law in December of 2011, and the U.S. Supreme Court endorsed the practice by denying an appeal, earlier this year.

With this redistricting season mostly behind us (except where plans are still in courts) lawmakers can take a little breather, but not for long. The next round will be here before we know it, and one thing we can be sure of: 2020 will bring its own set of legal developments, innovations, technology and population shifts to the drawing table.

The Impact on Elections

With the election just a month away, speculation over which party will have the upper hand is at a fever pitch. Many candidates face the uncertainty of running in new and untested districts; 428 congressional districts in 43 states (seven states have only one representative) and nearly all state legislative districts have been redrawn.

Because of the Republican landslide in the 2010 elections, the GOP had a clear political advantage over the redistricting process. Republicans unilaterally controlled redistricting for 210 congressional seats (in 18 states) and 2,498 state legislative seats (in 21 states).

Democrats unilaterally controlled the process for 44 congressional seats (in six states) and 885 state legislative seats (in eight states).

Since 2010, 193 court cases have been filed, and 68 are still active. This is far more than the 149 cases (40 states) filed in the 2000s and the 150 cases (41 states) filed in the 1990s, according to data compiled by NCSL. Courts have redrawn plans in Colorado, Connecticut, Kansas, Minnesota, Mississippi, New Mexico, Nevada, New York, Texas and Wisconsin.

Critical Thinking

1. How have demographic trends and new technology affected the latest round of redistricting?

2. What are the goals of shifting responsibility for redistricting from state legislatures to independent boards or commissions? What have been the results?

3. What is "preclearance" in the context of the Voting Rights Act of 1965 and what does "putting prisoners in their place" mean in the context of redistricting? What further decisions about the Voting Rights Act of 1965 has the U.S. Supreme Court rendered since this selection was first published in late 2012?

Create Central

www.mhhe.com/createcentral

Internet References

Fair Vote: The Center for Voting and Democracy
www.fairvote.org/redistricting#.Um5tPVOOCLd

Testimony of Peter Wagner, Prison Policy Initiative, Connecticut General Assembly
www.google.com/url?sa=t&rct=j&q=&esrc=s&source=web&cd=1&ved=0CCsQFjAA&url=http%3A%2F%2Fwww.cga.ct.gov%2F2011%2FJUD

data%2FTmy%2F2011HB-06606-R000321-Peter%2520Wagner%2C%2520Executive%2520Director%2C%2520Prison%2520Policy%2520Initiative-TMY.PDF&ei=w21uUvy1LcHayAHJ8oCYCA&usg=AFQjCNFnIGDJw0QlaQDLyX4z618do4oM1A&sig2=sS4-z5Nz_65XX74L4PDgzg&bvm=bv.55123115,d.aWc

U.S. Census Bureau: Redistricting Data
www.census.gov/rdo

MORGAN CULLEN covers redistricting issues for NCSL. MICHELLE DAVIS is a senior election law analyst for the Maryland Department of Legislative Services.

Article   Prepared by: Bruce Stinebrickner, *DePauw University*

Caperton's Coal

The Battle over an Appalachian Mine Exposes a Nasty Vein in Bench Politics

JOHN GIBEAUT

Learning Outcomes

After reading this article, you will be able to:

- Explain how litigation or the threat of litigation by a big corporation can intimidate and sometimes "ruin" a smaller business or an individual.

- Assess how the election of judges in West Virginia (as in most states) can contribute to judicial corruption or the appearance of judicial corruption.

- Summarize the difficulties with respect to "judicial disqualification," "recusal," "impartiality," and "bias" as they relate to state and local judges.

T he Harman mine in southwestern Virginia's Buchanan County was a rickety skeleton when lifelong coal man Hugh M. Caperton purchased it in 1993. But Caperton, a native of Slab Fork in neighboring West Virginia, saw gold in those Appalachian hills.

The mine yielded high-grade metallurgical coal, a hot-burning and especially pure variety that steel mills crave to fuel the blast furnaces used to make coke needed in their production process. By the end of 1993, the mine's yield had increased to 1 million tons a year, quadruple its previous output. Caperton also replaced the contract workers who used to ply the precious bituminous with 150 union miners in one of the nation's poorest states.

Then along came A.T. Massey Coal Co. and its CEO, Don L. Blankenship. Massey, which has headquarters in Richmond, Va., wanted the high-grade coal too. But Caperton at first was unwilling to sell, despite what he described as warnings from Blankenship: "He basically threatened me and said, 'Don't take me to court. We spend a million dollars a month on lawyers, and we'll tie you up for years.'"

Blankenship wasn't lying. Through a series of complex, almost Byzantine transactions, including the acquisition of Harman's prime customer and the land surrounding the competing mine, Massey both landlocked Harman with no road or rail access and left Caperton without a market for his coal even if he could ship it.

Caperton finally cried uncle in early 1998 and agreed to sell. But on the day the deal was to go down, Massey got up and walked away, sending Caperton to court instead of the bank.

"On the day of the closing, at 2 o'clock in the afternoon, they called the whole deal off," Caperton recalls. "They tanked us at the last second. It forced us into bankruptcy."

So after a stop at the federal bankruptcy court to file a Chapter 11 petition, he hauled Massey into West Virginia state court on various allegations of fraud and tortious contract interference. He won a $50 million jury verdict.

Blankenship appealed until the last cow straggled home. Besides his efforts in the courtroom, Blankenship also plunged into judicial politics—West Virginia-style—raising some $3 million in 2004 on behalf of an unknown Charleston lawyer named Brent D. Benjamin, who wanted a seat on the West Virginia Supreme Court of Appeals, the state's highest court. Both sides knew the case undoubtedly would wind up there.

Benjamin defeated a controversial Democratic incumbent in the partisan contest for the 12-year term. Sure enough, the case wound up before a court that included new Justice Benjamin.

Concerned that the seven figures in campaign backing could influence the case's outcome, Caperton's lawyers asked Benjamin to disqualify himself. He not only refused but also twice cast the third and deciding vote to reverse the judgment against Massey, the last time on April 3 after rehearing.

But Caperton wasn't quite ready to shrivel and die. The U.S. Supreme Court agreed to review his case in mid-November. In arguments scheduled for March 3, the justices will ponder whether Benjamin violated Caperton's 14th Amendment due process right by accepting the millions in campaign support from Blankenship, then deciding the case anyway.

Benjamin declined comment. Calls to Blankenship and his company's lawyers went unreturned.

Critics complain that tossing around such big bucks jeopardizes the system's integrity and independence by suggesting that justice is for sale on some clearance rack parked behind the courthouse. And a sharp rise in contributions to judicial races moved the ABA Standing Committee on Judicial Independence to attempt to clear up the often foggy rules for disqualification. The committee plans to submit its recommendations to the

House of Delegates at the association's 2009 annual meeting in Chicago in August.

"Survey after survey reports that 80 percent of the public believes money influences judicial decision-making," says chair William K. Weisenberg, an assistant executive director for the Ohio State Bar Association in Columbus. "What we're dealing with here is a perception that just isn't right."

Appearances Matter

Judicial disqualification dates to Roman law, which liberally allowed parties to remove jurists deemed "under suspicion." As the English common-law tradition evolved, however, grounds for recusal tightened considerably, focusing nearly exclusively on whether the judge held a financial stake in the case.

As the American version developed, legislators, courts and model ethics codes had little trouble translating some specific conduct into black-letter grounds for recusal.

For example, judges can't hear appeals of cases they've tried. They can't sit on cases where they're material witnesses. Judges who worked as government lawyers can't hear cases in which they previously participated.

Still, there are remnants of British legal thought that create troubling practical and philosophical tensions to this day for U.S. judges facing recusal questions. For one, a duty to sit arose so cases in small jurisdictions won't go wanting for resolution in the absence of an unquestionably evenhanded jurist. The obligation to hear cases can become especially nettlesome for intermediate appeals courts and courts of last resort, where the pool of replacement judges is considerably smaller than at the trial level.

More difficult, however, are accusations of bias, because judges often equate recusal with a failure to impartially administer justice. Disqualification for bias was not an option in England.

In the United States, attempts to identify such situations through statutes and court rules have been less than successful.

Rule 2.11 of the ABA Model Code of Judicial Conduct requires disqualification "in any proceedings in which the judge's impartiality might reasonably be questioned." The ABA and the majority of court jurisdictions stress both actual impropriety and the appearance of impropriety.

While most states and the federal courts have emulated catch-all provisions like the ABA's, only two states have adopted a 1999 addition that demands recusal when a state judge receives a certain amount in campaign contributions from a party or lawyer.

West Virginia is not one of those. It is one of 39 states that picks its judges through some form of election. And while fundraising and consequent conflicts of interest can occur in any scheme—head-to-head partisan elections, nonpartisan races and retention ballots—most of the allegations of conflict seem to arise in partisan elections.

Not surprisingly, lawyers and business interests combine for anywhere from half to two-thirds of money donated to judicial candidates in a given year.

The big money breakout came in 2000, when candidates for state supreme court seats raised $45.6 million, 60 percent more than the $28.2 million raised just two years before, according to the Brennan Center for Justice at New York University School of Law.

That figure dipped to $29 million in 2002, then bounced back to $42 million in 2004. In 2008, state supreme court campaigns were projected to collect nearly $34 million, about the same as in 2006.

Although few judicial races involve fundraising with the intensity found in West Virginia, most judges have to guard against conflicts in their workaday worlds. Even federal judges, with lifetime appointments, must pay attention to what people and what documents pass through their courts. Personal, family, business and professional relationships also can sow seeds for a recusal motion alleging bias.

Still, many judges grope in the dark. No one even knows how often judges are actually asked to withdraw.

U.S. District Judge Charles N. Clevert Jr. of Milwaukee says pro se petitions almost always demand disqualification. Clevert says he relies on the reasonableness of the complaint.

"The first thing that goes through my mind is whether there is anything in the [recusal] motion relating to a prior decision or something in this case," says Clevert.

Even with regular litigators whom he knows, the more facts alleged, the more likely the recusal motion will succeed on grounds of bias in Clevert's court.

"If there are some facts in the reasonableness complaint that aren't way out in left field, then that certainly could trigger a situation that could give rise to a recusal," Clevert says.

In Missouri, state supreme court Judge Michael A. Wolff compares motions for disqualification to juror selection in high-profile cases, where prospective panelists are asked whether they can set aside outside knowledge and decide the case as it's presented in court.

"When the guy says yes, we usually go ahead and let him be seated," Wolff says. Judges especially need to apply that standard to the lawyers who appear before them, he says.

"Judges have special connections with lawyers," Wolff explains. "That's who our friends are. That's who we went to law school with. 'Can I set it aside?' If a judge says, 'Yes, I can,' then he probably can go ahead and sit. But you know what? It can look bad.

"If you can't explain it in a simple sentence, then you probably have something bad," he says. This is where the similarity to jury selection ends.

"Nobody cares who the juror is," Wolff says. "At the end of the case he goes home. He's anonymous. But the judge has a higher calling to set an example."

Weighing the Recusal

In 2003 the ABA offered up another, even stricter addition to the Model Code—since adopted in 11 states—requiring recusal when judges make statements outside court that appear to predispose them to rule a particular way in certain kinds of cases.

In 2002, the Supreme Court held in *Republican Party of Minnesota v. White* that such restrictions violate the First Amendment speech rights of judicial candidates.

Indiana University law professor Charles Geyh, author of a report supporting the ABA recommendations, says the states have yet to demonstrate a full understanding of the *White* case.

"When it does come, it will be harder to disqualify judges because it puts them at odds with the electorate when you can't do what you promised," says Geyh.

The dearth of case law or other documentation also makes it tough to determine exactly why judges reject disqualification attempts. Geyh's report offers some suggestions.

Judges, he says, may refuse motions because they truly believe they can act fairly. Others may decline if they detect an attempt to gain a more sympathetic venue.

In some cases, clever court operators could try to force recusals of unsympathetic judges by seeding their campaign funds with donations. And granting a recusal motion could seem an endorsement of accusations.

Most often, however, lawyers are reluctant to ask for recusal for fear of failure.

"I always say if you're going to shoot the tiger, you'd better kill the tiger," Wolff says. "If you don't kill the tiger, then you're going to have one angry tiger."

While disqualification proceedings usually go unnoticed in the shadows, many potential conflicts, such as modest campaign giving, simply don't rise to the level of disqualification.

Caperton's lawyers could face questioning from the Supreme Court justices on what amounts may affect due process and thus open a disqualification inquiry. Though White addressed verbal comments by candidates, the justices also have long held that campaign donations are a form of First Amendment expression. But cases like the $3 million lunker from West Virginia are hard to hide.

"The magnitude and timing of the campaign contributions here gave Justice Benjamin, in appearance if not in fact, a personal interest in the outcome of this case," the ABA argued in an amicus brief supporting Caperton's cert petition. "If the facts of this case do not implicate due process concerns, then few judicial contribution cases ever will."

Caperton's lawyers call the case one of a kind. Though Massey CEO Blankenship apparently had shown little interest in donating to other political campaigns for statewide offices like governor or the legislature, he didn't mess around in channeling millions of dollars and other means of support to elect Benjamin.

In motions asking Benjamin to recuse himself, Caperton's lawyers recited Blankenship's fundraising and spending in head-throbbing detail. One version regurgitates a 26-page chunk of factual recitations and argument along with 84 appendices and exhibits.

"It's been surreal—what happened in that litigation," says Caperton lawyer David B. Fawcett of Pittsburgh. "We've never seen anything like what occurred."

Upping the Ante

As his options began to wane for getting the $50 million judgment reduced or tossed out, Blankenship moved quickly.

In August 2004 he formed a section 527 organization—so named for the part of the Internal Revenue Code that allows such groups to collect money to support or oppose candidates.

Blankenship's 527, called And for the Sake of the Kids, was designed not to work for Republican challenger and political novice Benjamin, but to use televised attack ads to work for the defeat of Warren McGraw, the Democratic incumbent. McGraw was under intense public heat for joining an unsigned opinion that placed a convicted child molester on probation. Blankenship also maintained that "anti-business rulings" by McGraw poisoned the Mountain State's economic climate.

Of the $3.6 million the group raised, $2.4 million came from Blankenship, with 25 other contributors uniting to shell out the remaining $1.1 million. The organization ranked fifth nationally among other 527s in the amount raised in a state election. Blankenship also contributed $515,000 in direct support to Benjamin's campaign committee, while other donors chipped in the remaining $330,000 of the $845,000 the committee raised.

Then Benjamin went public.

"Nobody, including the people we practice law with, knew who Brent Benjamin was," says Caperton lawyer Bruce E. Stanley of Pittsburgh. "Then the billboards started popping up."

They asked a good question: "Who is Brent Benjamin?" Stanley realized a political machine had started its engine. Benjamin drove it right over McGraw in the November 2004 election, garnering 53 percent of the vote.

By November 2007, the Caperton case arrived at the state high court and was promptly ushered out on a 3-2 vote that reversed the $50 million award and included Benjamin in the majority. Benjamin supplied the decisive third vote on rehearing in April 2008 to again pitch the judgment.

Benjamin never acknowledged Caperton's disqualification motions. Caperton's lawyers never got to argue them orally or received an explanation for the decision.

Riviera Snapshot

Meanwhile, Blankenship's relations with other members of the high court began receiving notice in early 2008 when photos surfaced of Blankenship vacationing on the French Riviera with Justice Elliott "Spike" Maynard. Though he insisted he paid his own way and did nothing wrong, Maynard withdrew from the coal case in January 2008. His term as a justice ended last year with his defeat in the May primary. He did not respond to requests for comment.

Meanwhile, Justice Larry V. Starcher, an especially vociferous and public critic of Massey and its practices, had a run-in with Blankenship, who not only wanted him off the Caperton matter but also has asked the U.S. Supreme Court to use his harsh attacks to disqualify Starcher from another Massey case, *Massey Energy Co. v. Wheeling-Pittsburgh Steel Corp.*

Starcher, who retired in January, dissented in the first Caperton decision but withdrew before the rehearing. He declined comment, but in his written recusal he hinted that Blankenship had disrupted the state supreme court's business.

"The simple fact of the matter is that the pernicious effects of Mr. Blankenship's bestowal of his personal wealth, political tactics and 'friendship' have created a cancer in the affairs of this court," Starcher wrote.

Benjamin did not write an opinion when the court again held for Massey on April 3. Caperton asked the U.S. Supreme Court for cert on July 2. Three weeks later, Benjamin added a concurrence to the state court's April ruling.

Caperton had not accused Benjamin of acting improperly or actually being prejudiced by the campaign contributions. But from Benjamin's perspective, actual bias is all that counts in West Virginia.

"The fundamental question raised by the appellees and the dissenting opinion herein is whether, in a free society, we should value 'apparent or political justice' more than 'actual justice,'" Benjamin wrote in the concurrence, filed July 28.

"Actual justice is based on actualities," he asserted. "Through its written decisions, a court gives that transparency of decision-making needed from government entities. Apparent or political justice is based instead on appearances and is measured not by the quality of a court's legal analysis, but rather by the political acceptability of the case's end result as measured by dominant partisan groups such as politicians and the media, or by the litigants themselves. Apparent or political justice is based on half-truths, innuendo, conjecture, surmise, prejudice and bias."

The Fear Factor

Fawcett says it's too easy to simply blame the decision on a political atmosphere unique to West Virginia. He suggests that Massey's economic power also loomed large in the background. Massey is the nation's fourth-largest coal company and the state's major employer.

"There are certain people who will say that's just the way it is down there, including Don Blankenship," Fawcett says. "But people were afraid. He's the largest employer in the state. Who's going to call him out on that? Even the lawyers were quiet. They all were afraid."

In the short run, Fawcett, Stanley and their client are headed to Washington, D.C., where former Solicitor General Theodore B. Olson will argue their position to the justices. Long term, both lawyers are in agreement when asked how to solve the campaign contribution conundrum once and for all: "The easiest and simplest way to do it is through public financing."

Taxpayer funding may be the most viable option. Last spring, in *Duke v. Leake,* the Richmond, Va.-based 4th U.S. Circuit Court of Appeals affirmed North Carolina's state financing scheme, the nation's first for judicial elections. The Supreme Court declined to review its decision.

To be sure, disqualification issues involving bias still can arise in publicly financed systems. Nevertheless, state campaign funding appears to relieve pressure on judges and dampen the giving spirits of the usual suspects in recusal proceedings.

In an amicus brief filed with the 4th Circuit, former North Carolina judges maintained that the 2002 law works and has attracted participation by a majority of candidates. Perhaps more telling, contributions from business interests in 2004 judicial races were only a third of those in 2002. Contributions from lawyers dropped by 75 percent.

"As a result, the public is less likely to feel that wealthy parties with access to wealthy attorneys who have contributed to judicial campaigns are treated more favorably than those without such access," the former judges maintained.

Meanwhile, the ABA judicial independence panel postponed its proposals until summer in order to accommodate a decision in the Caperton case and to respond to comments on a draft report and recommendations circulated in October. As things stood in the fall, the committee planned to present a list of principles on which to base specific policies and procedures to govern disqualification.

"What we need to do is create clarity," says chair Weisenberg. "We run into a lot of gray here. We want to clear up the gray as much as possible to assist the judiciary." Highlights of the draft recommendations include:

- Disclosure by a judge, at the start of a case, of "all information known by that judicial officer that might reasonably be construed as bearing on that judicial officer's impartiality."
- Recusal decisions made by a judge other than the subject of a disqualification motion. In Illinois, for instance, disqualification motions are automatically reassigned. Judges can testify on their own behalf, but they are not required to do so.
- A more rigorous standard of appellate review, particularly in states where judges review their own recusal. While great deference is given to the decisions of a trial judge in most cases, the ABA argues that standard should change when the judge is, in effect, reviewing himself.
- Written response to a contested disqualification motion. By explaining a recusal decision, a judge reassures the parties and the public, and creates a record of his reasoning for use in any appeals.
- Peremptory challenges, which allow a lawyer to remove a judge without cause, much the same as in jury selection. Such challenges—already permitted in Arizona—would allow reassignment within 10 days and cannot be for delay.

At 53, Caperton says the case has taken its toll not only on his bank account, but also on his health.

"It's miserable," he says. "It's like living in purgatory. It's cost me everything I've got. I've spent every nickel I've ever had trying to right this wrong."

At the end of a two-hour interview, Caperton pauses to consider his daughter, born just a few months before the case was filed. The 11-year-old must figure her dad is a lawyer, Caperton says, because he regularly hangs out with them so much in court. "That's all she's ever known."

Critical Thinking

1. What steps did the A.T. Massey Coal Company take to thwart Hugh Caperton's profitable operation of the Harman coal mine in Virginia?

2. What was the outcome of the West Virginia jury trial that originally settled Caperton's suit against Massey for fraud and tortious contract interference?

3. How were campaign contributions and West Virginia's system of electing Supreme Court judges related to the outcome of Massey's appeal of the jury trial verdict?

4. What is "recusal" and what are some of the many competing ideas or rules for when recusal is appropriate or even required? In how many states are judges chosen through some sort of elections, and what "recusal" or "judicial disqualification" rules or practices apply to elected judges?

5. How long has the Caperton-Massey legal battle lasted and what effect has it had on Hugh Caperton, who filed the original lawsuit against the Massey Coal Company?

Create Central

www.mhhe.com/createcentral

Internet References

National Center for State Courts
www.ncsc.org

West Virginia Gazette.com
www.wvgazette.com/News/201304180082

Article   Prepared by: Bruce Stinebrickner, *DePauw University*

The No-Tax Pledge

In the nine states that don't levy a personal income tax, the politics of staying that course remains powerful.

JONATHAN WALTERS

Learning Outcomes

After reading this article, you will be able to:

- Consider the nine states that do not have a state income tax and what leads them to be different in this regard from the rest of the states.

- Assess the pros and cons of state income taxes in state governments' revenue-raising efforts.

In New Hampshire, it's called "taking the pledge," a quadrennial exercise that every gubernatorial candidate must sedulously pursue: He or she must vow neither to offer up nor support establishing a state personal income tax. To do otherwise is to commit political seppuku, minus the knife.

New Hampshire is one of nine states—including Alaska, Florida, Nevada, South Dakota, Tennessee, Texas, Washington and Wyoming—that doesn't raise revenues through an income tax. But with states desperately casting about for ways to balance budgets, it would seem that such ironclad vows demanded in New Hampshire might be softening. After all, many economists praise the income tax for its progressive nature and fortuitous tendency to grow over time.

In Texas, Dick Lavine, a senior fiscal analyst at the Center for Public Policy Priorities, argues that an income tax is a critical staple of a mature and balanced state tax system. "It's inevitable if you want to operate a modern and well run state," he says. "Sales taxes just aren't as elastic. They get hit sooner in a recession, and they stay down longer. Plus, an income tax helps offset the regressivity and performs better over the long run than a sales tax."

It would seem to be empirically true that an income tax is vital to a balanced and up-to-date revenue mix—after all, 41 states have one. But arguments like Lavine's haven't been getting much traction in the states that continue to raise cash primarily through sales, property and other taxes.

"Given how bad state revenues have been during this recession, you would think it would be a time when such a tax might become attractive," says Senior Fellow Don Boyd, who closely tracks state fiscal issues for the Rockefeller Institute of Government. "But given the attitude toward taxes around the country, it's highly unlikely."

Fiscal experts confirmed Boyd's hunch in most of the nine states. In some, legislators routinely float proposals for instituting an income tax, usually with some offset that tinkers with existing taxes. And in virtually all states where the proposition seems to be a non-starter, there were efforts in the recent past that considered where an income tax might fit into a state's overall revenue raising strategy. None, however, led to a new tax.

The last time anyone talked about it in Wyoming was a decade ago. Former Republican Gov. Jim Geringer and the Legislature convened a tax commission—the Wyoming Tax Reform 2000 Committee—to look at what many viewed as the state's fiscally unhealthy overreliance on minerals taxes.

"The commission came back with a recommendation to implement an income tax and the governor said, 'Forget it,'" says Dan Neal, executive director of the Equality State Policy Center in Casper, Wyo. "Then came the energy boom in 2001, and a healthy pile of mineral tax revenues with it."

John Schiffer, the highly respected Republican chairman of the Wyoming Senate Revenue Committee, concedes that the state's heavy reliance on minerals taxes—about 50 percent of the state's revenues come from such taxes—is still a concern, but quickly adds that there has been no serious discussion of implementing an income tax since the Geringer tax commission report. At that time, Schiffer remembers, "An income tax was proposed as a third leg under the table. But when the revenue committee brought it up, it just went nowhere."

Not that Wyoming is against new taxes. Recently the Legislature voted to tax wind—from wind farms, that is. In 2012, a wind turbine tax goes into effect.

The extent to which income taxes are a taboo subject seems to depend on the economic climate and who's in power. A decade ago, when Wyoming was seeing mineral taxes crash, it was at least acceptable to float the income-tax concept, especially when it was a Republican who was pushing the tax-mix analysis. Today, however, with the nation's economy limping along and a national debate occurring around whether taxes enhance or stifle economic growth, there's a sense that taxing income isn't politically viable in the states that don't levy it.

There's a sense that taxing income isn't politically viable in the states that don't levy it.

The last time the idea was discussed in Tennessee—in the early 2000s by former Republican Gov. Don Sundquist—the electorate's emotional response made it clear that Tennesseans wanted no part of such a tax, says Bill Fox, director of the University of Tennessee's Center for Business and Economic Research. "The Nashville radio talk shows got hold of it," he says, "and got people riled up." Not even such well respected politicians as former Democratic Gov. Ned McWherter and former Republican Sen. Howard Baker, who teamed up to tour the state and proclaim concern over the state's tax system, could sway minds. In what might be seen as a pre-tea party outbreak, a handful of citizens even tossed rocks at the Capitol.

If anything, Fox says, the current political atmosphere around government and taxes makes the proposition even more distant. "It's absolutely off the table," he says.

Illustrating the issue's long-standing political volatility in the pertinent states is South Dakota, which came one vote away from enacting an income tax in the 1970s. With Democrats controlling the Legislature and the executive mansion for the first time in decades, the bill had passed the House, and former Gov. Richard Kneip vowed to sign it upon the Senate's approval. But the Senate was deadlocked, and so it fell to Democratic Lt. Gov. Bill Dougherty (who died in July) to cast the vote that would put the tax over the top. "He was the governor's pick," says Jim Fry, director of the South Dakota Legislative Research Council, "and so you would think he'd be in his camp. But he had real political aspirations, so he voted against the tax."

Meanwhile, some states never talk of instituting an income tax. Florida, for instance, has a prohibition written right into the state constitution. "It's not a political litmus test here," says Robert Weissert, director of communications for Florida Tax-Watch. "It's completely off the table. We have a consumption-based economy here, and so we have a consumption-based tax system."

As if a constitutional prohibition wasn't enough, a recent voter initiative now requires that any new statewide tax can only be enacted with two-thirds of the votes in an election. "So that's why I can say unequivocally that barring a constitutional convention, it's just not in the culture here," Weissert says.

Like Florida, Nevada depends heavily on tourism and taxing consumption, and it has seen its revenues crash along with the tourist trade. There has been some talk of a corporate income tax, reports Patrick Gibbons, a policy analyst with the Nevada Policy Research Institute, but nary a mumble about one on personal income—in no small part because Nevada, like Florida, has the income-tax prohibition written into its constitution.

Nevada does, however, indirectly get at personal income: It taxes a business' total payroll at 1.3 percent. It's not exactly an income tax, nor is it a corporate income tax. The latter was going to be the subject of a legislative study this year, but even the idea of studying a corporate income tax wound up dead on arrival in Carson City.

Currently one state out of the nine is seriously considering enacting an income tax. This November, Washington state will include Initiative 1098 on the ballot. It proposes to enact an income tax on individual Washingtonians making more than $200,000 a year; $400,000 for couples filing jointly. By way of politically sweetening the deal, the ballot measure reduces state property taxes by 20 percent and eliminates the state's business and occupations tax—collected on gross receipts, not profits—for 80 percent of businesses in the state. If passed, the proposal would raise $1 billion in revenues. Use of that money is also specified in the measure: It would go toward reducing class size and funding the state's Basic Health program.

Initiative 1098 is the lagged result of a tax study commission convened about eight years ago and led by Bill Gates Sr. Gary Locke, who was governor at the time, had appointed the Gates Commission to look at the state's tax mix. By the time the commission reported its recommendations—which included enacting an income tax—the political climate was already swinging hard against the notion of a new tax. (In her 2004 and 2008 campaigns, Democratic Gov. Christine Gregoire did, in fact, take Washington's version of "the pledge," but she also proposed and won a considerable increase in state gas taxes shortly after taking office.)

This year though, backed by labor unions and a strong push from the elder Gates, proponents of an income tax in Washington managed to gather enough signatures to get the tax measure on the November ballot. Currently polls have the state split at just about 50-50 on the new tax.

Even if Washington voters enact the tax, it likely won't signal the beginning of any softening when it comes to other states' inclination toward expanding revenue options. The concept will no doubt continue resurfacing in some of the other eight states, depending on who's in power and the economy's condition. But right now, the anti-tax mood seems set, and Alaska appears to exemplify that mood. "It's in the air we breathe," says Lawrence Weiss, executive director of the Alaska Center for Public Policy. "This is 'no-income-tax' air up here."

Critical Thinking

1. What does "taking the pledge" mean in New Hampshire?
2. How many states do not raise revenues through a personal income tax?

3. What are the advantages of a personal income tax in the context of a state's overall tax system?

4. What are the electoral realities faced by any candidate for governor in a state without a personal income tax?

5. What economic circumstances make establishing a state personal income tax more likely? Are Republicans or Democrats generally better positioned to make such a proposal?

6. What particulars distinguish Wyoming from most of the other states without personal income taxes? Florida?

Create Central

www.mhhe.com/createcentral

Internet References

Americans for Tax Reform
www.atr.org

Tax Foundation
http://taxfoundation.org/article_ns/state-individual-income-tax-rates-2000-2013

From *Governing*, October 2010, pp. 39–40. Copyright © 2010 by e.Republic Inc. Reprinted by permission via Wright's Media. contract #77805.

Article   Prepared by: Bruce Stinebrickner, *DePauw University*

States of Conservatism

Beyond the Beltway, the Right Is Thriving

JOHN HOOD

Learning Outcomes

After reading this article, you will be able to:

- Summarize and discuss the implications of Republicans' recent successes in state and local politics.

- Assess the political transformation of the Solid South and its implications for state and local politics and policies.

- Identify the connection between Republican successes in state legislature elections and Republicans' majority control of the U.S. House of Representatives since 2011 under Speaker John Boehner.

Inauguration Day 2013 was a moment of jubilation for conservatives. After four years of lackluster economic growth and a series of personal and policy mistakes, the incumbent chief executive, a history-making Democrat, was replaced by a conservative with an attractive policy agenda and a skillful campaign team. In a concise, hopeful inaugural address, the newly elected Republican leader of the executive branch promised to focus the administration's attention and resources on job creation and economic growth in the short run, while setting the stage for long-term solutions to the government's fiscal woes.

I'm describing the inauguration of Pat McCrory, North Carolina's first Republican governor in 20 years. His election to replace retiring one-term Democrat Bev Perdue, the state's first female governor, was one of the few bright spots for the GOP last November, so McCrory got more national attention than the incoming governor of the nation's tenth-largest state would normally have received.

In general, however, Republican success in state and local politics is an underreported story. It extends far beyond the Tar Heel State. The post-2012 talk of conservatism's electoral weakness and policy failures is disconnected from the personal experiences of many politicians, journalists, analysts, and activists who work at the state and local levels. While grassroots conservatives were disappointed at the reelection of President Obama and Republican misfires in races for the U.S. Senate, they continue to enjoy unprecedented influence and success in state capitals—while local liberals feel alienated from the governments and institutions they long dominated.

Even after giving up some of their 2010 legislative gains thanks to Obama's 2012 coattails, Republicans still control more state offices than they have in generations. They hold 30 of 50 state governorships and 58 of 98 partisan legislative chambers. The nonprofit news service Stateline reports that in 25 states, comprising 53 percent of the U.S. population, the GOP controls both the executive and the legislative branch. Only 13 states, with 30 percent of the U.S. population, have unified Democratic governments. In addition, Republicans are strongly represented in local government, albeit primarily at the county level rather than in the increasingly Democratic big cities. In some states, such as my native North Carolina, the GOP's local success has no modern precedent: A majority of the state's 100 county governments are now under Republican control, which hasn't been the case since General Sherman's army was camped outside Raleigh.

As it happens, the political transformation of North Carolina and other states in the formerly Democratic "Solid South" is a big part of the story. In the 2012 cycle, voters in the last state of the old Confederacy with a Democratic legislature—Arkansas—gave Republicans control of both chambers. In the broader South, only Kentucky's house of representatives retains a Democratic majority. Elsewhere in the country, Democrats regained some legislatures they lost in the Republican-wave election of 2010, such as those in Minnesota and Maine. But the GOP retained its recent gains in other presidential-blue states, such as Michigan and Wisconsin.

The regional dynamic reveals much about the ideological effects of recent political trends. Partisan affiliation doesn't always predict political views or voting behavior. In the past, there were significant numbers of center-left Republicans and center-right Democrats. Members of the latter group traditionally held many congressional, gubernatorial, and legislative seats in the South and Midwest. But the days of boll weevils and blue dogs are approaching dusk. Once southern and midwestern state electorates became more amenable to the Republican label for state and local offices, the two parties began to polarize by ideology. Individuals who might once have run and served in office as center-right Democrats have either become Republicans—usually moving rightward to win their primaries—or yielded to GOP candidates with even more reliable conservative inclinations. Both phenomena have red-shifted the ideological spectrum in state government.

Another way to think about these political trends is as a giant switcheroo. From 1968 to 1988, Republicans won popular-vote majorities in five of six presidential elections while Democrats were firmly ensconced as the majority party of state governments and the U.S. House. But from 1992 to 2012, Democrats have won popular-vote majorities in five of six presidential elections while Republicans have gained the advantage in House races and the states. (Control of the U.S. Senate hasn't precisely tracked the other results.)

The Founders intended the U.S. House to represent popular will through direct election and the U.S. Senate to represent popular will as channeled through state legislatures. Since the ratification of the 17th Amendment, popular votes have decided all races—but, interestingly, state legislatures have come to exercise a significant influence over the House. Responding to recent Voting Rights Act jurisprudence and using sophisticated data-analysis techniques, Republicans have redrawn congressional maps to their party's advantage. To an extent that remains underappreciated in Washington, the power of Speaker John Boehner and other Republican leaders of the House to challenge President Obama and the Democratic Senate originated with GOP success in legislative races and depends on its continuation, as does resistance to the implementation of Obamacare.

How did Republican candidates and conservative ideas become more competitive at the state and local levels? A number of factors are at work. The migration of GOP-leaning voters from northern and midwestern states to the South during the 1970s, 1980s, and 1990s helped strengthen southern Republican organizations at the local level. More generally, the Republican party has channeled significant resources, including money and political talent, into state and local politics from coast to coast. The process began in 1978, when former Delaware governor Pete du Pont founded GOPAC to recruit and train Republican candidates for state and local office. It ramped up when Newt Gingrich, then a House backbencher, took over GOPAC operations in 1986.

Separately, conservative donors began to create a panoply of new institutions—independent-expenditure committees, grass-roots organizations such as Americans for Prosperity and Freedom Works, the American Legislative Exchange Council to advise conservative state lawmakers, and state-based think tanks—to promote conservative principles in general, to fashion free-market policies, and to propel these policies through the legislative process. Using print, broadcast, and online media, they transformed the flow of information to policymakers, activists, and the voting public. Where liberal academics, special-interest lobbyists, and government staffers once monopolized the crafting of legislation, conservative think tankers and policy experts now offer different ideas to governors and lawmakers. Where liberal media outlets once monopolized the coverage of legislative issues and political scandal,

new conservative media (such as the statewide newspaper I publish, the *Carolina Journal*) now play a role in setting the political agenda and exposing wasteful or corrupt government programs and office-holders.

The donors and policy entrepreneurs who spent the past two decades building a strong conservative movement at the state and local levels knew exactly what they were doing. The policy environment matters a great deal in state politics. If you are a successful, goal-oriented conservative who is thinking of running for public office, you consider more than just the possibility of getting elected. You wonder what it will be like after the election. Will you be a lonely voice in the wilderness, fated to champion doomed bills and subject to constant attack and ridicule by the liberal establishment? Or will you be joined in office by other thoughtful conservatives, and receive support and encouragement from like-minded opinion leaders and effective, well-financed public-policy groups?

In the past, many able conservatives took a look at their bleak post-election prospects and decided against running for governor, the legislature, or county office. Now, many of them seek office with the expectation not only of winning in November but also of winning subsequent battles over taxes, government spending, regulation, education, and other issues they care about. Greatly improved candidate recruitment has proved to be one cause of Republican political success at the state and local level.

Understandably depressed about the 2012 federal elections and the manifest inability of Washington to take on the nation's economic, fiscal, and foreign-policy challenges, some conservatives might be tempted to dismiss the significance of down-ballot political trends. They might well ask what difference it makes who controls the governor's offices in Virginia and Ohio, or the legislatures in Michigan and Florida, if the Obama campaign still won these states' electoral votes and conservatives couldn't win their U.S. Senate seats. I would answer that conservatives should not place such a strong emphasis on Washington and the daily to-and-fro of Capitol Hill politics.

Often without a great deal of national attention, conservatives have turned their electoral victories in the states into legislative victories on many policy issues. These victories include Wisconsin's initiatives on tort reform and public-sector unionization, Michigan's passage of right-to-work protection, the implementation of criminal- and civil-justice reforms in Texas, and successful referenda in a dozen states—nearly all governed by Republican majorities—to enact constitutional amendments outlawing eminent-domain abuse. These victories are important not only on their own terms but also because they can build institutional knowledge, conservative confidence, and momentum for future battles, including those in the nation's capital. Two examples merit a closer look: fiscal policy and education reform.

America's fiscal problems aren't confined to short-term federal deficits or unfunded liabilities in federal entitlement programs. According to the Tax Policy Center, total government spending made up a record 37 percent of America's GDP in 2010, a statistic that fell only a single percentage point in 2011. State and local expenditures accounted for roughly one-third of these amounts, and even more if you consider that much of the federal "stimulus" package consisted of bailing out profligate states with supplemental Medicaid, education, and unemployment-insurance funds. Moreover, underfunded state and local pension and health-care plans add trillions to the nation's long-term liabilities.

The good news is that, while conservatives are properly frustrated at the inability of Republican politicians in Washington to make major headway on spending restraint and tax reform, the new generation of GOP leaders elected to state office over the past few cycles has a far better record. Both case studies and statistical comparisons demonstrate that partisanship makes a difference in state budgeting. Until recently, that wasn't the conventional wisdom, because analysts focused too much on governors. When it comes to fiscal policy, legislative control matters much more.

Writing in *The Journal of Politics* in 2000, James Alt of Harvard and Robert Lowry of Iowa State described their study of more than four decades of state budgeting and partisan affiliation. They found that "Democrats nearly everywhere target a larger share of state incomes for the public budget than Republicans," and that when either party enjoyed unified control of a state's legislature, it tended to get its way on fiscal policy even when the governor was of the other party. In 2006, University of Oklahoma economist Robert Reed examined 40 years of state tax data and found something similar: States with Democratic governments consistently had higher tax burdens than states with Republican ones. And once Reed adjusted for partisan control of the legislature, partisan control of the governorship had little effect.

At the onset of the Great Recession in 2007, states and localities found themselves with falling revenue forecasts and escalating service demands. Their responses reflected party and ideology. Democratic governments tended to raise taxes across the board. Republican governments tended to say no to new taxes, or at least to broad-based tax hikes, while cutting budgets. According to the Tax Foundation's analysis of 2010 data from the U.S. Census, the ten states with the highest combined state and local tax burdens took an average of 11.2 percent of their residents' income in 2010. The average for the ten lowest-taxed states was 7.9 percent. Put differently, the high-tax states took 42 percent more of the typical person's money. Nine of the ten most-taxed states had Democratic legislatures. Most of the ten least-taxed states had Republican legislatures, and three others were southern states with relatively moderate Democratic legislatures. Since 2010, all three have been replaced by more conservative Republican legislatures.

It's not just in overall spending and tax amounts that the new generation of Republican leaders is having an effect. Governors and legislative leaders in several states are now pushing sweeping reforms of their state tax codes, seeking to reduce or eliminate punitive taxation on investment and job creation. For Democrats, tax reform is about filling "loopholes" to make government larger. For Republicans, tax reform is about eliminating biases to make the private economy larger.

As for education, those who expected rising Republican power in state and local government to result in universal vouchers and large-scale privatization of public schools were guilty of inventing either utopian or dystopian fantasies, depending on their point of view. In reality, conservative leaders and policy experts had fashioned a strategy for education reform by the mid-1990s that included several elements: 1) higher academic expectations with rigorous assessments of student progress; 2) reform of teacher tenure and compensation policies; and 3) greater choice and competition in the delivery of education services.

Once they achieved electoral success, conservative policymakers set higher standards and instituted annual testing. They challenged teachers' unions on performance evaluation, pay, and work rules, especially in the Midwest and South. Nearly every state now allows the creation of independent public schools, run by private entities with government charters. As of the 2011–12 academic year, there were some 5,700 charter schools in operation across the country, enrolling about 2 million elementary and secondary students. That's up from only 1,650 charter schools in 2000–01. As for helping parents send their children to private schools, the Friedman Foundation reports that 22 states have some kind of tax deduction, tax credit, educational savings account, or scholarship program in operation—often more than one. Almost all of these programs have been implemented since the 1994 Republican-wave election transformed state capitals, although many of the bills have received bipartisan support.

Perhaps the best example of the conservative strategy in action can be found in Florida. Republicans took control of its senate in 1992 and its house in 1996—marking the first time since Reconstruction that both legislative chambers in a southern state went red. Two years later, Jeb Bush was elected governor on an ambitious platform of education reforms including higher standards, new testing, letter grades for every public school, alternative teacher certification, management reforms, and school-choice programs focused on students who had special challenges or were trapped in low-performing schools. The results have been difficult for even left-wing critics to dispute, although some have tried. Graduation rates are up 20 percent. According to the Thomas B. Fordham Institute, which grades state educational systems, Florida's math standards leapt from an F to an A from 2005 to 2010, and its English standards rose from a C to a B. Once mired near the bottom of the list in National Assessment of Education Progress scores, Florida has posted dramatic gains during the past decade. And in the latest international study of reading performance, released in December, Florida excelled—outscoring 48 of 52 participating education systems and tying the others.

Since leaving office in 2007, Jeb Bush has advised governors, legislators, and education leaders across the political spectrum. For the most part, however, his Republican audiences have responded most favorably. Last year, Indiana and Louisiana enacted sweeping education-reform bills crafted by conservative leaders (including Mitch Daniels and Bobby Jindal) that built and even improved on Bush's ideas, including tenure reform and a greatly expanded role for private schools.

I don't mean to suggest that Florida has been the only incubator of education innovation. Years before Bush was elected, other states acted separately to implement elements of the strategy with impressive results. Minnesota, for example, enacted the nation's first charter-school law in 1991. A couple of years later, Massachusetts pioneered the idea of raising academic standards and using rigorous annual testing to measure progress. North Carolina implemented both ideas in tandem in the mid-1990s. As it happens, Minnesota, Massachusetts, and North Carolina joined Florida among the highest-achieving education systems on recent international math tests. In these three states, the reforms of the 1990s emerged from divided governments, as the election of Republican governors or legislatures created opportunities that bipartisan coalitions then translated into legislation. Because Governor Bush had a Republican legislature to work with, however, he was able to fashion a more comprehensive approach.

W e should not be naïve. New Republican governments at the state and local levels haven't always produced conservative leadership, and conservative leaders still have a lot of work to do if they seek to transform state and local governments into smaller institutions that promote economic growth, refrain from encouraging dependency, and deliver a bigger bang for the taxpayer buck.

And state Republicans' successes can be difficult to apply at the federal level. The federal government lacks elements of the required institutional framework for conservative victories of the type found at lower levels of government. Enforceable rules against funding operating deficits with debt have been critical, and state experience suggests that an item-reduction veto (i.e., giving the governor the ability to reduce spending on a line item rather than vetoing the item or the entire bill) is a key tool for governors who want to cut spending. Without enacting some kind of balanced-budget requirement or constitutional cap on federal spending, and without strengthening the president's veto power, Republican success in future federal elections will likely prove insufficient to the task of imposing fiscal discipline on Washington.

What I am suggesting, however, is that the conservative movement should stop wallowing in its recent failures and start studying and replicating its recent successes. You'll find those successes, and most conservatives, far from the banks of the Potomac.

Critical Thinking

1. What is an important "underreported story" in recent electoral politics in the United States?

2. What was the "Solid South" and how is its demise relevant to the partisan composition of state governments in regional terms today?

3. How have recent electoral and partisan results affected fiscal policy and educational policy in many states?

Create Central

www.mhhe.com/createcentral

Internet References

The Solid South
    http://umich.edu/lawrace/votetour8.htm
Tax Policy Center
    www.taxpolicycenter.org

Mr. Hood is the president of the John Locke Foundation, a public-policy think tank in Raleigh, N.C., and the author, most recently, of *Our Best Foot Forward*.

Article

Prepared by: Bruce Stinebrickner, *DePauw University*

The Progressive Tax Rebellion

Local and state governments are gaining the ability to restore basic services and infrastructure.

SASHA ABRAMSKY

Learning Outcomes

After reading this article, you will be able to:

- Assess the significance of Proposition 13 and the prospective significance of Proposition 30 for California's state and local governments.

- Determine the similiarities and differences among tax-related measures put before voters in California, Michigan, and Florida in November 2012.

- Evaluate your own position on taxation and spending in states and localities in the United States.

On November 6, a solid majority of California voters supported Proposition 30. The ballot initiative, which temporarily raises the sales tax and increases income taxes for the wealthy, will generate an estimated $6 billion per year to help stabilize the state's dismal finances. The vote was a landmark event in California, the state that launched a national anti-tax revolt by passing Proposition 13 in 1978. And for Governor Jerry Brown—who was serving as a much younger governor back then—the triumph was particularly sweet.

In many ways, Brown was seeking redress for the crisis unleashed by Prop 13. That initiative—which capped the property tax rate that communities can impose and established a two-thirds majority requirement for any legislative effort to increase state or local revenues—torpedoed public finances in California for a generation. Prop 30 is by no means a cure-all, but it does offer a salve for the state's ailing public sector. California had already cut tens of billions of dollars from education spending in recent years. If Prop 30 had failed, Brown would likely have had to cut many billions more, and his latest tenure as governor would no doubt have been written off as an abysmal failure. By persuading the electorate to back his tax plan, Brown has paved the way for a much more favorable reading of his legacy.

The significance of Prop 30 resonates beyond California, of course. Thirty-four years after the passage of Prop 13, voters across the country have decided that the strategy behind it

doesn't work. That doesn't mean they've become overnight converts to notions of "big government." But it does mean that the "starve the beast" approach of Americans for Tax Reform president Grover Norquist—who once famously declared he wanted to shrink government until it was small enough to drown in the bathtub, and has compelled nearly every aspiring Republican to sign his "no new taxes" pledge—is no longer dominant. And the injection of nuance into the national discourse on taxes and spending is already making a huge difference.

Slowly but surely, local and state governments are gaining the ability to restore basic services and rebuild infrastructure that has corroded over decades. That can only be bad news for Norquist (who did not return calls relating to this article). After all, the appeal of his message relies on the assumption that government always delivers lemons. Improve the caliber of public service, allow schools and other parts of the public sector to deliver once more, and the talismanic power of his "no new taxes" slogan dissipates.

Norquist and his acolytes had a terrible day on November 6. First there was the presidential election, fought, at least in part, around the issue of raising taxes on the wealthy. Then there were the Senate races, in which liberals like Elizabeth Warren won and Tea Party–backed candidates like Richard Mourdock lost. (A month after the election, South Carolina Senator Jim DeMint, a Tea Party kingpin, resigned to head up the Heritage Foundation, his strident views no longer quite so seductive on the Hill.) The GOP retained its majority in the House, but as Republicans struggled to come to terms with the debacle, Speaker John Boehner replaced a number of conservative committee members with more moderate appointees. Finally, there were the initiatives—not just in California but also in Florida, where voters shot down a proposal to restrict property taxes severely, and in Michigan, where voters rejected a constitutional amendment that would have required supermajority votes to pass any tax increases. Across the country, voters looked at proposals to eliminate taxes and said no, or they looked at proposals to increase taxes and said yes. Several anti-tax initiatives did pass—including a supermajority requirement in Washington. But no state ballot measure was as high-profile, or as significant to the national debate, as Prop 30.

Norquist's power hasn't vanished, but the 2012 election shows that he has lost the ability to bend government to his whim automatically. During the "fiscal cliff" negotiations, dozens of prominent House and Senate Republicans went on record saying they'd be willing to renege on their pledges to him in order to achieve a workable compromise. It's true, as *The Washington Post*'s Ezra Klein pointed out in late November, that the Norquist pledge has "worked" in the sense that Democrats must wage a fierce fight for even the smallest tax increases. But there are clear signs that Norquist's star is on the wane, and nowhere is this more evident than in California—a state with a long history of leading the way on social and political change.

Across the country, voters looked at proposals to eliminate taxes and said no, or they looked at proposals to increase taxes and said yes.

"It's a big deal," says Marshall Ganz, a longtime community organizer and senior lecturer at Harvard's Kennedy School of Government, who served as a field director for Brown during an earlier gubernatorial campaign in the late 1970s. "California's got the opportunity now to really create some tax history. It'd be a wonderful end to the Prop 13 era if California said, 'Been there, done that. It didn't turn out so well. We destroyed our schools.' It's a huge opportunity for California to teach the rest of the country something."

This is why you need taxes

In recent years, Prop 13 and the makeup of the California legislature have made it very difficult for the state to get its fiscal house in order. The majority Democrats had enough votes to limit some of the worst spending cuts proposed by the Republicans. But the minority Republicans had enough votes to block revenue increases. When times were flush, the state could muddle through. It borrowed large amounts of money to fund its operations and juggled bills to help subsidize struggling localities. Even before the financial crisis of 2008, California was stretched thin. Education cuts began kicking in a few years before the crash. When the national crisis hit, California's mess became a catastrophe; crippled by some of the country's highest foreclosure and unemployment rates, the state's tax revenues imploded. The public infrastructure was so badly hit, and the political process so calcified, many experts concluded that only a constitutional convention could set California on the right path. Leaders proposed one draconian cut after another, while voters reformed the primary process to try to bring more stability to the political system. Budget fixes brought temporary respite—but only until the next dire revenue prediction resulted in a new round of cuts. Finally, Brown offered voters a choice: put up the money or accept the fact that the state would no longer be able to support the kind of public services necessary to nurture and sustain middle-class prosperity. In early 2012, his team wrote a proposition and began gathering signatures. Then they found themselves in negotiations with the California Tax Reform Association and

duh.

other progressive groups pushing for a "millionaire's tax." A compromise in March led to a revised draft of the initiative. The new proposal temporarily raised the state's sales tax rate by 0.25 percent and jacked up income taxes on individuals earning more than $250,000 per year. The money generated would, in the main, be used to shore up the state's educational system. As a side benefit, Prop 30 would virtually eliminate the budget deficit, leading the state's Legislative Analyst's Office to predict that surpluses would be possible within a couple of years. The state might even be able to implement another of Brown's ambitions: creating a durable rainy-day fund for California.

With the reworded initiative in hand, the Prop 30 campaign team enrolled public sector unions and other groups in a four-week scramble to qualify it for the ballot. At the height of the campaign, thousands of activists were spread out across the state. "We gathered an unprecedented number of signatures," says Gale Kaufman, a campaign strategist who helped coordinate the effort.

But that, it turned out, was the easy part. Next came the hard stuff: persuading a majority of California's infamously cynical electorate to support a tax hike. Vote no on Prop 30, the governor warned, and the consequences would be immediate and severe. Even if the legislature could be persuaded to approve a tax increase, he suggested, he would veto it. In a game of bluff and counter-bluff, Brown repeatedly assured the voters that he meant what he said. Proposition 30 really was a do-or-die moment.

"Jerry Brown is involved in everything," says Ace Smith, a political strategist whose San Francisco–based firm SCN Strategies has worked with Brown for many years. "Everything that is important in Jerry's world, he is eyeball deep in." Smith, balding with a ring of white hair around his pate, smiles gently as he recalls the hands-on approach Brown took to SCN's most recent media campaign. In the weeks leading up to the election, Smith says, he and Brown would talk ten times a day, give or take, as they worked out a strategy to sell Prop 30 to an electorate long suspicious of Sacramento politics and taxation.

Despite the scale of the educational crisis, the Sacramento punditocracy was convinced for much of the summer and early autumn that the "No on 30" people, and the anti-tax lobby coalesced around the Howard Jarvis Taxpayers Association, would win. (The association didn't return calls related to this article.) Conventional wisdom had it that any proposition relating to taxes for which the support even momentarily dipped below 50 percent was dead in the water come Election Day. In a Grover Norquist world, this theory suggested, momentum would always run against tax increases. Thus Prop 30 had to have at least a ten-point cushion going into the final weeks of the campaign in order to stand a chance.

The Prop 30 strategists were confident that Californians would not tolerate any more cuts to the state's tottering education system.

go young voters

By contrast, private polling commissioned by SCN found that support was much more solid. SCN's analysis suggested that voters—especially younger voters, Latinos, African-Americans and women—really did get the seriousness of the problem. In the office pool, SCN partner Sean Clegg bet that Prop 30 would ultimately get 54 percent of the vote.

The "Yes on 30" strategists were clear-eyed about Californians' longstanding aversion to big government. But they were confident that residents weren't going to tolerate further cuts to the besieged school and university systems. The state already ranked near the bottom for per-pupil expenditures. Schools had seen class sizes soar. Extracurricular activities and courses had been cut; libraries had been shuttered; school bus routes and summer school programs had been eliminated in many districts. There was simply no fat left to trim from the budget.

College and university fees had been massively hiked in an effort to gain some ground, but the increases prompted a public outcry. Activists were voicing their outrage—in Sacramento, at local school board meetings, at city halls. University campuses around the state had witnessed roiling protests and extraordinarily violent police responses that ultimately put California's plight in the international spotlight. In the fall of 2011, at Berkeley, activists were clubbed by riot police. A few days later, students at UC Davis were pepper-sprayed. Protests against the regents of the state university system also met with a violent response.

Teachers and support staff were under assault as well. "Our union has had 15,000 members laid off in the last several years," explains Dave Low, executive director of the California School Employees Association. "We have had a decade of cuts," he says. "It's in the neighborhood of $20 billion."

As the parent of two school-age kids, I've seen the impact of these cuts firsthand. At my kids' school, kindergarten class sizes have increased from around twenty-five students a few years ago to well over thirty. After funds were cut three years ago, the school library stayed open, though with reduced hours, only thanks to donations and parent volunteers. There is no longer a resident school nurse. When teachers want to set up after-school clubs, the district charges rent to keep the school building open. Earlier in the school year, the principal could be found cleaning the cafeteria and school grounds, and then raising the flag—duties she acquired after morning hours for janitors were cut. Parents volunteer as crossing guards when school lets out.

And that's a good school in a relatively affluent part of Sacramento, a school in which a fair number of students have parents with government jobs and a pretty sophisticated understanding of how to leverage services. In poorer schools in less well-connected communities, the damage has been even greater. In September 2009, the *Los Angeles Times* reported that some class sizes in the city had risen to fifty students, with some kids sitting on the floor. In poorer neighborhoods in Oakland, ninth graders reported that they weren't being offered science classes—even though such classes are a prerequisite for college.

As the Prop 30 campaign geared up, the state's coffers were again running out, and California's budget was once more spiraling into uncontrolled deficits. Absent passage of the ballot measure, parents were told, billions of dollars would be cut from K–12 funding; the academic year would be shortened by several weeks; and the community colleges, state university system and University of California campuses would forfeit hundreds of millions of dollars in revenues already promised by the state.

"There was talk of turning away 20,000 fully qualified high-school graduates" from the state university system, says Lillian Taiz, professor of history at California State University, Los Angeles, and president of the California Faculty Association. "It really was going to take an already pretty terrible situation and make it worse. People have seen opportunities shrink and shrink and shrink and shrink, and have finally gotten their heads around the reality that we're all going to have to take responsibility and pay up."

In the final weeks of the campaign, the momentum shifted toward the no vote when a massive influx of anonymous soft money from Arizona funded an $11 million ad campaign attacking Prop 30. The paper trail eventually suggested, though never conclusively proved, that the funder was a front for the Koch brothers. In a widely seen ad, a "mother" (in reality, a paid actress) claimed that the initiative would raise her gas taxes and complained that the money wouldn't even go to the schools. SCN ran online tests and determined that the ad had the potential to sink the campaign. In a series of meetings and conference calls, Brown—flanked by his wife, Anne, and other top aides—crafted a rapid-fire response: a commercial featuring a genuine educator who announced, "I'm a teacher, not an actress," and then set the facts straight. Teachers support Prop 30, she said, because it would inject billions of dollars into the state's tottering education system.

Billionaire attorney Molly Munger (heir to Berkshire Hathaway executive Charles Munger) complicated matters further when she poured millions of her own funds into an ad campaign for a separate tax-hike initiative. Proposition 38 had little chance of passing, but it threatened to split the vote of those who supported raising taxes. When Munger set aside $14 million to run attack ads against Prop 30 in the early autumn, Brown responded by urging every major newspaper board in the state to dissuade her from her slash-and-burn strategy. His tactic worked: faced with a barrage of criticism, Munger pulled her commercials with more than $7 million unspent. The "Yes on 30" campaign was also assisted by Brown's appearance in a series of soothing infomercials touting the glories of the Californian dream and the sense of possibility that could be unleashed if the state's schools were once again adequately funded.

From then on, the polling stabilized in Prop 30's favor. Brown and his campaign team became quietly confident that they had the vote in the bag.

SCN's strategy and Brown's gamble paid off on November 6, with great help from an extraordinary get-out-the-vote effort by public sector unions and activist groups. When the final numbers were tabulated, Prop 30 came in with approximately 55.3 percent support—1.5 percent more than Brown received when he won the governorship in 2010. It was a majority built largely of the same demographic components as those that secured President Obama his re-election.

For campus leaders at the California State University and UC systems, the result was a great relief. They had pushed the envelope to educate (though not to lobby) the campus community about Prop 30, helping fund student voter registration efforts; giving press conferences alongside Governor Brown on the impact of education cuts; personally endorsing the measure, as individuals rather than as campus spokespeople; and encouraging the UC Board of Regents, which is allowed to take stances on propositions, to endorse Prop 30.

"We're on the cusp of an important new coalition," explains University of California president Mark Yudof, "where we're all pulling our oars in the same direction—to protect the greatest public university system in the world. We see a path forward. If California can move in this direction, maybe other states can as well."

Yudof doesn't see the vote as a rubber stamp for lavish new outlays. Rather, he sees it as part of a package of reforms intended to give a once-vaunted educational system enough oxygen to keep it alive while leaders negotiate additional ways to raise money.

"Taxes are not nearly as taboo as the forces of the right have made them out to be," argues Nicholas Johnson, vice president for state fiscal policy at the Washington-based Center on Budget and Policy Priorities. "The election made clear some of the possibilities to tell a more hopeful story about the future."

In the end, Prop 30 was just one of a handful of Election Day victories in California that will help set the state on a more prosperous and sustainable course. Proposition 39, which closed a number of corporate tax loopholes and will likely provide the state with an additional $500 million to $1 billion annually, also received majority support. Several large municipalities passed their own temporary tax increases to keep services such as public libraries functioning. And voters delivered supermajorities to the Democrats in both the State Assembly and Senate, an outcome few pundits predicted—and one that could allow the party's legislators to increase taxes, if needed to preserve vital public services, without a single GOP vote.

All of which should make Jerry Brown happy, perhaps even self-congratulatory. But that's not how California's quixotic governor does things. Sitting in his war room at the Sheraton Grand Hotel in downtown Sacramento, where his team had gathered to monitor the results on Election Night, Brown realized shortly before 11 PM that Prop 30 had won. He barely cracked a smile. Instead, he turned to Smith and Clegg and said, "Success is ephemeral. On to the next thing." Smith laughs as he recalls the moment: "Whatever the opposite of a touchdown dance is, that was it."

One day later, asked to comment on the Democrats' new supermajority, the governor responded with a Zen mantra: "Desires are endless; I vow to cut them down." Clearly, the floodgates haven't been opened by Proposition 30. In all likelihood, voters came out in favor of it only because they trusted Brown not to go on a spending binge. But the endless cuts to education have stopped, at least for now. And whatever Brown may say, that achievement is hardly ephemeral.

continuous improvement

Critical Thinking

1. What is the central contrast between Proposition 13 and Proposition 30, which Californians passed in 1978 and 2012, respectively? What referendum results in Michigan and Florida in November 2012 can be compared and contrasted to the passage of Proposition 30 in California?

2. Who is Jerry Brown and what role did he play in the passage of Proposition 30?

3. How did Molly Munger's support for Proposition 38 threaten the fate of Proposition 30 in California?

Create Central

www.mhhe.com/createcentral

Internet References

Americans for Tax Reform
www.atr.org
California Tax Reform Association
http://caltaxreform.org
Office of Governor Edmund G. Brown, Jr.
http://gov.ca.gov/home.php

Sasha Abramsky, *a Nation* contributing writer, is the author of several books, including, most recently, *Inside Obama's Brain Breadline USA* and *American Furies*. His next book, *The American Way of Poverty,* will be published by Nation Books in the fall.

Article   Prepared by: Bruce Stinebrickner, *DePauw University*

Portland Fluoride: For the Fourth Time since 1956, Portland Voters Reject Fluoridation

RYAN KOST

Learning Outcomes

After reading this article, you will be able to:

- Assess the pros and cons of fluoridating public water supplies.

- Address the striking fact that Portland, Oregon, is the only one of the nation's most populous cities that does not have a fluoridated water supply.

Fluoride supporters, it appeared, had everything going for them.

Five Portland city commissioners had voted to add fluoride to the city water supply. Health advocacy groups, and many of the city's communities of color, lined up behind the cause. And proponents outraised opponents 3-to-1.

But none of that was enough. For the fourth time since 1956, Portlanders on Tuesday night rejected a plan to fluoridate city water, 60 percent to 40 percent.

"There's a libertarian component to Oregon politics . . . a kind of opposition to what the establishment might want," said Bill Lunch, a political science professor at Oregon State University. "Those who have more money, despite the kind of popular presumptions in this regard, don't always win elections."

The lesser-known of two issues on the Portland ballot passed easily. Voters approved a third renewal of the city's Children's Levy with more than 70 percent in favor. The levy directs more than $9 million a year to programs that support about 14,000 children annually in areas such as child abuse prevention, after-school activities and foster care.

The campaign to renew the levy, however, took a back seat to the fight over fluoride, which intensified in the weeks leading to Election Day.

In Portland, where a largely Democratic electorate often finds liberal candidates struggling to differentiate themselves, the fluoride debate created stark, and heated, divisions.

Both campaigns accused the other of stealing yard signs. A thinly veiled anti-fluoride push poll went out to voters. Opponents were described as insensitive to equity issues, while proponents were accused of wanting to willingly pollute the city's famously pure water.

The issue also wound up politicizing a statewide health report that showed falling cavity and tooth decay rates in the state over the past five years. One of the report's authors said she felt pressured by Upstream Health, the group spearheading fluoridation, to present the findings in a certain way.

More than $1 million was spent on the campaign, a considerable total for a Portland-only election. But Portland finds itself back where it has historically been, as the only city among the nation's 30 most populous to not approve fluoridation.

Clean Water Portland, the group leading the opposition, was hesitant to claim victory, but it was clear an hour after the 8 p.m. ballot deadline that the measure didn't have enough support.

Still, said Kellie Barnes, a spokeswoman for the group, when you really get down to it, clean water is a universal issue.

"When citizens took a look at the information, they decided for themselves that the risk wasn't worth it."

Barnes wouldn't discuss possible next steps, although the group has said it would like a ban on fluoride written into the city charter.

"I think we're going to take a little rest and reevaluate where we are."

The pro-fluoride group Healthy Kids, Healthy Portland conceded defeat early. "Disappointed" was the word of the night.

"The results are certainly disappointing, but I think they're mostly disappointing because, at the end of the day, we were not able to provide this preventative measure" to people who need it, said Alejandro Queral, co-chair of the group's steering committee. "The issue doesn't go away at the end of the election."

Dana Haynes, Mayor Charlie Hales' spokesman, said Hales had no plans to come back at the issue but shared supporters' frustration.

"The measure lost even with my own 'yes' vote," the mayor said in a statement. "Disappointing, but I accept the will of the voters."

Portland has been at odds with fluoridation for more than half a century.

In the 1950s, residents considered the question of fluoridation about the same time many of the nation's other large metro areas were adopting the practice as a way of fighting tooth decay. Portland voters bucked the trend and rejected the proposal. They said no again in 1962.

It seemed Portlanders had come around to the idea in 1978 when they approved a fluoridation plan. But two years later, they reversed course and voted to scrap it.

Since then, fluoridation has remained a constant political issue, on par with mandatory gas station attendants, occasionally coming up at the Legislature but never finding any traction.

That changed in September when, after a year of pro-fluoride lobbying, the Portland City Council quickly approved a plan to add fluoride at 0.7 parts per million beginning in March 2014.

The decision affected not just Portland, but 19 other cities, including Gresham, Tigard and Tualatin, that contract with the city to buy water from the Bull Run Reservoir. All told, the fluoridated water would have reached 900,000 people.

Early estimates put the project at $5 million for startup costs and $575,000 annually after that.

Opponents, however, quickly moved to get fluoride on the ballot.

In the months leading to the election, Healthy Kids, Healthy Portland focused on making the issue about equity. The group pulled together support among communities of color and raised more than $800,000 in cash and in-kind contributions. The group sold fluoridation as a scientifically sound method for fighting what they called the state's dental crisis, continuously noting that nearly three-fourths of Americans drink fluoridated water.

Despite its financial disadvantage, however, Clean Water Portland proved better at mobilizing an electorate wary of adding a chemical to one of the nation's cleanest sources of drinking water. Signs calling for residents to reject "fluoridation chemicals" popped up on lawns across the city even as stories in the national media popped up, poking fun at the city's resistance to a common practice.

"The simplicity of their message was certainly an advantage," said Queral from Healthy Kids, Healthy Portland. "I think the opponents did a very good job of casting doubt on the science. I think they homed in on their message and they hammered away on it."

Critical Thinking

1. What explanations are there for Portland being the only city among the 30 largest U.S. cities not to have fluoridated water, even though Portland residents are known to be liberal-inclined voters, who typically favor fluoridation?

2. What was the "Children's Levy" and did the voters of Portland approve or reject it at the same time they were rejecting water fluoridation?

3. In the fluoridation campaign, which side had more money and more support among the mayor and city council members of Portland?

Create Central

www.mhhe.com/createcentral

Internet References

Centers for Disease Control: Community Water Fluoridation
www.cdc.gov/fluoridation
Fluoride Action Network
http://fluoridealert.org
Why Portland Is Wrong about Water Fluoridation (*Scientific American*)
http://blogs.scientificamerican.com/but-not-simpler/2013/05/22/why-portland-is-wrong-about-water-fluoridation

Article   Prepared by: Bruce Stinebrickner, *DePauw University*

Public Meetings and the Democratic Process

Public meetings are frequently attacked as useless democratic rituals that lack deliberative qualities and fail to give citizens a voice in the policy process. Do public meetings have a role to play in fostering citizen participation in policy making? While many of the criticisms leveled against public meetings have merit, I argue that they do. In this article, I explore the functions that city council and school board meetings serve. While they may not be very good at accomplishing their primary goal of giving citizens the opportunity to directly influence decisions made by governing bodies, they can be used to achieve other ends, such as sending information to officials and setting the agenda. As a complement to deliberative political structures, public meetings have a role to play by offering a venue in which citizens can achieve their political goals, thereby enhancing governmental accountability and responsiveness.

BRIAN ADAMS

Learning Outcomes

After reading this article, you will be able to:

- Identify and assess six purported democratic functions that public meetings serve.

- Evaluate some critiques of public meetings commonly voiced by scholars.

- Weigh the notion that public meetings can play significant roles at the beginning and end of the participatory process.

Most local governments hold regularly scheduled meetings to discuss and decide public issues. Opportunities for citizens to voice their opinions are usually a part of these meetings. Public input may take the form of comments on specific issues before the governmental body, or it may be general comments on issues that citizens care about. In either case, citizens are given a specified period of time (frequently two to three minutes) to state their opinions and are usually prohibited from engaging other citizens or officials in dialogue.

In this article, I examine city council and school board meetings in a mid-sized city (Santa Ana, California) and ask what role public meetings have in the participatory policy process. Can they play a constructive role by allowing citizens to voice their concerns and influence policy decisions, or are they a hollow ritual that merely provides a facade of legitimacy? If we want to incorporate greater public participation into the policy process, is there a place for public meetings? I add to the literature that examines the role of public participation in policy analysis (Thomas 1990; Walters, Aydelotte, and Miller 2000) by exploring what function public meetings serve and how they fit into the larger institutional context of citizen input into the policy process.

I argue that public meetings serve an important democratic function by providing citizens with the opportunity to convey information to officials, influence public opinion, attract media attention, set future agendas, delay decisions, and communicate with other citizens. Meetings are a tool that citizens can use to achieve political objectives. This tool is ill-suited for fostering policy deliberations or persuading officials to change a vote on a specific issue. But meetings serve another purpose: By giving citizens a venue in which they can achieve political goals, public meetings can enhance the political power of citizens and, consequently, improve governmental responsiveness to citizens.

If we keep in mind the functions that public meetings can and cannot perform, their role in the participatory policy process becomes clearer. Public meetings can complement the structures that foster citizen deliberation (such as citizen panels, forums, and roundtables) by providing citizens with the opportunity to engage in the political process before deliberations commence and after citizens have developed a set of recommendations or a consensus policy position. Even though public meetings themselves are not deliberative, they can facilitate citizen participation and the development of good policy by assisting citizens in achieving their political goals. In this article, I hope to show the purposes that public meetings serve and how they fit into a larger scheme of citizen input into policy making.

Institutional Design and Citizen Participation

In recent years, many scholars have argued for an enhancement of the extent and quality of citizen participation in policy making (Fischer 1993; deLeon 1995, 1997; King, Feltey, and Susel 1998; Roberts 1997; Schneider and Ingram 1997; Dryzek 1990). They contend that we need to develop structures and institutions to provide citizens with opportunities to participate effectively. But how do you design institutions to allow citizen input into the policy process? There are many ways that citizens can be brought into the policy process: Public hearings, citizen juries, roundtables, and electronic town meetings are examples of institutions meant to create opportunities for citizen participation.

One of the most common methods of citizen participation is the public hearing: A survey of city managers and chief administrative officers found that over 97 percent of cities use it as a strategy for dealing with citizens (Berman 1997, 107). Public hearings, which are usually required by law, allow citizens to comment on a specific issue or proposal before a governmental entity makes a decision. Despite its widespread use, public hearings are not held in high esteem. The most common critique—made by participants, academics, and governmental officials alike—is that citizen comments do not influence policy outcomes (Cole and Caputo 1984; Checkoway 1981). Citizens march up to the podium, give their two-minute speeches, the presiding official says "thank you very much," and then officials proceed with their business irrespective of the arguments made by citizens. Citizens may speak their mind, but officials do not listen and usually have their minds made up before the public hearing. Hearings, in this view, are mere democratic rituals that provide a false sense of legitimacy to legislative outcomes: Officials can say they received input from the public, and it can give their decisions the respect afforded to democratic processes, even though citizen input has no impact. Rather than a means for citizen input, hearings allow officials to deflect criticism and proceed with decisions that have already been made (Rowe and Frewer 2000; Kemp 1985; Checkoway 1981).

A second critique of public hearings is that they are a poor mechanism for deliberation (King, Feltey, and Susel 1998; Kemmis 1990, 51–53; Checkoway 1981). Citizens go to the podium, speak their peace, and then sit down. There is rarely dialogue between citizens and officials; in fact, such dialogue is usually forbidden. While citizens have a chance to state their position and support it with a reasoned argument, public hearings do not allow them to engage elected officials or other participants in a dialogue to try to persuade them to change their opinions. Public hearings do not afford citizens a venue where they can engage in public discussions about common problems and try to reach understanding with their fellow citizens and elected officials. Further, public hearings frequently degenerate into the worst sort of debate: Rather than citizens stating their opinions and offering supporting argumentation, they will employ sound bites, hyperbole, and falsehoods to criticize and demonize opponents—hardly a model of citizen deliberation.

Hearings are also criticized for attracting an unrepresentative sample of the population (McComas 2001a; Gastil and Kelshaw 2000). People who show up to meetings are more likely to be extremists on the issue being discussed because they have greater personal incentives to participate. Hearings may be dominated by those with very strong views on the subject being discussed, crowding out moderate voices that may represent large segments of the community. This dynamic has two repercussions: It undermines the legitimacy of the hearing as a venue for assessing public opinion, and it provides officials with an excuse to ignore public comments (because they believe they are not representative of what the public really thinks).

While even defenders of public hearings acknowledge they are a poor venue for deliberation, some research indicates that hearings can be an effective form of citizen participation and citizens can, at times, be representative of the public at large. In studies of the California Coastal Commission, Mazmanian and Sabatier (1980) and Rosener (1982) found that citizen participation at public hearings had an impact on the denial rate of permits under consideration by the board. Others have argued that under the right conditions (for instance, meetings held at a convenient time and advertised extensively), hearings can be effective at influencing policy and attracting a representative sample of the citizenry (McComas 2001b; Chess and Purcell 1999; Gundry and Heberlein 1984; Gormley 1986).

Dissatisfaction with public hearings as an outlet for participation has led many scholars and practitioners to develop alternative methods for involving the public in policy making. One alternative has been to modify the format of public meetings, discarding the structured and nondeliberative hearing format in favor of a roundtable or small group setting. These settings differ from traditional public hearings in that citizens have an opportunity to discuss the issue at hand and deliberate with fellow citizens and officials. Roberts (1997) argues that the public deliberation occurring at these meetings should be the foundation of an alternative way to solicit public input, and Weeks (2000) describes successful attempts to integrate meetings into a deliberative policy process.

National Issues Forums, a network committed to enhancing civic life and public involvement in politics, has experimented with alternatives to the traditional public hearing for almost 20 years. Here, citizens deliberate over public problems with the goal of developing a plan of action to address the issue (for descriptions of the type of deliberation fostered in such forums, see Mathews 1999; Doble Research Associates 2000a, 2000b, 2001). America Speaks, a nonprofit organization, promotes and organizes electronic town hall meetings that allow citizens to deliberate over policy issues. Using a mix of face-to-face deliberation and communication through technology, America Speaks attempts to empower citizens to voice their opinions and inform governmental action (America Speaks 2002).

One common obstacle to public meetings concerns size: The more people who show up at the meeting, the more difficult it is to have the type of face-to-face interaction and discussion that deliberation proponents desire. While America Speaks and other organizations have addressed some of the logistical problems caused by size, fostering deliberation in large groups is still problematic. One response has been to convene citizens panels or citizens juries to deliberate on issues (Crosby, Kelly, and Schaefer 1986; Kathlene and Martin 1991; Haight and Ginger 2000). These panels are representative samples of the public, and thus can act as a proxy for deliberation among the entire public; because it is not feasible for everyone to deliberate on an issue, selecting a representative sample to do it for them is the next best thing. Fishkin's (1991, 1995) deliberative opinion polls are a variation on this theme: Select a random sample of the public to deliberate on an issue (or an election), and their recommendations will reflect what the public at large would have decided if they had deliberated themselves.

Finally, surveys and focus groups are often considered to be a form of participation, although a qualitatively different form than those already listed. Surveys do not allow for any deliberation, nor do they allow citizens to express their individual voices, as hearings do. While focus groups allow for greater voice and deliberation, they are still limited by a structure that is meant to solicit opinions, not form them. Even though surveys and focus groups by themselves do not offer much opportunity for citizens to participate in policy making, they can be used to enhance other participation tools, such as the ones described earlier, making for a more meaningful and rich participatory structure (for examples, see Weeks 2000; Kathlene and Martin 1991).

I have described various mechanisms by which citizens can provide input into the policy process. The question I pose is this: Where, in this landscape of meetings, panels, surveys, and forums, do local city council and school board meetings fit? What role can they play?

Data and Methodology

The arguments presented in this article are based on research conducted in a mid-sized city, Santa Ana, California. Located just south of Los Angeles, Santa Ana has a population of about 320,000. At one point in its history, Santa Ana was a suburb of Los Angeles, but its links to Los Angeles (in terms of its reliance on Los Angeles for employment, shopping, and entertainment) have diminished over the past few decades, and now it can be considered a city in its own right. Fifty-five interviews with citizen participants were conducted between March and July 2001. Respondents were selected through a variety of means: Some names were gathered through newspaper reports of citizen activities, some were culled from the minutes of city council and school board meetings, and other names were given to the researcher by respondents already interviewed. Through these methods, a list was compiled of these citizens who were most active in Santa Ana politics. Most respondents were involved in civic organizations, such as neighborhood associations, PTAs, and city advisory committees. While many held formal positions (president, treasurer, etc.) within these organizations, few could draw upon extensive institutional resources to achieve political ends, and thus were relatively less powerful than many other political actors, such as union leaders and developers.[1] Generally, the respondents were citizens

who were highly involved in local politics but could not be considered "political elites." There were four exceptions: three former elected officials (one city councilman and two school board trustees) and the president of the Santa Ana Chamber of Commerce.

Interviews were semistructured and asked participants about their activities in trying to influence city and school district policy (the city and school district are separate entities, but both were included in this study). After some general questions about the activities they engage in when trying to influence public policy, respondents were asked to list two or three policies they had personally been involved with, and then were asked follow-up questions on each, including questions about their strategy and effectiveness.

Attending city council and school board meetings is a very common form of participation: 98 percent of respondents reported having attended at least one meeting during the past 10 years, and most indicated they attend meetings on a regular basis.[2] Even though almost everybody stated they went to public meetings, there was some disagreement about their effectiveness. While a few respondents said that attending meetings was the most effective form of participation, most did not (the most frequent response was talking or writing to elected officials directly). Many echoed the common complaint that elected officials already have their minds made up before the meeting. Despite this widespread belief, many respondents offered other reasons why attendance at public meetings is effective. These explanations form the basis for the findings that follow. These are not meant to characterize the aggregate opinion of the respondents, as opinion varied too much to reach any firm conclusion about the attitude of respondents toward public meetings. Rather, the findings that follow describe some functions that public meetings perform and offer reasons why we should maintain this institution.

I do not present Santa Ana as a typical or representative city. Future research on other cities may find that citizens go to meetings for different reasons than they do in Santa Ana, and thus the findings that follow may not be generalizable to other cities. That said, they are valuable because they offer insight into the potential for public meetings to have a constructive role in the policy process. The findings that follow are evidence that public meetings can serve a valuable function for citizens, not that they serve those functions in all contexts or situations.

The Functions of Public Meetings

Public meetings of city councils and schools boards in California are governed by the Brown Act, which requires that all meetings of local governments be open to the public and allow for public participation. The Brown Act gives the public the right to comment on items before the legislative body, and it also stipulates that "time must be set aside for the public to comment on any other matters under the body's jurisdiction" (California DOJ 2002, vii). Thus, citizens have an opportunity to speak about agenda items, as well as any other local issues they feel are important. There are six ways that citizens can use these opportunities to accomplish their political goals.

Provide Information

Public meetings can be an effective way to convey information about public opinion to officials. One piece of information that needs to be communicated is interest in a particular issue: Letting officials know that you are out there is a necessary first step to participation. One respondent stated that attending public meetings was important because "it seems like if you don't show up at the Council meetings, the council says 'well, maybe this is a non-issue.'" Another participant made a similar point, arguing that getting a lot of people to a council meeting is critical to showing that people care about an issue (in this case, a traffic issue). There are, of course, other ways to let officials know that a particular issue is important to citizens: They may circulate petitions, write letters, or call officials directly. In some circumstances, however, attending a meeting can be the most effective way of indicating interest. Gathering a group of citizens to go to a meeting not only is relatively easy, but also clearly communicates to officials that there is interest in an issue.

Some respondents also felt that attendance at meetings was important to counterbalance opposing views and to get their message out. A common theme among respondents was that there is power in numbers, and turning out the masses at city council or school board meetings provides a political advantage by adding force to their message. This dynamic was evident on both sides of a highly contentious debate over the siting of a new school. A supporter of the school stated that "we wanted to have a lot of parents with school children there [at the public meeting] because otherwise you were going to have an imbalance." School opponents also noted their attempts to bring out large numbers to meetings, and both sides claimed they had outnumbered their opponent. Having numbers turn out for meetings is important because one common discourse in local politics concerns which side of the debate has more popular support. Absent scientific polls, actual levels of support are not known, leaving participants free to convince elected officials that they, in fact, have more support. Turnout at public meetings may be seen by officials as evidence of popular support (although frequently weak support, given the unrepresentativeness of those who attend), and thus can be used as a debating point. Lacking other information sources, elected officials may rely on turnout at public meetings, however unrepresentative, to gauge public support for or opposition to a given policy.

The comments of two former elected officials indicate they use public meetings as a source of information. One former school trustee said she kept tallies of supporters and opponents on an issue to get a feel for what the community thought. A former city councilman, talking about a proposal for a permit-parking district in a residential neighborhood, told this story:

> We were told that this was going on and the neighborhood is happy with it and the staff was happy with it, and they worked it out and it was all ready to go. Then it came before us to vote on it, all of the sudden we had a swarm of people who were against it. . . . I was prepared to go ahead and vote with it from the information I had, but then

when this large constituent [sic] of business owners came out I said this is something I hadn't planned on. I can't vote on it. We need to sit down and work this through to see if we can't make both sides a little bit happier. Those groups of people got to me. . . . I would do my homework, and my colleagues—we did our homework. . . . We may have had our minds made up with the facts that we had been given, but when we would have a group come and speak against it, I wouldn't ram it on through, but make a motion to continue it. Let's hear more of what the people are trying to say and sit down and talk to them, again get that dialogue going so we can really find out what their concerns are and what we can do to alleviate it.

For this city councilman, a public hearing provided information about where his constituents stood on an issue. He did not state that public comments had persuaded him to change his thinking on an issue by offering new ideas or new interpretations. He did not say the citizens appearing at the hearing had changed his mind on an issue, or persuaded him that he was mistaken in his support for the proposal. He did, however, change his actions based on the opposition to the proposal that was evident at the public hearing. The public hearing provided new information that altered the actions he took, even if it did not persuade him that his views were mistaken. Rather than acting as a deliberative forum where ideas are exchanged and people's opinions change based on rational persuasion, the view of meetings that emerges here is of a forum in which constituents provide their elected officials with new information about their views on an issue, prompting altered behavior on the part of officials.

Officials, of course, may have other sources of information about public opinion, such as surveys, focus groups, forums, letters and phone calls from constituents, conversations with others, and media reports. Some of these, such as surveys and focus groups, reflect public opinion more accurately because the participants are more representative of the population as a whole. Despite this shortcoming, public meetings have some benefits as a vehicle for voicing public opinion. First, public meetings are useful in measuring the strength of opinion on a particular issue. Officials know that citizens who take the time to come to a meeting care about the issue under discussion, while surveys make no such indication. Further, meetings are open to anyone who wishes to speak, while surveys, focus groups, and advisory panels have restricted participation. While not having restrictions may introduce bias into the opinions presented, the open meeting has an advantage in terms of legitimacy: Citizens who feel their voices are not being represented in survey results or panel recommendations have an opportunity to express views that may be a bit off the beaten path. By providing a venue for citizens who wish to present alternative opinions, meetings can add legitimacy to the policy process. By themselves, public meetings do not provide an accurate picture of public opinion on local issues, but they can act as a valuable and important supplement to other forms of public opinion, providing both additional information and legitimacy.

A Show of Support

One recurring theme among respondents was the importance of supporting friendly elected officials who take controversial policy stands and expressing displeasure with officials who take stands they disagree with. On controversial issues, elected officials are forced to take a position that may alienate some constituents—not a desirable position for politicians who prefer to please everyone. When an elected official takes a position that is unpopular with some, his or her supporters will frequently make a point of coming to a meeting to agree with the stand taken, in a show of support for a politician in an uncomfortable situation. For example, one participant made this comment about supporting a decision on a new school: "We certainly gave Rob and Audrey [two school board members] counter high-ground to stand on. They could say, 'look. These people, our constituents, the parents of the children, they are here to support.' This gave them a public high ground to stand on to shape the argument. . . . It didn't change anybody's mind, but it certainly helped to direct the flow of discussion."

Sometimes, officials need political cover for taking unpopular stands, which can be provided by supporters at a public meeting. If a politician is supporting the view of a small minority (for example, of one particular neighborhood) that is highly unpopular, he or she could take a major public relations hit; he or she could be characterized as out of step with the majority, catering to special interests and the like. These characterizations can be even more potent if they are out there all alone, without any support, while opponents are banging away. Citizens at public meetings, however, can provide some cover by showing public support for an unpopular position. For example, one participant explained why he had attended a meeting in support of a restaurant desiring a liquor license: "It makes it easier for them [the city council] to make a decision if they have support, rather than you making that decision on your own because you know it's right and its best for the community. It takes some of that burden, some of that responsibility, from the Council if there's public support." While the politicians supporting the liquor license might still take some political heat (there was opposition from nearby businesses), at least they can point to a group of citizens and say, "I have some support in the community for my position." From a public relations standpoint, a show of support can be critical, providing cover for a politician in a tight spot and diffusing some of the criticism. Public meetings are an excellent venue to provide this support because they are usually televised and sometimes covered by local newspapers, allowing supporters to get their message out.

Supporting sympathetic officials does not affect votes on issues, nor is it meant to. But it does have an impact. First, it strengthens the relationship between a politician and his or her supporters and creates channels of communication. Elected officials, seeing who supports them during the tough times, will be more likely to return phone calls, arrange face-to-face meetings, and listen to those constituents. Politicians appreciate support on controversial issues and, as a consequence, will be more willing to listen to their constituents on other issues. In other words, public meetings allow citizens to identify themselves as supporters, giving them an opportunity to create relationships with officials. Second, it provides an avenue by which citizens can help officials whom they want to remain in office. Popular support for a controversial vote is an important political cover: Without it, elected officials are susceptible to accusations during the next election that they are out of touch with their constituents and out of step with public opinion. Public meetings provide a means by which citizens can provide political cover for supportive politicians, thus reducing their exposure during the next election.

Shaming

Most citizens at public meetings are not there to support, but to criticize. Elected officials frequently complain about citizens who are silent until they want to vent about a decision they disagree with. At first blush, this type of behavior may seem futile. Yelling and screaming at a meeting is not likely to change the votes of elected officials, so why do citizens go to meetings to complain? One function it serves is to shame elected officials for disagreeable actions. As I have mentioned, support at a meeting can provide political cover for officials; the converse is also true. Criticizing officials in a public forum can create the perception they are out of touch with the community. This is particularly important from a media perspective: The local newspaper or television newscast is likely to report that officials were criticized by their constituents at a meeting, particularly if it is a highly controversial issue. Even if the citizens at the meeting are not representative of the community at large, the image of an official being hammered by his or her constituents is a powerful one, and one that may have important electoral implications.

One example of the shaming dynamic was seen when a group of parents went to a city council meeting to criticize a councilwoman. The issue was a proposed school that was generating a lot of controversy due to its location: The wealthy white neighborhood next to the proposed school opposed it, while many citizens in other parts of the city supported it. The decision to build or not to build was a school district decision (which is a separate entity from the city), but one councilwoman, Lisa Mills, was at the forefront of the opposition to the school. A group of school supporters went to a city council meeting to complain about Councilwoman Mills's activities on the issue and her divisive comments. One leader of the group explained why it was necessary: "[Lisa Mills] was very divisive . . . it was really a lot of lies that were coming down the pipe. A lot of people that weren't involved with the school district, that's all they were getting. So it was very important to counterbalance that. And you had to do it with numbers, you had to do that with a lot of people." Another leader of the group made this comment: "When [Mayor] Dan Young said after the meeting that he'd never ever seen anything like that before in his life, it was like 'ok, we got our message across.' To get up there and publicly censure Lisa Mills for her activities. That was something that . . . it was a distraction and a lot of energy that we didn't need to continue to fight that so we went in and we hit hard and she wasn't really heard from much on that issue after that."

Since the council had no authority over the issue, school supporters were not trying to change the outcome of any policy decision: Their only purpose was to shame Councilwoman Mills. This served two purposes. First, it swayed the terms of the debate and public perceptions by indicating the amount of support the school had. Also, it gave Councilwoman Mills a political black eye, which could have been a liability during the next election (she decided not to run for a second term).

Another example illustrates the effectiveness of shaming officials at public meetings. The issue was a proposed park and community center for Delhi, a working-class Latino community. The city had been promising to build the park for years but never came forward and provided the funding. After repeated stonewalling and delays by the city, supporters decided to force the issue by going to a city council meeting. Here's how a supporter relates what happened:

> So we organized a meeting at City Council, we took about 150 people to that meeting. . . . And the questions were very simple. They were like: why haven't you kept your promises? And I think in many ways, we sort of shamed people, we shamed them because, you know, why haven't you kept your promises? . . . And so what happened was that was aired on Comcast [the local cable company] throughout Santa Ana. . . . [S]o before you know it, I had people calling [me] . . . they were saying "they can't do this to you guys. They can't just put all the money into north Santa Ana. They have to pay attention to all these neighborhoods." People starting coming out of the woodworking, you know, they said they have to make this project for this community. So I think they [the City Council] were probably receiving those kind of calls. And the day after the meeting . . . at the meeting, the Mayor and the rest of the Council, they were kind of cool about things, very evasive, didn't act like they were disturbed in any way. But I'll tell you, the next morning, the Mayor was begging me to meet with him. He said, "please, let's sit down and let's try to work something out."

The value of this shaming strategy lies not in its capacity to persuade the council that the park was a good idea; accusing the council of lying and breaking promises is hardly the way to accomplish that goal. Rather, by embarrassing the council, it was forced to pay attention to the issue and take action (the council eventually did provide some funds for the park, although not as much as requested). A public meeting was the ideal venue for carrying out this shaming strategy. It was televised, and thus many people in the community heard the park supporters' message, placing additional pressure on the city council.[3] For council members, having to sit through a meeting at which 150 angry residents are accusing you of lying and breaking promises while other constituents watch on television is hardly an enticing prospect. We should not be surprised that this strategy bore fruit and got the city to move on the park project.

The capacity to publicly attack officials is an important aspect of democratic governance: Citizens need a venue in which they can counter what their elected officials are doing or saying. Public meetings provide that venue. They give citizens the ability to gather in one place and express opinions that run counter to what officials are saying. While citizens have other venues in which they can criticize officials—such as writing letters to the editor, staging street protests, or voting against officials in the next election—public meetings present a unique opportunity because they are public, easily accessible, and allow citizens to speak their minds. Elected officials never look good when they are being yelled at, and thus venting at public meetings can undermine and weaken the positions of elected officials. Much of the criticism that officials receive may be unjustified and unfair, and I certainly do not mean to imply that citizens are always correct or that elected officials always deserve derision. Fair or not, the ability to criticize elected officials is a cornerstone of democratic politics, and public meetings provide an excellent opportunity for citizens to do so.

Agenda Setting

The power of elites to set the agenda is well documented in the urban power literature (Bachrach and Baratz 1962; Crenson 1971; Gaventa 1980; see Polsby 1980 for a critique). Much less studied is how and under what conditions citizens can influence the agenda. We generally think of public meetings as venues where policy decisions are made, not where agendas are formulated. While in most cases this is true, meetings do provide opportunities for agenda setting by citizens. In Santa Ana, both the city council and school board allow for public comments on nonagenda items, allowing citizens to discuss issues that have not yet been formally taken up by officials. Some participants, when asked whether speaking at public meetings is effective, stated that attending a meeting the day an issue is going to be decided is useless, but going earlier in the process is very effective as an agenda-setting device. One respondent, who was both president of her neighborhood association and president of the library board (a city advisory board), has this to say about whether meetings are valuable:

> You have to be smart when you do it. Like we started speaking a while ago about the library budget because they won't make their decision, they're starting to make their decisions now [March], but they'll make final decisions in June and July. I think they're thinking, too, if you speak on the agenda items, well no, its totally done before it comes to the committee. So you have to speak now about. . . . Like we spoke about CenterLine [a light rail proposal]. . . . We spoke about CenterLine before it even came up at all. And they said "why are you talking about this today?" and we said "because we know you are going to make a decision on it soon. We know you are. We've heard the buzz. So we are going to get a voice now, even though its not an agenda item or anything." I think that's where you have to be smart.

The respondent is making two interrelated points about the value of speaking at public meetings on nonagenda items. First, she is highlighting the importance of early participation. By the time a decision reaches the city council or school board, it has already been in the works for quite some time, with advisory committees, staff, and interested parties providing input. Compromises may already be built into the policy, with the key players working out agreements among themselves. Further, supporters or opponents of a policy may be able to convince elected officials of the merits of their position well before it ever gets to a formal vote. Participation, therefore, is most effective before positions harden, compromises are worked out, and advisory committees make recommendations; showing up at a city council or school board meeting on the day a policy is scheduled to be approved is, in many cases, too late in the process to make an impact. Thus, speaking on an issue to be decided that night is not the most effective way to influence decisions. Speaking at a public meeting well before a decision is made, however, can be effective: By speaking early in the process, citizens are able to get their opinions heard while officials are still deciding how they want to resolve the issue. This is why it was smart to comment on the CenterLine proposal well before it came up for a formal vote (at the time, it was unclear how the city council was going to vote).

Speaking at public meetings can also influence the agenda by making officials pay attention to issues they ordinarily would not. The respondent just quoted illustrates this with her comment about the library budget. Usually, the city does not pay much attention to the library budget and rarely provides additional funding. By speaking up early at a public meeting, citizens can establish an issue (in this case, library funding) as one that needs to be addressed. Another respondent, when asked why speaking at budget hearings is effective, said that it has some impact because "even though they've already made up their minds, it could stay up in their minds for the next budget meeting."

Agenda-setting effects tie into my first point about public meetings sending information to officials: The reason speaking at meetings may help set the agenda is that elected officials may use it as a measure of citizen interest in a topic. If citizens are coming to meetings to talk about the CenterLine proposal months before a decision is due, officials may conclude it is a highly controversial issue that deserves more attention than they are giving it. Conversely, if nobody raises the library budget as an issue, it will likely be ignored by officials (as it usually is). Not only can officials use public comments at meetings to gauge where their constituents stand on the issues of the day, but they can also use them to determine which issues are important and deserve their attention. With limited time at their disposal (elected officials in Santa Ana work part-time), they need to pick and choose the issues that get on their agenda, and citizens showing up to discuss an issue at a meeting may influence those decisions.

That said, public meetings are not the most effective way to influence governmental agendas. Motivating a group of citizens to attend a meeting to discuss an issue that will be decided far in the future is difficult. Further, elected officials may forget about public comments by the time decisions need to be made. Other forms of participation, such as writing letters, circulating petitions, or speaking directly to officials may be more effective at getting them to pay attention to certain issues. Public meetings, however, can be used in conjunction with these other methods and can further advance the agenda-setting goals of citizens. They are particularly useful in making demands on officials public. More private forms of participation, such as letter writing and speaking directly to officials, may get some attention, but they are likely to get more attention if they are coupled with a public display. One chief virtue of public meetings is that they are public, and thus can reach a larger audience than just officials and a small group of participants. They may not be a very effective method by themselves, but they can serve an important agenda-setting purpose if used along with other methods.

Many of the other participatory structures discussed previously, such as citizens' panels, forums, and roundtables, already assume an agenda that is decided by officials. Sometimes, officials use these structures to define agendas (Weeks 2000), but usually the issue to be discussed is identified and framed by officials beforehand. Citizen comments at public meetings can play a role in deciding which issues to convene panels or roundtables for and how those issues will be framed. Public meetings can provide the raw opinions and ideas that can start more deliberative (and ultimately constructive) processes to address public issues.

Delay

While it is rare for elected officials to change their votes based on citizen comments at a public meeting, it is much more common for votes to be delayed because of public outcry, especially if it is unexpected. In some cases, officials may delay to avoid making unpopular decisions with people present, hoping fewer people will be present at the next meeting. In other instances, citizens may desire a delay. One respondent told of a planning commission meeting that was discussing a development mitigation plan. A neighborhood resident, seeing the planning commission was prepared to vote against the plan, stated, "We told them we need to know what our rights are, and we asked them for a 30-day extension, and they granted it to us." This gave the neighborhood residents time to develop a strategy for accomplishing their goals. In some cases, citizens may not find out about an issue until the last minute, and thus they may not have time to take actions such as circulating petitions or organizing a letter-writing campaign which could apply pressure on officials. A delay may create time to work over officials or to gather more support in the community.

Public meetings are an excellent venue for asking for a delay: Elected officials may find it hard to ignore citizens who are merely asking for more time to study an issue, try to reach a compromise, or (as in the previous example) figure out what actions they can take. Asking for a delay is not an unreasonable request, increasing the pressure on elected officials to accommodate it. The ability of citizens to publicly ask for a delay and to provide reasons why the delay is necessary adds to the force of the request. Privately requesting a delay (in a letter or in a phone conversation) does not allow citizens to publicly state their argument in favor of a delay, and thus it is not as politically forceful. Public meetings provide the best opportunity for citizens to ask elected officials to delay a decision because they can publicly present arguments that attest to the reasonableness and wisdom of the request.

Networking

While the primary channel of communication at public meetings is from citizens to elected officials, citizens can also use meetings to communicate with each other. Communication among citizens is not easy because they usually lack the money to send out mailings and frequently lack the time to knock on doors or organize phone trees (although citizens do engage in these activities on occasion). Public meetings allow citizens to get their message out to other citizens relatively cheaply and without a significant time commitment. Usually, only citizens who are active in local politics attend or watch the meeting on television, so they are not a good venue for communication to the citizenry at large. But they are good for communicating with other citizens who are active. Public meetings can create and maintain social networks among active citizens by allowing them to let others know what they are doing. We saw one example of this with the citizen who was advocating a new park for the Delhi neighborhood. She mentioned that after the public meeting, people from other parts of the city called her about the park issue, fostering networks between her group and other neighborhoods and organizations. Of course, citizens have other ways to communicate with each other, and I do not mean to imply that public meetings are a primary, or even an effective, means of building networks. But they can help citizens get their message out and reach out to other citizens in the community.

Influencing Votes

Public meetings can serve other functions in addition to influencing the votes of officials. The six functions just listed are examples of how citizens can use meetings to achieve political goals that may indirectly influence votes by altering the political context in which the votes are taken, but they do not directly change a specific vote. Whether public meetings are effective at the latter is a point of contention in the literature. To round out my picture of the role and place of public meetings, in this section I will discuss the conditions under which meetings may be effective at directly influencing votes. Rather than claim that meetings are effective or not effective, I will explore under what conditions meetings might be influential and why.

My research uncovered one case in which a public meeting unequivocally changed the outcome of a city council decision. The issue was a citywide redevelopment project that, according to its supporters, was proposed to raise money for needed infrastructure projects such as parks and schools. Going into the meeting, most observers expected it to pass. In the weeks before the meeting, a few activists who opposed the redevelopment plan rallied citizens to go to the meeting to voice their opposition. Their efforts worked better than they had hoped: According to newspaper accounts, more than 2,000 citizens showed up to protest. After hearing a handful of irate speakers, the city council voted unanimously to table the item, and it was never brought up again. According to all sources, the redevelopment plan would have passed if it had not been for the outpouring of opposition at the meeting.

This incident illuminates some conditions in which public meetings can effectively change votes. First, elected officials were surprised at the turnout and the opposition.[4] If they had known it would generate so much opposition, they likely would have postponed the decision until they could marshal more support. Or, if they had had the resolve, they might have voted for it despite the opposition. Here we have a case in which meetings conveyed new information to officials (that is, the amount of opposition in the community) that had a direct impact on the vote. The reason it had such a profound impact was that officials did not have the luxury of a public opinion poll to gauge opposition, and thus were blindsided at the meeting. The conclusion to draw is this: If elected officials misjudge public support or opposition, meetings may change votes because they provide new information that changes officials' political calculations.

Two other conditions contributed to the public's ability to change the vote: the sheer numbers of people who appeared, and the absence of supporters. An attendance of 2,000 at a public hearing is phenomenal, particularly in a city of 320,000 people. This unusual show of force must have indicated to officials that the vote could have serious political ramifications and prompted them to change their votes on the spot. Further, the fact that all present were opposed, made a yes vote politically dangerous. As I have mentioned, having support provides political cover. None was present here, making an affirmative vote more difficult.

One more condition may have contributed to the vote change which was not present during the redevelopment incident: the ambivalence of elected officials. Some issues may be more important to citizens than to elected officials, and the latter may be willing to change their votes based on comments at a hearing because they do not have strong feelings either way. This is not likely because elected officials are usually in tune with the wishes and demands of their constituents. But it may happen on occasion.

Whether public meetings are more effective than other forms of participation at influencing the votes of elected officials is a research question that is beyond the scope of this article. My point is not that attending meetings is the most effective strategy for changing legislative decisions, but that, under some circumstances, meetings can be used to accomplish this goal. Adding this argument to the previous section's description of other functions that meetings serve illustrates the usefulness of meetings for citizens. They may not be the best tool for accomplishing political goals, but they do add a weapon to the citizen's political arsenal which can be marshaled to enhance the effectiveness of citizen participation.

Conclusion

At the core of democracy is citizen deliberation and rational persuasion: Citizens deliberate over pressing public issues and make arguments to persuade officials (and each other) to take desired actions. Public meetings do not contribute to either of these goals: They are not deliberative, and they are not an effective vehicle for rational persuasion. Public meetings, however, have a role to play in maintaining a democratic system. Around the core of deliberation and rational persuasion is a democratic periphery of political maneuvering and pressure tactics that are essential parts of a democratic process, and this is where public meetings come into play. Meetings are a tool in the citizen's participatory toolbox that can help them accomplish political objectives—such as supporting allies, embarrassing enemies, setting the agenda, and getting their voice heard—which can add to their influence and effectiveness. The findings from Santa Ana demonstrate some ways that meetings can be used to citizens' advantage.

How do public meetings fit into the overall scheme of citizen participation and policy making? Public meetings do not directly contribute to the process of formulating effective policy solutions to public problems; other devices, such as roundtables, forums, and citizens' panels, are more effective at this task. But meetings, by helping citizens to be more effective, can enhance the responsiveness and accountability of government. Citizen deliberation and discussion on tough policy choices may lead to the formulation of better policy but, by itself, does not make government any more responsive to citizens. If citizen recommendations go unheeded, then the whole process is for naught. This is where public meetings fit in: They provide a venue for citizens to carry out a political struggle to have their voices heard and recommendations heeded. After citizens deliberate on an issue, weigh policy choices, and make recommendations, they can go to a public meeting to make their case. This is not the current role that meetings play, as most speakers at public meetings argue for their personal opinions, not collective opinions derived through deliberation. But, if additional deliberation structures are put into place, public meetings could have a valuable role by enhancing the political power of citizens and, consequently, increasing the chances that government will be responsive to their recommendations.

Public meetings can also assist citizens at the front end of the policy process by providing a venue for citizens to set the agenda and frame policy issues. In many participatory venues, the issues to be discussed are identified beforehand and a framework for discussing the issue is set. While this may be necessary to foster constructive deliberation, it limits the voice of citizens, preventing them from altering the structure of the conversation or changing how an issue is framed. At public meetings, citizens are free to identify issues that need to be discussed and offer new frameworks for understanding issues already under discussion. Before deliberation in forums, panels, or roundtables commences, citizens should have the opportunity to propose what issues need to be discussed, how the issue should be understood, and the manner in which the process should work. Public meetings could give citizens the opportunity to influence the way citizens participate, rather than having government officials decide for them.

Thus, public meetings have a role to play at the beginning and the end of participatory processes. Designing institutions that allow for citizen participation in the policy process requires us to create deliberative and constructive outlets for citizen input. But this positive political power needs to be supplemented by other forms of participation that allow citizens to flex their political muscle (see Rimmerman 1997 for a description of different forms of political participation). Both types of power are needed for a healthy democratic policy process. A process that lacks opportunities for constructive citizen deliberation will lead to disillusionment among citizens and reinforce the disconnect between citizens and their government. On the other hand, a process that allows citizens constructive input but limits their capacity to fight political battles, influence legislative votes, or criticize officials will reduce governmental responsiveness. Without the political power to back up citizen input, much of it will be duly filed, never to see the light of day again. The power to pressure, lobby, and cajole government officials is an essential complement to positive power, as constructive citizen deliberation is only valuable if officials pay attention to it. Thus, public meetings, as a venue where this can occur, cannot be replaced by more deliberative or constructive venues.

In this article, I have explored the value that public meetings have for citizens. But why would local officials want to hold them? By giving citizens an opportunity to accomplish their political goals, public meetings reduce the power and control exercised by officials. There are, however, two reasons why officials would desire to keep public meetings. First, they can provide information to officials about public opinion, particularly which issues citizens feel are important and the strength of their opinions. Second, because public meetings are an open forum in which any citizen can speak, they provide a measure of legitimacy to the policy process. As many scholars have noted, citizens are cynical about politics and government (Rimmerman 1997; Berman 1997; Harwood Group 1991), and thus likely to approach a roundtable, forum, or other project with a wary eye. By providing an open forum for citizens to express their opinions, public meetings enhance the legitimacy of the policy process, a desired commodity for public officials. While public meetings benefit citizens more than they do officials, the latter do derive some benefit and would be wise to maintain the institution.

Notes

1. Political actors commanding significant resources were intentionally excluded. The study was limited to focus on how citizens without institutional power or other resources can use public meetings as a political tool.

2. While this number is high, other forms of participation also ranked very high: 92 percent reported having circulated a petition, and 100 percent reported having spoken to an elected official. Because respondents were chosen based on the fact that they were active, we should expect such high numbers.

3. I do not know the television ratings for city council meetings, but I imagine very few people watch them. That said, those who do watch are most likely politically active, which explains the significant reaction to this meeting.

4. This observation is based on the comments of opponents who were interviewed for this study.

References

America Speaks. 2002. Taking Democracy to Scale: Reconnecting Citizens with National Policy through Public Deliberation. Paper presented at the Taking Democracy to Scale Conference, May 8–10, Warrenton, VA.

Bachrach, Peter, and Morton S. Baratz. 1962. Two Faces of Power. *American Political Science Review* 61(4): 947–52.

Berman, Evan M. 1997. Dealing with Cynical Citizens. *Public Administration Review* 57(2): 105–12.

California Department of Justice, Office of the Attorney General. 2002. *The Brown Act: Open Meetings for Local Legislative Bodies*. Informational pamphlet.

Checkoway, Barry. 1981. The Politics of Public Meetings. *Journal of Applied Behavioral Science* 17(4): 566–82.

Chess, Caron, and Kristen Purcell. 1999. Public Participation and the Environment: Do We Know What Works? *Environmental Science and Technology* 33(16): 2685–92.

Cole, Richard L., and David Caputo. 1984. The Public Hearing as an Effective Citizen Participation Mechanism: A Case Study of the General Revenue Sharing Program. *American Political Science Review* 78(2): 404–16.

Crenson, Matthew A. 1971. *The Un-Politics of Air Pollution: A Study of Non-Decisionmaking in the Cities*. Baltimore, MD: Johns Hopkins University Press.

Crosby, Ned, Janet M. Kelly, and Paul Schaefer. 1986. Citizens Panels: A New Approach to Citizen Participation. *Public Administration Review* 46(2): 170-78.

deLeon, Peter. 1995. Democratic Values and the Policy Sciences. *American Journal of Political Science* 39(4): 886–905.

———. 1997. *Democracy and the Policy Sciences*. Albany, NY: State University of New York Press.

Doble Research Associates. 2000a. Public Schools: Are They Making the Grade? Report prepared for the Kettering Foundation, Dayton, OH.

———. 2000b. Our Nation's Kids: Is Something Wrong? Report prepared for the Kettering Foundation, Dayton, OH.

———. 2001. Money and Politics: Who Owns Democracy? Report prepared for the Kettering Foundation, Dayton, OH.

Dryzek, John S. 1990. *Discursive Democracy*. Cambridge: Cambridge University Press.

Fischer, Frank. 1993. Citizen Participation and the Democratization of Policy Expertise: From Theoretical Inquiry to Practical Cases. *Policy Sciences* 26(3): 165–87.

Fishkin, James S. 1991. *Democracy and Deliberation: New Directions for Democratic Reform*. New Haven, CT: Yale University Press.

———. 1995. *The Voice of the People: Public Opinion and Democracy*. New Haven, CT: Yale University Press.

Gastil, John, and Todd Kelshaw. 2000. Public Meetings: A Sampler of Deliberative Forums that Bring Officeholders and Citizens Together. Report prepared for the Kettering Foundation, Dayton, OH.

Gaventa, John. 1980. *Power and Powerlessness: Quiescence and Rebellion in an Appalachian Valley*. Urbana: University of Illinois Press.

Gormley, William T. 1986. The Representation Revolution: Reforming State Regulation through Public Representation. *Administration and Society* 18(2): 179–96.

Gundry, Kathleen G., and Thomas A. Heberlein. 1984. Do Public Meetings Represent the Public? *Journal of the American Planning Association* 50(2): 175–82.

Haight, David, and Clare Ginger. 2000. Trust and Understanding in Participatory Policy Analysis: The Case of the Vermont Forest Resources Advisory Council. Policy Studies Journal 28(4): 739–59.

Harwood Group. 1991. Citizens and Politics: A View from Main Street America. Report prepared for the Kettering Foundation, Dayton, OH.

Kathlene, Lyn, and John A. Martin. 1991. Enhancing Citizen Participation: Panel Designs, Perspectives, and Policy Formation. *Journal of Policy Analysis and Management* 10(1): 46–63.

Kemmis, Daniel. 1990. *Community and the Politics of Place*. Norman: University of Oklahoma Press.

Kemp, Ray. 1985. Planning, Public Meetings and the Politics of Discourse. In *Critical Theory and Public Life*, edited by John Forester, 177–201. Cambridge, MA: MIT Press.

King, Cheryl Simrell, Kathryn M. Feltey, and Bridget O'Neill Susel. 1998. The Question of Participation: Towards Authentic Public Participation in Public Administration. *Public Administration Review* 58(4): 317–26.

Mathews, David. 1999. *Politics for People: Finding a Responsible Public Voice*. 2nd ed. Urbana: University of Illinois Press.

Mazmanian, Daniel A., and Paul A Sabatier. 1980. A Multivariate Model of Public Policy-Making. *American Journal of Political Science* 24(3): 439–68.

McComas, Katherine A. 2001a. Public Meetings about Local Waste Management Problems: Comparing Participants to Nonparticipants. *Environmental Management* 27(1): 135–47.

———. 2001b. Theory and Practice of Public Meetings. *Communication Theory* 11(1): 36–55.

Polsby, Nelson W. 1980. *Community Power and Political Theory: A Further Look at Problems of Evidence and Inference*. New Haven, CT: Yale University Press.

Rimmerman, Craig A. 1997. *The New Citizenship: Unconventional Politics, Activism, and Service*. Boulder, CO: Westview Press.

Roberts, Nancy. 1997. Public Deliberation: An Alternative Approach to Crafting Policy and Setting Direction. *Public Administration Review* 57(2): 124–32.

Rosener, Judy B. 1982. Making Bureaucrats Responsive: A Study of the Impact of Citizen Participation and Staff Recommendations on Regulatory Decision Making. *Public Administration Review* 42(4): 339–45.

Rowe, Gene, and Lynn J. Frewer. 2000. Public Participation Methods: A Framework for Evaluation. *Science, Technology and Human Values* 25(1): 3–29.

Schneider, Anne Larason, and Helen Ingram. 1997. *Policy Design For Democracy*. Lawrence: University Press of Kansas.

Thomas, John Clayton. 1990. Public Involvement in Public Management: Adapting and Testing a Borrowed Theory. *Public Administration Review* 50(4): 435–45.

Walters, Lawrence C., James Aydelotte, and Jessica Miller. 2000. Putting More Public in Policy Analysis. *Public Administration Review* 60(4): 349–59.

Weeks, Edward C. 2000. The Practice of Deliberative Democracy: Results From four Large-scale Trials. *Public Administration Review* 60(4): 360–72.

Critical Thinking

1. What six important democratic functions, according to Brian Adams, can local government public meetings serve?

2. What are some common criticisms that scholars have voiced about local government public meetings and public hearings?

3. What data did Brian Adams use in his research on local government public meetings in one California city?

4. What conditions, according to Brian Adams, make it most likely that public meetings can change the outcomes of local government officials' votes?

5. What does it mean to say that public meetings "have a role to play at the beginning and the end of participatory processes"?

Create Central

www.mhhe.com/createcentral

Internet References

Access to State and Local Government Meetings
www.dmlp.org/legal-guide/access-state-and-local-government-meetings

Conducting Public Meetings and Public Hearings (New York State)
www.google.com/url?sa=t&rct=j&q=&esrc=s&source=web&cd=1&ved=0CCkQFjAA&url=http%3A%2F%2Fwww.dos.ny.gov%2Flg%2Fpublications%2FConducting_Public_Meetings_and_Public_Hearings.pdf&ei=lsmMUpruF8LbyQHC5ICgDA&usg=AFQjCNGqELBDZdAEGOIxN0U4Q9534TF0Eg&sig2=6JP-Af50WowEuchd2Ll7wA&bvm=bv.56643336,d.aWcl

Planning and Conducting Public Meetings (Ohio State University)
http://ohioline.osu.edu/cd-fact/1555.html

Article   Prepared by: Bruce Stinebrickner, *DePauw University*

Embracing the Future

PAUL STEINLE AND SARA BROWN

Learning Outcomes

After reading this article, you will be able to:

- Assess the roles and vulnerabilities of state and local newspapers in the digital age.

- Explain some of the ways that newspapers are embracing the Internet in their efforts to survive and even prosper in the digital age.

- Weigh the prospects that hard-copy newspapers as we know them today will continue to exist a quarter-century or a halfcentury from now.

good question

Is the newspaper industry dying or is it "managing through a transition of consumer habits" en route to a successful new business model? Christopher Mayer, publisher of the *Boston Globe*, believes the latter is true. And his view is widely embraced in the profession.

Mayer sees his formerly newsprint-centric news organization expanding its reach while transforming into a multimedia, multiplatform news and information company.

Given that intent, can the "transformational newspaper" refinance a declining industry or does it face insurmountable hurdles?

Over 13 months in 2010 and 2011, we visited 50 newspapers across the United States—one in each state—to discover firsthand how newspapers are doing.

With the assistance of state press associations, we selected a cross section of leading daily and weekly newspapers. We interviewed each newspaper's publisher, editor and Web site manager and published our reports on a Web site: www.WhoNeedsNewspapers.org.

We discovered a rapidly evolving industry that is troubled but not dying.

The newspaper business' core financial challenges have not yet been solved, but many initiatives are producing new, digitally enabled products to support news operations.

Despite the challenges, there is optimism the new revenue centers will grow, and confidence newsprint-generated revenue will be sufficient to finance professional news operations during this transition.

Here are our key findings from the 50 newspapers we visited during this Internet-driven revolution.

I. What's Stayed the Same at Successful Newspapers?

- **The keys to success**

  "A good newspaper is like a community talking to itself," says John Bodette, executive editor of Minnesota's *St. Cloud Times*. "I want this newspaper to continue to be the place the community goes to have those conversations."

  Bodette's mantra was echoed in every newsroom we visited. Emphasizing local news, providing watchdog reporting, facilitating community dialogue and serving the public remain the fundamental keys to success.

- **Vetted, edited, ethically managed reporting**

  "If a newspaper doesn't have its credibility, its audience figures it out real quick. And its audience turns away," says Thomas Dewell, coeditor of Wyoming's *Jackson Hole News & Guide*.

  "I really feel like we do something important for a lot of people from all kinds of different walks of life," says Keith Magill, editor of the *Courier* in Houma, Louisiana. "In this community, I feel that . . . if we don't tell people, they don't know."

- **A cadre of community service-driven journalists.**

  "The classic contribution" we make "is shining a light on things," says Carole Tarrant, editor of the *Roanoke Times*. "We have this huge megaphone, and we can point out things that are good and things that are bad . . . I think everybody in [our] newsroom has a general interest in leaving the community a better place."

- **Publishers dedicated to their community's success.**

  Copublishers Kurt and Paula Johnson purchased the weekly *Aurora News-Register* in Nebraska because Aurora was a growing community, and they believed the newspaper should take an active role in community leadership. "I think it's important in a town like this that the newspaper just not be an observer," Kurt Johnson says.

[handwritten margin note, left: The only thing that's changed is the medium]

II. What's Changed at Successful Newspapers?

- **Newspapers are embracing digital delivery**

  Every newspaper we visited operates a news and information Web site. "The way it is now, when we get together for our morning meeting each day, we're not thinking print first; we're thinking Web first," says Dennis Anderson, managing editor of Kansas' *Lawrence Journal-World.*

- **Digital delivery requires complex content management software**

  As news platforms have diversified, more complex content management systems are needed to handle text, photos, graphics and video, and shape them for print, Web sites and mobile platforms. Newspapers owning radio and TV operations also need software to manipulate newspaper copy for use for broadcast and vice versa.

- **Newspapers are producing multimedia reports (and multimedia advertising)**

  Most newspapers have added video, digital databases and social media to their reporting tool chests. Some metros, such as the *Providence Journal*, have staff dedicated to producing video packages.

  Because it requires additional skills and time-consuming editing, many smaller newspapers have struggled with video, but most of the newspapers we visited see video news and advertising as a potential source for new revenue.

- **Some print, some don't**

  Newspapers are rationalizing their printing costs in three main ways. Some newspapers, like the *Boston Globe*, streamlined their printing operations. Others, like the *Northwest Herald* in Crystal Lake, Illinois, outsourced printing to other daily newspapers to cut overhead costs.

  Newspapers with state-of-the-art printing plants, like the *Opelika-Auburn News* in Opelika, Alabama, treat their printing business as a profit center. The *Opelika-Auburn News* earns incremental revenue by printing several regional dailies and weeklies.

- **Breaking news is back**

  "We've changed the way we think. We're more real time," says Sara Scott, community news director of the *Citizen Patriot* in Jackson, Michigan. "We have veteran reporters who can recall the days when they were . . . on deadline and they loved it, and now they're back on deadline again."

  [handwritten margin note, left: good change? more efficient]

  All the daily newspapers in the WNN sample post breaking news on their Web sites whenever local news events occur.

- **Print circulation has shrunk, but readership has expanded**

  As the Internet's impact has grown, newspaper circulation has declined, but newspaper readership has grown.

  "We have never had more consumers of our content," says *Boston Globe* Publisher Mayer. "We have over

  50 percent penetration in this marketplace between print and digital." Expanded readership is the norm.

- **News staffs are smaller**

  Almost every newspaper in the WNN report has cut its news staff in recent years. In his book, *Newsonomics: Twelve New Trends That Will Shape the News You Get,* industry analyst Ken Doctor estimates newsroom staffs shrunk about 20 percent between 2005 and 2010.

- **Fewer reporters dictates focused coverage**

  Vermont's *Burlington Free Press* no longer has the space to be the "paper of record" for its town, says Executive Editor Mike Townsend. "We can't spread ourselves out like that anymore."

  The *Free Press* emphasizes watchdog journalism and coverage of what Townsend calls "passion topics": politics, the environment, local food and culture. This is a common trend.

- **"Swiss Army Knife reporters" are needed**

  "If you're in [journalism] because you don't like technology, it's just not possible anymore," says Meg Heckman, Web editor of New Hampshire's *Concord Monitor*, who uses the "Army Knife" phrase to describe the phenomenon. "You need to know a little bit of everything."

  "I think the skill set is much different," says Frank Scandale, former editor of the *Record* in Bergen County, New Jersey. "Right now, if you're in the game, if you're not in school, you have to train yourself or seek the training."

- **Hyperlocal Web sites are blossoming**

  An Internet-savvy innovation within the WNN sample is the hyperlocal Web site. At lasvegassun.com, readers are encouraged to provide their ZIP codes; the Sun's Web site responds with a list of ZIP code-centric neighborhood events, a neighborhood crime blotter and neighborhood ads.

  The *Times of Northwest Indiana* in Munster, Indiana, serves a growing region of contiguous small towns. Its strategy is to create "communities"—custom Web sites for each venue in its coverage area. There are now 20 *Times* community sites, which showcase hyperlocal news and local ads and draw on the nwitimes.com Web site for regional news.

- **Some newspapers use community journalists**

  Many newspapers in our sample explored using nonprofessional community reporters with mixed results, but two newspapers are deeply committed to tapping into such reporting.

  Clark Gilbert, president and CEO of the *Deseret News* in Salt Lake City, says his newspaper is building a cadre of 4,000 unpaid community journalists, creating what it calls "Deseret Connect."

  In Cedar Rapids, Tim McDougall, vice president of products and the publisher of the *Gazette*, is finding local experts and tapping into their perspectives to create "dense networks around a topic."

- **Newspapers might aggregate news from non-newspaper sources**

    Aggregation is rare, but at the *Seattle Times*, Executive Editor David Boardman says the newspaper has partnered with local blogs. "They do a level of coverage we never did . . . We never covered neighborhoods like that. So our thinking was, 'Hey, they're doing great work. Let's see if we could create a network for which we could be a convener.' "

III. What are the key problems?

- **News audiences are fractionalizing**

    When A.J. Liebling wrote, "Freedom of the press belongs to the man who owns one," he did not envision the Internet. The torrent of blog and social media postings has further fractionalized the news audience, so assembling and retaining an audience is difficult.

- **No single "silver bullet" revenue source has been discovered**

    Joe DeLuca, publisher of the *Tampa Bay Times*' Tampa edition, says "there is no silver bullet" to ensure the economic viability of newspapers, which have lost much of their advertising. "The basic business model remains the same," says DeLuca, but "there will be many different revenue streams" to support it—"that kind of creative thinking needs to go into building a model for digital publishing."

- **10 percent won't pay the bills.**

    More competition and ease of entry to the Internet keep digital advertising rates low. Newspaper organizations are increasing readership but, according to Tom Rosenstiel, director of the Project for Excellence in Journalism, even as the audience grows, print-based advertisers "are not migrating with newspapers to their Web sites" to purchase ads there.

    Also, when advertisers do purchase ads on newspaper Web sites, the news organizations earn revenue at rates of about 5 percent to 10 percent of comparable newsprint advertising rates, according to WNN reporting.

- **The 2008–2011 economic downturn still hurts**

    A "tsunami" has been "going through our industry and all of society," says Gary Farrugia, publisher of the *Day* in New London, Connecticut. The downturn has been caused not only by the industry's transformation but also by the "oppressive recession" that has hit, "particularly hard, businesses that rely on advertising as a major source of revenue."

- **Gauging investment in digital assets is problematic.**

    "Technology is important to us," says *Seattle Times* Publisher Frank Blethen, "but you can't be a captive of [it]. When [digital news] is only 10 percent of your business, you just can't dump all your resources into it."

- **Selecting new digital tools is daunting**

    "I don't want to be the leader [in new technology]; I want to be two steps behind," says Publisher Jim Thompson of Idaho's *Coeur d'Alene Press*. But,

Thompson adds, "I don't want to get any farther back than that."

- **Digital news delivery requires newsroom reorganization**

    The *Day* in New London went from 66 FTEs (full-time equivalents) in the newsroom in 2001 to 57 in 2012, but their jobs are vastly different. Now the paper has "videographers, video producers, digital directors and breaking news editors," says Publisher Farrugia. These changes required a "deconstruction" of the traditional news and copy desks.

- **Selling digital ads takes new skills**

    At North Dakota's *Grand Forks Herald*, Advertising Director Zach Ahrens needed to convince his ad staff that online journalism is here to stay. "Some of the veteran staff thought, 'If we just wait this out—it's the latest fad—it will go away,' " Ahrens says. An accelerated bonus plan motivates the Herald sales staff to sell both print and online ads.

IV. What are the key opportunities?

- **Newspaper readership persists**

    "I think the newspaper form has at least 15 years," says Stephen Borg, publisher of the *Record* in Bergen County, "because you have people who are ingrained in the habit, where, if we don't mess it up, they'll die with the habit."

- **Newspapers have unique compelling attributes**

    The newspaper has distinctive storytelling advantages. In New Orleans, we watched a local TV news story about a man who had dined in every restaurant in the city.

    The local paper, the *Times-Picayune*, ran a feature story about this same man. Beneath his picture was a list of the 740-plus restaurants at which he had dined. Readers could immediately absorb the immensity of his project and determine if their favorite restaurant had been included.

    The newspaper used its unique print attributes to tell the story graphically. Random access, serendipitous story presentation and easy portability also distinguish newspapers.

- **More news platforms can earn more revenue**

    Some newspapers charge readers for stand-alone online products. The *Austin American-Statesman* sells access to a www.hookem.com Web site for University of Texas football junkies.

    The *Roanoke Times* is seeing success from "Daily Deal," a partnership with advertisers in which the newspaper earns revenue when readers purchase a featured daily deal from a local business posted on the Times' Web site. "We're brokering the sale, rather than just selling advertising to our customers," says *Times* President and Publisher Debbie Meade. "It's quickly grown into a very nice revenue stream for us."

In Portland, Oregon, an alternative weekly, *Willamette Week*, says 17 percent of its total revenue comes from producing public arts, culinary and entertainment events.

And newspapers are learning since new digital initiatives are relatively inexpensive, they can try and fail and try again until they design a winning product.

"We have to be doing stuff that other people aren't or can't," says Kathy Best, managing editor of the Seattle Times. "First, you've got to be a really passionate journalist. Second, you've got to be willing to change. . . . You've got to be willing to experiment and fail.

"But," she adds, "fail fast."

- **Newspaper Web sites can charge for their services**

After years of giving away their digital content, more and more newspapers are erecting paywalls. Some newspapers are adapting a two-tier subscription strategy. They publish local headlines, calendars and Associated Press copy on a free site. But only paid subscribers get access to the complete array of digital news and information.

"If you've got two products—one's a print product and one's the Internet product—and they're basically substitutes for each other, and you're asking people to pay for the print product and you're giving the Internet product away, you're driving people to the Internet," says Jay Seaton, publisher of the *Daily Sentinel* in Grand Junction, Colorado. "That's just simple economics. And that's an unsustainable business model."

- **Midsize, smaller and weekly newspapers have more time to transform**

"Smaller newspapers have a better place into the future because what they do is unique," says newspaper industry analyst Doctor. "To the extent that they do not have editorial competition and [have] lesser advertising competition, they're far less endangered than metro papers."

Also in smaller communities, the digital revolution is not moving so fast. Small-town merchants are still learning how to advertise online, and print delivers some kinds of advertising—like Sunday inserts—more effectively than the Internet.

Our visits to 50 newspapers across the country suggest that the newspaper industry is not ready for hospice care. The newspapers we checked out have become transformational news companies.

They have reduced staff and streamlined costs, admittedly reducing their newsgathering capacity. But they have also reshaped their missions to seize the opportunities of the digital era.

Before 1995, newspapers were traditional newsprint-bound, three-dimensional media—text, graphics and photos. Since then, at widely varying rates of speed, they have become multimedia, multiplatform news and information outlets.

The leading transformational newspapers are trying to reshape their industry. They've added video reporting and video advertising (a new revenue source). They are matching sellers and buyers to create transactional revenue streams. They are devising local mini-Web sites to assemble special interest audiences for niche advertisers.

Some newspapers—those that do not have the potential to aggregate vast, Amazon-sized audiences—are erecting two-tier Web sites: one free, with weather and headlines, and another, behind a subscription paywall, with all the news organization's content. This strategy has reduced the loss of paid circulation revenue at such newspapers as the *Arkansas Democrat-Gazette* in Little Rock, a pioneer in charging for digital content.

Predicting the long-term future of the newspaper industry is beyond the scope of this report. But we invite readers to visit the WhoNeedsNewspapers.org Web site, meet the people who are fighting to transform these newspapers and judge the level of their intelligence and commitment. You'll find bright, energetic, community service-oriented journalists and business people.

Their progress and missteps are writing a compelling, high-stakes drama. It's a business story about whether the public is willing to pay for valid, vetted, professionally gathered news, and whether the embattled newspaper community can recapture the public's imagination.

And it's a cliffhanger.

Critical Thinking

1. What has reportedly stayed the same at successful newspapers?
2. What are the most significant changes that have occurred at successful newspapers?
3. What are key advantages that newspapers have over competing media and for what key reason does one publisher say that "the newspaper form has at least 15 years"?

Create Central

www.mhhe.com/createcentral

Internet References

Hyperlocal On-line News Start-ups (Columbia Journalism Review)
   www.cjr.org/news_startups_guide/online-news-websites/coverage/hyperlocal-news.php
Who Needs Newspapers?
   www.whoneedsnewspapers.org

Paul Steinle and Sara Brown traveled from June 15, 2010, to July 15, 2011, visiting 50 newspapers in 50 states to report for their WhoNeedsNewspapers.org Web site. Steinle is an adjunct professor at Quinnipiac University and professor emeritus at Southern Oregon University, with 30 years professional experience as a reporter and news manager. Brown was a human resources manager at Washington's *Vancouver Columbian* and the *Los Angeles Times*, and a national newspaper management consultant.

Article   Prepared by: Bruce Stinebrickner, *DePauw University*

Cross Examination

Local prosecutors are the last sacred cow in journalism. But some journalists have found the value of a more thorough cross examination.

STEVE WEINBERG

Learning Outcomes

After reading this article, you will be able to:

- Assess the notion that prosecutors serve as judges and juries in about 95% of all criminal cases and consider alternatives to the way the criminal justice system currently operates.

- Evaluate the significance of Maurice Possley's "Ephiphany."

- Weigh the assertions that appellate court rulings and observation of interactions between–and performances by–prosecutors and defense attorneys are important activities in assessing how well and fairly a local criminal justice system is functioning.

Some journalistic epiphanies take a long time to form. In my case, 30 years. That is how long it took me to realize somebody needed to conduct a systematic examination of the nation's 2,341 local prosecutors' offices.

During an era when journalists tend to be skeptical about the performance of elected and appointed government officials at all levels, prosecutors qualify as the last sacred cow: assumed to be acting in the public interest, rarely scrutinized and, if covered at all, covered favorably.

In lots of newsrooms, the shorthand for the criminal justice beat is "cops and courts." That traditional label says a lot by what it fails to mention—the prosecutor. My painfully slow epiphany is that prosecutors are the linchpin of the criminal justice system. They receive information from the police about an alleged crime before any defense attorney or judge receives information, and information is power. No case can move forward without the prosecutor's assent. In most jurisdictions, about 95 percent of the crimes charged never reach trial; that means 95 percent of the time, prosecutors are acting as judge and jury combined, all behind closed doors. Furthermore, when a case does reach trial, no matter how wisely or unwisely judges, defense attorneys and juries act, it is usually won or lost because of the way the prosecutor presents the evidence.

Every day, prosecutors in district attorneys' offices throughout the United States decide if people arrested by local police should be:

- Charged with a crime.
- Placed back on the streets, or jailed.
- Allowed to sign a plea agreement, or proceed to trial.
- A candidate for the death penalty if the law permits that outcome.
- Heard after imprisonment because new evidence suggests a wrongful conviction.

Counting the elected district attorney at the top of the office pyramid and the lawyers appointed by the district attorney to serve justice, there are about 30,000 prosecutors working in the United States. Many of these prosecutors are dedicated, skilled public servants. Many others are mediocre. Some should never have been allowed to wield power. But few people know much about their local prosecutors. Most of the time, in most of those 2,341 jurisdictions, journalists are nowhere to be seen as new prosecutors are hired, as veterans are promoted, as other veterans retire or are forced out.

The sacred cow syndrome blessedly appears to be fading in some newsrooms, however. One factor: In cases with DNA evidence, the number of documented wrongful convictions is approaching 200. They demonstrate like nothing else the fallibility of prosecutors. Everybody makes mistakes. But in a system supposedly devoted more to serving justice than to winning at all costs, in a system supposedly loaded with safeguards, how do prosecutors allow innocent people to be charged with a crime, indicted by a grand jury, incarcerated for months or years while awaiting trial, convicted and sentenced?

The Center for Public Integrity Comes Through

Hoping to find somebody to support a national examination of prosecutors, I approached Charles Lewis at the Center for Public Integrity in Washington, D.C. Lewis is a former CBS 60

Minutes producer who had his own epiphany about 15 years ago. He left his job to start an organization that would conduct investigative journalism in the public interest, in-depth, on topics normally ignored. Against gigantic odds, the Center for Public Integrity has not only survived, but thrived.

Lewis and his staff raised money from foundations and individuals to make my idea a reality. The Center hired two individuals to work with me—Neil Gordon, a Baltimore lawyer who wanted to change careers, and Brooke Williams, a recent University of Missouri Journalism School graduate.

For three years, we gathered information about the performance of every local prosecutor's office in the United States and about as many of the individual district attorneys as we could identify. In several dozen newsrooms, reporters have used our specific findings about the local prosecutor's office, posted at www.publicintegrity.org at the "Harmful Error" icon, to produce insightful follow-ups. In addition to our specific findings, our general conclusions ideally will inform future coverage of prosecutors in every newsroom.

Maurice Possley's Epiphany

To some degree, we stood on the shoulders of giants while conducting our research. Chicago Tribune reporter Maurice Possley is renowned today for his coverage of Cook County prosecutors who break the rules to convict the guilty, and sometimes the innocent. Possley, with colleagues Ken Armstrong and Steve Mills, changed the world in ways most journalists only dream about: Because of their prosecutorial misconduct exposés, first the Illinois governor and legislature, followed by officials in other states, imposed a death penalty moratorium as well as spearheading procedural reforms to the criminal justice system.

But until a few years ago, Possley was part of a widespread newsroom problem—indifferent coverage of prosecutors. Possley saw them one-dimensionally, the way so many other journalists do—as good guys trying to put bad guys behind bars.

Possley covered federal courts in Chicago, first for the Sun-Times, then for the Tribune. He might evaluate a prosecutor's courtroom performance, but gave little attention to the decision-making outside of public view leading to the trial.

In 1995, Possley started covering local courts, which tend to be grittier than the federal system. He began to see the inflexibility of prosecutors as he honed his approach to trial coverage by telling each day as "a separate story with a beginning, middle and end. I tried to always balance the day with some flavor of cross-examination, sometimes saying it was unsuccessful. Sometimes the cross-examination became the lead. . . . Quite a few prosecutors would make remarks about my inclusion of cross-examination. They had seen (the questioning of prosecution witnesses by defense lawyers) as meaningless or not damaging their case and questioned why I would even report it."

Possley realized that "for most prosecutors, it is a one-way street—their way. And I understood that to be a condition of the beat. Along with these realizations came the knowledge that while the prosecution does usually win, that doesn't mean the truth got found out. There were cases where you couldn't really tell where the truth was, and I could see that for many prosecutors, it was all about winning. Still, I mostly thought they got the right guy—some cases were just closer than others. . . . The thought that innocent people were being convicted or that justice was being undermined was really not on my radar."

The epiphany Possley needed arrived during the murder trial of Rolando Cruz in DuPage County, Ill. Police and prosecutors originally said Cruz and two other men killed a 10-year-old girl. Some police officers and prosecutors believed early on that the arrests were misguided—especially after a fourth man, a convicted murderer, confessed. The DuPage County prosecutor refused to credit the confession.

In 1995, Cruz won a directed acquittal from a judge in a trial covered by Possley. After the acquittal, a court-appointed special prosecutor recommended that seven DuPage County prosecutors and police be charged with criminal offenses for their conduct.

Possley received a question from an editor: How often does it happen that a prosecutor is indicted for misconduct? Possley had no idea, so he studied decades of reporting by the Tribune and other Chicago-area news organizations. He found himself "astounded to see how prosecutor-oriented the coverage was." During the early stages of the research, Possley continued to cover the Cook County prosecutor's office. "Many prosecutors still thought of the beat guy and the Tribune largely as their allies. . . . I think many of them never imagined that the result of our reporting would be critical."

Armstrong joined Possley to document 381 cases back to 1963, the date of the U.S. Supreme Court decision *Brady v. Maryland,* in which the justices said convictions could be reversed if prosecutors presented evidence they knew to be false, concealed evidence suggesting innocence, or both. The Tribune's January 1999 series put prosecutors and readers on notice that a new era of coverage had dawned.

Then, in November 1999, Armstrong and Mills published a new revelatory series, examining murder cases in which Illinois prosecutors sought the death penalty. The journalists identified 326 reversals attributed in whole or part to the conduct of prosecutors. Armstrong and Mills wrote themed articles as part of the series, examining how prosecutors use confessions extracted through police torture, perjured testimony of jailhouse informants seeking rewards and unreliable hair/fiber analysis from law enforcement forensic laboratories.

When interviewed in July, Possley was collaborating with Mills on a new project, preparing for the launch of his second book (about a Chicago murder case) and planning his fall teaching leave at the University of Montana journalism school.

Without question, Possley has become skeptical about prosecutors. Today, he says, "I try to persuade defense attorneys to provide discovery (from the prosecutor) to me. I try to actually interview witnesses before trials. I spend more time covering pretrial motions, when significant evidence often comes out and evidence that tends to contradict the prosecution often is aired. And I adhere to the belief that not everything said is the truth, even if it's under oath, and that many things are said as truth but with such semantic gymnastics as to be ridiculous."

It Takes a Village

Possley came to his epiphany alone. When he started acting on it, though, he shared it with two reporting partners, Armstrong and Mills, who helped mine the possibilities of prosecutor coverage.

Dallas Morning News reporter Holly Becka has teamed up professionally, too. In fact, she learned last year it takes a village of journalists to provide exemplary coverage of a scandal that crosses beat lines, involving prosecutors, police and judges.

Becka, a veteran cops and courts reporter, became one of those village members when a Dallas fake-drug scandal emerged: Defendants were being charged, convicted and imprisoned for possessing or selling what appeared to be narcotics, but in fact was billiards chalk planted by police informants or police themselves. Instead of asking the right questions to halt the scam, prosecutors proceeded against the hapless defendants.

"The story started on the police beat and spilled to the criminal courts beat and then to the federal beat," Becka said. "A senior general assignments reporter also pitched in during the early months of the scandal to look at policies in the district attorney's office that helped lead to the scandal. . . . Most of the stories in the early months were written by the two then-criminal courts reporters because prosecutors were dismissing drug case upon drug case, and the effects were being felt by defendants-turned-victims, their lawyers and the court system in general. More recently, our federal beat reporter has handled the story . . . because of the FBI investigation and the federal civil-rights lawsuit." Becka also credits a Morning News editorial writer, journalists at WFAA-TV and the alternative weekly Dallas Observer.

In an April 27, 2003, story that skillfully weaves together seemingly stray strands to create a new reality for readers, Becka and fellow reporter Tanya Eiserer explain how police blame prosecutors for the scandal, while prosecutors blame police. For example, prosecutors say police learned earlier than previously acknowledged that the primary drug informant lacked credibility. While corrupt informants were fooling police officers, prosecutors accepted the cases without asking the tough questions, then hammered out plea bargains with presumably guilty defendants without running the allegedly illegal seized substances through drug testing.

As stories about the scandal kept coming, Becka still had to find time to cover the routine aspects of the beat, such as profiling the Dallas assistant district attorney who was recognized as the top prosecutor in Texas. Becka used a feature lead, telling how the assistant district attorney saw prosecutors as heroes even when he was a child—heroes with the same stature as movie star tough-guy John Wayne. For 19 years, Becka explained, the child hero worshiper has been living his dream as a real-life prosecutor. Such stories inform readers of the positive and help build relationships on the beat.

Becka recently moved from the criminal courts beat to a newly created criminal justice enterprise role. "I've had so many people—members of the public, the criminal defense bar and even a few prosecutors—credit the media with forcing public officials here to do the right thing after the scandal erupted," she said. ". . . The sentiment I've heard is if the media had been asleep or uncaring, innocent people would have remained in jail."

The Value of Appellate Court Rulings

Rob Modic, a Dayton Daily News reporter since 1979, knows what the best beat reporters, including Becka, know: When keeping tabs on prosecutors, study every appellate court opinion that comments on their conduct.

The upside of studying appellate court rulings is huge: They are official records, they often contain nuggets of news amidst the normally dry prose of judges, and those rendering opinions are often former prosecutors who know first-hand what to look for when examining state conduct. An appellate ruling can be a platform for discussing a specific issue, such as whether local prosecutors regularly withhold evidence from the defense in violation of U.S. Supreme Court mandates; use jailhouse snitches as witnesses, without fully checking the snitches' accounts or fully disclosing the quid pro quo to the defense; coach state witnesses or discourage potential defense witnesses from cooperating; cross the line during trial, perhaps during opening statements, perhaps during cross-examination, perhaps during closing arguments.

Part of a three-person criminal justice team, Modic and colleagues "get together regularly to discuss filed cases at every stage," including the appellate stage. "We look at search warrants, motions to suppress (evidence), preliminary hearings. We talk to parties about overcharging and undercharging. We collect string, then put the twine together for a story."

Watch the Interactions Carefully

As a longtime St. Louis County courthouse reporter for the Post-Dispatch, Bill Lhotka knows almost all the prosecutors and defense attorneys who work opposite sides of criminal cases. Tuned-in reporters watch "for veteran prosecutors taking advantage of neophyte defense attorneys or public defenders. The reverse is also true: veteran defense attorneys running circles around new prosecutors." Neither scenario leads to the closest approximation of the truth. Winning is ingrained in prosecutors and defense counsel, but, Lhotka says, that is no excuse for cutting corners to win a case, to obsess over percentages of victory and defeat because of career advancement plans or personal vanity.

Tim Bryant covers the St. Louis City courthouse for the same newspaper. He and Lhotka sometimes compare notes, especially because the same defense attorneys often appear in both jurisdictions. The reputation of individual prosecutors among defense attorneys and judges is usually easy to learn after trust is built on the beat, Bryant says. That information can also be supplemented through close observation. "Attendance at court proceedings early in a case may be helpful," Bryant said. "For example, a prosecutor's performance in a preliminary hearing or an evidentiary hearing could likely provide clues to his effectiveness. Was he prepared? Did he show proper courtesies to the judge and the opposing lawyer, especially in a proceeding where jurors are not present? Does the prosecutor have the respect of his office's investigator and the police detectives on his case?"

Jury selection provides more evidence, but lots of reporters are absent from that stage of the trial. "Was jury selection contentious to the point that the prosecutor was accused of removing potential jurors because of their race or gender?" Bryant asked. "Then there is the trial itself. Did the defense lawyer make more than a typical number of objections? Were disputes serious enough to merit sidebar conversations with the judge, or even recesses in the trial?"

Seek Access, and You Might Find It

Access granted to journalists by district attorneys might increase understanding of the daily difficulties faced by prosecutors—and everybody wins when that occurs. But it appears that journalists rarely ask to be a fly on the wall.

Gary Delsohn of the Sacramento Bee asked. Elected district attorney Jan Scully said yes. The only restrictions: Delsohn could not write anything for his newspaper during his year inside; nobody would be quoted by name without consent; personnel matters could be ruled off-limits by Scully; Delsohn would provide periodic reports on his observations if requested. (Scully never made such a request.)

In return, Delsohn would be provided a semiprivate writing space, could wander freely, pose questions and attend meetings. "There were more than a few people in the office who thought Scully was insane," Delsohn said, " . . . but for the most part people were extremely open and accessible. Prosecutors and investigators freely discussed the most sensitive aspects of their cases in front of me. I was allowed to sit in on meetings with victims, defense attorneys, judges, police and witnesses. I was almost never told something was off limits, and after I had been showing up for a few weeks, most of the resistance that I was aware of had disappeared."

Much of what Delsohn learned appears in his book, published in August by Dutton. The book, "The Prosecutors," subtly emphasizes Delsohn's special access in the subtitle: "A Year in the Life of a District Attorney's Office." It is a primer for any outsider journalist who wants to think about how to cover prosecutors more effectively.

Prosecutors Rarely Admit Their Mistakes

Ofra Bikel is a producer of documentaries for the PBS program Frontline. After turning her attention to the criminal justice system 15 years ago, she produced the "Innocence Lost" trilogy about the mishandling of child sexual abuse cases in Edenton, N.C. In 1999, her documentary about three prison inmates exonerated by DNA testing aired as "The Case for Innocence." Last year, Frontline aired "An Ordinary Crime,"

Bikel's account of a North Carolina armed-robbery prosecution beset with problems.

Bikel says she is baffled by the refusal of the prosecutor to reopen the conviction of Terence Garner, given post-trial evidence that the wrong man is in prison. Baffled but not surprised, because Bikel has watched prosecutors in previous cases dig in.

"There are a few problems with prosecutors," she said. "First, because it is an adversarial system, and the defense's job is to defend their client in any way they can—within the boundaries of the law, which is quite flexible. The prosecution, as the adversary, wants to do just the opposite of the defense: Convict the defendant in any way they can. So it is a contest. The problem is that the prosecution has a double function. Besides being one side in a contest, they are supposed to represent the people and to see that justice is done. This double-headed function in a cutthroat adversarial system is very hard to maintain. Unfortunately, I have not met too many prosecutors who spend sleepless nights over the fact that they won a case but sent an innocent person to prison. The prosecutors are not villains, but they look at a case, and they see people who they think are guilty go free because of smart-ass, manipulative attorneys, and they are furious. So they, too, cut corners, and blind themselves many times to the truth, or at least to doubt."

Expect to Be Verbally Attacked by Prosecutors

Edward Humes wrote about prosecutorial error and misconduct in the office of the Kern County, Calif., district attorney. The incumbent responded with a 154-page document attacking the journalist and his findings. Both used incendiary words. Humes' book, published by Simon & Schuster, is "Mean Justice: A Town's Terror, a Prosecutor's Power, a Betrayal of Innocence." The district attorney's reply is "Junk Journalism: Correcting the Errors, False Claims and Distortions in Edward Humes' Mean Justice."

Humes, like Possley, took awhile to reach the realization that prosecutors are not always the good guys. First as a newspaper reporter, then as the author of high-end true crime books, Humes usually found defendants' claims of innocence filled with holes.

He began to change his attitude while investigating the conviction of Pat Dunn, a Bakersfield educator and businessman, for murdering his wife, Sandy. Convinced after extensive research that Dunn is innocent, and appalled at what he believed to be prosecutorial misconduct in the case, Humes examined the actions of the district attorney and his deputies over several decades. The research resulted in what appeared to be questionable patterns of behavior among specific prosecutors handling specific types of cases.

Humes possessed an advantage over Bakersfield-based journalists. He was writing a book, then would probably leave the jurisdiction to pursue a different book. Beat reporters, on the other hand, who examine prosecutor conduct sometimes see sources dry up not only in the district attorney's office, but also in other law enforcement quarters.

Investigative reporting about prosecutors' performance, Humes said, "is likely to be met with strong, even bizarre, resistance from prosecutors, who may be prone to suggesting that anyone who criticizes their actions must be a) in league with criminals; b) in league with criminal defense lawyers; c) are criminals themselves; or d) worst of all, political liberals."

The Horrible Power of Self-Delusion

Dorothy Rabinowitz has carved out a specialty in her place on the Wall Street Journal editorial board. That specialty: problematic prosecutions of alleged child molestation rings.

Her first Journal exposé, published in 1995, centered on the Fells Acres Day School in Malden, Mass. Prosecutors charged Gerald Amirault, his sister Cheryl plus his mother, Violet, the founder of the day care center, with monstrous multiple molestations based on the word of preschoolers—and without a shred of physical evidence.

As Rabinowitz chronicled other fantastic-sounding child molestation cases in New Jersey, Florida, Washington State and California, an awful question occurred to her: What if the prosecutors did not believe in the guilt of those they brought to trial? What if they filed the charges to appease community outrage, to build support for a re-election campaign or a higher office? After all, the evidence of molestation seemed unbelievable when evaluated using common sense.

Rabinowitz worked up to raising her unpleasant question in her 2003 book "No Crueler Tyrannies: Accusation, False Witness, and Other Terrors of Our Times." What did the prosecutors think? she mused. "Did they actually believe in the charges they had brought, of naked children tied to trees in full public view and raped in broad daylight, as in the Amirault case; in the testimony of child witnesses who had recited obvious whoppers about robots, being stabbed with swords, and the like?"

Some prosecutors actually believe those seemingly ludicrous scenarios, and some do not, Rabinowitz concluded. Both patterns of thought are scary. One type of prosecutor cares nothing about the justice that is part of the office's sworn duty; won-lost records are paramount. The other type of prosecutor is blinded by passion, too close to the emotional residue of little children being victimized.

"The prosecutor's propensity to believe in the guilt of anyone accused of the crime of child sex abuse (is) overwhelming," Rabinowitz said. "That belief (is) fueled by investigators who share the same propensity and interrogated the children accordingly."

Critical Thinking

1. About how many local prosecutors' offices are there and what important roles do they perform in the criminal justice system?

2. What does it mean to say that prosecutors serve as judges and juries in about 95% of all criminal cases?

3. What did *Chicago Tribune* reporter Maurice Possley and his colleagues do to "change the world in ways most journalists only dream about"?

4. In what ways can appellate court opinions be helpful in studying the conduct of prosecutors?

5. What can be learned from watching prosecutors in public court proceedings?

6. What is the "double-headed function" of a prosecutor and why is it hard for him or her to maintain it?

7. What is meant by the "horrible power of self-delusion" relating to prosecutions of alleged child molestation rings?

Create Central

www.mhhe.com/createcentral

Internet References

American Bar Association: Prosecution Function
www.americanbar.org/publications/criminal_justice_section_archive/crimjust_standards_pfunc_blk.html

Maurice Possley Investigates
www.mauricepossley.com

National and State Prosecutors Websites
www.eatoncounty.org/departments/prosecuting-attorney/144-departments/prosecuting-attorney/prosecutorinfocom/461-national-a-state-prosecutor-association-web-sites

STEVE WEINBERG is a freelance magazine writer and book author in Columbia, Mo. He served as executive director of Investigative Reporters Editors, based at the Missouri Journalism School, from 1983–1990. He teaches from time to time at the Journalism School.

Article   Prepared by: Bruce Stinebrickner, *DePauw University*

Ready, Set, PAN

As newspapers close their capitol bureaus, the value of public affairs networks increases.

STEVEN WALTERS

Learning Outcomes

After reading this article, you will be able to:

- Assess the importance of television or Internet coverage of live proceedings of state legislatures and other state government public proceedings.

- Consider the difficulties and problems that can arise from state government funding of those who provide live coverage of state government proceedings.

- Evaluate NAPAN's "best practices" for covering state governments.

Move over "Survivor!, The Bachelor" and "The Amazing Race." There's a different kind of reality TV available for the more discriminating viewer. Public affairs networks provide real-time and taped coverage of the sometimes messy, but always fascinating, art of lawmaking in state legislatures.

Networks and broadcast systems began offering real-time and archived coverage of state legislatures in the 1990s. If time and resources allow, they also cover the executive and judicial branches of state governments. The trend has exploded in recent years, as many newspapers closed their capitol bureaus.

"As newspapers have pulled back on statehouse coverage, it is arguably more important than ever that the basic proceeding of state government be televised, just as the U.S. Congress is on C-SPAN," says a 2011 Federal Communications Commission report.

Lights, Camera, Action!

Almost every state has some type of network or broadcast system providing legislative coverage—although the landscape of organizations that do so varies widely, according to a survey by NCSL. The largest, most sophisticated and independent organizations belong to the National Association of Public Affairs Networks (NAPAN). The association's president, Paul Giguere,

who runs CT-N, The Connecticut Network, estimates that about 24 states have public affairs networks (PANs), most of which rely on tax or public funds to varying degrees.

Some of the larger networks include Connecticut, Florida, Michigan, Ohio, Pennsylvania, Washington and Wisconsin. They broadcast real-time and archived legislative coverage, produce Emmy-award winning programs on complex issues and trends, travel around their states to cover cultural and historical events, and offer regular news updates.

WisconsinEye, for example, taped 147 face-to-face interviews with candidates for Congress and the Legislature before the Nov. 6 election. It also rebroadcast and archived dozens of candidates' debates, forums and news conferences.

The Pennsylvania Cable Network, with 37 employees and a $4.5 million budget, "helps bring perspective to major issues by interviewing lawmakers one-on-one and hosting call-in programs with lawmakers, various commentators and analysts," says Pennsylvania Senate Majority Leader Dominic Pileggi (R).

A second tier of capitol coverage networks has survived by blending public funds and other fund-raising partnerships, including with public broadcasting channels. These networks turn to whatever broadcasting systems are available—including public, educational and government (PEG) channels—to stay afloat. In other states, legislative coverage is provided by employees who work directly for legislative leaders, or for their public information offices.

Some state networks, such as Hawaii's, cover the legislature only during session. Others, like the Minnesota Channel, borrow legislative staff to get the job done.

How coverage of state affairs is produced and distributed varies by state. Viewers can watch their government in action via livestreaming over the Internet, or on cable channels, public TV networks and PEG channels.

A Fine Line

Large or small, most public affairs network professionals strive for independence in determining what and how they cover government activities. State employees who make capitol coverage decisions can walk a fine line, since their budgets often depend on the lawmakers they must cover.

In states like Arizona, New York and Michigan, coverage is determined by legislative leaders and taped by their employees.

Tom Posey, public media director for the South Carolina ETV Channel and a NAPAN board member, says it's a balancing act to decide what to cover while working for a state agency the legislature funds. He was asked to start livecasting Senate Finance Committee meetings, for example, even though his agency has been downsized in recent years. He assigned a camera operator to those meetings.

"Each state has a political challenge" of how their house and senate want to be covered, says Posey. "We have evolved to the point where we balance our political relationships with our role as a state agency. At the end of the day, we govern ourselves by our editorial standards."

In an effort to help its members navigate the tricky waters of political reporting, NAPAN developed a set of "best practices"—standards to follow in order to operate as independently as possible. They include:

- Cover of all three branches of state government.
- Keep coverage decisions free from political influence.
- Engage citizens by offering real-time debates, as well as archives.

It is possible for public affairs networks and lawmakers to coexist peacefully. Wisconsin Senator Fred Risser (D), the longest-serving legislator in the nation, says he's received "positive feedback" from citizens about WisconsinEye, and that state lawmakers act no differently when cameras are present. "Quite honestly, WisconsinEye has had a minimal impact on legislative activity. The Legislature functions as if it did not exist," he says.

Washington House Speaker Pro Tem Jim Moeller (D) supports his state's network, TVW, because it provides transparency, which leads to "a better government, a better democracy." And even though TVW has had to absorb $2.5 million in state aid cuts since 2008, the network's subsidy remains a "very bipartisan appropriation. It's pretty much looked at as a 'hands-off' sort of thing," Moeller says.

And . . . Cut!

Many networks struggle with funding since state legislative allocations have been cut in recent years. Added to that are the high costs of keeping up with the constantly changing technologies that come with every new model of smartphone, tablet and other high-tech toy.

The only network that receives no public funding, the non-profit WisconsinEye, has relied on cable fees, donations and loans for its $1.2 million operating budget. But the 10-employee network, which fed coverage of collective bargaining protests at the state Capitol in 2011 around the world, has accumulated more than $2 million in debt. Even so, WisconsinEye's governing board turned down a state loan offer from lawmakers, fearing it could compromise its independence. Network president Jon Henkes is working to find new financial backers and develop a long-term development approach.

In Ohio, the network has been "flat-funded for 10 years, which has begun taking its toll," says Executive Director Daniel Shellenbarger. The Ohio Channel creates its own programming and does contract work, in addition to covering government. It also gathers and replays programs about the state's history and public affairs.

The Florida Channel has lost about 25 percent of its staff since the recession hit, forcing it to reorganize and cut back its coverage of legislative committees. But things are looking up, says Executive Director Beth Switzer, since there have been no new cuts in public funding in the last two annual budgets. She's even been hiring new staff. With a current budget of $3.5 million, the channel prides itself on enterprising shows like "Capitol Update," "Florida Crossroads" documentaries, "Face to Face" interviews and a new "News Brief" show that recaps daily state government news.

Other state networks have experienced cuts as well. Michigan Government TV had to cut staff hours, its operating budget and out-of-town productions. CT-N in Connecticut, which gets 99 percent of its budget from public funds, has postponed growth because of the recession but has avoided layoffs.

In North Carolina, Ivy Hoffman retired last April, after a cash-flow problem shut down the Agency for Public Telecommunications (APT), which she ran for decades. She is looking for $2 million to start a new network, and says she has interest—although no cash yet—from North Carolina's cable industry. "I think people agree that we need a PAN, but getting folks together to start detailing out what needs to be done just takes time," she says.

Giguere says the slow progress in North Carolina is not unusual. "In any state that's ever launched a network, the groundswell of interest and support has taken time to build," he says.

It's a Wrap

Constantly evolving technology provides opportunities—as well as obstacles—in the effort to offer full-time coverage in all states. Network executives worry about the future of cable, the cost of maintaining and replacing equipment, and whether they must provide closed-caption and Spanish translation programming, for example.

Giguere says public affairs networks must forge ahead in the face of changing technology, and continue to sell their message—that what they do is essential. "It's about cultivating a philosophy . . . that these networks are important, valuable to viewers and worth the bandwidth or 'shelf space' needed to include them in their offerings," he says.

Pennsylvania's Pileggi agrees, pointing out that such coverage is important because citizens can watch their government, and are often prompted to weigh in on the debates. "The programming is invaluable, both in terms of being able to explain the work we're doing in the Capitol in greater depth, and in hearing directly from residents across Pennsylvania."

In Washington, Moeller says viewers enjoy following the "high drama" of state budget debates, and did not hesitate to make their opinions known during the controversy over legalizing same-sex marriages.

Those who are passionate about making sure citizens can watch their government in action are not likely to give up the good fight, says Giguere. Public affairs networks introduce citizens to the capitol, where they can watch everyday decisions being made that affect their lives, he says, and learn how to participate in that process.

"That is incredibly empowering."

Critical Thinking

1. How do the organizations that cover state legislatures vary in their funding by and connections with state governments?

2. What is "the fine line" that state government employees who cover state legislatures must walk?

3. What are three "best practices" for covering state governments developed by NAPAN?

Create Central

www.mhhe.com/createcentral

Internet References

National Association of Public Affairs Networks (NAPAN)
http://napan.org

National Council of State Legislatures: Broadcasts and Webcasts of State Legislatures
www.ncsl.org/GoogleResults.aspx?q=broadcasts%20and%20webcasts%20of%20state%20legislatures

---

STEVEN WALTERS is a senior producer for WisconsinEye and a former bureau chief for the *Milwaukee Journal Sentinel*.

Unit 4

UNIT

Prepared by: Bruce Stinebrickner, *DePauw University*

Government Institutions and Officeholders

Government institutions are to state and local political systems what skeletons are to people. They shape the general outlines of government policymaking processes in the same way that bones shape the outlines of the human body. For state and local governments, as well as for the national government, institutions are critical elements in the governing process.

There are important state-by-state variations in executive, legislative, and judicial structures and in the degree to which citizens have access to the policymaking process. In strong governor states, chief executives hold substantially greater appointive, budgetary, and veto powers than those in weak governor states. The roles of parties, committees, and leaders differ among state legislatures, as does the degree of professionalism among legislators. The roles of state courts vary according to the contents of state constitutions, as well as a state's political and judicial traditions. In some states, the state's highest court plays a role that is roughly comparable to that of the United States Supreme Court at the national level. The highest courts in most states, however, are generally less prominent. States also differ in whether judges are elected or appointed. With respect to policy making and government as a whole, some states allow for direct citizen involvement through the devices of initiative, referendum, and recall, while others do not. Many of these structural details of state governments are spelled out in each state's written constitution, although state constitutions generally do not play as prominent or symbolically important a role in state government as the United States Constitution does in national government.

Local governments do not incorporate the traditional three-branch structure of government to the extent that state and national governments do. Legislative and executive powers are often given to a single governing body, with the members choosing one of themselves to be the nominal chief executive or presiding official when the body meets. For example, school boards typically elect their own board president to preside over meetings, but they hire a professional educational administrator, called a superintendent, to manage day-to-day affairs of the district and provide educational leadership. What is true of school districts is roughly paralleled in some but not all other local governments. In contrast, the structures of strong-mayor cities resemble executive-legislative arrangements in national and state governments. The traditional notion of an independent local judiciary as a third branch does not apply in a straightforward way at the local government level. Local courts, to the extent that they exist, do not restrain the other branches of local government in the way that state and national courts are empowered to restrain their respective legislative and executive branches. As with state judges, some local judges are appointed and some are elected.

This unit on institutions is organized along traditional legislative, executive, and judicial lines. The first section treats state and local legislatures, with the latter category including city and town councils, school boards, town meetings, and the like. The second section turns to governors and local government executives, while the third and last section treats state and local courts.

Article

Prepared by: Bruce Stinebrickner, *DePauw University*

The Legislature as Sausage Factory

It's about Time We Examine This Metaphor

When you get right down to it, making sausage is a lot different than making laws, no matter what the old saw says.

ALAN ROSENTHAL

Learning Outcomes

After reading this article, you will be able to:

- Assess the utility of the metaphor "legislature as sausage factory" in understanding the legislative process.

- Propose one or more other metaphors for the state legislative process as you understand it.

If you spend any time hanging around legislatures or around Congress for that matter, you will inevitably hear the expression, "There are two things you don't want to see being made—sausage and legislation." Attributed to Otto von Bismark (1815–1898), Germany's chancellor, the metaphor of sausage making and lawmaking has had a remarkably long run. But, I wonder, does it still apply or are today's sausages and legislation on separate tracks, unlike in the 19th century?

In connection with a book I am writing, I have been closely observing lawmaking in four states. So when I had the opportunity to observe sausage making at the Ohio Packing Company, I took it.

Established as a neighborhood butcher shop in 1907, Ohio Packing has two processing facilities in Columbus, one of which turns out 40,000 pounds of sausage a day. As sausage factories go, this is a medium-sized plant. Larger plants are more automated and have more bells and whistles, but the process is nearly the same. Rick Carter, the quality control manager in the facility, served as my guide.

The Guts of Sausage Making

Sausage making occurs in distinct stages, each of which takes place in a specified room or area. First comes the raw materials cooler, where sausage ingredients are mixed according to computer formulations. A vat will hold 2,000 pounds of one-quarter fat trimmings and three-quarters lean trimmings. At the second stage, the raw materials proceed to the sausage kitchen.

A grinder processes up to 40,000 pounds per hour, a blender allows water and seasoning to be added, an emulsifier reshapes the content into a new form, and natural hog casings are stuffed with ingredients.

The Cooking Process Is The Third Stage. Huge Processing Ovens Dry, Smoke, Cook Or Steam The Sausage. A Gas Fire, Using Hickory Chips, Provides Natural Smoking. The Chilling Or Holding Area Is The Fourth Stage. Here, The Sausage Sits Around Waiting To Be Packaged, Which Comes Fifth And Is Accomplished By Three Large Machines. With The Assistance Of 10 To 15 Packagers, The Machines Wrap Multiple Sausages In Plastic Film. Sixth Is Storage In A Huge Freezer With A Capacity Of About A Million Pounds. Finally, Seventh Is The Shipping Area Where Wrapped, Packaged Sausage Waits To Be Loaded On Trailer Trucks.

The Sausage Link

At first glance, sausage making and lawmaking would appear to be a lot alike.

Just as pork, beef and chicken make their way stage by stage to the shipping docks, so a bill is introduced, reviewed by a committee, considered on the floor of one house and then further reviewed by committee and on the floor of the other house. The two houses have to concur before the bill proceeds to the governor for his or her decision to sign, not sign or veto. In sausage making what you see is what you get. However, the "How a Bill Becomes a Law" formulation that is supposed to describe the process in Congress and state legislatures is way off the mark. So, let's compare the processes of sausage making and lawmaking in some of their significant dimensions.

Accessibility. It is not easy to get into a sausage factory, unless you work there or are a raw ingredient. Because of the possibilities of liability and contamination, the public is barred. I could not get in on my own recognizance, but had to secure a letter of introduction from the president of the Ohio Senate. Such a letter is not needed to get into the legislative process. The statehouse is most accessible. Public tours are offered.

In Search of the Perfect Metaphor

The legislature has been compared in other metaphors as well as Bismark's—among others, to a circus, marketplace and zoo.

Two interesting metaphors are offered by John A. Straayer in his book, *The Colorado General Assembly*. First is the legislature as an arena in which "a score of basketball games are progressing, all at one time, on the same floor, with games at different stages, with participants playing on several teams at once, switching at will, opposing each other in some instances and acting as teammates in others."

Second is the legislature as a casino, where there are lots of tables, lots of games, the stakes are high, there are winners and losers, but the outcome is never final, for there is always a new game ahead.

Just because the legislature as sausage factory does not stand the test of empirical examination doesn't mean there isn't a metaphor that can do the job. State Legislatures invites legislators, legislature staff and other readers to offer metaphorical candidates, even ones that only apply to part of the process or apply only in part, but not entirely.

Mail your submissions to Sharon Randall, NCSL, 1560 Broadway, Suite 700, Denver, CO 80202 or fax to 303–863–8003 or e-mail to Sharon.Randall@ncsl.org.

More important, people can observe the legislature indirectly through the media and more directly through C-Span coverage, which is aired in almost half the states. Constituents can visit with their legislators at home or in the capital. Furthermore, members of the public not only are observers, but, mainly through interest groups and their lobbyists, are also participants. They can make demands and help shape what comes out. Contamination is welcome in the legislature; it is a major element of democracy.

Coherence. The 60 people of Ohio Packing who make sausage work in different areas and engage in different operations. But they are all part of one team, making a variety of products according to specification. No one tries to introduce a substitute sausage or attach a bratwurst amendment to a frankfurter. No one wants to prevent a sausage from coming out. In the legislative process, there may be as many teams as there are individual members of the particular legislature. There is a Republican team, a Democratic team, a House team, a Senate team, a liberal team, a conservative team, an urban team, a suburban team and so on. Often, as in Congress and many states today, these teams are quite evenly matched. These teams are not in the business of producing the same product, but often are competing with one another over legislation and over the state budget.

Regularity. Sausage making strives for uniformity. Constant testing takes place to ensure the proper measurement of ingredients—fat content, moisture, seasoning and so forth. The process is strictly regulated by the U.S. Department of Agriculture, whose applicable regulations currently run into thousands of pages (there were only 86 pages of federal regulations in 1914) and whose inspector makes at least one visit a day to check on the

operations of the Ohio Packing Company. In addition, the process is monitored diligently in-house by quality control personnel.

Not so with the legislative process, where uniformity is virtually unheard of, measurement of content is illusory, and just about every bill—and certainly every important bill—gets individualized treatment. At the outset, one can predict what will come out of the sausage factory. It is impossible to predict what will come out of the legislature. We are pretty sure that every year or two we will have a budget, but that is as far as certainty goes.

Efficiency. Sausage making has to be efficient if Ohio Packing is to survive and prosper. Only a few weeks elapse from the time the raw materials are unloaded at the shipping dock to the time when the finished products are loaded onto trucks bound for distributors and retailers. And most of that time is spent on a shelf, waiting for orders to arrive. Not so with the legislative process. Noncontroversial bills may be enacted within a month or so, but significant legislation may take years before enactment. Not infrequently, the legislature fails to meet its budget deadline, as New York has failed for 17 consecutive years, or fails to finish its budget before constitutional adjournment, as is the case of Minnesota this year. Legislatures are hardly efficient if any economic sense. Nor should we expect them to be.

Comprehensibility. The process of making sausage ought not be minimized; it is complex. But it is also comprehensible. In an hour-and-a-half tour, I could figure it out. I have been a student of the legislative process for more than 30 years, but I still can't figure it out. The legislature is too human, too democratic and too messy to be totally comprehensible.

Product. There is no denying that sausage comes in many varieties. Ohio Packing produces 250 different items, although most are variations on the same theme: breakfast and Italian sausage, bratwurst, frankfurters, bologna and salami are the major items under the sausage umbrella. The brand names that Ohio Packing supplies also vary. Harvest Brand is the company's own label. Through a license agreement with Ohio State University, it also manufactures and sells Buckeye Hot Dogs and Brutus Brats; and it is the coast-to-coast distributor of Schmidt's Bahama Mama (a spicy, smoked sausage).

Whatever the brand, however, the labeling required by USDA provides consumers with more information than they could possibly absorb: the brand name; product name; ingredients by proportion, including seasoning; nutrition facts; inspection legend; net weight statement; signature line (that is, who manufactured the sausage); and a handling statement.

New Metaphor Needed

Legislation is much more diverse than sausage, law is much greater in scope. And it is much more indeterminate. Consumers can read the enactment and the bill analyses leading up to it, but they can never be sure of how a law or program will be funded and implemented and how it will actually work. No accurate labeling system has ever been devised.

The products as well as the processes of sausage making and lawmaking are almost entirely different. Bismark has been at rest for more than a century; his metaphor ought to be laid to rest also. We can search for another metaphor, although I doubt that we will find one. The legislative process in Congress and the state is *sui generis,* incomparable, not like anything else in our experience—and pretty much the way it ought to be.

Critical Thinking

1. What is the well-known statement by Otto von Bismark that linked legislation and sausage?

2. What are differences and similarities between sausage-making and legislating with respect to accessibility, coherence, regularity, efficiency, comprehensibility, and product?

3. Why, according to Alan Rosenthal, is a new metaphor needed to illuminate important elements in the legislative process?

Create Central

www.mhhe.com/createcentral

Internet References

Alan Rosenthal obituary (NY Times)
www.nytimes.com/2013/07/12/nyregion/alan-rosenthal-who-reshaped-legislatures-dies-at-81.html?_r=0

National Council of State Legislatures
www.ncsl.org

ALAN ROSENTHAL is a professor of political science at the Eagleton Institute of Politics at Rutgers University.

Article   Prepared by: Bruce Stinebrickner, *DePauw University*

What Legislatures Need Now

The prescription for change offered 40 years ago in "The Sometime Governments" has run its course, but legislatures still face plenty of institutional challenges.

KARL KURTZ AND BRIAN WEBERG

Learning Outcomes

After reading this article, you will be able to:

- Evaluate the 1971 recommendations of the Citizens Conference on State Legislatures about the operation of state legislatures.

- Assess the twelve questions about contemporary state legislatures posed by Karl Kurtz and Brian Weberg at the end of their article.

T he challenges of today's legislatures are complex. They involve questions of integrity, will, commitment and trust, and the solutions are not at all clear. The realities of today's government and politics require a new approach to strengthen legislatures. What's needed is a process that clarifies the current problems, what changes are needed and how to put those remedies into place.

In the 1970s, the Citizens Conference on State Legislatures launched a remarkable movement to strengthen our nation's legislatures by publishing "The Sometime Governments: An Evaluation of the 50 American Legislatures."

The book included sweeping recommendations for change. The guidelines were designed to give legislatures more resources of time, compensation, staff and facilities. Forty years later, that agenda for reform has been largely accomplished or is no longer as relevant.

In large measure, "The Sometime Governments" succeeded in igniting two decades of effort by legislatures in every state to build capacity—the amount of session time, the number of members, committee organization, facilities and staffing.

It provided state-specific marching orders and a battle plan to reform-minded political troops ready and able to carry out its agenda. At the time of its publication, American politics were in transition. The one-person, one-vote court decisions of the 1960s and subsequent redistricting after the 1970 census opened state legislatures to a surge of new members in the 1974 elections.

They were a generation inspired by Kennedy, but also battered by the Vietnam War and the Watergate scandal. Armed with ideas set out in "The Sometimes Governments" and fueled by private foundation support, they transformed state legislatures.

'The Sometime Governments'

The Citizens Conference on State Legislatures was a private nonprofit organization formed in 1964 to improve state legislatures. With a major grant from the Ford Foundation, it launched a 50-state study of legislatures in 1969 and published "The Sometime Governments: An Evaluation of the 50 American Legislatures" in 1971.

Based on criteria for "functional, accountable, informed, independent and representative" legislatures, the book evaluated state legislatures and ranked them from one to 50. The rankings caused a considerable stir among state lawmakers, and were an effective call to action: No state wanted to remain ranked in the bottom half of the list or to be below its neighbors or rivals.

The book contained both general recommendations for all states and specific recommendations for each legislature. The recommendations focused on such things as the length of the session, number of members, committee organization, facilities and staffing. They were highly prescriptive and specific.

During the study, the Citizens Conference was directed by Larry Margolis, former chief of staff to California Speaker Jesse Unruh, who led the transformation of the California Legislature into a full-time, professional body in the late 1960s. The implicit standard of "The Sometime Governments" was that all legislatures should look like California's, which, not surprisingly, came out No. 1 in the rankings.

For the next two decades, legislative leaders in almost every state engaged their members, the public and others concerned about legislatures in efforts to redesign and rebuild their institutions. These efforts were historic in scope and accomplishment. Legislatures became more muscular, agile, intelligent and independent than at any other time in American history.

The reform agenda of "The Sometime Governments" fell on hard times in the 1990s. There was a backlash, fueled by growing public cynicism about government, that developed against what political scientists call the "professionalization" of state legislatures. In almost all of the 24 states that allow voter initiatives, measures were placed on the ballot to limit the terms of state lawmakers. Virtually all of them passed, though some were later invalidated by courts or repealed, leaving 15 states today with term limits.

An NCSL study in 2007 showed term limits had significantly weakened state legislatures, especially in relation to the governor. Other initiatives placed limits on the tax and spending powers of legislatures in many states.

In this atmosphere of public distrust and cynicism toward government, it became difficult for legislatures to strengthen and grow in the fashion advocated by "The Sometime Governments." In the last 20 years—outside of the area of technology, which has its own momentum and societal drive—legislatures mostly have stopped taking steps such as adding staff, building more facilities or increasing the amount of time spent on the job. By the 1990s, the Citizens Conference's recommendations had run their course. They had done their job of stimulating positive change.

In the last 20 years legislatures mostly have stopped taking steps such as adding staff, building more facilities or increasing the amount of time spent on the job.

Problems Persist

While some of the issues raised in "The Sometime Governments" have been resolved, new ones have emerged.

The process of legislative improvement is never-ending, requiring constant tinkering and adjustment, state by state. Partly as a result of the previous success of strengthening legislatures, they face new problems today. In his book, "Engines of Democracy: Politics and Policy in State Legislatures," Rutgers University political scientist Alan Rosenthal identifies ailments confronting contemporary representative democracy.

- **Partisanship.** Strong party allegiance can organize conflict and disagreement, but in excess can lead to incivility and a lack of willingness to negotiate and compromise. Hyper-partisanship, as some have called it, undermines political trust and support for democratic institutions. Some state legislatures today, but by no means all, suffer from excessive partisanship.
- **Integrity.** The overwhelming number of state lawmakers behave ethically. The misdeeds of a few members, however, tar the entire institution. The public believes the majority of legislators are out to serve themselves, and they are for sale to the highest bidder.
- **Deliberation.** The work of standing committees, which was a major focus of the earlier legislative strengthening movement, has been undermined in many states in recent years. Partisan considerations have been a detriment to substantive study, analysis of and deliberation on all sides of an issue. Top legislative leaders and party caucuses too often bypass or downplay the committee

process. Term limits have also weakened committees as they have been deprived of experience and expertise.
- **Responsibility.** Rosenthal is concerned about the unwillingness of some legislators to make difficult fiscal decisions because of constituent opposition, the growing tendency for committees to fail to screen out bills that lack support or merit and the practice of lawmakers not voting against someone else's bill for fear that he or she will vote against their own.
- **Public cynicism.** Today's excessive public mistrust of democratic institutions is harmful. Cynicism discourages qualified people from running for office, promotes a reluctance by members to address unpopular but necessary issues, encourages simplistic institutional reforms such as term limits, and increases the public's unwillingness to comply with legislative decisions.
- **Institutional commitment.** Rosenthal writes that lawmakers often pay little attention to the institution and distance themselves from it. "If they do not devote themselves to their institution's well-being, who can they expect to do the job for them? The responsibility is primarily theirs—and it is not being adequately shouldered."

New Set of Questions

Rosenthal's list of ailments ring true and it's vital they be addressed and remedied. But it's important to emphasize that not all states have experienced all of these problems. The need for legislative improvement differs from state to state. The only problem on the Rosenthal list that is common to all the states is public cynicism, and even then there are a few states—Alaska, Idaho, North Dakota and Wyoming are examples—in which the legislature has relatively high public opinion ratings. As the Citizens Conference recognized 40 years ago, an agenda for legislative strengthening needs to be state specific.

But how can we create a state-specific agenda?

We suggest a basic set of questions that legislators, legislative staff, political scientists and interested citizens should ask and answer about the performance of their legislature. These questions are standards of a sort, expectations of what a good legislature should be.

1. Does the legislature effectively share power with the governor? Does the legislature initiate and enact its own legislation and make independent decisions about the state budget? Does the legislature provide effective oversight of executive actions?
2. Does the redistricting process for the legislature result in reasonably compact, contiguous and competitive legislative districts that do not provide an undue advantage to one party and incumbent legislators?
3. Do the members provide effective constituent service including answering requests for information, casework, local projects and public expenditures? Is the proportion of women and racial and ethnic minorities in the legislature reasonably reflective of the population of the state?

4. Does the legislature take into account interests of the state as a whole instead of the cumulative interests of districts and constituencies?

5. Is there a reasonable balance in the legislature between the need to have strong, effective leaders who guide members on procedural and policy choices and the need for internal democracy that disperses power and protects the rights of individual members?

6. Does the majority party have enough clout to get things done? Are the rights of the minority party protected?

7. Is the degree of partisanship in the legislature reasonable? Does the legislature engage in consensus-building? Are opposing sides willing to negotiate differences and find compromises to difficult problems?

8. Does the legislature have integrity? Do the members of the legislature and the capitol community behave in ethical ways?

9. Do individual citizens and organized groups with an interest in an issue have the opportunity to participate in the lawmaking process? Are all viewpoints heard and treated fairly by the legislature? Is the influence of moneyed interests that contribute to political campaigns appropriate relative to their role in the state's economy and well-being?

10. Does the legislature study and deliberate on issues effectively? Does it allow give-and-take and the open exchange of ideas at all stages of the formal and informal legislative process, especially the committee stage? Are legislative committees strong, attentive and involved in critical decision making?

11. Do the members of the legislature care about and protect the well-being of the institution? Is there adequate continuity in the membership of the legislature to promote institutional values, build up expertise, and pass on knowledge and skills? Are the leaders and members committed to educating the public about the legislative institution and defending its values?

12. Does the legislature have adequate resources—staff, time, facilities, technology—to do its job, and are those resources managed effectively? Is there an appropriate balance between partisan staff who provide strategic advice and guidance to members and nonpartisan staff who provide unbiased analysis and manage the institution?

Solutions Are the Challenge

Each state—depending on its history, traditions and culture—will have different answers to these questions, and people within the same state will disagree. But if the answer is "no" on any set of questions, this is an area to strengthen.

Once those areas are defined, finding solutions becomes the challenge. Most 21st century problems in legislatures will not be solved by throwing more resources at them or even by structural and procedural changes. The remedies for these ailments are more likely to come through education, training and cultural changes in the institution—all of which may be difficult to bring about.

> **Most 21st century problems in legislatures will not be solved by throwing more resources at them or even by structural and procedural changes.**

Legislators, staff, academics and committed citizens need to come together to draw up a new agenda to strengthen legislatures.

The reformers of the 1970s had a difficult task of transforming state legislatures into something more than "sometime governments." But, in retrospect, their task seems easy compared to today's work of building integrity, will, commitment and trust.

The challenges facing today's more robust legislatures are even more daunting. But that shouldn't stop them. They need to find the mechanisms and a spirit similar to those of a previous generation of dedicated people who improved America's state legislatures.

Critical Thinking

1. What were the main points of the 1971 publication entitled *The Sometime Governments: An Evaluation of the 50 American Legislatures*?

2. How did state legislatures, in general, respond to prescriptions in the *The Sometime Governments*?

3. What new set of problems did political scientist Alan Rosenthal identify in his *Engines of Democracy* book that appeared several decades after *The Sometimes Governments*?

4. What basic set of questions do the authors of this article present for legislators, legislative staff, and others to use in evaluating state legislatures today?

Create Central

www.mhhe.com/createcentral

Internet References

Alan Rosenthal obituary (NY Times)
www.nytimes.com/2013/07/12/nyregion/alan-rosenthal-who-reshaped-legislatures-dies-at-81.html?_r=

"History of US": National Council of State Legislatures
www.ncsl.org/bookstore/state-legislatures-magazine/sl-mag-the-history-of-us.aspx

---

KARL KURTZ runs NCSL's Trust for Representative Democracy. BRIAN WEBERG directs NCSL's Legislative Management program.

From *State Legislatures*, July/August 2010, pp. 47–50. Copyright © 2010 by National Conference of State Legislatures. Reprinted by permission.

Article

Prepared by: Bruce Stinebrickner, *DePauw University*

Legislatures: All Over the Map

Karl Kurtz and Brenda Erickson

Learning Outcomes

After reading this article, you will be able to:

- Assess the variation in annual compensation that state legislators earn and consider whether fairly well-paid legislators (California: more than $95,000) or those earning very small sums (New Hampshire: $100) are likely to perform better.

- Weigh the pros and cons of unicameral and bicameral legislatures.

- Evaluate the pros and cons of state legislatures with relatively large numbers of seats and those with fewer seats.

A s most of the country's 7,383 state lawmakers prepare to dive into session, it's interesting to note the diversity among full- and part-time legislatures. But it's a bit tricky to define the criteria. No matter the length of sessions, state lawmakers' work is full time. When not in regular session, legislators are assisting constituents, doing interim committee work, studying up on issues, campaigning, giving speeches, attending luncheons, returning phone calls and even riding in parades.

Nevertheless, NCSL has grouped the 50 state legislatures into three major categories: Green, White and Gold. Green legislatures tend to be in states with larger populations and are the most full-time, with longer sessions, bigger districts, larger staffs and higher salaries. White legislatures are hybrids, representing states in the middle of the population range, where lawmakers typically spend about two-thirds of a full-time job in their legislative roles and earn less money than their counterparts in green states. Gold state legislatures are in less populated, more rural states and are often called traditional or citizen legislatures. Lawmakers in gold states tend to work part time, have few if any personal staff, and generally require other sources of income.

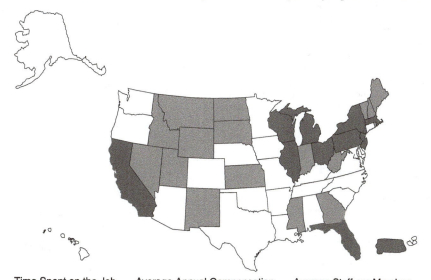

Time Spent on the Job	Average Annual Compensation	Average Staff per Member
80%	$68,599	8.9
70%	$35,326	3.1
54%	$15,984	1.2

Note: The portion of a full-time job spent on legislative work includes time in session, constituent service, interim committee work and election campaigns. The estimated compensation includes salary, per diem and unvouchered expense payments. And the ratio of all staff to all legislators does not indicate how many staff work directly for each legislator.

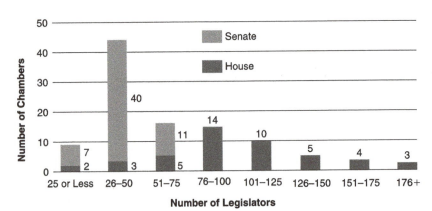

Number of Legislators per Chamber

Note: Includes states and territories, but not unicameral legislatures.

Trivial Pursuit

New Hampshire's 400-member House is the largest state chamber in the country and pays members the least amount per year, $100.

- California legislators earn the most per year, $95,291.
- Forty-nine states and three territories (American Samoa, Northern Mariana Islands and Puerto Rico) have bicameral legislatures—which include an upper and lower chamber.
- Nebraska, the District of Columbia, Guam and the Virgin Islands are unicameral, having only one chamber.
- Nebraska and American Samoa are the only non-partisan legislatures in the country.
- The number of legislative seats nationwide increased by one—to 7,383—after the November election. Which state added a seat? Find the answer at www.ncsl.org/magazine.

What's in a Name?

Official titles of lawmaking bodies

The Body

Legislature	31
General Assembly	19
Legislative Assembly	3
General Court	2
Council	1

Upper chamber

Senate	52
Legislature	3
Council	1

Lower chamber

House of Representatives	44
Assembly	4
House of Delegates	3
General Assembly	1

Note: Names include territories and District of Columbia.

Critical Thinking

1. What is the variation in annual compensation that state legislators earn? Does the amount of variation surprise you? Why or why not?

2. How common are unicameral legislatures among the 50 states, D.C., and U.S. territories? What are likely differences in what unicameral bicameral legislatures produce or do?

3. How much variation is there in the number of members in legislative chambers? Does the amount of variation surprise you? Why or why not?

Create Central

www.mhhe.com/createcentral

Internet References

National Council of State Legislatures
   www.ncsl.org
Nebraska legislature: On Unicamerlism
   http://nebraskalegislature.gov/about/on_unicameralism.php

Article   Prepared by: Bruce Stinebrickner, *DePauw University*

Newbies

Thanks to term limits and anti-incumbent fervor, half the lawmakers across the country have less than two years' experience.

ALAN GREENBLATT

Learning Outcomes

After reading this article, you will be able to:

- Assess the pros and cons of a large proportion of members of a legislative body having little or no prior experience in the legislature.

- Evaluate the pros and cons of term limits on state legislators.

- Assess the temptations and dangers that "over-reaching" poses for good government in a state such as North Carolina.

Jim Fulghum is 68 years old and a successful neurosurgeon, but he still finds freshman orientation a little overwhelming. Fulghum was elected in November to the North Carolina House and, as he's the first to tell you, he has a lot to learn.

"I'm not mechanically up to date on how to file a bill," he says. "I'll know within a month how much I don't know, but I know I don't know a lot."

If Fulghum is feeling a little lost, he's not alone. He's part of a big freshman class just now coming in, following the decennial redistricting process. His class joins an even bigger group of sophomores who rode to power, in Raleigh as elsewhere, on the gigantic Republican wave in 2010. Altogether, nearly two-thirds of the legislature in North Carolina is now made up of sophomores and freshmen.

North Carolina is not unique. Nationwide, roughly half the state legislators in the country have two years of experience or less. The 15 states with term limits in place are accustomed to such mass turnover, but now it's happening everywhere. "Half the people weren't here two years ago," says Texas state Sen. Robert Nichols. "They simply weren't here."

That means a lot of old hands are missing at a time when states face a raft of complicated questions, including ongoing budget problems, a decline in financial help from the federal government and the job of implementing (or continuing to resist) Obamacare. "All of us run on the premise that we're smarter than the people in there, but you get there and find out

there's a lot to learn," says Brian Cronin, a recently retired legislator in Idaho. "In the committee process, you develop a certain amount of expertise over the years. Without that, you're left with legislators voting on things that frankly they don't understand all that well."

The North Carolina General Assembly has long been considered a strong branch, with experienced "gangs" of seven or eight leaders able to stand up to any governor and avoid being rolled over or finessed. But the House alone has just lost two former speakers. Harold Brubaker, a Republican, was considered a leading expert on the budget, and Democrat Joe Hackney was a master at guiding bills through the process—or making sure ones he didn't like got bottled up in committee.

The current crop of leaders, including Speaker Thom Tillis, believes that what the newcomers bring to the body in terms of new ideas and freedom from the status quo outweighs any negatives that might be associated with lack of experience. They may not yet have mastered the art of presenting a bill to committee, Tillis says, but with their MBAs or experience handling complicated cases as attorneys or their work in local government, they'll catch on just fine. "I've learned that I can't do complicated things without listening and studying first," Fulghum says. "You can't go into an operating room without making a plan."

There's also strength in numbers. Tillis keeps a set of veto override messages under glass on the conference table in his office, testimony to the Republican majority's ability to get what it wanted—including passage of last year's budget—despite the opposition of Democratic Gov. Beverly Perdue.

Perdue is now out, replaced by Republican Pat McCrory, who becomes the first Republican governor to enjoy a GOP-controlled legislature since 1869. (That governor, William W. Holden, was impeached essentially for fighting the Ku Klux Klan.) McCrory, Tillis and Senate President Pro Tempore Phil Berger spent the transition period following the election batting around draft bills that aim to overhaul education and tax policy, and ease regulations on business.

With Republicans in firm control of all the political branches in North Carolina, there aren't likely to be a lot of veto overrides—or vetoes, for that matter. But the legislature—its freshman members included—will still have a strong hand in negotiations. North Carolina followed another nationwide trend last November, giving the GOP a two-thirds supermajority in the House to match the supermajority Republicans won in the state Senate back in 2010. (Legislative chambers in half the states are now controlled by supermajorities of one party or the other.)

That much power can breed problems of its own—particularly for freshmen who arrive with a lot of enthusiasm to make wholesale changes. Tillis says it's imperative that his caucus remains focused on what is already an ambitious agenda shared by the governor. It would be both easy and tempting to try to do more, given his party's big majorities but, he says, "You typically lose when you fight on too many fronts."

"On paper, there's nothing we can't do, so that raises the bar," says Tom Murry, a House member first elected in 2010. Murry, a pharmacist in his life outside the Capitol, has been listening to "All the President's Men," the classic book about Watergate, while driving between drug stores. He says it offers a reminder of the potential dangers of overreaching. "The 'we can do anything we want' mentality is dangerous," he says.

Mainly, Murry senses opportunity. He notes that he was born a year after Harold Brubaker (the former GOP speaker) first joined the House, and argues that a younger generation can accomplish things in new ways. He cites Twitter as a tool for organizing and communicating that some veteran members still aren't entirely comfortable with.

Although he didn't get to chair a committee in his freshman term, Murry says he still was given plenty of responsibility. Freshman members over the past couple of years have been able to carry significant pieces of legislation to the floor in North Carolina. Now, as sophomores, they feel ready for more responsibility. "When you've got 500 years of legislative experience that retired over the interim," Murry says, "that leaves a lot of opportunity for sophomores to fill that gap."

Paul Stam, who's been in the House since 2003 and served as the House majority leader during the last term, says that over the last two years, he acted as a primary sponsor of legislation along with 32 separate Republicans. "They would have the [policy] expertise and I would help them through the maze," Stam says. "A lot of them were freshmen."

In this role of mentor, Stam sent out email blasts to the caucus on more than a daily basis with background material on a particular issue, or offered a simple rejoinder to releases from interest groups. He wouldn't tell caucus members how to vote, but he would tell them what he was thinking, either about the issue or the particular lobbyist. "I wouldn't call it hand-holding," Stam says. "What I would call it is equipping, or arming."

Stam last month was selected as speaker pro tem for the new session. He had been one of three Republicans angling for that job, while three others had sought to replace Stam as House majority leader. This points to a potential problem for Republicans, says Democratic state Rep. Larry Hall, the newly selected House minortiy leader. When a party is growing, it can be difficult for leaders to keep all its members happy. "They've got 77 mouths to feed," Hall says, referring to the size of the House GOP caucus. "How do you keep that group together?"

In part to pass out plums themselves, Democrats during their long years in power had created more than 40 standing committees in the House alone. Tillis and the GOP cut that number back significantly and, Tillis says, it would be a mistake to create more gavels in order to make members feel special. Tillis admits that he faces a challenge in elevating junior members without angering their many classmates, but says there will be plenty of work to go around for everybody.

Two years ago, says Senate President Berger, "We didn't have anybody who had chaired an appropriations committee. That's something if you sit back and think about it." But two years have passed, and as Berger notes, he and his committee chairs might have been new to leadership, but they weren't all new to the process. That's the difference between a place like North Carolina and the states with term limits. As massive as the freshman and sophomore classes may be, there's still a cadre in place of veterans with 12 or 20 years' experience who can act as shepherds. "We're in constant conversation with the leadership and that makes you confident," says Jeff Tarte, a freshman senator. "Over half will be freshmen and sophomores, but we have excellent, sound leadership with experience to help guide us."

Having a guide though, doesn't guarantee you'll want to follow his lead. Most of the time, legislative neophytes become members of the Mushroom Caucus—kept in the dark and fed bull. But huge classes can create their own identities. Those elected en masse typically share a common agenda and believe they have the mandate to carry it out.

In North Carolina, as in other states, there has been some tension between the Tea Party-aligned members of the Class of 2010 and more established, business-oriented veterans. That tension is likely to heighten in the coming weeks as legislators grapple with the question of whether to raise taxes on employers to fill a $2.8 billion gap in the unemployment trust fund, even as promoting job creation remains a singular focus for the GOP.

Like teenagers, neophyte legislators tend to see things in black and white and believe they know more than they actually do. Having so many of them running around the Capitol—and giving them a good-sized share of power—only makes this problem worse. Freshmen, whether in high school or the state House, aren't known for their patience. "It used to be that you kept your mouth shut for a term or two, but that isn't the norm anymore," says Hackney, the former Democratic speaker. "They realize eventually that they didn't know as much as they thought they did, but it takes a while for that to happen."

Freshman and sopohomore legislators themselves joke about how they're like teenagers—specifically, like a high school class where some are more popular or more ambitious or considered most likely to succeed. One of the most important things they have to learn is who their true friends are. Fulghum, the freshman legislator, says he's been "overwhelmed with business cards" and lobbyists looking to set up first dates ever since Election Day.

Newcomers may be wary of lobbyists, but quickly come to realize that they're an integral part of the process—they can act as "an extension of your staff" in a state where there's no funding for individual members to have staff, says Tarte, the freshman senator. In turn, lobbyists—who may be in mourning at the departure of their buddy, the 20-year committee chair—must earn legislators' trust anew. Obviously, they're going to plead their case, but they can't stretch the facts too far without gaining a bad reputation.

They have to learn to possess the patience that new legislators sometimes lack. Newcomers might slip in ways that lawmakers who have already sat through 4,000 committee meetings won't, but calling them out on such blunders leads to "a long session," says John McMillan, a longtime lobbyist in Raleigh.

Republicans in North Carolina made plenty of rookie mistakes during their first term in power, says Hall, the Democratic representative. With first-time responsibility for writing the budget, some legislators would question why they couldn't move money from Pot A over to Pot C, where the need seemed greater. "Well, that money is devoted to a trust fund," Hall says. "You can't take that money and move it to the general fund, or you'll never see a dime of that money again."

McMillan says it's easy to bemoan the passing of an older and allegedly superior generation. "Thirty years ago, people said, 'You'll never replace these people.'" People have always been nervous about the old hands leaving, he says, but somehow the place still functions.

Freshmen and sophomores will eventually find their way, in large part by asking questions of others, whether it's leaders or lobbyists they trust. Much of the work of the legislature, after all, is less about the technical data backgrounding each bill than it is about relationships. It may take time to build a sense of trust among so many new faces. But just as in high school, people soon get to know each other pretty well, for good and for ill.

"It's important to keep yourself out of the ditches in terms of your relationships with people," says Senate President Berger. "The biggest thing you learn is that the person who opposes you today is the person you're working with tomorrow."

Critical Thinking

1. What proportion of current state legislators have two years of experience or less? Why are fifteen states accustomed to such turnover, while it is a new phenomenon for most of the other states?

2. What are some of the pros and cons that various North Carolina government officials have raised about having so many newcomers in the North Carolina legislature?

3. What is meant by the "Mushroom Caucus" in the context of this article? Which legislators often become members of it, willingly or not?

Create Central

www.mhhe.com/createcentral

Internet References

National Council of State Legislatures
www.ncsl.org
North Carolina General Assembly
www.ncleg.net

Article   Prepared by: Bruce Stinebrickner, *DePauw University*

Are City Councils a Relic of the Past?

One of America's oldest political institutions isn't adapting very well to 21st-century urban life.

ROB GURWITT

Learning Outcomes

After reading this article, you will be able to:

- Assess the role that St. Louis ward aldermen play in governing the city of St. Louis.

- Evaluate the pros and cons of relatively large and small numbers of seats on a city council.

- Consider what "balkanization" means in the context of urban governing and identify its likely causes in American cities.

You notice two things right off about the 19th Ward in St. Louis. The first is that pretty much everywhere there's construction, there's also a large sign reading, "Assistance for the project provided by Michael McMillan, Alderman." The second is just how limited Alderman McMillan's domain happens to be. Walk a few minutes in any direction, and you're out of his ward. You don't see the signs anymore. You also don't see as much construction.

Within the friendly confines of the 19th, St. Louis looks like a city busily reviving. There are new high schools being built, scattered apartments and loft projects underway, efforts to rejuvenate the historic arts and entertainment district, and a HOPE VI retrofit of an enormous public housing facility. While all this activity has some powerful people behind it, just one person has had a hand in all of it, and that is McMillan himself. Only 31, he has been on the St. Louis Board of Aldermen for six years, and in that time has made it clear that his ambitions for his ward—and by extension, himself—are high. "I don't have other obligations," he says. "I'm not married, I have no kids, I have no other job. It's one of my competitive edges."

Cross the ward boundary, and you find out what "competitive edge" means in St. Louis politics. North of the 19th, and for some distance to the east, stretch a series of neglected, depopulated neighborhoods that do not in any way suggest urban revival. This is, in part, a consequence of private market decisions: These neighborhoods don't have much clout within the corporate suites where such decisions are made. But equally

important, they don't have much clout in local government, either—at least not when it comes to large-scale development projects.

That's because in St. Louis, each of the 28 ward aldermen is the gatekeeper of development in his or her little slice of the city. If they're shrewd and well connected, like Michael McMillan, the ward does fine. If they're inattentive, or maladroit at cutting deals, or on the outs with local developers, or just plain picky, which is the case in more than a few wards, hardly anything gets done. "You don't see a Mike McMillan coming out of some of these devastated wards," says one City Hall insider. "They have a voice, but if it's weak, what do they really get?"

To be sure, even the weak aldermen in St. Louis have their uses. They get potholes filled and streetlights fixed, offer advice on how to handle code violations or deal with housing court, and see that garbage gets picked up in alleyways where contractors dump it illegally. This hands-on attention is hardly a bad thing. In the words of Jim Shrewsbury, who as president of the Board of Aldermen runs at large and is its 29th member, the city's deeply entrenched system of political micro-management "protects neighborhoods and gives people a sense of influence." As members of a democratic institution, that's what city councilmen are supposed to do. But when that's about all many of them do, in a city that is struggling to emerge from years of economic debility, even Shrewsbury agrees that something is wrong. The system, he says, "creates a sense of parochialism and feudalism. We become the Balkans."

Feuding and Hot Air

The concept of balkanization could be applied these days to councils and boards of aldermen in many of America's biggest cities—perhaps most of them. Look around the country and you can quickly compile a dossier of dysfunction.

Sometimes it is a case of pursuing tangents, as the Baltimore City Council likes to do. In a recent commentary about what it called "the hot-air council," the Baltimore Sun suggested that frequent resolutions on foreign affairs, hearings on the differences between telephone exchanges, and debate about counteracting "the negative images of Baltimore, as portrayed in 'real-crime' fiction, TV dramas and movies" suggested that the members didn't have enough real work to do.

Other councils become so embroiled in internal maneuvering that they lose their relevance. In Philadelphia, where a former mayor once referred to the city council as "the worst legislative body in the free world," there was a brief period of council influence in the mid-1990s, when John Street was council president and worked closely with Mayor Ed Rendell. Now, however, Street is mayor and finds himself in regular tangles with various council factions. "It's like an opera where everybody has a different libretto," says Mark Alan Hughes, an urban affairs professor at the University of Pennsylvania and columnist for the *Philadelphia Daily News.* "The melodrama is clear, it's just the meaning that's completely obscure."

There are councils where bickering and infighting are so intense that the entire body acquires an image of irresponsible flakiness. In Detroit recently, one member charged that supporters of the city's mayor had sabotaged the electric massager in her desk chair to give her a jolt when she used it. Not surprisingly, the public's response was disdainful—what most people saw was a group of elected officials engaged in sabotaging its own reputation.

There are places where, if you want to find the future of the city being pondered, the council chamber is the last place you'd look. "What you have," says a close watcher of civic affairs in Pittsburgh, "is a group of people who primarily deal with very mundane, housekeeping things in their districts. That's what they do, it's what they're interested in, and it's the way they see their power." The real power lies in the mayor's office and with the city's still-strong civic and corporate leadership.

Finally, there are councils whose problem has not been an absence of energy but a hyperactive compulsion to argue over everyday management decisions and prevent important decisions from being made. In Hartford, Connecticut, the city charter for years gave most of the political power to the council, but the council had a long history of intervening in the day-to-day administration of city services and tying itself up in petty squabbles corrosive to the morale of residents, as well as city employees. In the 1990s, the council essentially torpedoed the program of Mayor Mike Peters, who appeared to have broad voter support for his economic reform and revival ideas. Small surprise that when they were finally given a straightforward chance last November to change things, the city's voters opted to create a new form of government that strengthened the mayor at the council's expense.

None of this is to say that councils in large cities never tackle important issues or play a key role in crafting policy. Council members in Los Angeles, for instance, have a great deal to say about basic infrastructure issues, in their districts and across the city. And for all its infighting, the Philadelphia City Council did help to re-shape Street's ambitious urban renewal program, the Neighborhood Transformation Initiative, to be more responsive to neighborhood concerns.

But in all too many large cities these days, the power of councils is, at most, the power to stop things. The wellsprings of citywide innovation and progress lie elsewhere. It is telling that until this past year, neither of the two major national organizations speaking for cities addressed the specific concerns of big-city councils. The National League of Cities is dominated by small- and medium-sized jurisdictions; the U.S. Conference of Mayors, which focuses on larger cities, doesn't address council members at all. "We're literally locked out of the one national group that deals with big cities," observes Nick Licata, a Seattle council member.

Licata, who was struck by the dearth of representation from places like his when he first attended a League of Cities meeting, has put together a new "Central Cities Council" at the League, for council members in the 100 or so largest cities to share information and strategies on common issues. "We're not communicating on a regular basis, we're not exchanging information on local programs we can learn from, and on the national level, when we should be lobbying, we don't have our act together," he says. "This should help us link up."

Still, the sense of floundering one often gets watching big-city councils isn't really a surprise. Over the years, as mayors have moved to get a handle on crime, economic development and even school management, and as semi-private institutions— redevelopment authorities, stadium authorities, transit authorities, convention center authorities, tax increment finance districts—have proliferated, the role of councils in the most critical issues of urban governance has atrophied. Individual council members, the Michael McMillans of the country, may still have a share of power and influence, but the bodies on which many of them serve have lost their identity. "I think city councils have been neutered in most cases," says Dennis Judd, an urban affairs specialist at the University of Illinois-Chicago. "They are engaging in the most trivial aspects of urban government, rather than the most important aspects."

Under these circumstances, it is hard not to wonder whether city councils are becoming relics of the political past, poorly adapted to making the decisions of 21st-century urban life. In all too many cases, they seem in danger of becoming the dinosaurs of American local government.

Out of the Loop

There was a moment not long ago when the St. Louis Board of Aldermen managed to command national attention, but it's one local politicians would rather forget. In the midst of a tense and racially charged ward redistricting debate in 2001, Alderman Irene Smith was conducting a filibuster when she asked whether she could go to the bathroom. Told by Board President Shrewsbury that the rules required her to yield the floor to do so, she summoned her supporters, who brought in a trash can and surrounded her with improvised drapes while she appeared to urinate into the can. "I was mortified," says a St. Louis politician who happened to be watching on cable television at the time. "If you've been in the aldermanic chambers, they call to mind a time when the city was a powerful city, a grand place. To think of her staging that in there! The stock of the entire board of aldermen went down." Smith was later indicted on charges of public indecency but was acquitted in January on the reasoning that no one could know for sure whether she was actually urinating or simply pretending to do so.

To those who spend their time in City Hall, the incident was puzzling, because Smith, a lawyer and former judge, is generally seen as one of the more careful and thoughtful members of the board. "She's bright, she knows how to read the law, she asks tough questions in committee hearings," says one aldermanic insider. But to many in the city at large, there was little question about how to interpret her outburst: Not even its own members accord the board much respect any longer.

The fact is, for all the opportunities that ambitious aldermen have to promote development within their own neighborhoods, it's been a while since the board has played a significant role in shaping matters of vital interest to St. Louis as a whole. One of the biggest issues on the plate of Mayor Francis Slay—himself a former board president—is a new stadium for the St. Louis Cardinals baseball team, and while pieces of the complex deal he has put together will require aldermanic approval, the board itself has had very little role in constructing it.

"When I was in City Hall," says a former aide to one of Slay's recent predecessors, "I only went to the board if I absolutely had to. The truth is, I never felt the need to involve people there on the front end in order to get something passed on the back end. In the 1970s or '80s, if a mayor had a stadium project, he'd have had to line up five or six people on the board before he even went public with it." Because that didn't happen in the current situation, the aide argues, this stadium deal is just a stadium deal—it is not part of any broader city commitment to, say, refurbishing public sports facilities or community centers in the neighborhoods.

There are any number of theories about what has led the board of aldermen to its diminished citywide import, and many of them focus on its size. The 28 wards were created in 1914, when St. Louis had 680,000 people. They remained in place when the city reached its peak of 850,000 in 1950. And they're still there, half a century later, when it's down to 340,000. This means that each alderman represents about 12,500 people. Chicago's 50-member city council, which is one of the largest in the country, would have to grow to 200 members if its wards were the same size as those in St. Louis.

If all you expect of an alderman is close attention to garbage pickup and street repairs, of course, small wards are just fine. But they have a cost, as well. For one thing, they form a low barrier to political entry. In some wards, a politician needs as few as 800 votes to get elected. When the city was larger, says former Mayor Freeman Bosley Jr., "you had to be a real leader to get on the board, someone who could put together thousands and thousands of votes. That plays into your ability to put people together and pull them in a direction. So as the years have gone by, the number of go-to people has diminished."

To be sure, it's possible to overstate the case. "Just because we were once a city of 800,000 people doesn't mean we had rocket scientists serving on the board of aldermen," notes Jim Shrewsbury. "I don't think someone makes a decision between running a corporation and being an alderman." But it's equally true that city councils are, in essence, a political proving ground—former U.S. House Minority Leader Richard Gephardt, for instance, got his start on the St. Louis Board of Aldermen. The less skill and vision they demand of their members, the poorer a city's civic life is likely to be.

"If you can make the council a place where young people who are interested in public policy think they ought to be, then it serves as a farm system to create people who understand how local government works and who have sympathy for it," says Mike Jones, a former alderman who now runs the regional Empowerment Zone. "Because the real question is, Where do you get local leadership from? On a city council where you've got to work hard to get elected, it takes good political instincts and hones them into political and policy-making skills."

Ironclad Privilege

Over time, the small size of the constituencies and the rules of the institution itself have combined to make the lure of parochialism more and more irresistible. In the 1950s, following passage of the federal Urban Renewal Act of 1949, aldermen in St. Louis suddenly found themselves with real power in their neighborhoods as the arbiters of development. That law, says Lana Stein, a University of Missouri-St. Louis historian, "brought a huge pot of money, and the aldermen had to pass bills authorizing urban renewal projects and highway projects. They were courted by Civic Progress [the group of corporate movers and shakers at the time] and by the mayor. Even though there were working-class people and saloon keepers elected to the board, they became a much bigger deal because of what they were voting on."

But if the urban renewal money brought the board instant influence, it also led inexorably to parochialism. As requests grew for new housing or redevelopment in the wards, they ran into the ironclad principle of aldermanic privilege—the notion that no member of the board would interfere in matters affecting another member's ward.

Fifty years later, developers still need help from the city, and that usually means a vote from the aldermen, supporting a "blighting" provision or providing a tax abatement or creating a tax-increment financing district. If you happen to live in a ward with an active, responsive alderman who knows how to put together development deals, you're fortunate. But there's scarcely anyone left on the board looking at what makes sense for the city as a whole. Aldermen rarely feel any right or responsibility to look closely at deals being made in others' wards.

When a group of downtown residents recently challenged plans backed by their alderman to demolish a historic, marble-fronted building to make way for a parking garage, the board deferred to the alderman's wishes by essentially ignoring the protest. The demolition plans were backed by the mayor and by his allies, and the developers insisted that the garage was vital to their plans, even though there are underused garages within a block's walk.

The local residents, part of a small but growing group of loft dwellers who form one of the few tangible signs of hope for St. Louis' downtown, attended the one aldermanic hearing on the matter and found no one to talk to. "It was a farce," says Margie

Bodies Large and Small

Size of selected city councils

City	Number of Districts	Average Size of District
Los Angeles	15	246,000
Phoenix	8	165,000
New York	51	157,000
Kansas City	6	74,000
Memphis*	9	72,000
San Francisco**	11	71,000
Milwaukee	17	35,000
Minneapolis	13	29,000
Richmond	9	22,000
St. Louis	28	12,000

*Two districts have three members each, the others each have one, for a total of 13 members

** City/county supervisors

Source: Governing research

Newman, one of their leaders. "There was no opportunity to make our case. Literally, there was an alderman with the Sunday comics held up in front of his face, and of the six on the committee, three were wandering in and out. Remember, this was at our one opportunity to bring our case."

Indeed, confirms Matt Villa, a young alderman who represents the city's far southeast, there is little incentive on the board to pay attention to what others are doing when you don't have to. "In our neighborhood," he says, "there's a neighborhood association and a housing corporation, and we sit down to plan the next five years and never take into consideration what other wards are doing. I don't even know how a citywide plan would be embraced by 28 aldermen."

And because the board itself doesn't have an independent capacity to look carefully at measures that come before it—it has very few staff members, and those who want help, such as Michael McMillan, raise funds on the side to pay for an assistant—it often approves important decisions with scarcely any scrutiny at all. "We give pay raises and pension raises and things like that," Villa says, "without really knowing the fiscal impact. The alderman who's sponsored it explains, we pass it, and years later it turns out it wasn't a $5 million impact, it was a $50 million impact."

Charter Changes

If there's anyone unhappy with this state of affairs, it's Jim Shrewsbury, who as president would like the board to become more independent and active. "The truth is, most legislation and ideas originate with the administration," he says. "The vast majority of bills are administration-sponsored bills; they have the resources and the interest and the concentration.

Sometimes, I wish we were more careful and would scrutinize them more carefully. And I wish there were more innovation, that more legislation originated here." But he is also quick to point out that in the calculus of the 28 politicians who serve alongside him, that may be more of a risk than they want to take. "I know that on Election Day, the one thousand people who hate me will be there," he explains. "I don't know how many of the thousands who like me will be. I'm prepared to lose my office for something that was in *Profiles in Courage*. If it's not, you start to wonder whether it's worth getting involved."

Yet it's possible that change will come to the St. Louis Board of Aldermen anyway. Although St. Louis is technically a "strong mayor" city, the political reality is that the mayor is constitutionally among the weakest in the country for a city this size. Power has to be shared with a half-dozen other elected officials; the state controls the police through a board on which the mayor has only his own seat; budget decisions and city contracts have to be approved by two of the three members of the Board of Estimate and Apportionment, which is made up of the mayor, comptroller and aldermanic president. "St. Louis is probably the nation's best case of an unreformed government," says the University of Illinois' Dennis Judd, referring to the nationwide movement early in the last century to give mayors enhanced authority. "It's as if it never was touched by the reformers."

Like the board's awkward size, all of this is a result of the 1914 city charter, which is still in effect. But last November, voters statewide approved a home-rule provision for St. Louis that will allow it to take up charter change. Although most of the attention is likely to go to placing more power in the hands of the mayor, there is plenty of sentiment among civic leaders for shrinking the size of the board of aldermen.

This is happening in other big cities with similar problems. Contraction is on the docket in Milwaukee, where some aldermen themselves have proposed shrinking the Common Council from 17 to 15 members, and in Baltimore, where voters last November approved trimming the city council from 19 to 15. Baltimore's initiative, backed by a coalition of labor unions and community organizations, was opposed by most of the city's elected leadership, but it passed overwhelmingly.

It's unclear how much impact tinkering with council size will really have, in St. Louis or anywhere else. But it's clear that some fundamental changes will have to take place for city councils such as these to maintain any real relevance at all in coming years.

By any standard, there is still important work for these bodies to do. Cities need robust political institutions, and by all rights, city councils ought to be among them—they are, after all, the one institution designed to serve as the collective voice of residents and communities, whether their members are elected in districts or at large. But when little is expected of them, because a city's most important decisions are made elsewhere, it's no surprise that over time the ambitions of their members shrink to take in smaller and smaller patches of turf.

There are undeniable benefits to this. Two decades ago, voters in St. Louis overwhelmingly turned down an initiative to cut the number of wards. They felt, says Shrewsbury, "that government had gotten so complicated and big, the only way their voice could be heard was having an alderman who paid close attention." It may be that all most people really want from their city council is the kind of personal stroking that is often hard to come by elsewhere in a big city. But it's also hard to escape the feeling that, as Judd puts it, "when citizens are consulted these days, it's about things that are less and less consequential. What we're seeing is the slow strangulation of local democracy."

Critical Thinking

1. In what sense is every St. Louis ward alderman the "gate-keeper of development" in his or her ward?

2. What are some pros and cons of St. Louis's "deeply entrenched system of micro-management"?

3. What sorts of "tangents" do some city councils pursue?

4. What does it mean to suggest that small wards in a city result in a "low barrier to political entry"?

5. What is meant by the "principle of aldermanic privilege" and how is it connected to parochialism in the functioning of the St. Louis city council?

Create Central

www.mhhe.com/createcentral

Internet References

City of St. Louis, Missouri, website
https://stlouis-mo.gov/government

St. Louis Again Considers City-County Merger (Associated Press, 19 Nov 2013)
http://stlouis.cbslocal.com/2013/11/19/st-louis-again-considers-city-county-merger

Article   Prepared by: Bruce Stinebrickner, *DePauw University*

Should School Boards Be Expelled?

DYLAN SCOTT

Learning Outcomes

After reading this article, you will be able to:

- Assess the notion that school boards should be abolished.

- Consider and evaluate various alternatives to governance of public education by school boards.

- Consider and explain how home-schooling, which is growing in the United States, would fit with the "abolish school boards" idea.

"Kill all the school boards." That was the suggestion from the Center for American Progress' Matt Miller in 2008 as he outlined his vision for remaking how we govern education. It was a striking statement then, and it still is. But it's also not nearly as far-fetched as it might sound.

The notion of drastically redrawing the school governance structure has quietly but steadily gained support in the education reform era that began under No Child Left Behind and has continued with the Obama administration's Race to the Top program. There are many reasons, foremost among them that U.S. student achievement seems to have stagnated. There's also a growing perception that big money has started to corrupt the school board system. Look at the Los Angeles elections in March, where an estimated $4.4 million—a record high—was spent, much of it from outside groups supporting reform candidates.

Advocates contend that the school board structure gives communities a direct voice in governance and that members are held accountable through the election process. But there's an increasing sense among others that it may be time to eliminate school boards altogether. The idea has crossed party lines. The Center for American Progress is a generally liberal institution, but Chester Finn, president of the conservative Thomas B. Fordham Institute and a former assistant education secretary under President Ronald Reagan, has issued similar decrees. "School boards are an aberration, an anachronism, an education sinkhole," he said in 2006. "Put this dysfunctional arrangement out of its misery."

But what would take the school board's place? A number of real-world models are emerging. In cities like New York,

mayoral control has persevered. Michael Bloomberg has set an ambitious reform agenda as the head of his city's school system. "There's this movement toward getting these general-purpose governments back into education policy," says Michael Petrilli, executive vice president at the Fordham Institute and a former education official in the George W. Bush administration. "The point of school boards was to take politics out of education. But these school boards are easily captured by special interest groups."

The rise of charter schools has provided another new frontier. The entire concept of charter schools is that they're publicly funded but independently controlled—outside the purview of a school board. Nearly every state now authorizes charters in one form or another, and the number of students enrolled in them more than quadrupled in the past decade.

"I could imagine a future where every school is a charter school," Petrilli says, "so you no longer have a school board that's overseeing an entire city."

Some states and localities have experimented with recovery school districts, jurisdictions not bound by geography but instead built around having one body oversee failing schools. New Orleans pioneered the model in the wake of Hurricane Katrina, but it's also gained support in Michigan and Tennessee. Some education experts have suggested taking things further and handing complete control back to the states, which would serve as the higher authority for individual schools, cutting out the school board.

Don't expect a national move to disband school boards. Any changes will likely happen on a crisis-by-crisis basis. The Columbus, Ohio, City Schools, for example, have been thrown into chaos recently by a data-scamming scandal that touches the top levels of the district's administration. Some have suggested that Mayor Michael Coleman take a more active role as public outcry mounts.

"Because of our fragmented system, this stuff is going to be piecemeal. Some of these ideas are going to spread faster than others," Petrilli says. "I think they're going to spread the fastest in places where people see the biggest problems."

Critical Thinking

1. What seems to be the biggest reasons that the idea of abolishing school boards is gaining traction in the United States?

2. What are some alternatives to governing public schools through local boards of education?

3. What seems the most likely way that changes to the school board model of school governance will change? Why?

Create Central

www.mhhe.com/createcentral

Internet References

National Alliance for Public Charter Schools
www.publiccharters.org

National Association of Private and Home Schools
http://naphs.net/

National School Boards Association
www.nsba.org

Scott, Dylan. From *Governing*, May 2013, p. 9. Copyright © 2013 by e.Republic Inc. Reprinted by permission via Wright's Media.

Article

Prepared by: Bruce Stinebrickner, *DePauw University*

Altered States

Governors used to emphasize pragmatism not ideology. But more and more, they're pursuing agendas that reflect their party's partisan interest.

RONALD BROWNSTEIN AND STEPHANIE CZEKALINSKI

Learning Outcomes

After reading this article, you will be able to:

- Assess whether the central phenomenon described in "Altered States" is a desirable development for the American political system and its people.

- Consider the 1970s–1990s and determine how those decades differed from the contemporary scene with respect to beipartisan collaboration among governors and the cross-party flow of policy ideas.

- Assess whether the explanation for the "altering" of states that is given in the article is persuasive.

Even for longtime advocates on both sides of the emotional gun-control debate, the events of March 8 were enough to induce whiplash.

On that day, South Dakota became the first state to explicitly authorize school employees to carry guns, when Republican Gov. Dennis Daugaard signed legislation sent to him by Republican majorities in both chambers of the Legislature. The bill represented a resounding victory for the National Rifle Association.

That same day, after an exhaustive debate approximately 525 miles away in Denver, the Democratic-controlled state Senate, joining the Democratic House, gave preliminary approval to Colorado's most sweeping gun-control package in years—including measures to impose universal background checks on gun purchases and to prohibit the sale of ammunition magazines containing more than 15 rounds. Despite strong opposition from gun-owner groups and Republicans, Democratic Gov. John Hickenlooper signed the legislation later in March, capping a decisive victory for gun-control supporters.

That sort of jarring juxtaposition has become increasingly common across the United States. Exactly one week after Colorado and South Dakota split on guns, the Republican-controlled Legislature in North Dakota approved the nation's most restrictive abortion law on the same day the Democratic-controlled

Legislature in Maryland, fulfilling one of Democratic Gov. Martin O'Malley's top priorities, voted to repeal the state's death penalty. One day before that, Louisiana Republican Gov. Bobby Jindal, catching a rising wave among GOP state executives, proposed to eliminate the state's personal income and corporate taxes, replacing the lost revenue with a vastly expanded sales tax. And just two days earlier, Colorado's House gave final approval to legislation authorizing same-sex civil unions, while gay-marriage legislation cleared committees in the Minnesota House and Senate, both controlled by Democrats.

Some of these initiatives will not become law. But in their ambition, and proliferation, they show how the same pressures that have polarized the parties in Washington are reshaping policy-making in the states. Across the full range of economic and cultural issues, Democratic and Republican state officials are pulling apart far more than they did as recently as two decades ago. On gun control, gay marriage, immigration, taxes, and participation in President Obama's health reform law, among other issues, states that lean red and those that lean blue are diverging to an extent that is straining the boundaries of federalism. "I can't recall any time in American history where there was such a conscious effort to create such broad divisions, without any sense of how it is all going to turn out," says Donald Kettl, dean of the public-policy school at the University of Maryland and an expert on public administration.

In many places, this widening gap is recasting the role of governors. Well into the 1990s, state executives considered themselves more pragmatic than members of Congress; they regularly shared ideas across party lines and often sought to emerge nationally by bridging ideological disputes. Some of that tradition endures. But now, governors are operating mostly along parallel, and partisan, tracks. On each side, they are increasingly pursuing programs that reflect their party's national agenda—and enlisting with their party on national disputes such as health care reform. "Everything has been infected with the national political debate," says Bruce Babbitt, who served as Arizona's centrist Democratic governor for two terms and later as President Clinton's Interior secretary. "And it's really destructive." Tommy Thompson, who launched a flotilla of innovations emulated by governors in both parties during his four terms as Wisconsin's Republican chief executive, agrees. "Anyone who looks at this in an impartial way has to say we have become a more partisan nation," he says. "I think we have [become] much more doctrinaire with our philosophies and much more locked into our positions."

Blue Revival

The last time *National Journal* examined the trends in state policy-making (*see "Separate Ways," NJ, 7/23/11, p. 16*) the energy and ambition was greatest among the flood of GOP governors who surged into office in the electoral wave of 2010. Republicans, either newly empowered or fortified with expanded majorities, marched confidently through the Rust and Sun Belts into confrontations over spending, restricting collective-bargaining rights for public employees, and social issues.

Across the states, Republicans continue to push sweeping agendas. The change is that in blue-leaning states, Democrats, perhaps invigorated by Obama's 2012 campaign and reelection, are now pursuing left-of-center programs of comparable ambition. In Maryland, for instance, O'Malley since 2012 alone has helped to steer through ballot initiatives legalizing gay marriage and providing in-state tuition to the children of illegal immigrants. He also engineered the passage of legislation repealing the death penalty and tightening gun control, as well as measures authorizing the medical use of marijuana and providing driver's licenses to illegal immigrants.

Gun control probably captures the shifting dynamic most clearly. Since the 1990s, the NRA and gun owners have dominated the debate. Over the past quarter-century, through a wide swath of states, the NRA first won approval of "shall issue" state laws authorizing citizens to carry concealed weapons and then in recent years has returned to loosen the restrictions on that right, winning permission in some states for those with permits to carry their weapons in bars or on college campuses. At the furthest edge on that continuum, Arizona and three other states allow residents to carry guns without getting any permits.

But the atmosphere in the states has shifted notably since the elementary-school massacre in Newtown, Conn. last year, which also prompted Obama to declare gun control a top priority after almost entirely sublimating the issue in his first term. Against this backdrop, Democratic governors and legislators have recovered their voices on the issue, after a long silence. "We have had strong states for years . . . especially with California being able to pass a lot of strong laws," says Brian Malte, director of mobilization for the Brady Campaign to Prevent Gun Violence. "But, that said, the states with stronger gun laws hadn't passed [further] laws in a while. [Now] that's really ramped up."

In January, New York Gov. Andrew Cuomo signed legislation that expanded the state's assault-weapons ban, limited ammunition magazines to seven rounds, and required universal background checks. In March, Hickenlooper signed Colorado's bill limiting magazine size and imposing background checks. Maryland has approved a package that includes an assault-weapons ban and magazine limits, as well as a fingerprint requirement for handgun purchases. Connecticut Democratic Gov. Dannel Malloy last week signed into law a sweeping package that includes bans on assault weapons and large magazines, and background checks. Gun-control measures that include expanded background checks and magazine limits are also advancing through Democratic-controlled legislatures in California, Delaware, Oregon, and New Jersey, although Chris Christie, the Garden State's Republican governor, said he won't comment on the proposals unless and until they reach his desk. A bill to expand background checks also cleared a committee vote in March in the Minnesota state House but faces an uncertain future on the floor.

This fusillade of activity in blue states, though, hasn't breached the skepticism of gun control in red ones. In 2012, Ohio and Virginia both approved legislation loosening concealed-carry restrictions. This year, South Dakota has authorized the arming of school personnel, Virginia has barred state courts from disclosing information about concealed-carry permit holders, and Tennessee has allowed concealed-carry permit holders to transport guns in their car trunks, even without permission from private-property owners. Meanwhile, Republican legislators in Idaho, Michigan, Mississippi, Missouri, Texas, Virginia, and Wyoming have advanced, to varying degrees, mostly symbolic legislation to impede or block entirely the enforcement of new federal gun-control measures. Republican state Rep. Steve Toth has introduced legislation in Texas that would make it a crime for local officials to enforce any federal ban on assault weapons or large-capacity magazines.

Gun-control initiatives have faltered in some blue states this year, including Washington. But after years of inaction, the revival of activism in Democratic-leaning places has widened the chasm between blue and red states. The same pattern is evident on gay marriage. For most of the period since 2000, the story was the cascade of culturally conservative states that passed legislation or ballot initiatives banning same-sex marriages. But in more culturally liberal states, the momentum decisively shifted in 2011 when Delaware, Hawaii, Illinois, and Rhode Island all enacted civil-union laws, and New York trumped them by becoming the largest state to approve gay marriage. In 2012, three more blue states—Maine, Maryland, and Washington—became the first to pass ballot initiatives authorizing gay marriage; Minnesota voters rejected a ballot initiative to ban it.

This year, the momentum for advocates of same-sex marriage has continued, with the passage of the civil-union bill in Colorado (where a constitutional amendment still bars gay marriage), and votes by the Democratic-controlled Senate in Illinois and House in Rhode Island to move from civil unions to full-scale marriage recognition. Rhode Island's bill appears stalled in the state Senate, but the Legislature could still allow voters to decide the issue through a referendum. The powerful Illinois House speaker declared recently that the bill in his chamber was still a dozen votes short of passage, but supporters believe they are closer than that as a vote nears. "I'm optimistic," said Democratic Lt. Gov. Sheila Simon. "I have been making phone calls to House members. My advice to them is that if they are not persuaded by anything I have to say, listen to your kids."

Whatever happens in Rhode Island and Illinois, the trends on gay marriage have produced a striking contrast. The core blue states are the 18 that have voted Democratic in at least the past six presidential elections. Twelve of those 18 have approved either gay marriage or civil unions, and that number could rise to 14 if legislation passes in Minnesota and the Supreme Court upholds the lower-court decisions establishing the right to same-sex marriage in California. (Even if the high court overturns those rulings, polls show solid majority support in California for a potential ballot initiative to legalize gay marriage there.) By later this year, it's possible that only Michigan, Oregon, Pennsylvania, and Wisconsin among the "blue wall" states will have failed to join that list (the latter two states provide some "domestic partnership" benefits to same-sex couples).

Yet the only other states that have recognized marriage or civil unions are Iowa and New Hampshire (both of which have voted Democratic in five of the past six presidential elections) and Colorado, which has tilted demonstrably toward Democrats in the past two elections. Meanwhile, few of the remaining states that have banned gay marriage show signs of reconsideration. "The states that have already affirmed traditional marriage by constitutional amendment or other means are unlikely to reverse that action in the foreseeable future, because of the demographics of those states," says veteran social-conservative leader Ralph Reed, founder and chairman of the Faith and Freedom Coalition.

The Great Divergence

If the Supreme Court finds no right to gay marriage in the Constitution—an outcome that seems likely—the nation may in effect run the kind of experiment that the Court's *Roe v. Wade* decision preempted in 1973. As with abortion before *Roe,* gay marriage might be legal in some states but barred in others indefinitely. This sharp separation is presenting "really difficult and almost imponderable questions," Kettl says. "On issues of social policy, are we prepared for fundamentally dividing the country? When you have a couple that is legally married in one state that moves to another state where gay marriage is not legal, what happens to them? . . . We're going back through a hidden door we didn't know existed to envision what 'equal protection' means."

The great divergence in the states is even shaking the national right to abortion that the *Roe* decision had seemingly settled 40 years ago. In the months following their 2010 ascendance, Republicans pursued a towering wave of state laws to restrict abortion, including mandatory ultrasound examinations in states from Florida and Virginia to Arizona and Texas; measures to defund Planned Parenthood; stringent regulations on abortion providers; and expanded waiting periods. In 2011–12, seven Republican-leaning states (including Alabama, Kansas, and Louisiana) all barred access to abortion after 20 weeks; Arizona banned the procedure after 18 weeks.

Courts have blocked several of those laws, but this burst of activity has energized abortion opponents. "The momentum is very definitely on our side," says Charmaine Yoest, president of Americans United for Life. Advocates for legalized abortion

don't much disagree. Vicki Saporta, president of the National Abortion Federation, says that 2011 saw a new peak in the passage of state-level abortion restrictions, followed only by 2012. "The states that weren't necessarily hostile to abortion rights have become increasingly hostile," she says. "Bills, once they are introduced in one state, they make the circuit."

This year has seen some flicker of abortion activism in blue states, with New York's Cuomo pledging to introduce legislation to strengthen abortion rights. But the principal thrust continues to be restrictive. In Arkansas, the Republican-controlled Legislature overrode the veto of Democratic Gov. Mike Beebe to ban abortions after 12 weeks. That was quickly topped by the North Dakota legislation, which barred most abortions after six weeks; GOP Gov. Jack Dalrymple signed it in late March. (North Dakota legislators then agreed to place before voters a "personhood" constitutional amendment that would, in defiance of *Roe,* ban all abortions.) Alabama, Indiana, Kansas, Kentucky, and South Dakota are among the other red states advancing further restrictions. In Texas, Gov. Rick Perry is backing legislation to impose a 20-week ban and to tighten regulation of abortion clinics to a point that critics say would force most in the state to close.

"States are becoming more conservative around abortion issues," says Elizabeth Nash, who tracks state policy for the Guttmacher Institute. "It really is becoming a free-for-all."

The separation is only slightly hazier on the treatment of marijuana. With the exception of a few libertarian-leaning Western states (such as Alaska, Arizona, and Montana) almost all of the states that have authorized the medicinal use of marijuana lean Democratic in presidential elections, as do Washington and Colorado, the two that last fall approved recreational use.

And it's not only social issues that are separating the states. Although governors in both parties have curtailed public employees' retirement benefits, Republicans have often gone further and, in some cases (like Wisconsin's Scott Walker), vastly heightened the confrontation with state workers by seeking to simultaneously roll back their right to collective bargaining. Conservatives' plans to provide vouchers to parents or tax credits to help pay for private school, stalemated for decades at the federal level, have advanced in red states such as Alabama, Arizona, Indiana, and Louisiana (although the attempt in the latter has been blocked in court).

As the economy recovers, red and blue governors are diverging on taxes as well. GOP Govs. Bobby Jindal in Louisiana and Sam Brownback in Kansas proposed plans to eliminate the state income tax and replace the lost revenue by increasing the sales tax—a trade that critics complain will inevitably tilt the tax burden away from the affluent toward lower-income families. Although opposition forced Jindal to drop his plans this week, Republican legislators in Georgia and North Carolina have discussed similar proposals. Govs. Walker in Wisconsin, Mike Pence in Indiana, and John Kasich in Ohio, and GOP legislators in Missouri and Oklahoma are pursuing more modest income-tax cuts. In sharp contrast, Democrats Cuomo in New York, O'Malley in Maryland, Pat Quinn in Illinois, and Jerry Brown in California since 2011 have driven through tax increases, mostly on top earners, and Minnesota's Mark Dayton and Massachusetts' Deval Patrick are seeking to follow suit this year. Patrick, reversing the Brownback/Jindal formula, wants to raise income taxes to cut sales taxes.

On health care, the chasm between the parties is wider still. Only eight of the 30 Republican governors have agreed to participate in the expansion of Medicaid central to Obama's health reform law—and in Arizona and Florida, Republican state Legislatures are balking. Meanwhile, all 19 Democratic governors except West Virginia's Earl Ray Tomblin have already indicated their intent to expand. Likewise, just six Republican governors, compared with 17 Democrats, have agreed to either fully operate state-level health care exchanges or to run them in partnership with Washington.

"We believe that by being an early implementer of health care, we would have a competitive economic advantage over other states," says Maryland's O'Malley, who is both expanding Medicaid and opening a state exchange. "Those states that are incapable of shedding their ideology . . . will find themselves at a disadvantage."

A New Model

Tension between national imperatives and state flexibility has been a constant in the American political system since the Constitutional Convention rebuffed James Madison's desire to let Congress veto state laws. The nation has lived with enormous differences among the states that sometimes endured for generations. The United States existed as a "house divided" between slave and free states from the 1770s until the Civil War, and then allowed the South to maintain segregation from the 1880s until the 1964 Civil Rights Act dismantled it. The Supreme Court didn't override all state laws prohibiting interracial marriage until 1967, nearly two centuries after Pennsylvania became the first state to repeal its own ban. All states didn't mandate compulsory public education until 66 years after the first one (Massachusetts) did in 1852.

Yet the general scope of congressional lawmaking and judicial decisions through the 20th century was to narrow the differences among the states. That was both because Washington assumed more power to set national standards (on environmental regulation, wage and hour laws, and racial equality, for instance), and because the Supreme Court established more national rights that overrode variations in state law (on everything from school desegregation to abortion and interracial marriage).

Over roughly the final third of the 20th century, particularly once the divisive issues of civil rights receded and more states focused on a common agenda of economic development, this movement accelerated. State lawmakers converged around a burst of policy innovation that led some to describe the period as a second Progressive Era. From the 1970s through the 1990s, many of the most prominent governors in both parties prided themselves on recombining ideas from left and right on issues such as education, health care, transportation, and welfare. David Osborne, a consultant and author, profiled half a dozen leading governors during the 1980s for a seminal book on state innovation, *Laboratories of Democracy*. "They would communicate with each other across party lines, and when you'd go interview them, they would say things like, 'Governors from the different parties have more in common with each other than they do with colleagues from the

same party in Washington,'" Osborne recalled in a recent interview. "And for many of them, it was true."

Over those three decades, many ideas that first took root among governors in one party flowered among their colleagues in the other and ultimately influenced the national debate in Washington. President George H.W. Bush's landmark national conference on education reform in Charlottesville, Va., in 1989 grew from the push for stiffer standards from governors such as Democrats James Hunt in North Carolina, Dick Riley in South Carolina, and Republican Lamar Alexander in Tennessee. The charter-school movement began with measures in Minnesota and then California, drafted in each case by Democratic legislatures and signed by Republican Govs. Arne Carlson and Pete Wilson, respectively; the idea then became a central component of Clinton's national education agenda. Welfare reforms pioneered and tested by Tommy Thompson in Wisconsin and then-Gov. Clinton in Arkansas inspired the national reform legislation passed by the GOP Congress and signed by Clinton in 1996. The bipartisan Clinton-backed 1997 legislation establishing the State Children's Health Insurance Program for kids of the working poor was based on breakthrough efforts in states led by Minnesota. Even as late as 2001, President George W. Bush drew on state educational reform experiences, including his own in Texas, to design the No Child Left Behind Act.

Throughout this period, the gubernatorial model was eclectic, the barriers between the parties porous. Babbitt, Arizona's governor at the time, remembers consulting with Republican Sen. Alan Simpson of Wyoming as he drafted his landmark federal immigration-reform bill in 1986. Thompson worked with Democrats who controlled the Wisconsin state House to pass his path-breaking welfare reforms and learned from lunches with welfare recipients he invited to the state Capitol. "Most of my ideas came from welfare mothers," Thompson says. "I don't think you would see that today." During the national welfare-reform debate, Thompson and other GOP governors even publicly sided with Clinton to oppose a central component of the House Republican plan—something else Thompson doesn't think would happen now. "We were much more willing to take on individuals in our political party when we knew it was right for our state," he says. "Politically today that would not be a smart move. Back then it was much more of the right thing to do."

Differences between the two parties never entirely disappeared, but, politically and personally, governors frequently defined themselves in counterpoint to the Washington debate that grew steadily more polarized and predictable. The National Governors Association prided itself on finding consensus on issues that divided the parties in Congress, recalled Raymond Scheppach, now a University of Virginia professor of public policy, who served as the group's executive director from 1983 through 2010. "A lot of the times, 10 or 15 years ago, you would sit in the room with the governors and you couldn't account for who were the Republicans and who were the Democrats," he says.

This heterodoxy was rewarded. The governors who emerged as national figures—and, frequently, presidential candidates—were generally not the most partisan but those who most creatively blended ideas from the two parties. That list included such Democrats as Babbitt, Clinton, Michael Dukakis, James Hunt, and Dick Lamm; and Republicans such as Alexander,

John Engler, Tom Kean, Thompson, and Wilson. As late as 2000, George W. Bush rose from Texas in this mold, running initially as a "compassionate conservative" who worked with state Democrats to fight "the soft bigotry of low expectations" hobbling education for minority children.

Some of this traditional model is still visible in the performance of governors such as Republican Chris Christie in New Jersey, who worked closely with Obama on Hurricane Sandy relief and has praised his state's tough gun-control laws; the experiments in expanded preschool in red states Georgia and Oklahoma that helped inspire Obama's push on the issue; and in the decisions by New York's Cuomo and Maryland's O'Malley to pursue givebacks in pension benefits for public-employee unions vital to the Democratic coalition.

But, in most cases, the path to prominence for governors today is very different. In today's highly polarized political environment, they are more likely to emerge as national figures by championing and advancing their party's core ideas than by defying or rethinking them. Proposals still travel from state to state but along partisan tracks: Republicans draw inspiration from other Republicans, and Democrats from Democrats.

The change has been especially pronounced in the GOP. The Right, led by groups such as the American Legislative Exchange Council, has built a more robust transmission belt than the Left for moving edgy proposals from one state to another. And Republican state officials have hardened their own focus. During the earlier period, GOP governors usually argued that Washington should devolve more power to the states but accepted the premise that state government retained a large area of responsibility. Now, more Republican governors echo the arguments from congressional conservatives that the key to prosperity is retrenching government's role at every level. "It's not just states' rights: They don't want any government to do these things," says Neera Tanden, a longtime Democratic policy analyst who now is president of the liberal Center for American Progress. Republicans wouldn't phrase the shift in exactly those terms, but especially after the GOP's consecutive presidential defeats, many Republican governors seem determined to forge a model of small-government conservatism for the national party. Brownback recently touted his tax cuts to *The Wall Street Journal* by insisting: "My focus is to create a red-state model that allows the Republican ticket [in 2016] to say, 'See, we've got a different way, and it works.' "

This competition has inspired ambitious activity in both red and blue states. But many analysts question whether these initiatives really embody the "laboratory of democracy" ideal of state tinkering or rather reflect a centrally directed model in which states, often at the prodding of national interest groups, serially fall in line behind their party's national agenda. Babbitt expresses a widespread concern that states have diminished their capacity to genuinely innovate because their every choice is framed through the national partisan struggle. "The divergences in the laboratory-of-democracy idea ought to grow out of grassroots experience" in the states, he says. "It's not the case now. It's a top-down divergence being driven by national

ideological arguments. It's not an experimental model, and it's not a very productive exercise." Rather than ideas rising from the states to Washington, he says, governors are being "conscripted and corrupted into the national political debate."

Governors have adopted this more partisan posture in response to "bottom-up as well as top-down" pressures, notes Scheppach, the former NGA official. The pressure from below springs from the electorate's ongoing ideological re-sorting, which has tilted more states decisively toward one partisan side or the other, and simultaneously increased the pressure for purity and reduced the incentive for bipartisan compromise. Today, Republicans control both legislative chambers and the governorship in 24 states, and Democrats hold unified control in another 12, leaving an unusually small pool of states with divided government. The pressure from above is the same demand for greater party unity from party leaders, activist groups, and overtly partisan media of the Left and Right that has transformed Congress into a quasi-parliamentary institution. "I just think there's been a pounding by their respective parties in the very long run to get in line," Scheppach says. Thompson believes that ambition reinforces that dynamic, because many governors at least fantasize about seeking the presidency, and they recognize how difficult it's become to win a nomination with a record that challenges their party's ideological vanguard.

The causes may differ from place to place, but the common effect has been to send red and blue states hurtling in opposite directions on the critical choices they face. Not long ago, the states mostly operated as an exception to the war between the parties in Washington. Now they look more like an extension of it.

Critical Thinking

1. What is the central argument or central point of this selection? Is the central argument captured well by the title "Altered States"?

2. In policy areas such as gun control, same-sex marriage, and marijuana laws, what differences between states with Republican and states with Democratic governors have emerged?

3. Why does the current divide between Republican and Democratic states seem to have developed, after several decades in the late twentieth century during which there was much less of a clear-cut pattern?

Create Central

www.mhhe.com/createcentral

Internet References

Democratic Governors Association
   http://democraticgovernors.org
National Governors Association
   www.nga.org
Republican Governors Association
   www.rga.org

Brownstein, Ronald, and Czekalinski, Stephanie. Reprinted by permission from *National Journal*, April 13, 2013, pp. 12, 14–15, 18–21. Copyright © 2013 by National Journal Group Inc. All rights reserved. Reprinted by permission via Wright's Media.

Article   Prepared by: Bruce Stinebrickner, *DePauw University*

The Last Democrat in Dixie

Somebody forgot to tell Mississippi's attorney general that his party doesn't win in the Deep South anymore.

J.B. Wogan

Learning Outcomes

After reading this article, you will be able to:

- Explain how Attorney General Jim Hood, even though a Democrat, has held office in Mississippi for nearly a decade.
- Describe the political culture of Mississippi in which Attorney General Jim Hood operates.

Jim Hood speaks with a folksy twang. He says grace before dinner and styles his hair like the late country singer Conway Twitty. An American flag nearly as long as Hood juts from the brick portico of his suburban Jackson, Miss., home, and just inside the front door, he keeps a Good News Bible in plain view for guests to peruse. Out back he stores his tractor and guns in a woodshed and on days when he needs to get his mind off work as Mississippi's attorney general, he retreats to the shed, where he takes used ammunition casings from his weekend hunting excursions and reloads them manually, shell by shell.

You might say Jim Hood is about as Mississippi as you can get. In one respect, though, he's unusual for a politician in his home state: He's a Democrat—and, on certain occasions, a liberal one. He prosecuted a Ku Klux Klan member for a 40-year-old murder and sued pharmaceutical companies over high drug prices. He declined to join a challenge to the national health-care law, and believes his state should participate in the expansion of Medicaid. None of that has seemed to hurt him politically.

Every other statewide officeholder in Mississippi is a Republican. In fact, across the seven states of the Deep South, every other governor, attorney general and secretary of state belongs to the GOP. Yet Hood has held onto his job easily for nearly a decade. In the 2011 election, his third successful bid for attorney general, he won a higher percentage of votes than the successful Republican nominee for governor, Phil Bryant. His electoral victories raise a simple question with a complicated answer: How does he manage to do that?

One reason is that he has a knack for picking up independent votes—even though Mississippi is one of the reddest of the red states, with just under half the voters identifying as Republicans, according to Harrison Hickman, Hood's pollster. A little more than a third are Democrats. The rest call themselves independents. "Any Democrat who is successful in statewide politics in the South," Hickman says, "is somebody who can talk to independents, because you cannot be elected on the strength of Democrats."

And Hood can talk to independents. Bobby Moak, the Democratic minority leader in the state house, says Hood reaches independents because "he takes the right stance on God and guns."

To be sure, there are other explanations. In 2003, when he first ran for attorney general, winning wasn't quite as difficult as it is now for Democrats running statewide. Hood had been a district attorney for eight years in northern Mississippi and had the endorsement of the retiring four-term attorney general, Mike Moore. In all of his campaigns, he has been able to count on generous funding from trial lawyers across the country. Those things have mattered. Nonetheless, Hood's ability to cultivate a reputation as an average Mississippian begins with religion and firearms.

Hood's parents named him after the Book of James, which he points out, "talks about taking care of the least among us." He says "it's the job of the government to take care of the people who need it." Hood insists he isn't "one of those Bible thumpers," but religion plays a prominent role in the way he thinks about his career. Here's how he explains perhaps the biggest turn in his professional trajectory, when a scarcity of jobs in the oil and gas industry convinced him to go to law school: "I think the good Lord opens his doors and closes them."

As for guns, Hood earned a "B" on gun rights from the National Rifle Association in 2011. He comes to work every day armed with a 9mm handgun, and at home he keeps a stock of shotguns and rifles in a vault, including an antique bolt-action rifle that is the exact model his grandfather once owned. He hunts deer or birds almost every weekend in December and January.

So on one level, Hood's appeal is cultural—voters look at him and sense he is one of them. But he has also chosen issues that appeal across party lines. "Results matter more than party ID in most elections," says Rob McKenna, a friend of Hood's who served two terms as a Republican attorney general in a Democratic stronghold, Washington state. "I don't think most voters are comfortable with the idea of a highly partisan AG."

Much of Hood's agenda veers away from divisive political battles and addresses crime detested by Democrats and Republicans alike. He has targeted deadbeat dads who haven't paid child support, child pornographers on the Internet and men who abuse their wives or girlfriends. After Hurricane Katrina devastated coastal Mississippi, Hood recouped money for individuals and families who had been victimized by companies that engaged in home repair fraud.

During his second term, Hood seized on the fact that Mississippi had the fifth-highest incidence of domestic homicide of any state in the country. He created a protective order registry and a fee exemption for domestic violence victims seeking a restraining order. Under Hood, the rate of domestic homicides dropped to the 13th highest in the nation.

Republicans sometimes say that the nature of his job has made it easy for him to draw support across party lines. "It's real popular when you're locking up crooks," says sometime adversary Terry Brown, the Republican senate president pro tem.

But Hood has also taken up a few causes that have touched a sensitive Mississippi nerve. Early in his first term, he reopened the infamous 1964 case in which local Ku Klux Klan members brutally murdered three civil rights workers in Neshoba County for pushing black voter registration. In the original trial, federal prosecutors tried to prove former Klan preacher Edgar Ray Killen was a central figure in orchestrating the killings, but the jury determined that the evidence was too circumstantial. Four decades later, Hood secured three 20-year manslaughter convictions against Killen.

Because Hood's recipe for success hinges on his reputation as a political moderate, his adversaries often try to paint him as partisan. The opportunities for doing this usually involve a national issue with clear red and blue positions. In the summer of 2012, for example, Ceara Sturgis and her partner Emily Key applied to rent the taxpayer-funded Mississippi Agriculture and Forestry Museum for a same-sex wedding. The agriculture commissioner, Cindy Hyde-Smith, refused, citing state law that prohibits gay marriage. Hood supported the couple's right to hold the wedding.

Republican leaders implied that Hood's legal opinion against the agriculture commissioner was an attempt to keep pace with trends inside his own party at the national level. "Attorney General Hood's legal advice goes against the wishes of an overwhelming majority of Mississippians," Lt. Gov. Tate Reeves said at the time. "Based on my personal and religious beliefs, I strongly object to this," Hyde-Smith said in a press release.

Hood skirted the issue by making a distinction between a marriage and a wedding. His office ruled that there was a technical difference between a marriage, which involves a government license and confers legal rights on a couple, and a wedding, which amounts to a personal commitment ceremony. Current state law in Mississippi doesn't prohibit same-sex weddings, he said, only marriages.

Hood does disagree with his state's prohibition of same-sex marriage. "What people do in their private lives is their own business," he says. But he insists that, whatever his personal opinion might be, he would defend Mississippi state law in court. "The state constitution defines marriage as between a man and woman," he says, "and it's my job to defend that to the bitter end. I have my personal beliefs and I don't let them interfere."

On a day-to-day basis, Hood's job consists largely of negotiating with Republicans. One recent afternoon, he walked across the street to the state house in Jackson to ask for money from the senate appropriations chair, Buck Clarke. The informal get-together involved several potential lawsuits filed by the federal government, including one alleging that the state wasn't providing adequate care to the mentally ill. Hood had negotiated a deal with the U.S. Department of Justice specifying that if the state spent an initial $10 million on an independent monitor to jump-start an overhaul of the state's mental health system, the federal government wouldn't sue. If Mississippi didn't comply, the lawsuit could wind up costing the state millions in litigation fees, as had happened in other states already. The thrust of Hood's appeal wasn't moral, it was financial. He argued that the price of challenging the feds was too high.

That's something Hood likes to do: present his policy choices in fiscal rather than programmatic terms. On the same day he approached Clarke about mental health care, he talked about other potential lawsuits by the federal government over prison conditions and environmental cleanup. Some initial spending by the legislature, he said, might avoid much larger litigation costs. In every case, he persuaded Republicans to appropriate funds on the front end by making a case for financial prudence in the long run. In another state with less conservative politics, a Democrat might talk up the social benefits involved. In Mississippi, Hood avoids that strategy. Instead, he is quick to tout the more than $500 million he has recouped for the state since taking office in 2003.

"I look out for the coffers. That's the way I look at it," he says, describing his philosophy in giving the state advice on legal matters. "Are you going to cost the state money by dragging out this litigation and defending a losing case?"

When Hood declined to sign onto the lawsuit in protest against the Affordable Care Act—much to the chagrin of state Republicans—his explanation was once again financial, not moral. "I just didn't think that the state of Mississippi needed to spend any money on lawyers to file a 'me-too' brief," he says.

It's a fine line, though. Hood readily admits he thinks the health law's Medicaid expansion would be helpful in

Mississippi, a state with some of the worst health statistics in the country and a large population that can't afford health insurance. But, he says, it's just not his call.

At the time Hood was negotiating with Republicans in the legislature to avoid lawsuits from the federal government, Democratic lawmakers were threatening to defund Medicaid as a way to win health policy concessions from Republicans. Despite Hood's efforts to appear apolitical, the "D" by his name seems to automatically make him a player in such partisan dramas. When Hood wrote an opinion holding that Mississippi law empowered the insurance commissioner, a Republican, to set up a state-based health insurance exchange under the federal law, GOP Gov. Bryant dismissed Hood's interpretation as political, not legal. "This ruling by Attorney General Jim Hood is not surprising," said Mick Bullock, a Bryant spokesman, in a prepared statement. "Gov. Bryant understands that as a Democrat, General Hood was placed in an extremely difficult position."

"It's become more partisan now than when I was AG," says Mike Moore, Hood's predecessor and a Democrat who was attorney general for 16 years under Democratic and Republican governors. "It's been tough for Jim. At least I had other Democratic allies [in state government]. It makes it harder for him to promote legislation and get things passed."

Last year, for example, the Republican legislative majority enacted a "sunshine" law allowing state officials to hire outside counsel if they disagree with legal strategy prescribed by the attorney general. In the past, they could use outside counsel only if the attorney general declined to get involved in the case. Hood says the law is unconstitutional because it undermines his role as an independent legal counsel to the state government. It might mean the state will choose to settle in cases when it's in the public interest to go to trial, he says.

The new law also calls for scrutiny of payments to trial lawyers working for the state on contingency fees in lawsuits, typically against national companies. Corporations have long criticized this system, arguing that it is a form of patronage used to reward Hood's biggest campaign contributors. They see trial lawyers as the main reason why he wins re-election, and say he benefits from their financial backing and then rewards them with profitable cases afterward. The sunshine law undermines that patronage by discouraging the use of private-sector attorneys. It was a slap in the face by Republicans, says Danny Cupit, a trial lawyer who represented Hood's office in a lawsuit against the insurance company State Farm.

Despite the theatrics on both sides after the law passed, Democrats haven't challenged it in court and Republicans haven't disowned Hood as their legal representative. At least not yet.

Critical Thinking

1. What has enabled MIssissippi Attorney General Jim Hood to be the only Democrat who holds office as governor, attorney general, or secretary of state in the seven states of the Deep South?

2. How has presenting his policy choices in fiscal rather than programmatic terms been helpful to Mississippi Attorney General Hood?

3. How did Mississippi Attorney General Hood use a distinction between a "wedding" and a "marriage" to support a controversial legal opinion involving Mississippi's agricultural commissioner?

Create Central

www.mhhe.com/createcentral

Internet References

Jim Hood (Campaign to Re-elect Jim Hood, 2011)
www.jimhood.org
Office of the Attorney General of the state of Mississippi
www.ago.state.ms.us

Article   Prepared by: Bruce Stinebrickner, *DePauw University*

The Badgered State
Wisconsin Governor Scott Walker Is the Left's Public Enemy No. 1

ROBERT COSTA

Learning Outcomes

After reading this article, you will be able to:

- Assess the desirability of the policies that Governor Scott Walker of Wisconsin announced in February 2011, which led to protests and demonstrations at the Wisconsin state capitol that drew national and worldwide attention.

- Understand and evaluate the Wisconsin state senate rule that led fourteen Democratic state senators to go to Illinois.

- Investigate and weigh, from the perspective of several years later, the aftermath of Governor Walker's controversial announcement in February 2011 and of the tumultuous weeks in Wisconsin that began in February 2011.

Madison, Wis.

Snow is falling here. The coffee shops have closed. The college bars are shuttered. A lone police car inches along State Street, icy slush glazing its wheels. The heavyset patrolman eyes me warily: Trench coats and suit jackets are rare in these parts. We nod, and he continues on, spotlights floating through the Lake Monona fog.

Up on the knoll, a white dome gleams. In the midnight quiet, I trudge toward it, past a graybeard professor and hulking Teamsters. Near the door, a skinny girl decked out in a ruby University of Wisconsin sweatshirt smokes a cigarette. Her friend is hooked into her iPhone, texting her classmates, urging them to visit. I move inside, out of the cold. The marble hall is dark, dimly lit by sunflower-yellow lamps. There is a faint hum.

Ambling down the corridor, sidestepping grungy pillows, acoustic guitars, and empty pizza boxes, I near the center of this stately building. The humid, sweat-scented air flares the nostrils. The hum becomes a roar: Thousands are packed into all four wings of the building. They wear bright purple SEIU T-shirts, lime green AFSCME ponchos, and fraying flannel. Gently elbowing my way through the dreadlocks and past the stacked hand drums, I find myself under the rotunda, at the center of a bizarre, union-sponsored slumber party.

A couple of feet away, a high-school teacher grabs a bullhorn and, much as the shaman calls the rain, begins to lead those assembled in a sing-along of "Union Maid," a Woody Guthrie ditty. The scene is like a Grateful Dead concert without the plugged-in licks, a raucous temple for aging activists and impressionable youth. "Welcome to paradise," chuckles a capitol guard.

For much of February, the Wisconsin state capitol was occupied by labor leaders, undergraduates, and a potpourri of lefty radicals. They were loud and they were angry. On cardboard signs and sprawling banners, they railed against Gov. Scott Walker, the Badger State's rookie executive, who earlier in the month had proposed a budget-repair bill that would break the grip of public-sector unions in a state that has long been dominated by them.

Walker, a 43-year-old Republican, was skewered by liberal pundits. Protesters compared him to Adolf Hitler, Hosni Mubarak, and Darth Vader. But he ignored their cries and made a compelling, unflinching argument for fiscal prudence. For conservatives, it was an awe-inspiring sight. George Will observed that Walker's steely determination called up the ghosts of Ronald Reagan and Margaret Thatcher, who so famously tangled with union bosses three decades ago.

But Walker's fight was more than an echo of glory past: It emerged, with speed and fervor, as the definitive state-level budget battle in the Age of Obama. Since Walker rolled out his plan, a half-dozen states have seen similar union-fueled uprisings as they grapple with budget gaps and benefit-addicted government workers. Walker, an unassuming man who speaks with a nasal midwestern accent, is suddenly a nationally recognized fiscal hawk and, to many Republicans, a hero.

On Friday, February 11, days after the Green Bay Packers topped the Pittsburgh Steelers in the Super Bowl, Madison was a picture of placidity. Walker, still settling in, had few enemies. He did not need a Google alert for his name. Few national reporters were paying attention to him. Wisconsin's GOP stars—Rep. Paul Ryan, a leader in the U.S. House, and Sen. Ron Johnson, a Tea Party–inspired freshman—owned the spotlight.

One press conference changed that. Facing an immediate budget deficit of $137 million and a $3.6 billion shortfall over the next two years, Walker took to the podium behind his first-floor office at the capitol and told a handful of scribes that bold action was needed. "The path to long-term financial solvency for our state requires shared sacrifices from everyone," he said. Walker's plan asked state workers to contribute 5.8 percent of their salaries toward their pensions and to pay 12.6 percent of their health-insurance premiums. Most controversially, he aimed to limit collective bargaining for nearly all state employees by restricting future government-union haggles to wages and excluding pensions and other benefits. He unveiled this all softly, with none of the frank combativeness of Gov. Chris Christie of New Jersey, who gained headlines last year for his tussle with the public sector. Walker's aides say their boss saw the fiscal mess as spectacle enough—no need to wag a finger.

But he might as well have thrown acid at the Left. The eye-rubbing reactions poured in. Here was a greenhorn Republican governor taking on the unions in a state that in 1959 became the first to grant public workers collective-bargaining rights. A GOP nobody was going to throttle the political culture in a capitol where a statue of "Fighting" Bob La Follette, a progressive legend, stands vigil between the legislative chambers. For Democrats and their allies, it was almost unbelievable. Republican governors had come and gone, to be sure, but none had so fiercely and so quickly attempted to tear at the fabric of the state government's cozy, union-friendly culture.

Jill Bakken, a spokeswoman for the American Federation of Teachers in Wisconsin, spoke for many with her initial response. "State employees are shocked and bewildered about how 50 years of labor peace can be unraveled by a governor who has been in office for six weeks," she said. Fellow Democrats, sensing trouble, began to mobilize. Organizing outfits such as MoveOn.org stirred online buzz. By Sunday evening, hundreds were gathered outside the state capitol and the governor's mansion, demanding that Walker back down.

The crowds began to swell on Tuesday and Wednesday, when Madison-area teachers abandoned their classrooms in protest. Although teacher strikes are illegal in Wisconsin, teachers danced around the law and organized "sickouts." Supportive physicians scribbled phony doctor's notes for those in need. The Madison epidemic spread from Kenosha to Superior—schools were shut down across the state, and teachers reinforced their ranks at the capitol. "We teach the children!" one legion cried as they marched below Walker's office. "We are the mighty teachers!" bellowed another.

According to the *Wisconsin State Journal,* anti-Walker forces hit the 10,000 mark by Tuesday afternoon and 20,000 by Wednesday. Sleeping bags started to appear by committee rooms. Inflatable mattresses popped up near state senate offices. Police officers, themselves members of a union allied with the protesters, abstained from confronting the squatters. There were no metal detectors or other security measures, and the capitol doors remained wide open, day and night. Zero arrests were made.

Walker plowed ahead. He knew that he had the votes to pass his plan, regardless of the kicking and screaming. Republicans hold a 19–14 edge in the state senate and a 57–38–1 majority in the state assembly. But to have a vote, elected representatives have to show up: Specifically, the Wisconsin senate requires the presence of a 20-senator quorum before considering any fiscal measure. Knowing this, the 14 Democratic state senators promptly went on the lam.

By the evening of February 18, the entire Democratic caucus from the upper chamber was in hiding, holed up at hotels in northern Illinois and Chicago. They giggled with bloggers over the phone that, in Dick Cheney style, they were calling from "undisclosed locations." As the senators evaded state troopers dispatched by the state senate to haul them back to work, busloads of labor supporters began to arrive in Madison. The Left was digging in—and man, did they love it. MSNBC's Ed Schultz set up shop. Teaching assistants from the University of Wisconsin began to organize a commune of sorts, operating out of a hearing room on the capitol's third floor. Even President Obama jumped into the mix, calling Walker's maneuver an "assault on unions."

A week after Walker's initial presser, with a circus rollicking outside his office and the national press pouring into Dane County airport, the unions approached and dangled an offer: They would accept Walker's terms on pensions and health benefits but would not give up collective-bargaining power. "We will not—I repeat, we will not—be denied our rights to collectively bargain," said Marty Beil, the leader of the state employees' union. The chants around Capitol Square quickly picked up this spin. Public-school teachers wearing varsity jackets belted out: "It's not about the money!"

Walker responded coolly to the deal. He later told me that he immediately figured it to be a red herring. He argued that his budget fix was designed to help school districts and municipalities tighten their belts in coming years. Labor wanted to make the kerfuffle about his alleged thirst for "union busting," but the governor would not bite. If collective bargaining remained, he reasoned, then few local leaders would be able to balance their budgets—not with the unions holding all of the cards.

Astounded that Walker would not buckle, labor brass called in reinforcements. Richard Trumka, the national president of the AFL-CIO, convened a rally Friday evening. Jesse Jackson and others flocked to the scene. On Saturday, approximately 70,000 people showed up at the capitol, circling the building for hours. Firefighters marched hand in hand with teachers, corrections officers raised their fists in front of a nearby Starbucks, students scurried over from UW-Madison's campus. Out-of-state supporters flooded in.

So did the Tea Party. Thousands of Walker supporters appeared with Gadsden flags and Old Glory, cutting right through the labor masses toward the capitol. They set up a makeshift stage, their pro-Walker posters waving under the clear blue sky. Conservative favorites such as publisher Andrew Breitbart, presidential candidate Herman Cain, and Samuel "Joe the Plumber" Wurzelbacher cheered on the crowd and chastised the absent state senators. "Recall them all!" was a common chant. Walker loved it.

The day after the Saturday showdown, the governor and I met in his capitol office. He implored the on-the-run legislators to "come home." For the first time, I saw a flash of disdain from Walker, whose calm usually reminds me of a placid public-radio newsreader. This battle was dragging on with no conclusion in sight. But Walker would not budge and insisted that he could outlast the Democrats, even if protests swamped the capitol for months.

"They have no endgame," he said with a hint of exasperation. "They don't know what they are doing. They got caught up in the hysteria and decided to run, but that's not how this works. You have got to be in the arena."

Walker had seen this movie before. From 2002 to 2010, he served as chief executive of Milwaukee County, a blue community of nearly a million. He was elected to the post after county executives had lavished extensive pension perks upon themselves, inspiring an outbreak of flinty fiscal conservatism even in liberal voters—at least for a time. After nearly a decade as a state legislator, during which time he was a popular guest on Wisconsin's talk-radio circuit and was viewed as a rising Republican star, he found himself managing an out-of-control budget in a major Midwestern city. It was an abrupt change of pace.

From the outset, Walker led as an unapologetic conservative and began to make immediate, deep cuts. Budgets were slashed and public workers laid off. The local unions were apoplectic. Walker soldiered on and never once raised property taxes. The county's bond rating improved, and its debt was reduced. Walker, a low-key speaker but a pol with solid gut instincts, even donated thousands in salary back to the taxpayers. For a middle-class father of two teenage sons, that was more than a gimmick.

"We were dealing with many of the same fights I'm fighting right now: pension reform and health-care benefits," Walker recalled. "We were challenging the status quo. We reined in spending, reined in the size of government, and reduced the size of the work force."

Year after year, he roiled big-government Democrats with his streamlined county budgets. "People would sit in the chambers when I presented my budgets. I'd have whole sections of the gallery filled with AFSCME leaders in green shirts holding up signs that read 'Negotiate, don't dictate.' So I have great credibility when I talk about the need to change collective bargaining. I saw firsthand how the unions thumbed their noses at local elected officials."

"'We are not budging'—that is the unions' mindset," Walker sighed as the protesters rumbled beyond his door. "Even if you wanted modest changes in health-care and pension contributions, you could not get it. One year, I even tried a 35-hour workweek for a couple weeks, and they told me to forget it. 'Go lay people off,' they said, 'you'll be gone soon enough. We may not get our people back, but our benefits won't be reduced.' They had no interest in doing anything reasonable with local officials."

By late February, with Democratic state senators still roosting in Illinois, assembly Republicans hustled to pass the governor's budget bill. It was a slow, arduous process: Lower-chamber Democrats did not flee, but they did filibuster, via amendments and long-winded floor speeches, for 61 hours straight. On February 24, there were rumors that the Democrats would finally stop the theatrics. But they kept riffing well into the night.

At 1 A.M. on Friday, February 25, Rep. Bill Kramer, the GOP speaker pro tempore, decided he had seen enough. He grabbed his gavel, halted the debate, and called for a vote. It was over in seconds. Walker's bill passed 51 to 17, with nearly one-third of the sleepy chamber, including 25 Democrats, not voting—some were absent, others confused by the sudden end to the filibuster.

Bedlam ensued. Democratic legislators, clad in orange shirts like their union backers, took to the floor. They raised their arms and pointed their fingers at their GOP colleagues, echoing the chants of those huddled throughout the capitol. There were yelps and groans; some screamed "Shame!" at Republicans, others called the process undemocratic. The shout-fest was akin to the British House of Commons at its absolute worst. But Walker had won a crucial victory in the war to pass his bill. If that meant that the absentee Democratic senators stayed in Illinois and started rooting for the Chicago Bears, never to return home again, he could live with that.

At the end of my conversation with Walker, the throbbing drums of the protesters began to bleed through the granite. Walker shrugged off the noise. "These tens of thousands of protesters have every right to be heard," he told me. "But there are 5.5 million people in this state, and those taxpayers also have a right to be heard. I, for one, am not going to let the protesters overshadow, or shout out, the interest of the state's taxpayers. And I believe that they are with us in trying to balance this budget."

Indeed, Walker sees his brawl with union bosses as an important testing ground for other governors dealing with in-the-red budgets. "I was talking to former governor Tommy Thompson about this the other day," he said, his hands clasped. "Wisconsin set the table back in the Nineties on welfare reform. We were a leader there, and we were a leader on education reform. Now we are talking about budgetary and fiscal reform. Wisconsin, in many cases, sets the pace."

Scott Walker sees his brawl with union bosses as an important testing ground for other governors dealing with in-the-red budgets.

And Scott Walker intends to set the pace for Wisconsin.

Critical Thinking

1. What government office does Scott Walker hold and what did he do early in 2011 that produced fierce controversy and protests in his state?

2. Why did the entire Democratic caucus of the Wisconsin state senate go to Illinois in response to Governor Walker's proposal?

3. What government offices had Walker held before becoming governor?

4. In what two policy areas, according to Governor Walker, had the state of Wisconsin been a leader before the 2011 controversy over budgetary and fiscal reform?

Create Central

www.mhhe.com/createcentral

Internet References

Is Scott Walker Running? (*Christian Science Monitor*)

www.csmonitor.com/USA/Politics/2013/1120/Is-Scott-Walker-running-5-quick-takes-from-Wisconsin-governor-s-memoir/Mitt-Romney-didn-t-resonate

Office of the Governor: Scott Walker

www.walker.wi.gov

Wisconsin state website (State of Wisconsin portal)

www.wisconsin.gov/state

Article   Prepared by: Bruce Stinebrickner, *DePauw University*

Counter Cultures

Success in government demands a different set of skills than making it big in business.

MARTY LINSKY

Learning Outcomes

After reading this article, you will be able to:

- Assess each of the author's four key differences between politics and business and determine whether you find them persuasive.

- Evaluate whether each of the four differences have any practical use for a government office-holder.

M y third tour in government was as chief secretary to then Republican Governor Bill Weld in Massachusetts in the early 1990s. My portfolio was politics and personnel—aka "patronage."

It was the early days of the merger and acquisition craze. As a consequence, there were a slew of men and women with highly successful track records in business whose jobs had ended on someone else's schedule. With impressive resumés, paid-up college tuitions behind them, and enough money squirreled away to get by on a public secular salary, they "wanted to give something back" by serving in an important position in state government. Status was still important. For example, if you had been the president of a successful local bank that had been swallowed up, you might well be addicted to a certain level of authority.

We recruited lots of those folks into the Weld administration. Anecdotally, it seemed as if they either blew out pretty quickly or they made the transition well and made significant contributions to the public good, at least as we defined it. Almost no one was just so-so.

I remember noticing the pattern at the time. It got me to thinking about the difference between exercising leadership successfully in business and doing so in government and politics, and why it was so difficult for many in business to match their private sector success in the public arena.

What are the cultural and value differentiators between these two worlds?

While my academic colleagues might be eager to attack that question with an elaborate research design, I'm too much of a journalist—and politician—to resist taking a stab at naming the most important of these many differentiators.

So based on what I have experienced and observed, here are four key differences I see between succeeding in the world of business and politics.

No. 1: Data Versus Anecdotes

For business, systematic data are powerful. In politics, anecdotal evidence is not an oxymoron.

People in government and politics—for our purposes here, let's use "politics" or "political environment" to cover both elected and appointed officials in the public sector—have different ideas about the utility of systematic data versus anecdotes in decision making. At one end of the spectrum, academics and scientists use many, many cases to come up with a general theory, which is then applied to a particular situation. Legislators, on the other hand, are forced by the nature of their work to use individual cases to make general rules. To a scientist, systematic analysis trumps intuition or any individual case. To a politician, intuition is a resource, and individual cases are legitimate pathways to general laws. Business people fall somewhere in between.

No. 2: Politics Is Not the Problem

To be successful in a political environment, you've got to acknowledge, respect and engage in the politics of policymaking, not disdain it. In business, the politics is just as present, but being explicit about the politics is, well, politically incorrect.

You've got to acknowledge, respect and engage in the politics of policymaking, not disdain it.

I was a three-term member of the Massachusetts House of Representatives. It was the most honest environment in which I have ever worked, including, among others, law firms, academic institutions, consulting firms and newspapers. It was honest because politics, which pervades everything from families to corporations, was upfront and explicit.

In most organizations outside of government, politics is very much present but below the radar. When I first joined the faculty at the Harvard Kennedy School nearly 30 years ago, a trusted colleague and I were having a candid conversation about my career when he suddenly stopped and said, "You know, I will have this conversation with you any time you want, but we can never have it with anyone else in the room."

The message was clear: Normal, human ambition and strategizing about it were not appropriate subjects for public conversation. The Kennedy School was founded to train people to speak truth to power on the assumption that the world would be a better place if we could only take the politics out of policymaking.

Many of our unsuccessful appointees from the private sector had the same idea. They thought their job was to eliminate the politics, instead of engaging in it because it was so real and relevant to making progress.

The central difference between functioning well in politics and functioning well in business is not whether the politics exists, but whether politics is accepted as an appropriate and public factor in decision making.

No. 3: Everything Is Connected

Once you accept the legitimacy of politics, certain other differentiators result. The most important of these is No. 3: In politics, there are no discrete issues. Everything is connected to everything else.

People who are successful in politics think systemically. If I am coming to a meeting with you, I want to know what else you care about besides what is on the agenda, who your friends and your enemies are, what other pressures you are facing, and whether I have done anything for you lately, or vice versa. People in business tend to want to hold on to the fiction that they can solve a value-laden problem in one place without ramifications everywhere else. Unexpected consequences are the result of lack of good political or systemic diagnoses.

One of the reasons that people in business can ignore the politics is they tend to work in more or less homogeneous worlds, with clear lines of authority and a shared objective, namely the bottom line. Working in a political environment, you are thrown together every day with people who have very different values, priorities and preferred outcomes.

Personal power derives as much from relationships—and the informal authority that comes from those relationships—as from formal authority. And people are where they are because of their differences, be they policy preferences, issue advocacy or geographical constituencies.

No. 4: A World of Ambiguity

In business, you can enjoy the comfort of being on a team and agreeing on your role and scope of authority. But to be successful in politics, you have to revel in being in an environment of ambiguous authority, and relish confronting the "other."

To be successful in politics, you have to revel in being in an environment of ambiguous authority.

In this space I can only touch on some of the most important cultural, value and structural differences between government and business, and how the willingness and capacity to overcome those differences affect the success of business people in government and politics. This is a mother lode of a subject, and I have only scratched the surface here.

But ironically, in the turbulent times in which we live, some of those distinctions will blur.

With huge challenges and diminished resources, government bureaucrats and politicians will to have to look more to rigorous analysis on which to make—and justify—hard choices.

On the other side, with such rapid change and future uncertainties, people in business must increase their tolerance for ambiguity and less clear lines of authority, collaborate with people who hold very different values and perspectives, and make more intuitive decisions based on insufficient data.

Critical Thinking

1. How are the worlds of business and politics distinguished by "data versus anecdotes"?

2. How are the worlds of business and politics distinguished by whether "politics" itself is accepted as an appropriate and public factor in decision making?

3. Does the notion that "everything is connected" apply better to the world of business or the world of politics? Why?

4. In which world—business or politics—does ambiguity fit more comfortably?

Create Central

www.mhhe.com/createcentral

Internet References

Cambridge Leadership Associates
   www.cambridge-leadership.com

Marty Linsky profile (Harvard Kennedy School)
   www.hks.harvard.edu/about/faculty-staff-directory/marty-linsky

MARTY LINSKY is co-founder and principal of Cambridge Leadership Associates, a global leadership development consulting practice. He also is a longtime faculty member at Harvard's Kennedy School and a former three-term Republican representative in the Massachusetts House, where he served as assistant minority leader.

From *State Legislatures*, January 2011, pp. 20–21. Copyright © 2011 by National Conference of State Legislatures. Reprinted by permission.

Article   Prepared by: Bruce Stinebrickner, *DePauw University*

The Life of the Mayor-for-Life

Richard M. Daley may not have been the smartest guy in the room. But he knew how to run Chicago.

ALAN EHRENHALT

Learning Outcomes

After reading this article, you will be able to:

- Add your own assessment of the performance of Mayor Richard M. Daley.

- Critique the criteria that Alan Ehrenhalt uses to assess Mayor Daley's performance.

- Assess the thesis that Mayor Daley performed less well in his later years than in earlier years and consider whether that was almost inevitable for someone who served 22 years as mayor of a large city.

There's no doubt something to be said for being the smartest person in the room. In politics, though, power and success often flow to the less brilliant who accept their own limitations and take full advantage of the gaudier intellects around them.

That is, in many ways, the story of Richard M. Daley. Eldest son of the legendary Chicago mayor and political boss, Daley entered politics at an early age surrounded by doubters who considered him an inarticulate, unsophisticated mediocrity, incapable of maintaining the family legacy. The disparaging comments continued through his first two decades in Illinois public office and did not disappear even during the early stages of his mayoralty, which began in 1989. "There are smarter people than me," Daley once told a reporter. "I know that. I've met a lot of them. I don't say too much. I just listen and try to figure out where they're coming from."

But when he retired in 2011 after twenty-two years as mayor, Daley could genuinely be said to have had the last laugh. He had exercised power about as nimbly as his father had, turned Chicago into a laboratory for new ideas in urban management, and guided the city's transformation from a large but inward-looking midwestern metropolis to a place with legitimate global aspirations.

The odyssey of Richard M. Daley is laid out with scrupulous detail in *First Son*, a new biography by Keith Koeneman that takes Daley from his initial political venture as a state constitutional convention delegate to the final moments of his tenure on the fifth floor of city hall. The book wanders from its subject at times, and the prose is less than dazzling. But it is a valuable book, admirably fair and balanced, and vastly informative about four colorful and highly eventful decades in the life of America's third-largest metropolis.

Chicago is, for all of its attractions, a deeply flawed city, and Daley accumulated a long list of disappointments to go with his successes. Early in his tenure, he attracted national attention by taking personal control of the city's school system, but it was only marginally better when he left office than when he started out. The crime rate, and especially the murder rate, remained frighteningly high, fueled by a horrendous gang problem in the poorest neighborhoods. And while Daley prided himself, with some justification, on his skills as a financial manager, he left a heavy load of debt for his successor, Rahm Emanuel.

But all of this must, in the end, be measured against some developments more visible to the naked eye: the glittering downtown that hosts a cavalcade of visitors from virtually everywhere in the world, turning Michigan Avenue on a June Friday night into a promenade equal to what the brightest global cities have to offer; the boom in central-city residential life, which has converted once-dull avenues downtown into thriving corridors for the upwardly mobile and the affluent; the second wind of old working-class neighborhoods close to the center, blighted just a few years ago, as walkable enclaves of the Millennial generation.

Daley entered politics at an early age surrounded by doubters who considered him inarticulate, unsophisticated, and incapable of maintaining the family legacy. When he retired in 2011 after twenty-two years as mayor, he had the last laugh. He had exercised power about as nimbly as his father had, turned Chicago into a laboratory for new ideas in urban management, and guided the city's transformation from

a large but inward-looking midwestern metropolis to a place with legitimate global aspirations.

Daley did not create the inner-city comeback, but it is fair to conclude that his development policies and sensitivity to Chicago's physical character made possible changes that other cities are still laboring to emulate. Anyone who sees the visual evidence of Chicago's more successful neighborhoods is likely to ponder the career of Richard M. Daley and ask: What if he did make a few mistakes?

Of course, Daley's critics, of whom there are many, are likely to respond that there were more than a few, and they were more than mistakes. These people will argue that he was nearly as much of an autocrat as his father, becoming increasingly impervious to outside criticism as he grew older and more deeply ensconced in office.

To detractors, the most tangible evidence of autocratic mischief was his unilateral order to demolish Meigs Field, an in-town airport for private planes highly valued by much of the city's business elite. Meigs Field was destroyed in the dead of night in 2002, in order, Daley said, to create a park. Opponents said it was destroyed so Daley could prove his ultimate political control to anyone who doubted it.

It was episodes like the Meigs Field debacle that led to muttering about Daley as a not-so-benign dictator, pursuing the path set out by his father a few decades before. But those particular comparisons don't quite work. The elder Daley presided over a city divided uneasily by black and white, but he owned the meek loyalties of a political organization in which the white politicians were beholden to him and the black machine aldermen were willing to accept virtual table scraps of patronage in exchange for the votes that kept him in office.

The younger Daley never had a situation like that. He succeeded a pair of African American mayors, came in with the city's black community highly suspicious of him, and faced a political environment in which unified black opposition might threaten his mayoralty at any time.

Richard M. Daley's ability to work in this environment stands as perhaps his single most impressive political attribute. He saw the changing demographics of the city, with Hispanics drawing closer to their current one-third of the population, and reasoned that with sufficient Hispanic support he would never have to worry about a black challenger. He offered patronage and political assistance to Hispanic community leaders, and soon converted himself into a majority mayor rather than a minority mayor fighting to hang on.

But Daley cultivated other constituencies that were not part of his father's world. Soon after taking office in 1989, he served as grand marshal of the annual gay and lesbian pride parade. "I think it is important," he said, "for me to show my support of the gay community." Daley's conspicuous environmentalism—symbolized by his successful determination to place a "green roof" on top of city hall, won over many of the "lakefront liberals" who had constituted the only organized political bloc that

had opposed his father. "Talk about a tree person!" Daley once boasted to reporters. "Right here! I'm a tree hugger."

The early years represented Daley at his innovative best. In addition to taking personal charge of the city's school system and promoting numerous teaching and management experiments—a bold and valuable move, if a less than triumphant one—the mayor reorganized the slothful and patronage-ridden Chicago Park District, kept finances in good shape, personally supervised construction of the wildly successful Millennium Park along the downtown lakefront, and launched a widely copied series of cultural initiatives with his energetic and creative cultural affairs commissioner, Lois Weisberg.

Daley also led the city into a wide range of experiments in privatization, taking numerous city services and facilities out of public management, a step his father would no doubt have disdained. Foremost among these moves was the decision to sell off the Chicago Skyway, a troubled eight-mile toll road, for $1.8 billion. But nearly every annual budget through the 1990s included the privatization of one government function or another.

When scandals emerged in the Chicago Housing Authority, resulting in the temporary transfer of the city's housing programs to the federal government, Daley responded with the "Plan for Transformation," which featured the privatization of all housing management as well as the demolition of fifty dysfunctional public housing towers and the construction of new low-rise mixed-income developments to replace them. By the early years of the new century, nearly all the infamous towers were down, although many of the new projects remained to be built.

Koeneman makes a distinction between the mayor's widely praised early terms and the later ones, in which he was more autocratic, more impulsive, and less attuned to management detail. Whatever one thinks of this thesis, it is undeniable that the last few years served to tarnish at least a little bit of Daley's legacy.

For one thing, there were clear signs that the old tradition of shady political dealings had not faded away completely. Patronage ran up to and beyond the level of cronyism. The most egregious example was the Hired Truck Program scandal, in which it was disclosed that the city, as Koeneman tells it, "spent $40 million a year to pay private trucking companies to do little or no work." Some of these companies were run by close political allies of Daley's, as was the program itself. "I am embarrassed," Daley said when the scandal broke. "I'm angry, and I'm disappointed because I feel I've let the people down."

Beyond the evidence of graft that came uncomfortably close to him, Daley suffered serious public policy setbacks in the closing years. An expensive and broadly supported bid to bring the 2016 Olympics to Chicago was shot down in embarrassing fashion by the International Olympic Committee. City finances gradually deteriorated, in part a result of the Great Recession but also a consequence, as Koeneman points out, of a still-bloated city workforce and extravagant public pension commitments. By 2009, Chicago was running a large deficit.

Perhaps worst of all, in the public's mind, was Daley's last big privatization venture, the decision to lease the city's 36,000 parking meters to a private company for seventy-five years in return for $1.2 billion. It was an effort to help with the financial problems, but it led to a dramatic increase in parking charges. An inspector general brought in to assess the situation concluded that Daley should have asked for at least a billion dollars more in payments, or else the city should have held on to the meters, raised rates, and kept all the money for itself.

Chronicling the series of late-career setbacks Daley suffered, Koeneman writes that the mayor "appeared more and more like a prize fighter past his prime, a once-great champion who had stayed in the ring for one fight too many." But when it comes to measuring the entire twenty-two years, Koeneman ends up, albeit a little nervously, on the positive side. "The passage of time," he says, "would likely lead to history's judgment that Daley's achievements had outweighed his mistakes." The volume as a whole bears that judgment out.

Critical Thinking

1. What were some of the disappointing ventures of Chicago Mayor Richard M. Daley during his 22 years in office?

2. What were some of his successes?

3. What did Mayor Daley do to convert himself from a minority mayor "fighting to hang on" into a majority mayor?

Create Central

www.mhhe.com/createcentral

Internet References

City of Chicago website
www.cityofchicago.org/city/en.html

Richard M. Daley (*New York Times* profile)
http://topics.nytimes.com/top/reference/timestopics/people/d/richard_m_daley

Article   Prepared by: Bruce Stinebrickner, *DePauw University*

The Millennials in the Mayor's Seat

Young leaders are injecting cities with a new energy.

DYLAN SCOTT

Learning Outcomes

After reading this article, you will be able to:

- Assess the pros and cons for a city of having a young mayor.
- Evaluate whether indivduals in their twenties would be suitable to be mayors of the biggest of U.S. cities such as New York, Chicago, and Los Angeles.

Just in front of City Hall in Ithaca, N.Y., the mayor has a reserved parking spot. Or at least he did. When then-24-year-old Svante Myrick took office in January 2012, he decided he didn't need it. During his four years as a student at Cornell University, Myrick had gotten used to traversing the city of 30,000 on his feet and via public transit. As an environmentally conscious member of Generation Y, he wanted to set an example. So Myrick authorized city workers to construct Ithaca's smallest public park where his parking space once stood. They laid down turf and erected a small bench. Some evenings, he will sit out there and conduct a sort of open forum, letting residents come up and share their thoughts or concerns. A few feet away stands a "Mayor's Mailbox" that Myrick has installed, a comment box for citizens to leave their praise and scorn for the city government.

These small touches are reminders that Ithaca's youngest and first African-American mayor (he's actually biracial) does things a little differently. When Myrick wants public input on a road project, he doesn't wait for the 6 p.m. Tuesday City Council meetings, where folks have to fill out a comment card and get their allotted three minutes to speak. He posts a status on the city's Facebook page—a page he started—and lets residents share their thoughts. His new style "still freaks people out a little bit," Myrick says. "They're used to getting feedback in a certain way and through a certain structure."

"People aren't used to having unfettered access to public officials," he says. "But unfettered access is kind of what my generation is all about."

Just like his approach to governance, little about Myrick's journey to the Ithaca mayor's office is traditional. He grew up in Earlville, about 70 miles to the east, the son of a single mom and the third of four children. His mom worked two jobs, cooking at a hospital and nursing home, while caring for her kids between double shifts. Perpetually short on money, the family moved in and out of rundown apartments and homeless shelters. When Myrick was 11 years old, he started his first business. He and a friend would walk around Earlville with a bucket of water, offering to wash strangers' windows, mow their lawns or trim their hedges.

He grows noticeably quieter when talking about his childhood and how it might have impacted how he approaches his job, but he acknowledges the influence is there. Some months as a kid, he would have to choose between going on a school field trip and buying a new pair of shoes. "When the money didn't match up, and it never matched up, it was like, 'OK, what are we going to do?'" Myrick says. "It does make you grow up a little faster, and it does prepare you for the hard decisions that you have to make in this job."

That level of maturity is part of what it takes to be a young, new mayor. And Myrick is one of several young mayors around the country who represent a changing of the guard in city hall, bringing a fresh perspective and new energy to public office.

You can see it in Pittsburgh, where residents might catch 32-year-old Mayor Luke Ravenstahl at a City Council meeting one night and then out with friends at a local watering hole the next. In Manitowoc, Wis., where 25-year-old Mayor Justin Nickels can't go out on a date without his server asking about a pothole on her street. In Holyoke, Mass., where 23-year-old Mayor Alex Morse commuted from class at Brown University during his campaign. Or in Duluth, Minn., where 38-year-old Mayor Don Ness keeps a drawer full of toys in his desk for his young children when they make a surprise visit to the office.

Being a young mayor comes with its own set of challenges. There's skepticism from friends and family—not to mention voters—about whether you're prepared to move from the college dorm to city hall. Once in office, younger mayors are eager to shake things up with fresh ideas and new ways of doing business, only to be confronted with the same old challenges of overburdened budgets, drowning pension systems and struggling schools. And these mayors are still learning to strike a balance between public service and the private life of someone in their mid-20s or 30s.

"With this new generation of elected officials, I think you have people who see the potential in public service to establish a new framework to how we approach these things, to be solution-minded and to bring a sense of optimism," says Duluth's Ness. "Oftentimes, we look at optimism as a source of weakness, but I actually see it completely differently. I think optimism is the fuel for a willingness to take on the big problems and to feel like we have a chance to actually solve those problems."

The first step in running for office as a young person is convincing somebody—anybody—that you can do it. That usually starts with family. In 2011, when Holyoke's Morse sat down with his extended family (his parents, grandparents, aunts, uncles—everyone) and told them he wanted to challenge Elaine Pluta, the 67-year-old incumbent mayor, they voiced their support. But Morse says he sensed a little skepticism. "I'm sure they thought, 'We'll support him, but I doubt he can unseat an incumbent mayor.' Even if they thought I was crazy, though, they weren't going to tell me that."

Then comes convincing everyone else that you're ready for the responsibilities of public office. "People would laugh," says Pittsburgh's Ravenstahl, who ran for City Council at age 23 in 2003 and even had the advantage of having a father who had been a local judge and a grandfather who had been a state legislator. "At least one person told me, 'Look, I have kids your age. The last thing I would ever do is put them in that seat.' There were days that were very discouraging."

But the mayors overcame others' skepticism by conveying long-term visions for their cities. "Experience is important for mayors, but it's really not as important as inspiration and leadership," says Stephen Goldsmith, professor of government at the Harvard Kennedy School and former mayor of Indianapolis (and a contributor to Governing.com). "A person will be successful as mayor if they're able to galvanize enthusiasm and support for public goals. So in that sense, a young mayor is as capable as somebody older in filling that role."

Many of these executives have already achieved significant successes. In Duluth, Ness was facing a structurally unbalanced budget and $290 million in unfunded retiree health-care benefits. So he offered his plan to resolve those legacy issues. "There were a lot of derogatory statements—that I just didn't get it, that these were promises written in granite," he says. "But I explained that we either had to have the courage to face this today or be faced with bankruptcy in the future." In his first few years as mayor, Ness cut the city's annual budget by more than 9 percent and implemented reforms, including increasing copays and deductibles, to retiree health benefits, changes he says will save Duluth $4 million annually. He won a court case in 2011 to go through with his plan.

Pittsburgh's Ravenstahl campaigned in part on a promise to improve public schools. For years, he had watched friends with young children move away or send their kids to private schools because of public education's poor reputation. Now he's organized Pittsburgh Promise, a public-private partnership that awards college scholarships of up to $40,000 to public students who finish high school. So far the project has given out some

$25 million to more than 3,000 students, and graduation rates are on the rise.

Alex Morse saw Holyoke, a former paper mill town now facing 11 percent unemployment, as a dying city. He pledged to remake its economy around art, innovation and technology. Last year, he oversaw the ribbon-cutting at the Massachusetts Green High Performance Computing Center, a state-of-the-art energy efficient computing facility, as a start down that path.

In Ithaca, Myrick has said he wants to create a more affordable, livable and sustainable city. That's already resulted in plans for a 60-unit mixed-income housing project, an $800,000 commercial street rebuild with sidewalks and bike lanes, reforms to the zoning code to encourage denser development and a $10 million downtown redevelopment program. "Mayor Myrick is wise beyond his years," says Stephen Philip Johnson, vice president of government and community relations at Cornell, an important constituency in a town-and-gown place like Ithaca. "He has been able to make the tough decisions that the reality of our economic times have required."

In addition to these kinds of successes in somewhat traditional areas—education, fiscal reform, downtown redevelopment— there's a definite shift in style among this cadre of young leaders. They're injecting their cities with a hipper, cooler vibe that many residents say is bringing new energy and new attitudes about public service. Before Don Ness became mayor, he ran the Homegrown Music Festival (billed as "Duluth's annual showcase of rawk and/or roll devil music"), and when the alt-rock band Wilco performed in Duluth last summer, Ness, a fan, gave the members keys to the city. Each of these mayors regularly speaks at local schools or colleges about their experiences and why a life of public service is worthwhile. Ravenstahl created the ServePBH initiative in Pittsburgh, aimed at getting youth to volunteer and improve their city. Morse was recently approached by a 19-year-old Holyoke resident who wants to run for City Council after seeing what Morse has done as mayor.

Youth can be a double-edged sword. Ness, who was first elected to the Duluth City Council in 1999 at age 25, remembers the strange looks he got when he walked into a local chamber of commerce meeting dressed in shorts and a T-shirt. But as soon as he started speaking, displaying intimate knowledge of the local economy and the state politics that would factor into their ability to get it going, the mood changed, he says. "I could feel the room turn. Folks had been playing wait-and-see, wondering, 'Is this kid going to bring any real value or is it just a sideshow?'"

Manitowoc's Nickels noticed similar doubts as he sat in on some of his first department meetings after taking office in 2009. Longtime city workers seemed to talk around him as if he weren't even there. "I could tell sometimes that I wasn't a part of their conversation," he says. "But I think people finally get it now. They accept that a 25-year-old can do a pretty darn good job."

And then there's trying to have a social life. Balancing the role of running a city and living the life of a single 20- or 30-something can be tricky. Morse (who is gay) says that the biggest drain on his social life is fellow bar patrons asking if they can take a picture with him and post it on Facebook. In Manitowoc, Nickels recalls being on a date with another young professional, with roses set at the table's center and candles lit, while half a dozen residents kept walking up and sharing their complaints about the city government. It can all be a little jarring, says Ithaca's Myrick. "I've tried to adapt—I'm usually more comfortable with it than the people who are unlucky enough to go out with me."

Sometimes the tug of war between political and personal life can have very real consequences. That's true for any public official, of course, but especially for those unaccustomed to the limelight. Less than a year after he became mayor, Ravenstahl was criticized for appearing at a celebrity golf invitational sponsored by some groups, including a university medical center, that have frequent dealings with the city. The same year, he caught flak for driving a publicly funded homeland security SUV to a country music concert. Some of that scrutiny was probably connected to his age, Ravenstahl says, but he also admits that he didn't fully understand the attention that comes with being mayor in those days. "I underestimated the lens that I was under," he says. "I've learned a lot, and I do approach things a lot differently than I did in the beginning."

Ravenstahl assumed office in 2006 when Mayor Bob O'Connor died and Ravenstahl was sitting council president— a promotion he was granted only because he was viewed, in his youth, as the least threatening candidate by other council members. Some dubbed him "The Accidental Mayor." The stress of the position took a toll on Ravenstahl's personal life. He and his wife, with whom he shares a 4-year-old son, separated in 2009, when Ravenstahl was 29. While Ravenstahl says he wouldn't go back and change his mind about seeking public office, he acknowledges that the divorce has been one of the toughest unintended consequences of his decision to become a public figure at such a young age. "The hardest thing for me is how this job impacts my family and those that didn't choose to have their name in the paper and be a public servant," he says. "It's something that I didn't foresee or expect."

In the years since he took office, Ravenstahl has grown into the position and become a stronger leader, says Pat Altdorfer, a political science professor at the University of Pittsburgh. "You play the hand you're dealt. From that perspective, he did step up," Altdorfer says. "Everyone's got a learning curve, and I would certainly say he's a better mayor today than he was when he first started."

The bottom line, these mayors say, is that they don't see their youth as the defining aspect of their leadership. Sure, they may be more connected on Facebook and Twitter than their predecessors were. And they may be more open to unconventional solutions and ideas, like Myrick's pocket park in his parking space. But being an effective city leader is the same regardless of age. "I ran not because I wanted to represent the youth," says Myrick, "but because I cared about this place."

Critical Thinking

1. What positive attributes might we expect young mayors to be able to bring to the job because of their age?

2. What challenges might young mayors be expected to face because of their age?

3. What particular social and personal costs or inconveniences might young mayors face because of their age?

Create Central

www.mhhe.com/createcentral

Internet References

City of Duluth, MN, website
www.duluthmn.gov

City of Holyoke, MA, website
www.holyoke.org

City of Ithaca, NY, website
www.ci.ithaca.ny.us

City of Pittsburgh, PA, website
www.pittsburghpa.gov

Article   Prepared by: Bruce Stinebrickner, *DePauw University*

Watching the Bench

Justice by Numbers

Mandatory sentencing drove me from the bench.

LOIS G. FORER

Learning Outcomes

After reading this article, you will be able to:

- Assess the pros and cons of mandatory sentencing.

- Weigh whether Judge Lois Forer's decision to resign was justified and whether it was likely to have beneficial effects for the judicial system.

ichael S. would have been one of the more than 600,000 incarcerated persons in the United States. He would have been a statistic, yet another addition to a clogged criminal justice system. But he's not—in part because to me Michael was a human being: a slight 24-year-old with a young wife and small daughter. Not that I freed him; I tried him and found him guilty. He is free now only because he is a fugitive. I have not seen him since the day of his sentencing in 1984, yet since that day our lives have been inextricably connected. Because of his case I retired from the bench.

Michael's case appeared routine. He was a typical offender: young, black, and male, a high-school dropout without a job. The charge was an insignificant holdup that occasioned no comment in the press. And the trial itself was, in the busy life of a judge, a run-of-the-mill event.

The year before, Michael, brandishing a toy gun, held up a taxi and took $50 from the driver and the passenger, harming neither. This was Michael's first offense. Although he had dropped out of school to marry his pregnant girlfriend, Michael later obtained a high school equivalency diploma. He had been steadily employed, earning enough to send his daughter to parochial school—a considerable sacrifice for him and his wife. Shortly before the holdup, Michael had lost his job. Despondent because he could not support his family, he went out on a Saturday night, had more than a few drinks, and then robbed the taxi.

There was no doubt that Michael was guilty. But the penalty posed problems. To me, a robbery in a taxi is not an intrinsically graver offense than a robbery in an alley, but to the Pennsylvania legislature, it is. Because the holdup occurred on public transportation, it fell within the ambit of the state's mandatory sentencing law—which required a minimum sentence of five years in the state penitentiary. In Pennsylvania, a prosecutor may decide not to demand imposition of that law, but Michael's prosecuting attorney wanted the five-year sentence.

One might argue that a five-year sentence for a $50 robbery is excessive or even immoral, but to a judge, those arguments are necessarily irrelevant. He or she has agreed to enforce the law, no matter how ill-advised, unless the law is unconstitutional.

I believed the mandatory sentencing law was, and like many of my colleagues I had held it unconstitutional in several other cases for several reasons. We agreed that it violates the constitutional principle of separation of powers because it can be invoked by the prosecutor, and not by the judge. In addition, the act is arbitrary and capricious in its application. Robbery, which is often a simple purse snatching, is covered, but not child molestation or incest, two of society's most damaging offenses. Nor can a defendant's previous record or mental state be considered. A hardened repeat offender receives the same sentence as a retarded man who steals out of hunger. Those facts violate the fundamental Anglo-American legal principles of individualized sentencing and proportionality of the penalty to the crime.

Thus in Michael's case, I again held the statute to be unconstitutional and turned to the sentencing guidelines—a state statute designed to give uniform sentences to offenders who commit similar crimes. The minimum sentence prescribed by the guidelines was 24 months.

A judge can deviate from the prescribed sentence if he or she writes an opinion explaining the reasons for the deviation. While this sounds reasonable in theory, "downwardly departing" from the guidelines is extremely difficult. The mitigating circumstances that influence most judges are not included in the limited list of factors on which "presumptive" sentence is based—that an offender is a caretaker of small children; that the offender is mentally retarded; or that the offender, like Michael, is emotionally distraught.

So I decided to deviate from the guidelines, sentencing Michael to 11-and-a-half months in the county jail and permitting him to work outside the prison during the day to support his family. I also imposed a sentence of two years' probation following his imprisonment conditioned upon repayment of the $50. My rationale for the lesser penalty, outlined in my lengthy opinion, was that this was a first offense, no one was harmed, Michael acted under the pressures of unemployment and need, and he seemed truly contrite. He had never committed a violent act and posed no danger to the public. A sentence of close to a year seemed adequate to convince Michael of the seriousness of his crime. Nevertheless, the prosecutor appealed.

Michael returned to his family, obtained steady employment, and repaid the victims of his crime. I thought no more about Michael until 1986, when the state supreme court upheld the appeal and ordered me to resentence him to a minimum of five years in the state penitentiary. By this time Michael had successfully completed his term of imprisonment and probation, including payment of restitution. I checked Michael's record. He had not been rearrested.

I was faced with a legal and moral dilemma. As a judge I had sworn to uphold the law, and I could find no legal grounds for violating an order of the supreme court. Yet five years' imprisonment was grossly disproportionate to the offense. The usual grounds for imprisonment are retribution, deterrence, and rehabilitation. Michael had paid his retribution by a short term of imprisonment and by making restitution to the victims. He had been effectively deterred from committing future crimes. And by any measurable standard he had been rehabilitated. There was no social or criminological justification for sending him back to prison. Given the choice between defying a court order or my conscience, I decided to leave the bench where I had sat for 16 years.

That didn't help Michael, of course; he was resentenced by another judge to serve the balance of the five years: four years and 15 days. Faced with this prospect, he disappeared. A bench warrant was issued, but given the hundreds of fugitives—including dangerous ones—loose in Philadelphia, I doubt that anyone is seriously looking for him.

But any day he may be stopped for a routine traffic violation; he may apply for a job or a license; he may even be the victim of a crime—and if so, the ubiquitous computer will be alerted and he will be returned to prison to serve the balance of his sentence, plus additional time for being a fugitive. It is not a happy prospect for him and his family—nor for America, which is saddled with a punishment system that operates like a computer—crime in, points tallied, sentence out—utterly disregarding the differences among the human beings involved.

The mandatory sentencing laws and guidelines that exist today in every state were designed to smooth out the inequities in the American judiciary, and were couched in terms of fairness to criminals—they would stop the racist judge from sentencing black robbers to be hanged, or the crusading judge from imprisoning pot smokers for life. Guidelines make sense, for that very reason. But they have had an ugly and unintended result—an increase in the number of American prisoners and an increase in the length of the sentences they serve. Meanwhile, the laws have effectively neutralized judges who prefer sentencing the nonviolent to alternative programs or attempt to keep mothers with young children out of jail.

Have the laws made justice fairer—the central objective of the law? I say no, and a recent report by the Federal Sentencing Commission concurs. It found that, even under mandatory sentencing laws, black males served 83.4 months to white males' 53.7 months for the same offenses. (Prosecutors are more likely to demand imposition of the mandatory laws for blacks than for whites.)

Most important, however, as mandatory sentencing packs our prisons and busts our budgets, it doesn't prevent crime very effectively. For certain kinds of criminals, alternative sentencing is the most effective type of punishment. That, by the way, is a cold, hard statistic—rather like Michael will be when they find him.

Sentenced to Death

In the past two decades, all 50 state legislatures have enacted mandatory sentencing laws, sentencing guideline statutes, or both. The result: In 1975 there were 263,291 inmates in federal and state prisons. Today there are over 600,000—more than in any other nation—the bill for which comes to $20.3 billion a year. Yet incarceration has not reduced the crime rate or made our streets and communities safer. The number of known crimes committed in the U.S. has increased 10 percent in the last five years.

How did we get into this no-win situation? Like most legislative reforms, it started with good intentions. In 1970, after the turmoil of the sixties, legislators were bombarded with pleas for "law and order." A young, eager, newly appointed federal judge, Marvin Frankel, had an idea.

Before his appointment, Frankel had experienced little personal contact with the criminal justice system. Yet his slim book, *Fair and Certain Punishment,* offered a system of guidelines to determine the length of various sentences. Each crime was given a certain number of points. The offender was also given a number of points depending upon his or her prior record, use of a weapon, and a few other variables. The judge merely needed to add up the points to calculate the length of imprisonment.

The book was widely read and lauded for two main reasons. First, it got tough on criminals and made justice "certain." A potential offender would know in advance the penalty he would face and thus be deterred. (Of course, a large proportion of street crimes are not premeditated, but that fact was ignored.) And second, it got tough on the "bleeding heart" judges. All offenders similarly situated would be treated the same.

The plan sounded so fair and politically promising that many states rushed to implement it in the seventies. In Pennsylvania, members of the legislature admonished judges not to oppose the guidelines because the alternative would be even worse: mandatory sentences. In fact, within a few years almost every jurisdiction had both sentencing guidelines and mandatory sentencing laws. Since then, Congress has enacted some 60 mandatory sentencing laws on the federal level.

As for unfairnesses in sentencing—for instance, the fact that the robber with his finger in his jacket gets the same sentence as the guy with a semiautomatic—these could have been rectified by giving appellate courts jurisdiction to review sentences, as is the law in Canada. This was not done on either the state or federal level. Thus what influential criminologist James Q. Wilson had argued during the height of the battle had become the law of the land: The legal system should "most definitely stop pretending that the judges know any better than the rest of us how to provide 'individualized justice.' "

Hardening Time

I'm not sure I knew better than the rest of you, but I knew a few things about Michael and the correctional system I would be throwing him into. At the time of Michael's sentencing, both the city of Philadelphia and the commonwealth of Pennsylvania were, like many cities and states, in such poor fiscal shape that they did not have money for schools and health care, let alone new prisons, and the ones they did have were overflowing. The city was under a federal order to reduce the prison population; untried persons accused of dangerous crimes were being released, as were offenders who had not completed their sentences.

As for Michael, his problems and those of his family were very real to me. Unlike appellate judges who never see the individuals whose lives and property they dispose of, a trial judge sees living men and women. I had seen Michael and his wife and daughter. I had heard him express remorse. I had favorable reports about him from the prison and his parole officer. Moreover, Michael, like many offenders who appeared before me, had written to me several times. I felt I knew him.

Of course, I could have been wrong. As Wilson says, judges are not infallible—and most of them know that. But they have heard the evidence, seen the offender, and been furnished with presentence reports and psychiatric evaluations. They are in a better position to evaluate the individual and devise an appropriate sentence than anyone else in the criminal justice system.

Yet under mandatory sentencing laws, the complexities of each crime and criminal are ignored. And seldom do we ask what was once a legitimate question in criminal justice: What are the benefits of incarceration? The offenders are off the streets for the period of the sentence, but once released, most will soon be rearrested. (Many crimes are committed in prison, including murder, rape, robbery, and drug dealing.) They have not been "incapacitated," another of the theoretical justifications for imprisonment. More likely, they have simply been hardened.

Sentence Structure

Is there another way to sentence criminals without endangering the public? I believe there is. During my tenure on the bench, I treated imprisonment as the penalty of last resort, not the penalty of choice. And my examination of 16 years' worth of cases suggests my inclination was well founded. While a recent Justice Department study found that two thirds of all prisoners are arrested for other offenses within three years of release, more than two thirds of the 1,000-plus offenders I sentenced to probation conditioned upon payment of reparations to victims successfully completed their sentences and were not rearrested. I am not a statistician, so I had my records analyzed and verified by Elmer Weitekamp, then a doctoral candidate in criminology at the Wharton School of the University of Pennsylvania. He confirmed my findings.

The offenders who appeared before me were mostly poor people, poor enough to qualify for representation by a public defender. I did not see any Ivan Boeskys or Leona Helmsleys, and although there was a powerful mafia in Philadelphia, I did not see any dons, either. Approximately three fourths of these defendants were nonwhite. Almost 80 percent were high school dropouts. Many were functionally illiterate. Almost a third had some history of mental problems, were retarded, or had been in special schools. One dreary day my court reporter said plaintively, "Judge, why can't we get a better class of criminal?"

Not all of these offenders were sentenced to probation, obviously. But I had my own criteria or guidelines—very different from those established by most states and the federal government—for deciding on a punishment. My primary concern was public safety. The most important question I asked myself was whether the offender could be deterred from committing other crimes. No one can predict with certainty who will or will not commit a crime, but there are indicators most sensible people recognize as danger signals.

First, was this an irrational crime? If an arsonist sets a fire to collect insurance, that is a crime but also a rational act. Such a person can be deterred by being made to pay for the harm done and the costs to the fire department. However, if the arsonist sets fires just because he likes to see them, it is highly unlikely that he can be stopped from setting others, no matter how high the fine. Imprisonment is advisable even though it may be a first offense.

Second, was there wanton cruelty? If a robber maims or slashes the victim, there is little likelihood that he can safely be left in the community. If a robber simply displays a gun but does not fire it or harm the victim, then one should consider his life history, provocation, and other circumstances in deciding whether probation is appropriate.

Third, is this a hostile person? Was his crime one of hatred, and does he show any genuine remorse? Most rapes are acts of hostility, and the vast majority of rapists have a record of numerous sexual assaults. I remember one man who raped his mother. I gave him the maximum sentence under the law—20 years—but with good behavior, he got out fairly quickly. He immediately raped another elderly woman. Clearly, few rapists can safely be left in the community, and in my tenure, I incarcerated every one.

Yet gang rape, although a brutal and horrifying crime, is more complicated. The leader is clearly hostile and should be punished severely. Yet the followers can't be so neatly categorized. Some may act largely out of cowardice and peer pressure.

Fourth, is this a person who knows he is doing wrong but cannot control himself? Typical of such offenders are pedophiles. One child abuser who appeared before me had already been convicted of abusing his first wife's child. I got him on the second wife's child and sentenced him to the maximum. Still, he'll get out with good behavior, and I shudder to think about the children around him when he does. This is one case in which justice is not tough enough.

By contrast, some people who have committed homicide present very little danger of further violence—although many more do. Once a young man came before me because he had taken aim at a person half a block away and then shot him in the back, killing him. Why did he do it? "I wanted to get me a body." He should never get out. But the mandatory codes don't make great distinctions between him and another murderer who came before me, a woman who shot and killed a boy after he and his friends brutally gang-raped her teenage daughter.

I found this woman guilty of first-degree murder, but I found no reason to incarcerate her. She had four young children to support who would have become wards of the welfare department and probably would have spent their childhoods in a series of foster homes. I placed her on probation—a decision few judges now have the discretion to impose. She had not been arrested before. She has not been arrested since.

Of course, the vast majority of men, women, and children in custody in the United States are not killers, rapists, or arsonists. They're in prison for some type of theft—a purse snatching, burglary, or embezzlement. Many of these criminals can be punished without incarceration. If you force a first-time white-collar criminal to pay heavily for his crimes—perhaps three times the value of the money or property taken—he'll get the message that crime does not pay. As for poor people, stealing is not always a sign that the individual is an unreasonable risk to the community. It's often a sign that they want something—a car, Air Jordans—that they are too poor to buy themselves. Many of them, if they are not violent, can also be made to make some restitution and learn that crime doesn't pay.

Of course, to most of us, the idea of a nonprison sentence is tantamount to exoneration; a criminal sentenced to probation has effectively "gotten off." And there's a reason for that impression: Unless the probationer is required by the sentencing judge to perform specific tasks, probation is a charade. The probationer meets with the probation officer, briefly, perhaps once a month—making the procedure a waste of time for both. The officer duly records the meeting and the two go their separate ways until the probationer is arrested for another offense.

When I made the decision not to send a criminal to prison, I wanted to make sure that the probation system I sent them into had teeth. So I set firm conditions. If the offender was functionally illiterate, he was unemployable and would probably steal or engage in some other illegal activity once released. Thus in my sentencing, I sent him to school and ordered the probation officer to see that he went. (I use the masculine pronoun deliberately for I have never seen an illiterate female offender under the age of 60). I ordered school dropouts to get their high school equivalency certificates and find jobs. All offenders were ordered to pay restitution or reparations within their means or earning capacity to their victims. Sometimes it was as little as $5 a week. Offenders simply could not return to their old, feckless lifestyles without paying some financial penalty for their wrongdoing.

Monitoring probation wasn't easy for me, or the probation officers with whom I worked. Every day I'd come into my office, look at my calendar, and notice that, say, 30 days had passed since Elliott was let out. So I'd call the probation office. Has Elliott made his payment? Is he going to his GED class? And so on. If the answer was no, I'd hold a violation hearing with the threat of incarceration if the conditions were not met within 30 days. After I returned a few people to jail for noncompliance, both my offenders and their probation officers knew I meant business. (Few probation officers protested my demands; their jobs were more meaningful and satisfying, they said.)

Of course, probation that required education and work and payment plans meant real work for criminals, too. But there was a payoff both the probation officers and I could see: As offenders worked and learned and made restitution, their attitudes often changed dramatically.

Time and Punishment

My rules of sentencing don't make judgeship easier; relying on mandatory sentencing is a far better way to guarantee a leisurely, controversy-free career on the bench. But my rules are, I believe, both effective and transferable: an application of common sense that any reasonable person could follow to similar ends. What prevents Americans from adopting practical measures like these is a atavistic belief in the sanctity of punishment. Even persons who have never heard of Immanuel Kant or the categorical imperative to punish believe that violation of law must be followed by the infliction of pain.

If we Americans treated crime more practically—as socially unacceptable behavior that should be curbed for the good of the community—we might begin to take a rational approach to the development of alternatives to prison. We might start thinking in terms not of punishment but of public safety, deterrence, and rehabilitation. Penalties like fines, work, and payment of restitution protect the public better and more cheaply than imprisonment in many cases.

Mind you, sentencing guidelines are not inherently evil. Intelligent guidelines would keep some judges from returning repeat offenders to the streets and others from putting the occasional cocaine user away for 10 years. Yet those guidelines must allow more latitude for the judge and the person who comes before him. While some states' sentencing laws include provisions that allow judges to override the mandatory sentences in some cases, the laws are for the most part inflexible—they deny judges the freedom to discriminate between the hardened criminal and the Michael. Richard H. Girgenti, the criminal justice director of New York state, has long proposed that the legislature give judges more discretion to impose shorter sentences for nonviolent and noncoercive felonies. This common-sense proposal has not been acted on in New York or any other state with mandatory sentencing laws.

Current laws are predicated on the belief that there must be punishment for every offense in terms of prison time rather than alternative sentences. But when it comes to determining the fate of a human being, there must be room for judgment. To make that room, we must stop acting as if mathematic calculations are superior to human thought. We must abolish mandatory sentencing laws and change the criteria on which sentencing guidelines are based.

Why not permit judges more freedom in making their decisions, provided that they give legitimate reasons? (If a judge doesn't have a good reason for deviating—if he's a reactionary or a fool—his sentencing decision will be overturned.) And why not revise the guidelines to consider dangerousness rather than the nomenclature of the offense? If we made simple reforms like these, thousands of non-threatening, nonhabitual offenders would be allowed to recompense their victims and society in a far less expensive and far more productive way.

You may be wondering, after all this, if I have a Willie Horton in my closet—a criminal whose actions after release privately haunt me. I do. I sentenced him to 10 to 20 years in prison—the maximum the law allowed—for forcible rape. He was released after eight years and promptly raped another woman. I could foresee what would happen but was powerless to impose a longer sentence.

And then there are the other cases that keep me up nights: those of men and women I might have let out, but didn't. And those of people like Michael, for whom justice shouldn't have been a mathematical equation.

Critical Thinking

1. What is mandatory sentencing?
2. What led Judge Lois Forer to resign from her judicial post in Philadelphia?
3. Why, according to Lois Forer, was the book *Fair and Certain Punishment* so influential in fostering mandatory sentencing laws?
4. To what four main indicators did Judge Forer pay attention when deciding on an appropriate punishment for someone convicted of a crime?
5. What steps did Judge Forer take to monitor probation for those convicted in her court?

Create Central

www.mhhe.com/createcentral

Internet References

Families Against Mandatory Minimums (FAMM)
www.FAMM.org

Judge Lois Forer obituary (*Philadelphia Inquirer*)
http://articles.philly.com/1994-05-10/news/25826546_1_juvenile-rights-wrong-number-young-man

LOIS G. FORER, a former judge of the Court of Common Pleas of Philadelphia, is the author, most recently, of *Unequal Protection: Women, Children, and the Elderly in Court*.

Article   Prepared by: Bruce Stinebrickner, *DePauw University*

Under the Gaydar

How gays won the right to raise children without conservatives even noticing.

ALISON GASH

Learning Outcomes

After reading this article, you will be able to:

- Assess the "best interests of the child" standard in the context of granting custody of children to gay and lesbian parents and allowing gays and lesbians to adopt.

- Determine the persuasiveness of Alison Gash's argument in which she explains why same-sex marriage has been so much more prominent and controversial than gays and lesbians' right to raise children.

No one knows for sure how the Supreme Court will rule on the two high-profile gay marriage cases it is now considering. The betting, however, is that, regardless of the outcome, progress toward marriage equality will persist. A majority of the public now believe gays and lesbians should have the right to wed. Nine states and the District of Columbia have laws on the books conferring such rights. A stampede of Democratic elected officials have announced support for same-sex marriage, and in its March "autopsy" report the Republican National Committee hinted its members should do the same.

Although progress has been unusually swift, this story of same-sex marriage rights has followed a familiar path, one blazed by women and African Americans in their struggles for equality. Members of an out-group, advocating for their rights, demand a fundamental change in the legal interpretation of the Constitution, which causes a series of high-profile court cases, state and federal laws and counter-laws, and all of it accompanied by a broadly held national conversation that leads to a change in public attitudes, laws and legal interpretations.

But this isn't the only way that civil rights advance. A few decades ago, openly gay and lesbian Americans did not have the legal right to raise their own biological children, much less adopt. Today, more than 25 states recognize the same legal benefits and responsibilities of parenthood regardless of sexual orientation. It is now routine for gays and lesbians to jointly adopt, to be recognized as co-parents, and to collect child support or demand custody or visitation rights—even without a biological connection to the child in question. All this has happened

without the hallmarks of a traditional rights campaign. There were very few high-profile court cases, few legislative battles, and little public debate. In sharp contrast to marriage equality—where between 1993 and 2003 two pro-marriage rulings incited over 35 state bans—parenting litigation has provoked minimal public backlash.

At first blush, this would seem unlikely. Gay marriage, after all, is between consenting adults, whereas gay adoption involves children; one would think society would be at least as skittish about the latter as about the former. Even countries that pioneered marriage equality, such at Denmark, have been slower to extend full parenting rights to same-sex couples. And yet, paradoxically, in the United States we've seen the opposite: we've had a contentious, two-decades-long national debate about same-sex marriage—one that has repeatedly featured in battles for the presidency—but have allowed same-sex couples to quietly begin legally adopting and co-parenting with hardly any national discussion at all. Why the difference?

The answer is that same-sex parenting rights have successfully advanced precisely because the legal wrangling over them has remained largely below the radar—a fact highlighted by Justice Antonin Scalia's confusion about whether California even permits same-sex adoption during Supreme Court hearings on that state's Proposition 8 law. Where marriage-equality advocates had little choice but to engage in open political battles and bring high-profile constitutional court cases on behalf of their fundamental rights, the fight for same-sex parental rights has mostly played out in obscure family courts, with few reporters present, and with advocates consciously delaying or avoiding high court review. This below-the-radar strategy created a foundation of "facts on the ground"—tens of thousands of intact gay- and lesbian-headed families with children—well before most conservative activists were even aware the phenomenon existed, making their subsequent efforts to block same-sex parenting an uphill fight.

The legal struggle over same-sex parenting began in the 1950s and '60s. As divorce laws loosened, a growing number of closeted gays and lesbians came out to their heterosexual spouses, leading to legal disputes about custody and visitation rights over the couples' children. These cases were handled in local family courts, where records tend to be sealed. Few were ever covered in the newspapers. Fewer still resulted in victories for the gay spouses. Judges typically ruled that simply being homosexual made a parent unfit.

In one such case, in 1967, a lesbian woman named Ellen Doreen Nadler lost custody of her daughter to the child's heterosexual father. Nadler petitioned the California appellate court, which found that the previous court was wrong to base its decision solely on Nadler's homosexuality. Instead, the court wrote, the "primary consideration must be given to the welfare of the child." In a retrial, Nadler still didn't regain custody of her daughter, but the case set a key precedent: in custody cases, "the best interests of the child," a legal doctrine dating back to the mid-1800s, and not the sexual orientation of the parent, should be the deciding factor.

That precedent proved decisive in 1973, when an Oregon court ruled in favor of a gay father when the mother—who had not seen her children in over ten years—challenged custody because of the father's sexual orientation. The court determined that it was not necessarily in the "best interests of the child" to alter the custody arrangement, despite the father's homosexuality. Similarly, in two companion cases in 1978, the Washington Supreme Court ruled that withdrawing custody from two lesbian mothers who were raising children together from both of their previous marriages, would not serve the children's best interests. Although the court expressed some trepidation about the mothers' relationship, it determined that a change in custody would be more harmful to the children than maintaining the status quo.

While ground-breaking in many ways, these unorthodox rulings attracted little public interest, largely because they were focused on the particulars of the cases and not framed in terms of broader homosexual rights. This was in sharp contrast to the budding gay rights movement, which at that time was starting to push for statutory changes in the law. In 1977, for instance, gay rights activists convinced Miami-Dade County to amend its anti-discrimination ordinance to include gays and lesbians. In response, an anti-gay rights coalition called Save Our Children, was formed, with country singer and Florida orange juice spokeswoman Anita Bryant as its leader. "As a mother, I know that homosexuals cannot biologically reproduce children," she proclaimed, "therefore, they must recruit our children." Yet despite her rhetoric and the group's name, Bryant and her allies didn't focus on gay parenting. Instead they went after higher-profile anti-discrimination ordinances that included sexual orientation and, in some instances, tried to remove gay and lesbian teachers from public schools. The Florida legislature did subsequently pass a law barring single gays and lesbians, as well as same-sex couples, from adopting children, but only one other state, New Hampshire, followed suit.

In the 1980s, the same-sex parenting movement continued to move quietly forward. Family courts began to see cases where gay and lesbian couples with children were petitioning for parental rights for the non-biological partner. Because these "other" parents were essentially legal strangers to the children they were raising, they were often barred from engaging in the most routine—and important—parenting functions: picking up their kids at school, visiting them in the hospital, or listing them as dependents on health or life insurance policies. During that decade, family or lower courts in Oregon, Alaska, California, and Washington granted co-parent adoptions to same sex couples, with relatively little reaction from gay rights opponents.

Again, the secret to this progress was that gay parents and couples—who were by now aided by newly formed gay rights advocacy groups—fought these cases in family court, where judges had wide discretion and public scrutiny was minimal. Aware of the perils of drawing public attention to these cases, advocates from national gay rights groups worked hard to camouflage their efforts. They removed their names from briefs, provided behind-the-scenes support, and avoided appealing losses to appellate courts, out of fear that higher-level court approval would awaken the sleeping giant of public opposition.

Some even developed strategies to educate judges who were likely to hear same-sex parenting cases through seminars and bench books. They quietly met with judges to reassure them that their rulings would not be politicized. Says one advocate, "You have to take steps to keep it under the radar. I make sure to tell these judges that this is not a test case. We are not going to put you on the spot. I appreciate that you are an elected judge and I am not going to do something that will hurt you."

Eventually, same-sex parenting cases did make their way to higher courts in two states—ironically, in the same year, 1993, that gay marriage hit the supreme court docket in Hawaii (the case that launched a nationwide debate). But rather than rally opposition to both issues, conservatives chose to focus their attention only on same-sex marriage. Why?

For one, the co-parenting cases received relatively little attention from the mainstream press—again, because they were not being argued as matters of "gay rights." Also, many pro-family activists also assumed, or at least hoped, that anti-marriage efforts would limit both gay marriage and parenting progress. They theorized that same-sex marriage bans would, like anti-sodomy statutes, impose a chilling effect on judges. So while conservatives were busy getting the 1996 Defense of Marriage Act through Congress and initiating state-level bans on same-sex marriage, gay parents and their advocates continued to quietly amass significant court victories in Delaware, the District of Columbia, Illinois, Indiana, Maryland, Massachusetts, New Jersey, New York, Pennsylvania, and Vermont.

Meanwhile, by the end of 2004, anti–gay rights forces had won measures banning gay marriage in forty states. Hoping to leverage these gains, pro-family advocates finally turned their attention to parenting. Between 2004 and 2006 the pro-family movement initiated more than thirty-five attempts to limit same-sex parenting. In 2006, alone, sixteen states were poised to initiate bans on same-sex parenting legislatively or through the ballot process.

But—happily, for gay rights advocates—the anti-gay forces were too late. Despite dire predictions, almost none of these measures against same-sex parenting went anywhere. Legislation died in committee and proposed initiatives never made it to the ballot. All the while—on the strength of decades of precedents and facts on the ground—family, appellate, and state supreme courts continued "to recognize the parental rights of and grant adoptions to gay and lesbian parents."

Why did the backlash against same-sex parenting fail? It certainly wasn't public opinion. The handful of polls from 2006 that questioned participants about both same-sex marriage and adoption rights showed that average Americans were no more comfortable with gay parenthood than with gay marriage. In fact, they opposed both by well over 50 percent. And if we take their arguments seriously, it is precisely concern about gay parenthood that drives opposition efforts against marriage equality.

Rather, the main problem for conservatives was that they were trying to roll back gay parenting rights that had, in effect, already been granted. This proved a tough sell. The media didn't much cover the conservative campaign against same-sex parenting, and what few stories did run typically featured heartwarming narratives of gay and lesbian couples raising well-adjusted kids. Such families existed in the thousands precisely because the under-the-radar strategy had allowed them to flourish over the previous twenty years. Whereas gay marriage was still an abstraction that opponents could rally the public to prevent, gay families were a reality that the public would have to tear asunder to stop.

Also, by the mid-2000s social scientists had conducted studies on same-sex families. In general, this research demonstrated that children of same-sex couples were not appreciably different from kids raised by straight couples—including their propensity to identify as gay or lesbian. These studies were widely quoted in the media and used to foster support among child welfare experts.

All this made it a tough fight for anti-gay advocates. As an official at Focus on Family, a conservative Christian advocacy group, concedes, the issue was low on the "radar for pro-family conservatives" because of the "confusing rhetoric of same-sex adoption, the media bombarding the public with images of happy gay couples taking in disadvantaged kids," and the argument that "this kind of family is better than no family." Adds another opponent, "Trying to take the kids away . . . it's a ridiculous battle to fight."

That doesn't mean the fight is completely over. Taking a page from the playbook of parenting advocates, opponents of gay parenting have begun engaging at the level of family courts as well. They are now advocating on behalf of gay biological parents who are in custody battles with their estranged gay partners who are not the children's biological parents. Still, apart from such skirmishes, the right of same-sex parents to raise their kids seems well on its way to being secured.

Same-sex parenting advocates weren't the first to use an under-the-radar strategy to advance their cause, and probably won't be the last. John F. Kennedy employed low-visibility tactics to both attract black voters during his presidential campaign and to encourage voter registration after he was elected. Some disability advocates, in their attempt to secure group housing for their disabled clients, circumvent public notification procedures when looking for appropriate housing and instead procure the property, move the clients in, and wait to be discovered. And groups like the Nature Conservancy long ago figured out that instead of engaging in contentious public campaigns to get elected officials to do protect environmentally sensitive parcels of land, it is often easier to raise money and quietly buy the land themselves.

History books suggest that our society has made its greatest leaps on the shoulders of high-profile campaigns. But change can also be the result of quiet battles that play out in courtrooms, boardrooms and bedrooms all across the country. And it is often these hidden battles that most effectively propel our society forward.

Critical Thinking

1. How did the "best interests of the child" standard figure into state court decisions to grant custody of children to gay and lesbian parents in the 1970s?

2. Why did early state court rulings granting custody of children to gay and lesbian parents, including allowing them to adopt children, attract little public interest?

3. Why did backlash against gay and lesbian parenting fail in the early twenty-first century?

Create Central

www.mhhe.com/createcentral

Internet References

American Psychological Association: Sexual Orientation, Parents, and Children
www.apa.org/about/policy/parenting.aspx

Focus on the Family: Adoption (Cause for Concern)
www.focusonthefamily.com/socialissues/social-issues/adoption/cause-for-concern.aspx

Independent Adoption Center: LGBTQ Adoption
www.adoptionhelp.org/lgbtq-adoption

ALISON GASH is an assistant professor of political science at the University of Oregon. She is completing a manuscript entitled *Below the Radar: How Silence Can Save Civil Rights,* which will be published in 2014.

Gash, Alison. From *Washington Monthly*, May/June 2013, pp. 23–26. Copyright © 2013 by Washington Monthly Publishing, LLC, 1319 F St. NW, Suite 710, Washington, DC 20004. (202) 393-5155. Reprinted by permission. www.washingtonmonthly.com

Unit 5

UNIT

Prepared by: Bruce Stinebrickner, *DePauw University*

Cities and Suburbs, Counties and Towns

More than three-quarters of Americans live in cities or in surrounding suburban areas. In these densely populated settings, local governments face great challenges and opportunities. One challenge is to provide services such as policing, schooling, sanitation, water, roads, and public transportation at a satisfactory level and at a cost that taxpayers can and will bear. An accompanying opportunity is the possibility of helping to create a local setting that improves the lives of residents in meaningful ways. The challenges and opportunities arise amid a formidable array of urban and suburban problems: crime, violence, drugs, deterioration of public schools, racial tension, financial stringencies, pollution, congestion, aging populations, decaying physical plants, breakdown of family life, and so forth.

Cities are the local government jurisdictions that usually govern areas with relatively high population density. Major metropolitan areas usually have a large city at their center and a surrounding network of suburbs under a number of smaller local government jurisdictions. In smaller metropolitan areas, a single county can encompass both the center city and its surrounding suburbs. Smaller cities can be part of suburban rings around larger cities, or they can exist independently of major metropolitan areas, with their own smaller network of surrounding suburbs.

Cities of all sizes generally provide more services to their residents than other kinds of local government jurisdictions do. Residents of cities expect their city governments to provide water, a sewerage system, professional police and firefighting forces, public museums, parks and other such recreational facilities, and sometimes other services such as public transportation that are associated with city life. By contrast, local governments in rural areas are not expected to provide such services. Local governments in suburban areas typically provide some but not all of them. With the greater range of services provided in cities come higher taxes and more government regulatory activities.

Like urban areas, suburbs come in various shapes and sizes. Some are called bedroom or commuter suburbs because people live there with their families and commute to and from the central city to work. Others have a more independent economic base. Local governments in suburbs have often emphasized quality education (i.e., good schools), zoning plans to preserve the residential character of the locale, and keeping property taxes within tolerable limits. Generally speaking, suburbs have a greater proportion of whites and upper- and middle-class people than cities do.

One problem facing suburban governments today stems from aging populations. Older people need and demand different services than the young families that used to occupy suburbs in greater proportions. It is not always easy to shift policy priorities from, for example, public schooling to public transportation and recreational programs for the elderly. A second problem is structural in nature and relates to the overlapping and usually noncontiguous local government jurisdictions in suburban areas—school districts, sanitation districts, townships, counties, villages, boroughs, and so forth. The maze of jurisdictions often confuses citizens and sometimes makes coordinated and effective government difficult.

The goals of small suburban local governments, one or more counties, and the central city government in a single metropolitan area often come into conflict in policy areas such as public transportation, school integration, air pollution, highway systems, and so forth. Sometimes common aims can be pursued through county government, through cooperative ventures between suburban and city governments, or through creation of metropolitan-wide special districts. Sometimes, through annexation or consolidation, a larger unit of general-purpose local government is formed in an attempt to cope with metropolitan-wide issues more easily.

The New England town meeting is a remarkable institution that dates back to the earliest local governments in what are now the six New England states. Today town meetings seem feasible only outside major cities. In many rural, semirural, and suburban areas of New England, local government centered on annual town meetings remains the norm. In such traditional New England towns, policymaking or legislative authority is vested in an annual meeting in which every registered voter in the town is entitled to participate. The contrast between this traditional form of participatory local government and, for example, the government of the City of New York and its eight million citizens helps illustrates the diversity of local government structures in the United States.

Article   Prepared by: Bruce Stinebrickner, *DePauw University*

Merger Inertia

Despite strained finances, there's been no significant shift toward consolidation in recent years.

MIKE MACIAG

Learning Outcomes

After reading this article, you will be able to:

- Assess the pros and cons of the fragmentation and multiplicity of local governments in the United States.

- Evaluate the reasons why local government consolidation or mergers are relatively infrequent.

- Determine how your state and neighboring states rank in "governments per capita."

Hundreds of jurisdictional boundaries weave through the rolling hills and rivers that make up Pittsburgh and its surrounding suburbs. The region is carved into numerous neighborhoods, each with its own identity. But what makes the area unique is that many of these communities also have their own governments and separate services.

In fact, a total of 35 suburbs share borders with the city. Other public entities responsible for a range of services—often referred to as "special purpose" or "special use" districts—span the region as well. In all, more than 250 local governments serve city and Allegheny County residents, making life for public officials—not to mention taxpayers—complicated.

Given this level of fragmentation and public concerns about high taxation, one might expect calls for consolidation. Yet this hasn't happened in Pittsburgh. Indeed, it rarely has in most other metropolitan areas surrounded by a host of local governments and special-purpose districts. Figures from the 2012 Census of Governments signal no significant national shift toward consolidation in recent years. The survey, published in August, tallied 89,004 general and special-purpose local governments across the U.S. in 2012, down only slightly from 89,476 five years prior. Rather than merge, officials seem to be seeking answers to solve mutual problems cooperatively, but are doing so while leaving governmental boundaries and districts largely intact.

Robert O'Neill, the International City/County Management Association's executive director, said last fall that continuing fiscal pressures sparked talks of consolidation in a few localities, but that this hasn't resulted in any great push for mergers. Instead, municipalities explored tactics like shared services to curb inefficiencies,

an attractive option for economic development, transportation and other large-scale initiatives, according to O'Neill.

Government fragmentation has long been tugged at by two competing interests. On the one hand, many argue consolidation cuts costs and allows officials to better coordinate efforts. Citizens, though, are often emotionally attached to their local governments.

Many governments are packed into dense areas of the Midwest and New England. The Census Bureau counted 6,968 governments—including special districts—in Illinois alone, the most of any state, followed by Pennsylvania (4,905) and Texas (4,856). Not surprisingly, rural states harbor the most units of government per capita, with North Dakota, South Dakota and Nebraska recording the highest number of governments relative to population.

Voters, along with some states' rules and regulations, often impede consolidation. For most general-purpose government consolidations, residents of all affected communities must approve public referenda before a consolidation can proceed. In New York, only two of 18 votes for consolidation of towns and villages have passed since the state's government reorganization law was updated in March 2010.

But are all these distinct units of local government necessary? Myron Orfield, who leads the Institute on Metropolitan Opportunity at the University of Minnesota Law School, doesn't think so. Divided regions often experience disparity in quality of services. One of the most prominent such examples is the long-running statewide battles over education that pit cash-strapped school districts against their more affluent neighbors. Similarly, government fragmentation contributes to racial segregation in urban areas, Orfield says.

Another consequence of fragmented government is that competition among municipalities potentially hinders land use and economic development. "You have a lot of warfare between units of government to move shopping centers," Orfield says. "They spend a lot of time fighting with each other." By comparison, consolidated governments, such as the city-county systems of Indianapolis and Lexington, Ky., create more effective incentive packages to lure employers.

This doesn't mean fragmented regions can't successfully pursue ambitious projects, especially with involvement from nonprofits and the business community. It's this type of alliance that has contributed to Pittsburgh's revival, says David Miller, director of the Center for Metropolitan Studies at the University of Pittsburgh. "In a way, being so decentralized creates access into the civic community in ways that are remarkable," he says.

Miller says centralized metropolitan regions with fewer local governments typically perform best economically, as long as the state affords them a broad range of powers. He assesses fragmentation using a "metropolitan power diffusion index" he developed, which factors both the number of governments and distribution of expenditures. By this measure, the Chicago-Joliet-Naperville, Ill., metro area is the nation's most fragmented, with Pittsburgh close behind.

If there's one state that's a poster child for fragmented government, it is Illinois. The state's nearly 7,000 total local governments far exceed any other state. The bulk of these—more than 4,000—are special-purpose units, dating back to a previous version of the state's constitution that moved municipalities to create new governments to get around state-mandated debt requirements.

Today, Illinois still maintains a long roster of special districts. One law mandates coverage by a fire protection district for properties not served by municipal fire departments. Local boards oversee more than 20 streetlight districts. In some areas, elementary schools in multiple districts feed into a single high school.

But like Pittsburgh, the state has yet to experience significant consolidation. The state Legislature has explored the possibility of reducing special districts, forming a 17-member Local Government Consolidation Commission in 2011. However, consolidation is far more difficult to actually carry out, says Larry Frang, executive director of the Illinois Municipal League. Some cities, for example, lack the capacity to provide adequate protection for outlying areas if fire districts are eliminated.

Historical boundaries further explain why some areas have so many governments. In North Dakota, more than 1,300 sparsely populated civil townships stretch across the state, many of which are occupied by only a few families who've farmed the same land for generations.

Some state lawmakers have brought up the issue of consolidating townships, but the idea failed to gain traction. Part of the opposition stems from the state's culture. Larry Syverson, president of the North Dakota Township Officers Association, says many residents cling to their local control, resisting interference from outsiders.

"We're just used to the idea that somebody has got to be taking care of these things," he says, "so it's either we have to roll up our sleeves and do it or the next guy has to."

Critical Thinking

1. About how many local governments are there in the United States? Which states and which kinds of states have the most local governments per capita?

2. What factors work to impede consolidation of local governments?

3. How can fragmented local government potentially hinder land use and economic development?

Create Central

www.mhhe.com/createcentral

Internet References

City Mayors.com: Mergers
www.citymayors.com/government/mergers_locgov.html

Government Consolidation and Structure (Carl Vinson Institute of Government)
www.cviog.uga.edu/local-government-services

Article   Prepared by: Bruce Stinebrickner, *DePauw University*

The Sentient City

Cameras and sensors can make a city aware of everything happening on its streets, helping it do more for less.

ZACH PATTON

Learning Outcomes

After reading this article, you will be able to:

- Summarize the assistance that cameras and sensors can currently provide to those governing a city and imagine what future technologies might offer.

- Assess the pros and cons for residents of living in a "sentient city."

Call it City 2.0: a metropolis where officials instantly monitor all of the urban environment's constantly changing dynamics—the outside temperature; snow or rainfall; traffic; and perhaps most importantly, people moving through the streets, flowing from one neighborhood to the next. This system helps officials send resources to the street corner where gangs are converging, manage traffic before it becomes congested, and respond to emergencies seamlessly—automatically—before they're even reported.

It may sound like science fiction, but the idea of a living, sentient city—one in which managers use real-time data to respond to events as they occur—isn't the stuff of fantasy anymore. By creating intricately linked networks of cameras and sensors throughout an urban area, cities in the U.S. and elsewhere are already making great strides toward tracking weather conditions and traffic flow, to name a few, and then using that data to govern more effectively.

The ultimate City 2.0 vision is of a "highly networked, highly metered environment so that an administrator can oversee the inputs and the outputs," says Rob Enderle, a technology analyst with the Enderle Group. Tapping into all this real-time data, he says, means "you can run a city cheaper and have happier and safer citizens." The city, in short, becomes a more efficient place for people to live and work. It also means a government can do more with less.

The reality isn't that far away. Many of the building blocks are familiar, even mundane: sensors that monitor weather conditions and air pollution; smart-grid technology that helps deliver energy more efficiently; cameras that track the flow of pedestrians and automobile traffic; devices that measure and relay snowfall to the public works department; and access to Wi-Fi and cloud computing.

Alone, each of these blocks performs one discrete function for one purpose. But if a city fused all of those different data streams, it could create a place keenly aware of changes in the urban environment. With that awareness, a city could respond rapidly and efficiently where and when needed.

The sentient city is still an emerging idea, and managers will have to address many issues—technological and otherwise—before smart cities can flourish. But as more and more cities implement and refine the tools used to gather and assess all this data, the idea of City 2.0 is a vision that's quickly coming into focus.

The genesis of these ideas is decades old. Enderle likens the vision of sentient cities to the concept of "arcologies," the classic sci-fi notion of megalopolises made up of gargantuan, self-contained structures that house thousands of residents in an all-encapsulating environment. At the arcology dynamic's core is the idea that if you can contain all aspects of a city's life and needs, you can monitor and control what happens there.

While arcologies remain firmly ensconced in the pages of Utopian literature, cities have begun implementing technologies that approach somewhat similar ideals of monitoring the urbanscape as a whole. Traffic-light cameras, for example, are ubiquitous in many places. Some localities have gone further, installing video cameras throughout the city and creating a network of video streams. Chicago is the most prominent U.S. city to outfit itself with such a web of cameras. In 2004, the Windy City installed 250 surveillance cameras at sites thought to be at risk of a terror attack. Those devices were linked to 2,000 other cameras already spread throughout the city and networked into Chicago's emergency dispatch center. Mayor Richard Daley said his goal is to have a camera trained on every single intersection in the city.

Then there are gunshot location systems—a technology that uses audio sensors attached to rooftops and telephone poles to detect when a gun is fired and pinpoint the location. In 1995,

Redwood City, Calif., was the first in the nation to test this system, which lets police respond to shots without receiving a 911 call. Today more than 30 U.S. cities, including Chicago, Los Angeles and Washington, D.C., rely on the same acoustic sensors.

Surveillance cameras and gunshot detection were the first steps toward a fully sensor-equipped city. In more recent years as sensor technology has improved, the focus has broadened from public safety and emergency response to include subtler changes in environment. Matt Welsh, an associate professor of computer science at Harvard University, has spent the past four years designing and building a system of sensors to constantly monitor conditions in Cambridge, Mass. Welsh and his team have worked with the city to disperse nearly 30 sensors around the relatively small town. "We wanted to capture the ephemeral changes in environment," he says. Using the sensor data, Welsh hopes to gain understanding of how the city works on a minute level. He's recently begun looking at air pollution levels in areas with high automobile traffic, for example, and how those levels shift during the course of a day. The information from monitoring those outputs continuously on a city block, he suggests, could be extremely useful in the city's future decision-making.

Meanwhile, other cities are experimenting with monitoring residents' energy use in real time. Pilot programs that let citizens view their individual energy consumption as it's being used are up and running in Houston; Boulder, Colo.; and Dubuque, Iowa.

While the technology for a sentient city is already available, what's missing is the ability to connect all the different data streams to form a comprehensive picture of a city's happenings. Wilmington, N.C., however, is trying. In February, the city and surrounding New Hanover County launched a pilot that could make it the nation's first true smart city. Using cameras and sensors, the city will analyze and respond to everything from traffic congestion and fuel consumption to water quality and sewage capacity.

For the most part, though, cities have yet to make the leap to fusing different kinds of sensor data. "The concept of City 2.0, is that all these things would be networked," Enderle says. "But I don't see anybody doing a great job of connecting all these things together."

As with so many IT projects, the obstacles toward a fully networked sentient city aren't really technological. The issues are much bigger than that, says Mark Cleverley, the director of strategy for IBM's Global Government Industry. "It's about how technology is changing," he says, "but it's also about how society is changing."

It's also about getting a city's agencies to work together to share and analyze sensor data. And that can be a challenge. "The big problem is working through the political structure," Enderle says. "It can be very turf-oriented and very fragmented

when it comes to this kind of stuff." And what works for one city may not work for another. Cleverley worked with Stockholm to build a congestion-pricing system that utilized radio-frequency ID tags to track citizens' automobiles throughout the city. Cleverley says there's been widespread acceptance of the program and a general agreement that it's had a dramatic effect on reducing traffic congestion. But when New York City Mayor Michael Bloomberg floated the idea of congestion pricing in 2008, it took his citizens a New York minute to rebuke the notion.

Unsurprisingly there are privacy concerns. While most citizens probably don't mind the idea of pole-mounted devices collecting data on rainfall or air pollution, they are likely to be less receptive to the notion of cameras or traffic sensors that follow their movements throughout a city. Those kinds of concerns are not insurmountable, but they must be dealt with, says Cleverley, who notes that Chicago adopted a policy with its vast network of cameras that individuals' faces are, by default, blurred out. Law enforcement officials must go through an approval process, akin to obtaining a warrant, if they want to look for a specific person.

In the end, the collection of sensor data isn't what's important—it's how a city uses that information. "You can deliver better outcomes for society if you think about a city as a system of systems," says Cleverley. "What these technologies do is make it easier to track these systems. What they don't do is guarantee success."

Critical Thinking

1. How can modern technology be used to help city government leaders respond to urban events as they occur?

2. What different "data streams" can modern technology enable a city government to monitor in "real time"?

3. What privacy concerns arise in connection with a "sentient city" and what can be done to lessen such concerns?

4. What should be the ultimate objective of collecting sensor data reporting on multiple dimensions of urban life?

Create Central

www.mhhe.com/createcentral

Internet References

Chicago's Camera Network Is Everywhere (*Wall Street Journal*)
http://online.wsj.com/article/SB1000142405274870453840457453991041 2824756.html

ShotSpotter Helps Washington, D.C., police track gunshots (Homeland Security Wire)
www.homelandsecuritynewswire.com/dr20131106-shotspotter-helps-washington-d-c-police-track-gunshots

Article   Prepared by: Bruce Stinebrickner, *DePauw University*

Rebel Towns

Call it municipal disobedience: These communities are defying laws they deem illegitimate.

BARRY YEOMAN

Learning Outcomes

After reading this article, you will be able to:

- Assess the pros and cons of what the Community Environmental Defense Fund advises local governments to do when they are threatened by actions, especially corporate actions, that violate their sense of environmental well-being.

- Evaluate the utility of "rights-based ordinances" when local governments want to resist planned corporate actions that the governments oppose.

- Weigh the pros and cons of Dillon's Rule.

The 600 residents of Sugar Hill, New Hampshire, have done a laudable job of keeping the vulgarities of modern life at bay. There are no fast-food restaurants, no neon signs. Instead, the former iron-mining town has rambling country inns and a main road lined with Victorian and Arts and Crafts houses. Locals gather for breakfast, as they have since 1938, at Polly's Pancake Parlor, which grinds its own corn and wheat and uses syrup from the sugar maples that give the town its name. With tourism driving the economy, the village's biggest assets are its fall foliage, fields of lupines and uninterrupted views of the snow-capped White Mountains.

Each March, Sugar Hill's voters gather at the white meetinghouse—a converted church built in 1830 with a trio of gold-leaf clocks on its steeple—for their annual town meeting. Anyone who collects enough signatures can place an item on the agenda to be voted into law. That New Englander impulse toward self-government, combined with the feistiness that led Sugar Hill to secede from a neighboring town in 1962, might explain its residents' sweeping response when they learned in 2010 that an international electric consortium has proposed a high-voltage transmission line that would slice through the village like a giant zipper.

The Northern Pass, if built, would enter New Hampshire at the Canadian border and bisect some of the state's most intact forestland as it connects Quebec's hydroelectric dams with New England's power grid. Steel towers, some exceeding thirteen stories in height, would line the 180-mile route, which snakes through ten miles of protected national forest and seven miles of Sugar Hill. Conservationists say the project is unneeded and could degrade waterways and fragment wildlife habitats.

But what New Hampshirites fear most is that the Northern Pass will disfigure the state's visual landscape. "It could destroy our economy," says Dolly McPhaul, a lifelong Sugar Hill resident. "If people don't build their second homes here, where are the builders going to get their money? The plumbers? The grocery store that feeds these people?" McPhaul and her neighbors were particularly disheartened to learn that the Northern Pass required federal and state permits—but no local permits at all.

"You're shocked to find out you have no say," says Nancy Martland, a retired child-development researcher who moved to Sugar Hill in 2007. "Even your whole town. Even at town meeting. Even your Select Board. You have no power. People in New Hampshire—maybe everywhere, I don't know—we want to stand up for ourselves."

So they did. Last year, Martland and McPhaul campaigned for a local ordinance that would ban corporations from acquiring land or building structures to support any "unsustainable energy system." The ordinance stripped those corporations of their free-speech and due-process rights under the Constitution, as well as protections afforded by the Constitution's commerce and contract clauses. Judicial rulings that recognized corporations as legal "persons" would not be recognized in Sugar Hill. Any state or federal law that tried to interfere with the town's authority would be invalidated. "Natural communities and ecosystems"—wetlands, streams, rivers, aquifers—would acquire "inalienable and fundamental rights to exist and flourish," and any resident could enforce the law on their behalf. "All power is inherent in the people," the measure stated.

Sugar Hill's attorney suggested this was folly; local governments can't override state or federal law, much less the Constitution. Such an ordinance could attract a lawsuit, which the village could ill afford. McPhaul, a Republican and a charity volunteer and self-described "goody two-shoes," also worried about litigation. "But what is your option?" she asks. "To lie down, play dead and let them destroy your town?" After a two-month public-awareness campaign, Sugar Hill's residents took up the ordinance at their 2012 town meeting. It passed by a unanimous voice vote.

Thus, Sugar Hill became one of dozens of communities nationwide—mostly villages but also the city of Pittsburgh—that have reacted to environmental threats by directly challenging the Constitution and established case law. The leading champion of this confrontational strategy—which has its share of critics, even among progressives who share the sense of desperation that is driving it—is a bearish 43-year-old attorney named Thomas Linzey. These skirmishes, Linzey believes, are the first steps in a long campaign to wrest power from corporations and strengthen American democracy. He refers to the strategy as "collective nonviolent civil disobedience through municipal lawmaking."

Linzey runs the Community Environmental Legal Defense Fund, a Pennsylvania nonprofit that advocates for local self-government and the rights of nature. CELDF comes into threatened communities, educates residents about US legal history, and trains them to advocate for "rights-based ordinances" like Sugar Hill's. About thirty municipalities in Maine, New Hampshire, Massachusetts, New York, Pennsylvania, Maryland, Virginia, Ohio and New Mexico have enacted such measures, according to Linzey, following an earlier round of over 100 more modest laws. CELDF's organizers have helped citizens fight frackers, coal companies, factory farms, big-box stores, water bottlers and sewage-sludge dumpers. They've campaigned to overhaul the city charter in Spokane, Washington. And they aided the successful effort to confer rights on nature in Ecuador's 2008 Constitution. Linzey, whose baritone voice is filled with populist fire, has crafted a message whose appeal brings together liberals distrustful of big business and conservatives distrustful of big government.

Linzey's approach has evolved dramatically since 1995, when the organization he co-founded started assisting Pennsylvania communities that were battling polluters and developers. Newly admitted to the bar, the young Alabaman initially put his faith in the regulatory system. "It seemed to us at the time that people needed lawyers," he recalls. "The problem was not that we didn't have good environmental laws. The problem was, the world has gone to shit because we didn't have enough people enforcing those laws." So Linzey applied what he'd learned in law school. Faced with a proposed incinerator or landfill, "we would take the 400-page application and try to find places where it was deficient—gaps, omissions, those types of things." Based on these bureaucratic challenges, CELDF's clients often won their first rounds.

"Then the community group would have a victory party," he recalls. "Everybody would pat each other on the back and say the system works. Meanwhile, thirty, sixty days from then, the corporation would come back and submit a new and improved permit application, and the project would move forward. So we weren't stopping anything."

The attorney wondered what he was accomplishing by working within the system. "In many ways, the regulatory process is intended to exhaust communities, because it does not recognize—and neither does the broader structure of the law recognize—that communities have any power to make those fundamental decisions about energy or transportation or agriculture." Citizens could delay but not stop projects; the law was "merely regulating the rate at which the environment was being destroyed."

Behind Linzey's epiphany is almost 200 years of jurisprudence giving both constitutional rights and legal personhood to corporations. The Supreme Court's 2010 *Citizens United* decision, which used the First Amendment to permit corporations unlimited independent political spending, is just the latest in a chain of such rulings. Most famous is the 1886 case *Santa Clara v. Southern Pacific,* in which a railroad company argued that a particular tax law violated the Fourteenth Amendment's equal-protection clause. "The court does not wish to hear argument on the question whether the [clause] applies to these corporations," Chief Justice Morrison Waite said from the bench. "We are all of opinion that it does." Since then, courts have also used the Constitution's Fourth and Fifth Amendments, and its commerce and contract clauses, to expand corporate rights. Linzey believes these rulings are rooted in the very structure of the Constitution, which he says "puts the rights of property and commerce over the rights of people, communities and nature."

The Constitution also concentrates power by declaring itself, along with federal statutes, "the supreme law of the land." And starting in 1868, a judicial doctrine known as Dillon's Rule held local governments subservient to state legislatures, which "breathes into them the breath of life, without which they cannot exist," Linzey adds.

With communities holding so little authority, Linzey and his colleagues decided that the only way to fight environmental threats was through open defiance. He compares this to Northern jurors who refused to convict defendants in fugitive slave cases, suffragists who risked arrest to vote and African-Americans who sat down at segregated lunch counters. "Change does not happen by silver-tongued lawyers going into courthouses," he says. "The only way law changes is through disobedience." There was no reason, he concluded, that disobedience couldn't come from local governments—and he found eager allies in Pennsylvania's Republican-leaning farm country.

Linzey had started receiving calls from elected supervisors worried about the arrival of factory hog farms in their rural townships. The officials had tried to stave off the invasions by strictly regulating manure disposal, only to find their efforts pre-empted by Pennsylvania law. Now some were willing to butt heads with the state government. Linzey drafted an ordinance that would ban corporate farming altogether, drawing from similar laws passed by nine Midwestern states. About twenty townships enacted the measure, he estimates, followed by eighty that banned the importing of corporate-hauled sewage sludge for use as fertilizer on farm fields. (Despite industry assurances, some scientists consider the noxious sludge toxic. Two Pennsylvania teens had recently died after exposure to such sludge.) A few townships went further, refusing altogether to recognize the personhood of corporate sludge haulers.

Predictably, Pennsylvania's state government invoked its supremacy. It passed a law in 2005 empowering the attorney general to sue local governments that restrict "normal agricultural operations," then took legal action against two townships, East Brunswick and Packer. Both withdrew their sludge bans, though Packer's supervisors voted not to recognize the attorney general's authority to restrict their autonomy. A court voided that measure.

News of the Pennsylvania rebellion reached other places. In Barnstead, New Hampshire (population 4,600), a homeschooling mother named Gail Darrell, who lives in a Revolutionary War–era cabin with her piano-tuner husband, watched with alarm as a water bottler called USA Springs announced plans to extract 310,000 gallons a day from three bedrock wells in nearby Nottingham. A report by civil engineer Thomas Ballestero warned that the operations could deplete and contaminate the local water supply. Yet the project seemed to be moving forward.

Darrell had never been involved in local politics. But her children were getting older, leaving her with free time. So she volunteered to sit on a committee studying how Barnstead could protect its own water. There she learned about CELDF and invited Linzey to speak to the town's selectmen. Linzey's call to outlaw corporate privilege found a receptive audience in freedom-loving New Hampshire. (The state constitution authorizes its citizens to form a new government when the existing one starts serving private interests.) "It's always been a bit ornery up here," says Gordon Preston, who chaired the board of selectmen at the time. Preston had reservations about CELDF's approach: "The biggest fear of a small town is that they get their asses hauled into court and have little or no money to defend themselves." But he also shared Linzey's concern about corporate power and supported the principle of local self-government.

Darrell worked with the selectmen to put an anti-bottling ordinance on the 2006 town meeting agenda. Shortly before the vote, Linzey and historian Richard Grossman came to Barnstead to teach CELDF's Democracy School, an intensive seminar that traces the history of corporate and government power. It was a clarifying moment for Darrell. "I didn't really understand about the Constitution till I went through the school—that it wasn't about freedom," she says. "We grow up with that IV drip in our arm that tells us that we live in the greatest democracy that ever was." The seminar gave Darrell the momentum she needed to defend the ordinance, which passed overwhelmingly at the town meeting and was strengthened two years later. Barnstead not only banned corporate water withdrawals and stripped bottling companies of their presumed constitutional rights; it also threatened secession from any government that tries to overturn the ban or "intimidate the people of Barnstead." The measure was among the first to confer civil rights on natural systems like aquifers and rivers. Nottingham, which had initially rebuffed CELDF, followed suit with a similar measure.

"New Hampshire has always had an independent spirit," Darrell says. "The soil here is crap, and you really have to work hard to farm. When people came up here to settle, they were coming into no-man's land. You had to have enough gumption to stick it out, to stand up for yourself, and to make it through the winter. That spirit has carried out into the way we treat government. We believe that we have the inalienable right to govern ourselves. So to hear the language of the ordinance—that didn't seem foreign to people."

USA Springs later filed for bankruptcy, so it is hard to know whether these ordinances had any impact. But Darrell, who became CELDF's New England organizer, claimed a more tangible victory in Shapleigh, Maine, where residents passed a rights-based ordinance in 2009. Their target, the Nestlé subsidiary Poland Spring, pulled up its test wells and left four months later. "Without the town's permission to proceed on that project," says Mark Dubois, the company's natural-resource manager, "we had no project."

Nestlé's withdrawal felt particularly sweet because Shapleigh's citizens had defied both the company and their own elected officials. When the board of selectmen refused to put the rights-based ordinance to a public vote, calling it unconstitutional, bottling opponents convened their own town meeting and passed it 114-66. "Nobody is covering our asses out here," says Charles Mullins, a retired machinist who later served one term as selectman. "When the people up high don't do their jobs, then we've got to get out in the streets and do it ourselves."

Victories like Shapleigh's have inspired other threatened communities, but they're not really part of CELDF's long-term game plan. For Linzey, disobedient lawmaking is an organizing tactic, not a legal one. He knows municipalities violate the law when they assert supremacy over state and federal governments. He expects "lawsuits galore" and assumes judges won't permit these affronts to the Constitution. But he also believes that every courtroom defeat will trigger a bigger backlash against the status quo, leading to more municipal defiance. Over time, he expects to build the critical mass necessary to amend state constitutions and eventually the federal one.

CELDF considers this the only path to environmental sustainability, and its leaders freely criticize liberals who believe otherwise. "We're seen as not able to play well with others," says Ben Price, who leads the nonprofit's efforts in Pennsylvania. He admits that CELDF's uncompromising style can be off-putting, but he doesn't care. "Frankly, I'm not willing to suggest that the traditional progressive strategy is just as good" as the one CELDF is pursuing, and "we're just giving another tool in the toolbox—I don't agree with that. If trying to regulate the rate of destruction was working so well, we wouldn't be in the mess we're in environmentally."

Price says that when he chats with mainstream environmentalists, "what I constantly hear is, 'We need to have a seat at the table. If we're not sitting down when they're talking about these rules and regs, we're left out. Is that what you want?' My answer is yes. We need to stop legitimizing what they're doing by being invited to the table of power, and then having no power.'"

The criticism, though, runs both ways. Some progressives call CELDF's tactics pie-in-the-sky at best, dangerous at worst. "I'm concerned about how this can suck energy out of other avenues for change," says Jon Snyder, a Spokane City Council member who believes the resources spent on a

CELDF-sponsored ballot initiative cost his council the chance for its "first progressive majority." The 2011 measure would have amended the city charter to strip rights from corporations and give them to waterways, neighborhoods and workers. It lost by 1,000 votes out of 58,700 cast. That's a thin margin, but wider than the eighty-nine votes that would have elected a fourth progressive to the seven-member council. The liberal bloc has lost 4–3 votes on marriage equality, saving union jobs, utility rate reform, historic preservation, alternatives to incarceration and job-placement services for the poor, Snyder says.

Constitutional scholar Kent Greenfield believes CELDF's shortcomings go beyond misplaced energy. "I totally understand people's revulsion against corporations' misdeeds," says the Boston College law professor. "I think, though, that we shouldn't be squandering this political moment on organizational tools that, if implemented, would be a disaster. The reason we have a national government is because there are certain things we ought to decide at the national level and we can't let people opt out of." America's racial history, he says, is exhibit number one; if Barnstead can threaten to secede, so can a town that wants to resegregate its schools. "This is what we fought the Civil War over, for goodness' sake. This is what the civil rights movement was about. We cannot let the George Wallaces of the world stand in the schoolhouse door and say, 'Our community norm of segregation is going to control here in the face of the national norm of equality.' The assertion of power to rewrite the Constitution within one's own community is a nonstarter—and ought to be."

Linzey has heard the racial analogy before and rejects it. He argues that CELDF's ordinances expand rights, at least to flesh-and-blood humans. The Constitution and federal laws should be used, he says, to overturn local restrictions of rights. "Vehicles are only as good," he says, "as the values that animate them."

In the decade since it first took aim at corporate privilege, CELDF has jumped beyond its rural roots. It crossed the Rubicon in 2010, when Pittsburgh's City Council unanimously passed a rights-based anti-fracking ordinance. "It was a very, very assertive bill," says sponsor Doug Shields, who has since retired from the council. "It didn't mince words. And there was talk that if you do this, you'll be challenged the day after your vote." Sure enough, last year Pennsylvania's legislature passed a bill nullifying almost all local regulation of oil and gas extraction. (The state's Public Utility Commission says this includes the Pittsburgh ordinance.) The new law is currently in litigation.

Even before the Pittsburgh foray, CELDF started working internationally. After a handful of townships had given civil rights to "natural communities and ecosystems"—an idea floated forty years ago by legal scholar Christopher Stone in an essay titled "Should Trees Have Standing?"—CELDF was invited by an NGO to help draft a similar provision in Ecuador's Constitution. "Ecuador has been treated by multinational corporations as a cheap hotel," says associate director Mari Margil. "They come in, they make a giant mess, and then they leave." The new Constitution, adopted in 2008, gives nature the right to "respect for its existence and for the maintenance and regeneration of its life cycles." Courts have used that provision to crack down on illegal mining and road construction. Yet resource extraction continues, including the opening of 8 million acres of unspoiled rainforest to oil drilling. Margil and Linzey have also talked with activists in Nepal, Italy, India and New Zealand.

The heart of CELDF's work, though, remains in small American communities like those affected by the Northern Pass. Besides Sugar Hill, two other towns outlawed unsustainable energy projects by popular vote last year. Three others rejected or tabled the ordinance. For all of New Hampshire's iconoclasm, not everyone wants to register dissent through a vehicle that could be overturned in court. "Unfortunately, the state trumps anything the towns do," says Tom Mullen, developer of a resort that lies in the transmission line's path. "I want to focus on things that will stop this project now." For Mullen, that means working with the state government, which in 2012 led to a victory: legislators banned the use of eminent domain to obtain right-of-way for unneeded transmission projects.

Still, CELDF keeps minting activists who want nothing to do with government as usual. Alexis Eynon, a middle-school art teacher, started attending Democracy Schools—following them around New England—when she learned the Northern Pass would come within a mile of her home in Thornton. Eynon built her house from straw bale, framing it with salvaged timber from her five wooded acres and heating it with a geothermal pump and a wood stove. "The original concept was to disturb the land as little as possible," she says, which makes the nearby utility corridor that much harder to bear. "It takes a spectacular treasure that to me seems so rare in our country—these untouched places—and makes it mundane. It becomes like every other place that's been destroyed by some kind of industrial project."

Hearing Linzey speak, and attending the Democracy Schools, convinced Eynon that "nobody's going to help us here. We have to help ourselves." In March, she plans to present the rights-based ordinance at Thornton's town meeting in the hope that it will follow the lead of Sugar Hill, thirty miles away. Eynon knows that some of her neighbors are wary of a lawsuit and that others support the Northern Pass outright. She still considers such ordinances New Hampshire's only hope.

"The whole regulatory business feels like being a hamster in a hamster wheel," she says. "I want to put my track shoes to the pavement and just start running."

Critical Thinking

1. What are the primary objectives and chief methods of the Community Environmental Legal Defense Fund (CELDF)?
2. What is "Dillon's Rule" and how does it relate to CELDF's recommendation of "open defiance"?

Create Central

www.mhhe.com/createcentral

Internet References

The Community Environmental Legal Defense Fund (CELDF)
www.celdf.org

Town of Sugar Hill, New Hampshire
www.sugarhillnh.org

BARRY YEOMAN is a freelance journalist living in Durham, North Carolina. His work has appeared in *The New York Times, Mother Jones, Rolling Stone* and *Discover,* among other publications, and won numerous awards.

Article   Prepared by: Bruce Stinebrickner, *DePauw University*

267 Years and Counting

The Town Hall Meeting Is Alive and Well in Pelham, Mass

TOD NEWCOMBE

Learning Outcomes

After reading this article, you will be able to:

- Explain the history and function of town meetings in New England local government.
- Assess the pros and cons of town meetings as an institution of local government.

On a cool autumn evening, Kathleen Martell, town clerk for Pelham, Mass., unlocks the doors to the Town Hall, turns on the lights, starts a fire in the fireplace and helps arrange chairs in neat rows, enough to seat 115 townspeople. Soon she is joined by newly elected town moderator Daniel Robb and the Board of Selectmen: James Huber, William Martell and Edward Martin. By 7 P.M., town residents occupy most of the chairs, with the overflow sitting on simple wooden benches that line the meeting room's walls. A few minutes later, Robb calls the meeting to order, the noisy crowd quiets quickly and so begins a Pelham tradition dating back nearly three centuries.

Town meetings have been a fixture in New England since the first one was held in Dorchester, Mass., in 1633. But only Pelham can lay claim to having the oldest town hall in continuous use for town meetings. The wooden, two-story structure, which stands on a hill at the corner of Amherst Road and Daniel Shays Highway (named after the leader of a post-Revolutionary War rebellion of farmers who battled government soldiers on the Town Hall's grounds), was built in 1743. For 267 years, Pelham residents have annually walked, ridden horses, driven in wagons or carriages—and now, cars and trucks—to the simple clapboard hall to discuss and vote on vital town issues.

Upstairs, where the meetings were held for many years, the rear of the room is lined with narrow pews; the backs consist of a single pine plank more than two feet wide. Centuries of carving by bored or restless residents have scarred the pews with names, doodles and images—some so deep they've left holes in the thick planks. Two wood-burning stoves sit on the floor,

ready to provide heat. The entire structure is devoid of decoration, save for a small amount of wood carving in the form of two scallops on the wall near where a pulpit once stood. (The hall also served as a church until 1833, when Massachusetts formerly separated church and state with an amendment to the state constitution.)

These days, the meetings have been moved downstairs to accommodate disabled residents who can't climb the stairs to the second floor. At this year's fall gathering on Oct. 20, Robb starts by calling for a moment of silence for a sick town member, and then reads the five warrant articles the town will discuss and vote on. Technically the meeting that evening is a special one—it's not the annual meeting that takes place in the spring. Special town meetings are held to consider business that must be dealt with prior to the annual meeting, according to town historian Joseph Larson. And he's quick to admit that Pelham makes sure it annually holds a special meeting to maintain the designation of having the oldest town hall in continuous use.

Town meetings often are called the purest and most democratic form of government—direct democracy where the town's business is discussed, debated and voted on by members of the community. Yes, anyone can speak, but unlike the mock town meetings seen on TV and the Internet during the health-care debates, with their confrontational and hyperbolic politics, the meeting in Pelham is civil and the participants engaged. Moderator Robb quietly reminds the residents to introduce themselves and state where they live before speaking. In fact, the governance process that evening, regarding rules of order, is discussed with almost as much fervor as the articles.

It quickly becomes clear which topic will be the most contentious when Robb reads Article 2, calling for the town to vote to raise the salaries of Pelham's fire chief and its volunteer firefighters. The sums are modest—$9,230 for the part-time fire chief and $10,386 for the firefighters. It has been six years since the last salary increase was passed, but a number of residents raise questions about the article's timing and amount. The debate continues, and with the room full of volunteer firefighters (all wearing their uniforms), a motion is passed to vote on the article by secret ballot.

Before voting begins, Pelham Fire Chief Raymond Murphy makes an impassioned speech in favor of the raises. He points out that the dollar amount will raise the hourly rate for the firefighters from $7.45 to $10. "Some of you have the idea that the fire department is a social club, a place to hang out because there's no bowling in town," he says. "But we're a professional organization, run by dedicated firefighters, willing to risk our lives for the safety of the community."

The final comments before the vote come from Thomas P. Lederle, an elderly man in the front row who speaks eloquently in a clear voice about his recent medical emergency and how the town's firefighters arrived quickly and transported him to the hospital, "saving my life." He implores the town to pass the modest increase. When the voting is done and the ballots are counted, the salary increase passes by a large majority.

Except for the chirping of the occasional mobile phone (which draws admonishment from Robb), Pelham's town hall meeting hardly differs from those that took place decades, even centuries, before.

But the town meeting—once a fixture in New England—has been slowly buffeted by change. Urbanization and depopulation of the hill towns has reduced the practice—as well as participation. Starting in the 1960s, however, town meetings in New England underwent something of a revival, according to Frank Bryan, author of *Real Democracy: The New England Town Meeting and How It Works*. The notion of "small is beautiful," along with skepticism for large-scale solutions, began drawing people back to participate in this simple form of democratic government.

Today though, that revival is beginning to lose steam. In Vermont, for example, only 7.2 percent of the state population voted at the annual town meetings in 2009, according to its secretary of state. Other New England states have reported decreases in town meeting participation. Bryan attributes the more recent decline to "commuter-based lifestyles and other demographic and institutional dislocations."

But Larson is optimistic about town meeting democracy in Pelham. He points out that the town has seen its population dwindle to just a few hundred residents at the turn of the last century, only to have it slowly return to its current level of 1,440 (about the same level as in the early 19th century). "That increase has kept the attendance at meetings going well," he says. And Larson is sanguine about the long-term prospects for the Town Hall. At the October meeting, Article 4, which calls for appropriating $2,400 to hire a historic preservation consultant to evaluate the building's exterior, passes by a near-unanimous vote.

Critical Thinking

1. When was the first town meeting held in New England?
2. Why are town meetings often called the purest and most democratic form of democracy? What sorts of government decisions can and do town meetings make?
3. In what ways has the town meeting been "buffeted by change" in recent decades?
4. What percentage of Vermonters voted at annual town meetings in 2009?

Create Central

www.mhhe.com/createcentral

Internet References

Interview with Frank M. Bryan, author of *Real Democracy: The New England Town Meeting and How It Works*
  www.press.uchicago.edu/Misc/Chicago/077977in.html
New England Town Meetings (Participedia)
  http://participedia.net/en/methods/new-england-town-meetings
Town of Pelham, MA, website
  www.townofpelham.org

Unit 6

UNIT

Prepared by: Bruce Stinebrickner, *DePauw University*

Fiscal Matters and Economic Development

All governments need financial resources to carry out their activities. State and local governments rely on a variety of revenue sources, including sales tax, income tax, and property tax; user charges (for example, motor vehicle registration fees, college tuition, and swimming pool admission fees); lotteries and casinos; and grants of money from other levels of government. Despite this diversity of funding sources, the overall financial situation of state and local governments is often far from satisfactory, and the Great Recession of 2007–2009 significantly worsened their fiscal problems.

Conspicuous attempts to curb spending at all levels of government have occurred over the past four decades. An early and historically important success in this context was the passage of Proposition 13, an initiative that California voters approved in 1978. Proposition 13 imposed ceilings on local government property taxes and, in turn, curtailed the services and programs that California local governments could offer. The Proposition 13 tax revolt soon spread to other states. In the years after the passage of Proposition 13, measures designed to limit government spending were put into effect in states and localities across the country. Some observers see Californians' passage of Proposition 30 in 2012 as a turning point in the decades-long tax revolt in the aftermath of Proposition 13. Whether Proposition 30's four-year increase in sales taxes and seven-year rise in income tax rates for high-income earners actually constitutes such a turning point remains to be seen.

Unlike the national government, state and local governments receive a sizable portion of their revenues from intergovernmental grants. The national government provides funding to state and local governments along with a variety of attached conditions. Money can be given with virtually no accompanying strings or with considerable limitations on how it can be spent. Similarly, states provide funds to local governments with sets of conditions attached. Governments providing financial grants, of course, exercise control over the amount of funds available and the conditions associated with such funds. This, in turn, can cause uncertainty and administrative burdens for governments receiving money from other levels of government. As should be apparent, intergovernmental relations and the financing of state and local governments overlap considerably.

The financial situation of state and local governments differs from that of the national government in other important respects. The national government can try to affect the national economy by manipulating the money supply and by deliberately running budgetary deficits or surpluses. By contrast, 49 state governments and most local governments are legally required to balance their budgets. For those few state and local governments not required to have balanced budgets, it is difficult to borrow money for large and persistent budget deficits. The fiscal crises of New York City and other local governments during the 1970s showed that lenders will go only so far in providing money for state and local governments whose expenditures consistently exceed their revenues. The declaration of bankruptcy by Orange County, California, in 1994 reveals how tempting it is for local governments to pursue risky, although potentially very profitable, investment strategies, especially in financially difficult times. In 1997, several dozen school districts in Pennsylvania learned a similar lesson. Risky investment decisions made on their behalf by a reputed financial wizard resulted in the loss of millions of dollars and jeopardized the school districts' financial futures. But the bankruptcy or bankruptcy-like events just mentioned seem to pale into insignificance when contrasted with the number of state and local governments in fiscal strife in the aftermath of the Great Recession of 2007–2009, when a number of local government bankruptcies occurred. State governments have had to take over local governments that have gone "broke" (including the City of Detroit, Michigan), and many state governments found themselves in fiscal straits unrivalled since the Great Depression of the 1930s.

National, state, and local governments all try to promote economic development. New industries employ workers who pay taxes and, thus, increase government revenues for relevant government jurisdictions. What seems new in recent decades on the state and the local scene is the energy, persistence, and ingenuity with which states and localities compete with one another to attract new businesses to their jurisdictions.

Finances are a complicated but critical element of state and local government. This unit treats taxes, lotteries, and related revenue-raising matters, as well as economic development activities of state and local governments.

Article   Prepared by: Bruce Stinebrickner, *DePauw University*

The 'B' Word

Is the stigma of municipal bankruptcy going away?

LIZ FARMER

Learning Outcomes

After reading this article, you will be able to:

- Weigh the pros and cons of municipal bankruptcies for the overall well-being of state and local governments in the United States.

- Assess the desirability and fairness of reducing promised pension benefits for retired or retiring government employees.

Dan Keen knew what he was getting into. When he took the post of city manager of Vallejo, Calif., more than a year ago, Keen understood that Vallejo, a city of more than 100,000 people about 30 miles north of San Francisco, had just emerged from a grueling three-year bankruptcy case. The working-class port town had become the largest municipality to file for bankruptcy after it ran out of money in May 2008. Unable to pay its bills, Vallejo faced a $16 million deficit amid falling property tax revenue and soaring costs in employee compensation and pensions.

So when Keen arrived in Vallejo, he fully expected plenty of headaches. But it was the little things that got him.

"When I came here, the copy machine was on the fritz," Keen says. "As opposed to leasing a new copy machine, which you would do in other cities, that's not an option in Vallejo because they're not going to lease to you. You're a bankrupt city."

Many fiscal observers point to Vallejo as Exhibit A of why municipal bankruptcies are a bad idea. The city's credit rating plummeted, all but killing its borrowing ability. Cuts to services and public safety led to increased crime and prostitution. Even now, the city faces a looming collective bargaining battle with labor unions, and its 2013 budget draws several million dollars from rainy day reserves.

But the landscape may be changing. Since Vallejo, other cities have used bankruptcy filings to help restructure burdensome debts, overhaul pension obligations and renegotiate labor contracts. A handful of California cities are now using bankruptcy to take on that state's goliath pension system; the outcomes of those cases could spread far beyond California, changing the way other municipalities view bankruptcy. Filing for Chapter 9 will almost certainly remain a decision of last resort, but the stigma may not be what it once was. There's a growing sense among some leaders that municipal bankruptcy—unthinkable just a few years ago—may be a valuable tool in a city's financial toolbox.

A big part of the shift has to do with pensions. Employee pensions and other retiree benefits aren't the only cause of municipal distress, but they're a major factor. Cities' obligations to retired employees are gobbling up a larger and larger share of local budgets. In San Jose, Calif., for example, the city's pension payments jumped from $73 million in 2001 to $245 million in 2012, roughly 27 percent of that city's general fund budget. But tinkering with those obligations can be next to impossible. Fiscally distressed cities have sought relief by raising taxes and cutting services, but they often hit a brick wall when it comes to contract adjustments. And even in cases where they can negotiate a new labor agreement, existing pension agreements have legally been untouchable.

That was until Central Falls, R.I., declared bankruptcy. The finance-strapped town of 20,000 people, located on the northern outskirts of Providence, had been trying to renegotiate its pension contracts for months with no success. When it filed for bankruptcy protection in August 2011, the slate was essentially wiped clean. The city immediately moved to change its labor and retiree agreements. The new deal hammered out by Central Falls and the unions was essentially what the city had wanted all along, says Ted Orson, the attorney for the city's receiver. The final agreement slashed pensions by 55 percent (although funding from the state's general assembly reduced that cut to 25 percent for the first five years).

The difference, Olson says, is that Central Falls was the first city to use bankruptcy to make good on its promise to cut pension benefits. "Up until Central Falls, there was never what we call an 'or else,'" Orson says. "There wasn't any leverage to make concessions. However, after Central Falls, when [the labor unions] saw what happened, they understood it's better to negotiate a better agreement than to be in a position where something can be forced on you and you might not like what it is."

Central Falls showed cities that pensions were touchable. Now, two cases in California could cement that idea into law. In Stockton, which filed for bankruptcy in June, the city's bond insurer, Assured Guaranty, is challenging Stockton's Chapter 9 status because the city did not attempt to renegotiate its pension debt with the California Public Employees' Retirement System (CalPERS). In Southern California, San Bernardino is arguing that CalPERS should be treated like any other of the city's creditors. The pension system, says San Bernardino (which surpassed Vallejo last July to become the largest U.S. city ever to declare bankruptcy), should take a haircut right alongside the city's bondholders and other shareholders. If a judge rules that pension systems can indeed be treated like other creditors—many expect the case to make its way to the U.S. Supreme Court—it could forever change the notion of municipal bankruptcy and fiscal restructuring.

The whole definition of bankruptcy is rapidly changing, says University of Pennsylvania law professor David Skeel. "Each new significant bankruptcy has suggested that a type of obligation that more or less seemed to be off the table is on the table."

Needless to say, labor unions don't see the issue the same way. Steve Kreisberg, collective bargaining director for the American Federation of State, County and Municipal Employees, says it's erroneous to think that the country is entering some new phase when it comes to municipal bankruptcies. He rejects the notion that bankruptcy will be used as a tool for restructuring pensions and similar agreements. Case law, he says, still favors his side. "I really think this idea that somehow we're going to create a precedent in this country that public employee pensions are a debt like any other is misguided," Kreisberg says. "So that's why we're opposed to giving up anything that's accrued in terms of a benefit."

Kreisberg may be right. After all, only about half the states even allow cities to file for bankruptcy. Of the 13 cities, towns or counties that have filed since 2008, five cases have been dismissed by a court. And many of the rest of the filings tend to arise from special cases. In Westfall Township, Pa., for example, the city had been hit by a $20 million federal judgment granted to a developer. And Jefferson County, Ala., had filed because of a failed sewer project and corrupt financial dealings by local politicians.

Nonetheless, many legal observers think the outcome of the cases in California could open the door to a host of new bankruptcy filings. "I think you'll see cities looking at Chapter 9 as not some horrible thing, but as a business tool," says San Francisco-based bankruptcy lawyer Karol Denniston, who has helped numerous California cities restructure their finances. She adds that insurers would favor the move because restructuring is not being done "on the back of the bonds." "I think capital markets would be more receptive if there's that opportunity to restructure."

On the other hand, there's the possibility that such a ruling could actually reduce the number of future bankruptcies. If pensions are indeed deemed to be creditors, labor unions and retirees may be more willing to negotiate in the first place because

they know cities' threats are real—the "or else" that was demonstrated in Central Falls. "I think increasingly you'll see unions come around if they believe the city or town will qualify [for bankruptcy]," says Robert Flanders, who was the state-appointed receiver for Central Falls. "Because if it does qualify, unions are going to get taken to the cleaners in bankruptcy."

Indeed, after Central Falls, Rhode Island Treasurer Gina Raimondo pushed through major pension reform at the state level, reform that included raising the retirement age and adjusting benefits for current employees. Raimondo often used Central Falls in making her case for why the reform was needed.

Although many states underwent some kind of cursory pension reform last year, a few cities followed Rhode Island's dramatic lead. In California, San Diego and San Jose voters both approved changes to city pensions that targeted retirement age and restructured employee contributions.

Many believe those changes wouldn't have been possible a few years ago. "I think the lesson from all of this is that in cities across the country, there is a need for them to address their pension and health-care liabilities sooner rather than later," says Chris Hoene, executive director of the nonprofit California Budget Project. In the past, he says, "there's always been this thought of, 'We're not in crisis mode, we have time to sort out this problem.'"

Seeing other places file for bankruptcy has also raised public awareness about the fiscal burdens cities face. In San Diego, for example, retirement fund payments soared from $43 million in 1999 to $231.2 million in 2012. As residents have become more attuned to those kinds of budget obligations, the public outcry against municipal debt restructuring may have softened somewhat. The city of Pacific Grove, Calif., for instance, recently launched community forums to get input from its citizens on how the city should handle its retiree debt. And, says bankruptcy lawyer Denniston, who is helping the city host the forums, Pacific Grove's large community of retirees isn't shying away from the issue of balancing pension costs with the need for public services. "If you can get the conversation out in the open that this is a problem, then you get lots of people talking about solutions," she says. "They've watched what's happened: Nobody wants to be in the position of San Bernardino. They drove off a cliff."

Taxpayers are also becoming more aware of the fact that the bankruptcy process, by its nature, excludes them from decision-making. Chapter 9 cases deal with debtors and creditors. Taxpayers take a hit in the form of higher taxes and reduced services, but since they aren't creditors they don't have a seat at the table, says Skeel, the law professor. "The bankruptcy process isn't really designed to maximize their voice."

Perhaps the most important bottom line when it comes to bankruptcy is image.

In Vallejo, the bankruptcy process has bruised the city's ego as well as its morale, says Keen, the city manager. "You see it everywhere—the pace of work by employees, the police response time. We are not capable of providing what this community needs."

There's definitely still a dark cloud associated with bankruptcy, says Lou Schimmel, the state-appointed emergency manager in Pontiac, Mich. (which has not filed for bankruptcy). Bankruptcies restructure debt, but they don't address gross mismanagement, he says. During his 18-month tenure, Schimmel has struck new labor agreements, consolidated city resources, cut spending and sold off assets to bring Pontiac into a balanced budget. Bankruptcy, he says, doesn't stop a city from making poor financial choices in the future.

Still, many experts say more municipal bankruptcies are inevitably on the horizon. Hoene, for instance, notes that many cities in the Midwest and the Rust Belt have struggled for years, and some are likely too far gone to avoid bankruptcy. And Michigan recently passed a revised emergency manager law that could ease the restrictions allowing that state's cities to file for bankruptcy. Perhaps perversely, declaring bankruptcy could ultimately help a city's credit rating. That was the reasoning in Central Falls, where the bankruptcy court judge's focus was the city's credit standing and access to capital markets. If more places begin to see bankruptcy as a restructuring tool for pension obligations—and a route to better credit—the practice could become more common.

"The biggest hurdle," says Central Falls' Flanders, "is the stigma that's still associated with the 'B' word. Cities, towns and legislatures are deathly afraid of what that word means." If the process had another name, Flanders has said, cities would be much likelier to use it. It's still a very difficult choice to make, and he says he wouldn't want to recommend it. Still, as he said at a *Governing* event last fall, "Bankruptcy is not the disease for these cities and towns. It's the cure."

Critical Thinking

1. What precedent did the bankruptcy of Central Falls, Rhode Island, in 2011 set?
2. What interest do labor unions who represent government employees have in how municipal bankruptcy cases play out?
3. In what sense does a municipal bankruptcy exclude taxpayers from the decision-making process?

Create Central

www.mhhe.com/createcentral

Internet References

Bankrupt Cities, Municipalities List and Map (Governing)
www.governing.com/gov-data/municipal-cities-counties-bankruptcies-and-defaults.html
Biggest Municipal Bankruptcies in U.S. History (Forbes)
www.forbes.com/pictures/ejii45efkm/the-5-biggest-municipal-bankruptcies-in-u-s-histo

Article   Prepared by: Bruce Stinebrickner, *DePauw University*

Two Cheers for the Property Tax

Everyone hates it, but the property tax has some good attributes that make it indispensable.

STEVEN GINSBERG

Learning Outcomes

After reading this article, you will be able to:

- Assess the pros and cons of the property tax as a way for raising local government revenues and weigh its overall utility.

- Evaluate a number of proposed reforms that would improve property taxes as a revenue-raising instrument.

To most Americans, the property tax is about as revered as communism and as popular as a pro-lifer at a NOW rally. The reasons are not hard to understand. At first glance, the property tax system seems arbitrary, unreasonable, and just plain unfair. Every year property owners are hit with a large tax bill, demanding a nearly immediate lump-sum payment. In many jurisdictions, including our nation's capital, the government isn't even required to do you the courtesy of mailing that bill; if you miss the deadline, you must pay late fees whether you received your notice or not. Furthermore, as far as many homeowners are concerned, the manner by which both tax rates and individual property values are determined could not be more random if they were plucked out of a hat. In some cases this is because on-site assessments are only done infrequently—like every five or 10 years. This forces assessors to rely on unreliable estimation methods in the intervening years, such as setting the value of a property based on what neighboring real estate sold for that year, regardless of how the condition of those properties compares with that of the building being assessed. Thus a shack and a renovated loft in the same area can be valued at the same amount. In other communities, like those in California, property values are reassessed only when a building is sold. So a young family of four buying a home in San Francisco's pricey real estate market is slapped with an exorbitant tax bill, while the filthy-rich investment banker down the street is still paying the same amount in taxes as when he first purchased his home in 1979.

Property tax rates are just as varied. In each community, homeowners, businesses, and non-homestead residences (like apartment buildings) vie to lighten their portion of the tax load. Often, regardless of actual property values, whichever group happens to have the most lobbying clout gets a break, while the losing parties are left to shoulder more than their fair share of the burden. In Minnesota, for instance, between 1977 and 1990 homeowners were able to cut their share of property taxes from 45 to 36 percent, even as their share of real estate values rose from 51 to 56 percent. All of this financial finagling, of course, only strengthens taxpayers' conviction that the system is inherently unjust and highly politicized.

It's not surprising then that the property tax has earned such a bad rep among voters—and even less surprising that politicians have latched onto the issue. If you're looking to win votes, opposing the property tax is a no-brainer: It's like declaring that you're anti-drugs. Already, states as politically diverse as Oregon and New York have moved to defang the property tax.

But before we pop open the champagne to toast these developments, we need to take a close look at the upside of the property tax. (And, yes, there is a considerable one.) For although the list of the system's failures is long, people who advocate lowering or abolishing the tax outright are in many cases not considering the big picture.

For starters, contrary to popular belief, the property tax serves as a vital complement to other types of taxes. For instance, our income tax system may be geared to collect more from the affluent, but it also includes numerous loopholes that allow the rich to slip out of paying an amount of tax truly commensurate with their wealth. The property tax picks up where the income tax leaves off. Even if they manage to downplay their annual income, chances are, rich folks are going to buy property. They can't resist owning that summer home in Nantucket, that weekend home in the Hamptons, or that colonial mansion in Georgetown. After all, what's the point of having all that dough if you're not going to spend it? Thus the amount of property you own is as important an indicator of how well-off you are as the income you're officially pulling in each year.

Similarly, property taxes improve the accuracy with which the wealth of senior citizens—whose assets tend to dramatically outweigh their cash incomes—can be taxed. Without property taxes, many seniors would only be taxed on their fixed incomes—which often grossly underestimate how well-to-do they actually are. Now, we're not talking about the 70-year-old Brooklyn couple whose fixed income barely covers the taxes on the brownstone they bought 30 years ago. (An exemption can and should be made to ensure taxes don't force elderly people out of their homes.) But lots of seniors have invested in real estate other than their primary residences. Take the case of a retired speculator who bought property years ago and has watched gleefully as its value skyrocketed. He can enjoy the benefits of his good fortune long before he actually sells those investments. For instance, ownership of pricey real estate makes him eligible for large loans on which the interest is tax deductible. Furthermore, he can spend his fixed annual retirement income without a second thought—knowing that if he's ever low on funds, he can simply cash in his property. The property tax ensures that his tax bill reflects his good fortune. It's not surprising then, that the powerful AARP seniors lobby is pressuring states for an overhaul of the property tax system. And as baby boomers slide into their golden years, we can expect this branch of the anti-property tax lobby to grow even stronger.

Who Will Pick Up the Slack?

No doubt the rich and the elderly recognize that abolishing or lowering property taxes would deal a crushing blow to the schools in their communities—which is where the bulk of the tax's revenues go. But that's no skin off their noses: The rich can always send their kids to private school, and most old people's kids have already flown the nest. Of course, cash-strapped communities are unwilling to stand by as their schools are devastated and may raise other kinds of taxes—like sales taxes—to make up for lost revenue. But such taxes shift more of the burden onto the middle and lower classes, who must buy basic goods, even if they can't afford property.

If you have any doubts about the kind of fiscal havoc the elimination of the property tax can cause, you need only look at what's happened in the states that have "reformed" it. In Florida, the large and religiously anti-property tax seniors population has pushed lawmakers into reducing the property tax rates for some, and completely exempting others. The result is a maze of slimmed-down services and hidden "non-tax" fees that end up unfairly shackling the middle class. Worst of all, these alternative methods simply can't raise the same amount of revenue as the property taxes did. Consequently, notes Kurt Wenner, an economist with Florida TaxWatch, "the schools don't have much of a chance." Small wonder that Florida kids consistently place near the bottom in national reading and math tests, alongside much poorer states such as Louisiana.

In Texas, voters overwhelmingly approved Proposition 1, a ballot measure providing $1 billion in property tax "relief." The law's supporters in the legislature said they had to act "before there was a taxpayer revolt." Of course, almost immediately after the bill passed, school districts across the state announced that they would have to raise other taxes to make ends meet.

Taxpayers in Maine are looking to reduce their property tax bills by expanding the homestead exemption by $20,000, a measure that would rob the state of $200 million in funds. To compensate for the reduction in real estate taxes, Maine will be forced to extend its 6 percent sales tax to a wide range of everyday sources that directly hit middle-class wallets, including movie theaters, bowling alleys, beauticians, and barbers.

The situation is no different in New York; Governor Pataki, along with a slew of legislators, has vowed to cut property taxes. But as property taxes go down, local taxes, user fees, and college education prices continue to surge to make up the difference. The New York proposals are so unbalanced they prompted Patricia Woodworth, director of the budget for the State of New York, to complain to *Newsday* last April, "the benefits are going to go to those who have the greater monetary and financial interest in property holdings, which is not the average person. This plan is not truly tax relief."

But it is Oregon that gives us the most vivid example of what happens when property taxes are slashed. The northwestern state passed Measure 5 in 1990, putting a cap on all property tax increases. This, in turn, forced a massive transfer of state funds to support schools, which left the state with no choice but to cut spending on child welfare, prisons, and state police.

The bottom line: When property taxes are cut, other taxes must be raised to make up for lost revenues. And, as Chris Herbert, an economist at the Harvard-MIT Joint Center for Housing Studies, points out, the property tax is far more progressive than the alternatives. "Cutbacks in property tax have got to be made up and they're not going to be done by a more progressive tax," he says. "Localities can't get states to pick up the tab, so there's a big shift to user charges. You start getting taxes on trash collection and recreation facilities. With user fees things are becoming less progressive because you're paying as much as the next guy"—regardless of whether he happens to be a millionaire.

Mend It, Don't End It

But if we want to get the property tax off the political hit list, we need to address the legitimate problems with the current system. A handful of governments around the country have already started the ball rolling, instituting models that correct some of the more egregious flaws.

Washington state has perhaps the best system, having tackled the issue of favoritism head-on and passed a constitutional amendment declaring that statewide property tax rates must be uniform. For example, all real estate property is currently taxed at approximately 1.2 percent. In addition, all property tax revenues are split between the state and localities. This allows states to tap a deep vein of revenue and distribute it equitably. Under such a system, localities ultimately get to administer their portion of the pot, but the disparity between rich and poor districts is not so wide. "The real key is that the system is administered fairly," says Kriss Sjoblon, an economist at the Washington Research Council. "We have a good system of assessment that eliminates inequities, and the uniformity is vital. People should be treated fairly and folks shouldn't get deals."

Even jurisdictions with special needs can establish systems that are less arbitrary and that make sense to the average taxpayer. Pittsburgh, for instance, has initiated a "split-rate" system in an attempt to foster urban renewal. Property tax is really two separate taxes, one on land and one on building values; Pittsburgh simply separated these two values. The city then lowered the tax on buildings, giving property owners an incentive to maintain, build, and improve their properties, while at the same time increasing the levy on land values, thus discouraging land speculation and stemming urban sprawl. In Pittsburgh and other Pennsylvania cities where the "split-rate" is employed, 85 percent of homeowners pay less than they would with a flat rate, according to analysis by the *American Journal of Economics and Sociology*. The analysis also found that those who do pay more tend to be wealthier homeowners.

Most importantly, the system achieves its goal of encouraging economic growth in urban centers. A study conducted by University of Maryland economists Wallace Oates and Robert Schwab, comparing Pittsburgh to 14 other eastern cities during the decade before and the decade after Pittsburgh expanded its two-rate system, found that: "Pittsburgh had a 70.4 percent increase in the value of building permits, while the 14-city average decreased by 14.4 percent. These findings are especially remarkable when it is recalled that the city's basic industry—steel—was undergoing a severe crisis throughout the latter decade."

Aside from these more comprehensive systems, there are a number of basic steps localities could take to alter the perception of unfairness and ease the burden of property taxes:

- Use the property tax to pay for more than just schools. If seniors and the wealthy feel that the taxes support services they need, they will have reason to pause before directing their lobbying muscle against it.
- Raise the level of exemptions for people over 65. Property taxes do blindside some senior citizens, and there's no reason why they should have to move out of their lifelong homes because the market value of the house has gone up. A moderate raise in the exemption level would prevent poorer seniors from losing their homes, while still raising revenue from the wealthy.
- Stagger payments. A major reason property tax is so unpopular is that it's administered in huge chunks and

people aren't allowed much time before hefty late fees kick in. Distributing the burden over four or more payments a year, with more advanced notice, would take some of the sting out of the bill.
- Upgrade technology. Set it up so people can pay electronically. It's a small thing, but it will make a difference. Most cities allow offenders to pay parking tickets with credit cards, there's no reason they can't do the same with property tax.

Rooting out favoritism and slipshod assessment methods will help make the tax palatable to the majority of citizens. They will no longer see the property tax as a mindless ogre coming to swallow up their hard-earned money. Instead, they will see it as the soundest way to make sure that everyone, especially the wealthy, contributes his share to ensure a high level of public services. In short, they will see it for what it is.

Critical Thinking

1. Why, at first glance, does the property tax system seem "arbitrary, unreasonable, and . . . unfair"?
2. Despite the criticisms, what are the upsides of the property tax?
3. What inevitably happens when property taxes are cut?
4. What reforms would remedy many of the problems of local government property taxes as they currently operate?
5. What is the "split-rate" system of property taxing that Pittsburgh has used? What are the advantages of such a system?

Create Central

www.mhhe.com/createcentral

Internet References

Here We Go Again: Another Try at Property Tax Reform (Business Weekly, November 12, 2013)
http://businessweekly.readingeagle.com/here-we-go-again-another-try-at-property-tax-reform
New York State Property Tax Reform Coalition
www.nyspropertytaxreform.org

STEVEN GINSBERG is an editorial aide at *The Washington Post*.

Article   Prepared by: Bruce Stinebrickner, *DePauw University*

The (New) Rules of the Road

Cash-strapped states such as Virginia are turning to the private sector to help finance large infrastructure projects, but it may just be a way of forcing drivers to pay more in the long run.

FAWN JOHNSON

Learning Outcomes

After reading this article, you will be able to:

- Evaluate the pros and cons of private-public partnerships in the surface transportation sector.

- Explain accountability, tolls, profits, and "revenue risks" in the context of private-public partnerships in the surface transportation sector.

- Explain why the current state of the U.S. economy and increased fuel efficiency in cars each contribute to funding difficulties for surface transportation projects.

Dusty Holcombe had to look up his new boss on Google when he learned in 2011 that he would be transferred to a small government office with the sole mission of making deals with the private sector. Holcombe, a 13-year veteran of the Virginia Transportation Department, had never heard of Tony Kinn, the man tapped to head the commonwealth's newly minted Office of Transportation Public-Private Partnerships.

That's because Kinn had spent most of his career far away from government, honing marketing and business-development strategies for clients such as Macy's, General Foods, and Procter & Gamble. Not a typical civil servant, Kinn can sell you an island in Montana. "We're in the sales and marketing game," he declares. "Twenty percent of the time we're a state agency—the private sector gives not one tinker's damn about that. . . . We're dealing with them business-to-business."

Kinn's boisterous personality, his white hair, his overstuffed frame, his mile-a-minute chatter—it all seems to clash with the bureaucratic nothingness of this public office building in downtown Richmond. He's an imp, not a drone—the visiting uncle who sneaks the kids an extra dessert at Thanksgiving. "This is fun. Are you kiddin' me?" he says. "We've got limited money. We've got 50 competitors."

Kinn arrives an hour late to a meeting with *National Journal* and his top two staffers, Holcombe and project director Jacqueline Cromwell, because he was busy plotting with other state officials about the next round of public-private deals coming through his office. One project involves cultivating developers for land around Metrorail stops where Virginia owns air rights. He dangles tidbits about the other projects without further embellishment. In that way, he is also a tease. "One will be urban, one will be rural, and one will be really rural. I can't tell you any more," he says.

Like it or not, this tenuous marriage of business and government is the new normal. The salad days of massive federal investment in public services are long gone. The most recent surface-transportation measure to pass Congress, clocking in at $105 billion, didn't even make it past the halfway mark in terms of keeping pace with maintenance needs for the next five years. Absent a steady influx of taxpayer funding to build highways and transit systems, state governments are increasingly looking for help from the business world.

Holcombe's role is to serve as Kinn's opposite—the one who makes the gears turn in the office. He is a government whiz who can navigate a procurement process blindfolded. Buzzwords and acronyms pepper his dialogue. Holcombe, not Kinn, is the one you can picture leafing through back issues of *Public Works* magazine that lie in his office's reception area, the ones with profiles of heavy-duty excavator buckets and track-mounted crushers. Holcombe talks like this: "Our goal is to try to mature a project enough before we take it out for procurement. Get the environmental petition in place. Make sure sketch-level traffic and revenue studies are done. Make sure you've done your business model to define that it brings value."

Together, Kinn and Holcombe form the perfect blend of bureaucratic know-how and private-sector competitiveness, a relationship that is increasingly vital as state and federal budgets shrink. Like phosphorus and sulphur on a match, their combined aptitudes are intended to spark new and cheaper ways to allow people to travel about Virginia with less hassle.

Their solution is to woo corporate partners who aren't shy about boosting their own bottom lines. Such an unvarnished quest for profits can be off-putting to residents who just want the roads to be pothole-free. Why should a Wall Street firm make money from a taxpayer-supported utility? Typical public-private arrangements, such as leased roads or privately tolled tunnels, are often met with grumpy skepticism by drivers, who are just as likely to complain about traffic snarls along the Capital Beltway or I-264 into Norfolk.

Is the United States ready to make the shift from the Eisenhower-era national highway network—in which the public owns the roads and highways it supports with tax dollars—to a partially private, profit-based system that invites partners from Wall Street and even other countries?

The benefits of such a shift are rooted deeply in the tenets of capitalism, if not public works. Businesses looking for new markets have struck a gold mine of need, if they can respond to it, in the country's crumbling infrastructure. If market-based motives operate as capitalism dictates, the private sector should be able come up with new and innovative ways to solve complex traffic problems at a lower cost for a city or state. The disadvantages lie in the public's potential lack of access to a needed utility. If private companies run the roads, it's possible that those who are able to pay more would get better access because they could assume the higher cost of tolls.

We may not be quite ready for the shift. The Virginia Transportation Department is fighting to keep afloat a $2.1 billion public-private tunnel project in the Hampton Roads region after a Portsmouth judge ruled in May that the accompanying toll hike was unconstitutional. The case will likely wind up at the Virginia Supreme Court, putting at risk the department's ability to negotiate tolling authority with private investors, a near-essential component of public-private partnerships.

There is a history to this kind of objection. Texas Republican Gov. Rick Perry faced withering criticism for forging a deal with the Spanish infrastructure giant Cintra to build a 4,000-mile network of tolled highways. The project eventually died after the federal Transportation Department refused to sanction it in 2010. The state Legislature made sure to outlaw it in 2011.

Former Gov. Mitch Daniels fared better in Indiana. The Republican succeeded in completing a public-private deal to finance the 157-mile Indiana Toll Road, which secured $3.8 billion for the state. Yet critics still complain that truck tolls could increase more than 3,000 percent over the 75-year deal. Economists say the private dollars were a windfall for the state when the deal closed in 2006, but the agreement will wind up being a net loss for future generations.

"It's almost a kind of confidence game, where you're continually putting more debt into the future," says Phineas Baxandall, a federal budget and tax analyst with U.S. PIRG.

GOP Gov. John Kasich of Ohio recently opted not to pursue a leasing deal with a private infrastructure company to upgrade Cleveland's I-90 Innerbelt, because he didn't want the state to relinquish control of tolling on the road. Kasich is up for reelection, and Democrats say the move was a political ploy. Political or not, the decision shows the governor is sensitive about public wariness when it comes to handing over roads to unelected entities, no matter how efficient those businesses are at doing the work.

Public-private ventures can cause new kinds of headaches. Market investors don't run in the same circles as bureaucrats, and they barely speak the same language. (This is one reason Holcombe and Kinn make a good team: They can translate for one another.)

And that's not the only problem. In business, a cash return on an investment is expected, something generally not required of government-paid projects. Taxpayers stuck in traffic and having to pay out of pocket for the privilege get even grumpier.

Skeptical taxpayers and sketchy economics be damned: Officials such as Kinn and Holcombe are looking for creative ways to attract private investors to develop roads, tunnels, and government land because they see no other options. State budgets are not going to increase anytime soon, and tax increases are politically unpalatable. What's more, when private investors are looking for places to put their capital, why not take advantage?

"Gotta Freakin' Produce"

Virginia is far ahead of other states in courting private investors. Global analytical firm Inspiratia recently ranked the commonwealth as the top entity in the United States, and second in the world, for private-sector attractiveness. Virginia's deal-making seeds were planted in 1995, when the General Assembly passed a law encouraging transportation officials to chase private-sector dollars. Talks with investors went slowly at first because government funds were plentiful and public-private partnerships were in their infancy. By 2012, only three public-private projects had been completed under Virginia's law, but 18 others were in the works.

Kinn's job is to step up the pace, a goal he attacks with gusto. His office is one of the first government agencies in the United States to be judged on the private investment it attracts. Since it was formed in July 2011, it has secured $6.3 billion for Virginia, using $1.8 billion from taxpayers as seed money, a better than 3-1 ratio of private-to-public dollars.

Kinn prides himself on consistently badgering all of Virginia's agencies to seek out potential investors. "You gotta freakin' produce!" he says. "Our job is to drive these agencies, give them opportunities on a regular basis so that they don't even want to see us coming."

Kinn's office is wading into the real-estate market by courting investors who want to develop the land around several of Northern Virginia's Metro stations. They are concocting similar pacts for a NASA space-flight facility off Virginia's coast, looking for investors who might want to sell recreational rides into space.

"Kind of like King's Dominion on steroids," says Cromwell, the office's program director in charge of public relations, referring to the state's popular amusement park. "Where are you going to beat flames and shooting rockets?"

The office was the brainchild of the state's sometimes controversial Republican governor, Bob McDonnell, who has a geek streak when it comes to transportation. McDonnell is one of the few high-level elected officials to openly declare what transportation gurus have been saying for a decade without being heard: The gas tax is an antiquated way to fund roads. Without changes, highway coffers will dwindle over time as cars become lighter and more fuel-efficient. McDonnell was pilloried from both the right and the left for his proposal to replace Virginia's gas tax with new sales taxes, but he is to be commended for pointing out the elephant in the room. His gas-tax replacement bill became law in March.

Kinn and McDonnell are kindred spirits, but Kinn had not met the governor when he was asked to head the new office. "I got a phone call on a Friday afternoon from someone who says, 'Do you want to speak to the governor?' My response is unprintable in this interview," Kinn says cheerfully as he holds court, Falstaff-like, with Holcombe, Cromwell, and *National Journal* in a brightly lit conference room. "I said, 'Who are you? What are you calling me for?' . . . I told my wife after both interviews, 'I fixed that one. They'll never call me back.' "

Beyond Bureaucracy

Kinn was just the type McDonnell wanted for the job: a business-first operator who isn't happy unless investment opportunities are moving, moving, moving. Kinn met his team for the first time at an alehouse across the street from their Richmond office. "I talked to these people, and I thought, 'My goodness, if they just allowed these people to do their jobs, we can do just about anything we want,' " he says.

His attitude toward his staffers, whom he says he dearly loves, is an odd mix of contempt for government culture and awe of their individual expertise. It drives him crazy to see their ingenuity squelched in bureaucracy, and he insists they have to rise above it. "If I want the private-sector industry to play with us, then our people have to be held to a higher standard," he says. "They have to deliver." For example, Holcombe and his team created an interim agreement with two private partners to help finance the tunnel between Portsmouth and Norfolk, which got them in earlier than usual. That made everything work better. "We were both putting funds in for the development of the project," Holcombe says. "It matured the project a little bit more."

Holcombe and Cromwell, who each have decades of civil-service experience, are critical players in fashioning deals that are attractive to the private sector. They make sure permits are delivered on time and concurrently with construction plans. They navigate the matrix of federal, state, and local rules for the private companies. They schedule public meetings and contact all the stakeholders. They let the private partners in on the construction planning early so they can seek their own contracts in non-bureaucratic ways.

"You've got contractors that are not looking so much for change orders or more money or more time out of a traditional contract. They're looking to deliver on time, on budget for less than what they told you," Cromwell says. "It's a completely different way."

Public-private partnerships make sense only for the biggest and most complex infrastructure projects. Simple road paving, for example, needs nothing more than a standard "design-bid-build" process to seek out cost-effective contractors. It doesn't need a lot of up-front money, and the job can be completed in a few months or years.

Bigger projects that span five, eight, or 10 years—and probably a few electoral cycles—benefit from private-sector partners because the firms can infuse a state with cash at the front end.

They can also provide consistency in the design and construction phases even if political administrations change. No matter how sophisticated an infrastructure contract gets, private-sector partners add a tricky new dimension to an already difficult process. Unwieldy projects can run amok for any number of reasons, and that makes some people suspicious of the private partners from the get-go.

The biggest concern the public expresses, although often not in an organized fashion, is lack of accountability. Citizens carry the impression, true or not, that a big project is being turned over to a company that has no roots in the community and no reason to take the public's preferences into account. The reality tends to be more complex. Municipalities often have dueling political goals. Large projects tend to cross several local jurisdictions, which can make the political talks messier. Even without these local problems, transportation analysts acknowledge that elected bodies will always end up ceding some of their authority to a private entity in the course of these deals (witness the recent dustup over flaws in the Silver Spring Transit Center in suburban Maryland). That doesn't always sit well with the locals.

Such doubts were on display when Kinn's office sought private investors to operate what's called the Port of Virginia, composed of ports in Newport News, Norfolk, and Portsmouth. The administration thought a private operator seemed like the right idea because the port was not running efficiently. Yet the Virginia Port Authority's board of directors unanimously turned down multiple private offers in March and stuck with its existing nonprofit government operator. The unspoken reason, according to several observers, was that the nonprofit was a known and trustworthy entity to the port operators. The private bidders were unknowns, and the prospect of dealing with them made the businesses surrounding the port nervous.

The decision didn't go over well with the losers. David Narefsky, an infrastructure lawyer for Chicago law firm Mayer Brown, sees the failure to secure private operators at the Port of Virginia as a show of weakness by the McDonnell administration. Kinn's office could not overcome the general anxiety about a long-term private-sector lease for a highly visible Virginia asset.

Kinn even had to buck up his own staff lawyer when it was over; the lawyer thought they had lost the fight. "I said, 'You have won a major battle. You've changed the *Titanic*. You've created mileposts. You've created signposts on how the performance needs to be done, and our job is to do projects that benefit the citizens of the commonwealth.' "

Kinn and his staff spend a lot of time calculating and communicating the benefits of public-private partnerships. In January, they published a slick-looking set of fact sheets for members of the General Assembly highlighting the jobs and personal-earnings growth that come from projects such as new express lanes on the Capital Beltway and improvements to Virginia's Route 460. Fairfax County, for example, realized $425 million in additional personal earnings for its residents and got support for more than 13,000 jobs, according to the fact sheets.

It is imperative for the office's success, and the success of public-private partnerships anywhere, that these types of jobs and earnings numbers are repeated again and again. Complaints arise automatically when new projects are announced, especially if they involve tolls. By taking a more holistic view of the economic impact, Kinn and his team hope to expand the dialogue about privatization beyond just tolling and fees to also include jobs and earnings figures.

"Pay out the Kazoo"

Drivers hate tolls. That is the beast that Kinn's team is continually fighting, and it is also the biggest drawback to government's exploration of private-sector deals. Tolling is the most common characteristic of public-private transportation agreements because it is the private sector's way of collecting payment for its work.

Kinn ran into this problem almost immediately. His first task was to close a pending public-private deal to finance a new tunnel in the Hampton Roads area connecting Portsmouth and Norfolk. The negotiations were far along and relatively noncontroversial; they began in the administration of Virginia's Democratic former governor, Tim Kaine, and were heartily endorsed by McDonnell.

Kinn brought the agreement to the finish line in December 2011, less than six months after he took his job. The project is valued at $2.1 billion, with a taxpayer contribution of $420.5 million. The new Midtown Tunnel is slated to run parallel to an existing tunnel under the Elizabeth River. The two private-sector partners, the Australian Macquarie Group and the Swedish Skanska Infrastructure Development, will operate and maintain the tolling for both tunnels.

Here's the catch: Tolls will go up 25 cents per car in 2014. After that, they can go up annually, as much as 3.5 percent a year, for 56 years. The private partners will use the toll revenue to maintain the tunnels and subsidize bus and ferry services between Portsmouth and Norfolk. They will pocket the rest.

McDonnell hailed the agreement with Macquarie and Skanska as "a significant step forward for transportation improvements in Hampton Roads." Some constituents weren't impressed. "He outsourced this mega-billion-dollar contract to a foreign country and got our corner of the state to pay out the kazoo for the next 56 years to the tune of a guaranteed $20-something billion in profits," was one comment on the website for the local *Virginian-Pilot* newspaper.

"NO TOLLS!!! NO TOLLS!!! NO TOLLS!!! NO TOLLS!!!" shouted a commenter on the website for WAVY, the local NBC News affiliate.

Experts shrug off such pocketbook complaints, contending that the beauty of the deal isn't readily apparent to people forking over $1.84 every time they traverse a tunnel. The average Hampton Roads resident doesn't see, for example, that Virginia taxpayers no longer have to assume the "revenue risk" that comes from unpredictable traffic patterns, says Simon Santiago, a lawyer with the Washington-based Nossaman law firm, who helped broker the agreement with Macquarie and Skanska.

Transferring the risk to the private sector gives state officials the ability to "keep public contributions at their lowest," Santiago explains. Private companies, meanwhile, have incentive to "keep tolls at their lowest" to attract customers.

The rationale is cold comfort to many Hampton Roads residents. Regular commuters calculate that the initial toll hike will amount to $1,000 in yearly travel expenses. Truckers could pay as much as $15 to cross during rush hour, an expense that could force some of them out of business. As an added irritant, the contract calls for tolls to go up in February 2014, but the new tunnel isn't scheduled to open for two years after that.

The fate of the toll hike is in doubt after Portsmouth Circuit Court Judge James Cales Jr. ruled that the law used to craft the Midtown Tunnel agreement violates Virginia's constitution. Cales said in a court hearing that he agreed with the plaintiffs' assertion that the General Assembly cannot pass a law that cedes tolling and taxing authority to another entity. The agreement with Macquarie and Skanska does just that. An appeal will likely wind up at the Virginia Supreme Court, and it could prompt major queries about the ramifications of inviting Wall Street firms to finance public infrastructure.

"The principle of public accountability has to be stabilized," says Patrick McSweeney, the lawyer who represents a Portsmouth City Council member and hundreds of other residents in the case. "Elected officials are out of the picture for 58 years."

McSweeney says it is typical that big public-private infrastructure projects like the Midtown Tunnel go unchallenged because the public can't figure out how, or whom, to fight. They may be told one thing in an early public meeting and then, as a deal develops, some of the features of the project change. They may face divided opinions among their elected officials.

"The developers, the chamber, they have such an influence on government. The government officials don't realize they are being influenced in that way," McSweeney says.

It's hard to get the public's attention until it's almost too late. Despite the government's seemingly endless stream of postcard notices, public meetings, Web announcements, and communication to local media, someone will always be caught off guard.

"Throughout this whole process, you will still get individuals who indicate, 'Oh, I never knew about this project,' " Holcombe says.

Monster in the Closet

It is ironic that one of the most socialized parts of American society, the national highway system, came about out of fear of being overrun by communism. At the height of the Cold War, President Eisenhower saw the folly of a local, unconnected, and disorganized network of dirt roads if the country ever faced a land invasion or an atomic bomb. As supreme commander of the Allies in World War II, he had been inspired by Germany's autobahns and the ease at which goods and services (and weapons) were transported.

Less well-known is that Eisenhower originally proposed that the national highway system be funded by tolls. The Democratic Congress rejected that, and negotiators finally hit on the idea of a Highway Trust Fund fed by a tax on fuel. Half a century later, with fuel-efficient cars putting a big dent in Trust Fund revenue, states are scrambling for solutions. Still, the public by and large isn't ready to surrender its romantic, 1950s-era worldview. "Nobody wants to pay for something they think they are getting already for free," says Patrick Jones, executive director of the International Bridge, Tunnel and Turnpike Association, offering perhaps the best explanation for why public-private partnerships have not been used to their full potential in the United States.

Jones, who represents the tolling industry, believes the public negativity about tolling is misplaced yet understandable. After all, the only time tolling shows up in the news is when rates go up. This phenomenon is so pervasive that Jones's group is trying to counter what he calls the "niggling negativity" about tolling with a relentlessly upbeat public-relations campaign.

Last year, IBTTA hired a team of PR experts to make sure the industry is pointing out the positive aspects of tolling at every opportunity. When San Francisco's Golden Gate Bridge implemented all-electronic tolling, for example, the association applauded. "Tolling once meant, 'Stop.' But today high-tech tolling means 'Go, go, go,' " Jones says in the press release.

People may be willing to embrace tolls if they have few other choices. A recent poll from the infrastructure firm HNTB found that 46 percent of respondents preferred new roads funded by tolls if the only other choices were new roads funded by higher gas taxes (25 percent) or no new roads (28 percent).

People also feel better about tolls if they see a direct benefit from them. Seventy-one percent of respondents in the HNTB poll say they would be willing to pay a higher fare on a road or highway to save travel time.

Therein lies the problem. The benefits of tolling are frequently not obvious, and years of construction while tolls are still being collected further cloud the picture. It is difficult to walk back from an initial bad impression. The headlines about the improvements for Cleveland's I-90 Innerbelt highlight the traffic jams during construction. Regular users of the Hampton Roads tunnel fear similar delays. It's not hard to see how a toll hike becomes an additional affront to drivers.

Even when commuters are given the choice, they may not opt for the costlier, faster way around. The "HOT lanes" on I-495, another of Virginia's much-touted public-private partnerships that gives drivers the choice to pay to avoid Washington's Beltway congestion, posted an $11.3 million loss in the first six weeks of operation. Drivers simply didn't see the need to pay the extra money. "It's kind of expensive," one Virginia driver told *NJ.*

In Hampton Roads, Kinn thinks Virginia screwed up the public-relations effort because the toll hike was one of the first and most well-known facts about the project. "If timing is everything, the horse had left the barn" by the time the deal was inked, he says.

Kinn has a better way of explaining it, but his sound bite now comes off like an excuse for the toll hike instead of a big bonus for the area. He believes local drivers should not have had the opportunity to add up the annual costs of the toll hikes without taking into account reduced gas expenses and faster commute times. "Would you pay 18 cents a day to get home an hour earlier?" he asks.

Pleading the Case

Public-private partnerships have a distinct advantage in the current political climate. They bring in dollars from private investors willing to bet on the future flow of traffic so the state doesn't have to. The terms of such deals tend to be good for cities and states that are short on cash—they get two to three times the value of the taxpayer investment for a new road or bridge. They can then invest more state money in basic repairs.

"A city or a state says, 'There's no way we can raise money, and [a public-private partnership] puts money on the table,'" says Baxandall, the PIRG analyst.

That's more or less how it worked in Hampton Roads. The Midtown Tunnel has been the No. 1 transportation priority in the area for at least 10 years, but it is hugely expensive. The deal with Macquarie and Skanska definitely makes sense at the moment, with three-fourths of the up-front costs coming from two outside companies. It could turn out to be a worse deal later, and the residents would have no recourse.

"Twenty years from now, let's say, people may be cursing how high these tolls are. The people who put down the Hampton Roads project now won't get the blame for that," Baxandall says.

It is difficult to fault the Hampton Roads contract on any other grounds than a basic dislike for private-sector involvement in government and the long-term obligations it brings. The project gives an economic boost to the area with minimal risk to the taxpayer. The negotiators had the right expertise, did their homework, got all the technical specifications right, and touched base with all the right people. The Virginia Transportation Department and the attorney general's office are banking on a judicial reversal from their appeal, and the beginning stages of tunnel construction are going forward in the interim. If the contract is found to be unconstitutional, the department could find itself with a $1 billion financing hole to continue the project.

It wouldn't be the first time a deal like this threatened to crumble. A classic example of a public-private partnership gone awry is the South Bay Expressway, a 10-mile express toll road near San Diego. California negotiated the deal in 1991 with Macquarie, the same company partnering in the Hampton Roads project. In 2010, just three years after the road opened, the private operator hired by Macquarie declared bankruptcy. San Diego eventually bought the road back at fire-sale terms.

The South Bay deal was among the first of its kind in the United States, and it suffered from rookie errors. Delays and unexpected costs led to large budget overruns. A design-and-build team sued Macquarie over the construction timetables. The road opened for business at the start of a massive economic recession that hit Southern California especially hard. Both the costs of the lawsuit and the collapse of the subprime housing market were cited in the bankruptcy declaration.

Even here, the story has a happy ending. After the city took over the expressway, it was able to slash tolls by almost half to attract drivers. Usage went up 20 percent in just a few months. The road won't be paid off until 2042, but like any mortgage, the owner-taxpayers can use it while paying down their debt.

Since that debacle, government operators have learned a lot about how the pieces of a public-private partnership need to fit together to make sense to the public. Kinn likes to say that even the name is a misnomer. "They're not public-private partnerships," he argues. "They're public, private, political, publicity-type partnerships. We don't have any public-relations arm that's strong enough to deal with what we're facing."

That's why Kinn recently hired a political operator and an old friend, Rick McGeorge, whose main job is to go from town to town and make sure Virginia's local officials and opinion leaders are aware of potential public-private infrastructure projects in their areas. The worst thing the deal-makers can do to a city is blindside it, even if the projects on tap would be a boon to residents.

Kinn and McGeorge spend a lot of time on the road, gladhanding. "We've gotten to know the mayors. We've got to know the [metropolitan planning organizations]," Kinn says. "I've taken Rick on one of these junkets. It's tiring for Rick, and its tiring for me. But we don't walk in there as unknowns. Every key person is there. We've worked to earn that right, and now we've got to stay there."

These "junkets" seem more like political tours than business trips, but Kinn understands they are just as critical to a well-crafted deal as the final signatures in a CEO's conference room. Like politics, all business is personal. Local champions are essential when you blend government with business, because the agreements look smarmy and opportunistic without them.

The rules are simple: Get the mayor and city council on board; show the neighboring mayors and city councils that you have ideas for them, too; treat cities like equals with your private-sector partners; above all, do not underestimate the people by keeping them in the dark. Kinn's team is comfortable presenting at churches, county fairs, 4-H clubs, and any other community group that will have them. Still, it doesn't always work. They did all of this outreach for the Hampton Roads tunnel and still met considerable opposition in Portsmouth.

Even so, it's hard to imagine a transportation network operating in this budget climate without the influx of private-sector cash. The people who protest that investment, such as Portsmouth lawyer McSweeney, acknowledge that the government has its back up against a wall, that choices have to be made. "Maybe it's better," he says, "just to recognize we've bumped up against the debt limits."

Critical Thinking

1. How do private-public partnerships in the surface transportation sphere work?

2. How do accountability or lack thereof, tolls, profits, and "revenue risk" fit into private-public partnerships in providing highways, tunnels, bridges, and other such projects?

3. What was President Eisenhower's rationale for proposing the national government's Interstate highway system in the 1950s? How did he want to fund it? How, in fact, has it been funded?

Create Central

www.mhhe.com/createcentral

Internet References

CEO's Message—Indiana Toll Road
www.ezpassin.com/aboutITR.do;jsessionid=80E01A9C3BC8CEEF26831
89B653A3231

Public-Private Partnerships Aren't Just for Roads (*National Journal,* **September 23, 2013**)
www.nationaljournal.com/policy/insiders/transportation/public-
private-partnerships-aren-t-just-for-roads-20130923

Take the Public-Private Road to Efficiency (*Wall Street Journal,* **February 19, 2013**)
http://online.wsj.com/news/articles/SB100014241278873234780045783 0
4372344816256

Article   Prepared by: Bruce Stinebrickner, *DePauw University*

Snookered

The corporate tax incentive game is a money-loser, but states keep playing.

WILLIAM FULTON

Learning Outcomes

After reading this article, you will be able to:

- Assess the $80-billion a year decentralized economic development incentive system operated by state and local governments in the United States.

- Evaluate the suitability of the analogy between the operation of the economic incentive system and the role of the ante in a poker game.

If you sat down and drew up the ideal plan to invest $80 billion every year in economic development across the United States, you would think of a lot of exciting things. You could pour the money into research and form the basis for new product breakthroughs in a wide variety of fields. You could invest in America's workforce to make it more skilled and flexible. You might assist manufacturing companies in upgrading their factories and equipment, or help universities attract the best students from around the world for science and engineering programs, or improve our transportation infrastructure.

The one thing you almost certainly would *not* do with $80 billion a year is create a decentralized system of providing tax breaks and other subsidies to profitable businesses in different economic sectors, often with little accountability for how the money is spent and no recourse if the company goes south. Yet, as a highly publicized series in *The New York Times* last December showed, this is exactly the system that state and local governments around the country have created over the past four decades.

Though the issue of economic development incentives has been around for a long time, the *Times* used solid footwork and a lot of groundbreaking data analysis to draw the most complete picture of our incentive system to date. By combing through a variety of databases, the newspaper's reporters examined 150,000 incentive deals and came up with the $80 billion price tag. They also cast the story in David-versus-Goliath terms, clearly suggesting that unsophisticated government agencies—especially local governments—get snookered on a regular basis by slick corporations that often take the money and break their promise to deliver jobs.

The bottom line was depressingly familiar. When asked whether the tax breaks and subsidies actually created jobs, elected officials and economic development experts couldn't say for sure. All they knew—or so they said—was that they didn't dare *not* put these incentives on the table, for fear that the companies would locate or relocate elsewhere.

And therein lies the biggest problem with America's decentralized economic development incentive system: It may or may not work. In fact, there's considerable evidence that it doesn't work, but it operates kind of like the ante in a poker game. Throwing the money into the pot doesn't mean you'll win the game. All it means is that you get to play.

Whether you win depends a lot on how the business sectors you are dealing with approach the poker game. Sophisticated businesses tend to play their poker hands based on skill. "Sure, we'll take the money you ante up with, but that's not really what we are looking for," they'll say. "We also need a skilled labor force, a good transportation system, connections to research institutions, perhaps a favorable regulatory environment—because those are the things we really need to run our enterprises profitably and no amount of cash is going to make up the difference if these things are lacking."

Manufacturing in the South is undergoing a renaissance in large part because both governments and companies play this game with skill. "Yes, we have incentives, low taxes, and light regulations, but we also have the things you really need as well," government officials respond. It is no coincidence, by the way, that these other things are often place-based and hard to move, meaning the companies are less likely to skip town.

In other situations, however, governments and businesses play a very simple, bald game of up the ante. Some manufacturers insist on subsidies and promise jobs, but they take the subsidies and then leave town. General Motors' up-the-ante approach during its bankruptcy was the subject of much of the *Times*' reporting.

The film industry plays a similar game of, "If you're dumb enough to give me your money, I'm dumb enough to take it." Movie productions search all over the United States and Canada seeking ever more subsidies and tax credits. Some localities are just excited to land a Hollywood film shoot, while others try to use the shooting as a foundation to build a bigger infrastructure that will attract more value-added pieces of the business. But the bulk of the film business remains headquartered in Los Angeles, which has an enormous infrastructure that is virtually impossible to duplicate anywhere else. Even so, the studios still try to extract more subsidies out of the state of California, which is under constant pressure to up the ante—or else.

The great comedian Jack Benny had a running joke with Ed Sullivan, the host of his namesake TV show, one of the most popular in America in the 1950s and '60s. What would happen if Sullivan didn't show up for his own show? Being on the Ed Sullivan show was the biggest thing in American entertainment, but Sullivan himself didn't actually do anything. Pressed for an answer, Sullivan said he had no idea. Finally, Benny delivered his classic deadpan punchline: "Don't ever stay home to find out."

That's the dilemma states and localities in America face in dealing with financial incentives. A lot of the time they don't seem to do anything. But no one knows whether the companies would turn up in town without them. So the politicians follow Jack Benny's advice: They keep putting money on the table just to find out what will happen.

Critical Thinking

1. Approximately how much money do state and local governments spend on tax breaks and other subsidies every year? How much accountability and systematic evaluation are associated with that spending?

2. In what way(s) does the U.S. decentralized economic development incentive system operate like the ante in a poker game?

Create Central

www.mhhe.com/createcentral

Internet References

As Companies Seek Tax Deals, Governments Pay High Price (*New York Times*, 1 Dec 2012)
www.nytimes.com/2012/12/02/us/how-local-taxpayers-bankroll-corporations. html?_r=0

Economic Development Agencies (U.S. Small Business Administration)
www.sba.gov/content/economic-development-agencies

Fulton, William. From *Governing*, March 2013, pp. 20–21. Copyright © 2013 by e.Republic Inc. Reprinted by permission via Wright's Media.

Article   Prepared by: Bruce Stinebrickner, *DePauw University*

The Enticement Window

Millions of millennials will soon be putting down roots. Are cities ready?

WILLIAM FULTON

Learning Outcomes

After reading this article, you will be able to:

- Assess the implications for localities of young people moving to where they want to live and only then looking for a job.
- Weigh the sorts of characteristics that seem to attract millennials and determine whether you are attracted by those same things.

I knew the "brain drain" problem had reached a crisis point when they started talking about it in Boston.

You know the story: Kids move to where they want to live and then look for a job, not the other way around. They're drawn to a small number of hip metro areas (D.C., San Francisco, Seattle) and smaller cities (Boulder, Colo.; Missoula, Mont.; Palo Alto, Calif.) around the country and hip employers follow them. The result is an upward cycle of talent and jobs and business growth in the fashionable places, and a downward cycle everywhere else.

It's not unusual to hear people complain about this problem in Middle America, or in second-tier cities without a big university, or in populous but aging suburban locations such as Long Island, N.Y. But it's not a common thing to hear about in a place like Boston, which has the greatest concentration of universities in the country, lots of cool neighborhoods and a big chunk of the innovation economy.

The problem, Massachusetts economic development folks say, is that metro Boston is so expensive they can't keep the kids, especially after those kids begin to have their own kids. Yes, they can live in tiny city apartments, or maybe in a pleasant older suburb like Newton—if they can afford it. After that, they are living somewhere beyond Interstate 495 and the reach of most commuter rail lines. What Boston needs, the experts say, is more starter homes in interesting, transit-rich locations.

Don't we all. If Boston can't stop the brain drain, is there any hope for the rest of us? Yes, but it requires a concentrated effort to create compelling places to live and work—and *fast*.

Because of the demographics of young talent, the cities and suburbs on the downward cycle have a limited window to turn things around: ten years at most, and maybe no more than five.

Here are the facts most people know: For the foreseeable future, the so-called millennials (currently ages 18–30) will drive both the housing market and the fast-growing innovation economy. It's a huge cohort of about 70 million people. And as I mentioned above, they are gravitating toward a select group of metros and small cities.

But there are a couple of other facts that we don't usually think about. Most people settle down by age 35, and usually don't move from one metro area to another after that. And the demographic group behind the millennials is a lot smaller. Just like baby boomers, the preferences of the millennials will drive our society for two generations. They're making location decisions based on their idea of quality of life. And they're going to make all those decisions in the next few years—by the time they're 35.

So if you're not one of the hip places today, you have only a few years—the length of one real estate cycle and the time horizon for planning an infrastructure project—to become hip enough to keep your kids and attract others.

This might seem like a daunting, if not insurmountable, challenge, but frankly I'm encouraged by what I see. Over the last six months I've been to many second-tier cities—Omaha, Neb.; Oklahoma City; Richmond, Va.; Syracuse, Buffalo and Rochester, N.Y.; and Manchester, N.H., among them—that would not be good candidates for a hip urban core. Yet they're all developing one.

Nebraska's conservative Republican governor, Dave Heineman, took the opportunity of hosting a National Governors Association event in Omaha to show off downtown lofts and restaurants. In Oklahoma City, Republican Mayor Mick Cornett, who lives a block from City Hall, has championed urban reinvestment—one of his latest projects is a streetcar line. In Manchester, the old mills bordering downtown are being refurbished. In Syracuse, where the urban core is adjacent to a prominent research university, several hundred housing units have been created in historic buildings, attracting many new downtown residents, including my onetime roommate, who moved back downtown after 20 years of living in a ritzy, cutesy suburb.

The lesson for me is that even though the window is short, there's still time for second-tier cities and older suburbs to create the compelling places that will be required to succeed in the 21st-century economy. Most people—even millennials—want to live near their families and near where they grew up, meaning that if you can create interesting places, they're likelier to stay. And you don't need the endless hip urban fabric of New York or D.C. to compete. You just need a few great neighborhoods for people to live and work in. For most cities, that's an achievable goal.

In his recent book, *The New Geography of Jobs,* economist Enrico Moretti of the University of California, Berkeley, noted that the current pattern of winners and losers is good for the national economy even if it's bad for most cities, because the innovation economy thrives on agglomeration. That's probably true, at least in the short run. But in the long run, it's surely better to have more compelling places—large and small—that can attract their share of young talent and economic buzz. America's prosperity will be more enduring as a result.

Critical Thinking

1. What causes an "upward cycle of talent and jobs and business growth" in a (relatively few) fashionable places?

2. What do second-tier cities or other localities have to do to compete for millennials? According to William Fulton, how much time do they have to do so?

Create Central

www.mhhe.com/createcentral

Internet References

How Millennial Are You? (Pew Research Center quiz)
www.pewresearch.org/quiz/how-millennial-are-you

The Rise of the Creative Class by Richard Florida (*Washington Monthly*)
www.washingtonmonthly.com/features/2001/0205.florida.html

Article   Prepared by: Bruce Stinebrickner, *DePauw University*

The Secret Tax Explosion

Special districts are growing like weeds—and raising tax burdens as they proliferate.

FRANK SHAFROTH

Learning Outcomes

After reading this article, you will be able to:

- Explain what a special district is and why their numbers have grown so much in recent years.

- Explain why the rapid growth in the number of special districts in recent years has led to the Internal Revenue System questioning whether special districts are eligible to issue tax-exempt debt.

The structure of local government in America is changing. In the last half century, the number of school districts has declined by more than 80 percent and the number of counties and municipalities has either declined or barely budged. There has, however, been an explosion in special-purpose districts. A whole new kind of government is now the most prevalent form of government in the U.S.—and that's raising all sorts of taxing questions.

The Internal Revenue Service is asking whether these districts are eligible to issue tax-exempt debt. Similarly, rating agencies and some taxpayers question whether there's sufficient transparency and accountability in the taxing processes that special districts use.

The extraordinary growth in special districts appears to be a response, at least in part, to the spread of tax and debt limitations, as well as popular resistance to general tax increases. In Colorado, for instance, in the wake of the 1992 adoption of its Taxpayer Bill of Rights, there was a proliferation of new quasi-governments. By 2005, special districts accounted for 87 percent of all local governments in Colorado. The irony: A citizens' initiative to reduce the size and role of government achieved the obverse. The increase in special-purpose districts is due to local governments' seeking budget relief, while still desiring to maintain services.

Special districts, which generally provide services not being supplied by existing general-purpose governments, may serve multiple states or counties—or be as small as one person.

In Texas, for example, it only took one person to create a utility district out of 1,000 acres of Shiney Hiney Ranch. A former Dallas medical student, who'd moved to a trailer home on Shiney Hiney a month before an election, voted to create "a special district with rights to invoke eminent domain and to issue $400 million in bonds, along with setting a $1 property tax rate (per $100 of assessed value)," according to the *Denton Record-Chronicle*.

It's how these districts are supported that raises questions about tax burdens and transparency. When special districts are created to run enterprise activities—airports, harbors, hospitals, water and sewer utilities—they rely either entirely or predominantly on user fees. Special districts for non-enterprise activities, like fire and police, however, lean heavily on property tax as a revenue source.

The lines of revenue raising can be opaque. In Travis County, Texas, for example, 118 different entities can levy property taxes. Many of those entities tax only certain areas within the county, which means no one is taxed by all 118. Throughout the state, the number of entities with the power to levy property taxes has also increased. In 1992 cities and counties were roughly a third of those that could levy property taxes, school districts made up another third and the last third consisted of special-purpose districts. By 2010, special-purpose districts made up 87 percent of the growth in property taxing authorities over the last two decades. As a result, special-purpose tax districts constitute more than 40 percent of property taxing entities in Texas.

According to data provided by the comptroller's office, Texas' population has grown by more than 40 percent since 1992, even as property taxes have increased by 188 percent. Some of the money goes to counties, cities and school districts, but the bulk goes to special-purpose districts.

The upsurge in special districts has meant an explosion of new taxes. Ironically, this is happening in states that are often perceived as anti-tax. This unprecedented growth in special districts is leading to a showdown with the federal government over the ability of local governments to issue public capital debt and could preempt the authority of many states and localities.

Critical Thinking

1. How does a special district differ from a general-purpose local government?
2. Why has people's resistance to tax increases led to an extraordinary increase in the number of special districts in the United States in recent years?

Create Central

www.mhhe.com/createcentral

Internet References

Images for Special Districts

www.google.com/search?q=special+district&client=firefox-a&hs=K0O&rls=org.mozilla:en-US:official&channel=fflb&tbm=isch&tbo=u&source=univ&sa=X&ei=6UWRUse0IMyLqQGxlYGYDg&ved=0CGEQsAQ&biw=1024&bih=609

What Is a Special District? (Municipal Research Services Center of Washington)

www.mrsc.org/subjects/governance/spd/spd-definition.aspx

Shafroth, Frank. From *Governing,* September 2013, pp. 66. Copyright © 2013 by e.Republic Inc. Reprinted by permission via Wright's Media.

Unit 7

UNIT

Prepared by: Bruce Stinebrickner, *DePauw University*

Policy Issues

One only has to look through a daily newspaper to realize the multiple and diverse activities in which state and local governments engage. Indeed, it would be an unusual American who, in a typical day, does not have numerous encounters with state and local government programs, services, and regulations.

State and local governments are involved in providing roads, sidewalks, streetlights, fire and police protection, schools, colleges, daycare centers, health clinics, job training programs, public transportation, consumer protection agencies, museums, libraries, parks and swimming pools, sewage systems, and water. They regulate telephone services, gambling, sanitation in restaurants and supermarkets, land use, building standards, automobile emissions, noise levels, air pollution, hunting and fishing, and consumption of alcohol. They are involved in licensing or certifying morticians, teachers, electricians, social workers, childcare agencies, nurses, doctors, lawyers, pharmacists, and others. As these listings should make clear, state and local governments affect very many aspects of Americans' everyday lives.

Among the most important state and local government functions are those related to the well-being and development of children, with education being one particularly prominent such function. For the most part, public elementary and secondary schools operate under the immediate authority of more than 15,000 local school districts. Typically headed by elected school boards, these districts are collectively responsible for spending more than $600 billion a year and have no direct counterparts in any other country in the world. State governments regulate and supervise numerous aspects of elementary and secondary schooling, and school districts must operate within the usually considerable constraints imposed by their state government. In addition, most states have fairly extensive systems of higher education. Tuition charges are higher at private colleges than at state institutions, and taxpayers make up much of the difference between what students pay and the actual costs of operating state colleges and universities. While the national government provides some aid to elementary, secondary, and higher education and also involves itself in some areas of education policies, state and local governments have been the dominant policymakers in public education for decades. That having been said, the controversial No Child Left Behind law, enacted early in the George W. Bush administration, has undoubtedly increased the national government's profile—and influence—in public elementary and secondary schooling.

Crime control and order maintenance constitute another salient function of state and local governments. Criminal statutes, police forces, prisons, traffic laws (including drunk driving laws and penalties), juvenile detention centers, and courts all relate to state and local government activities in the area of public safety. Presidents and presidential candidates have sometimes talked about crime in the streets and what to do about it, but the reality is that state and local governments have traditionally had far more direct responsibility in this policy area than the national government has ever had. The September 11 terrorist attacks, however, have caused a reconsideration and readjustment of national, state, and local roles in protecting public safety.

Singling out education, one of several key state and local policy clusters involving children, and public safety in the preceding two paragraphs is not intended to slight the many other significant policy areas in which the state and local governments are involved: planning and zoning, roads and public transport, fire protection, provision of health care facilities, licensing and job training programs, and environmental protection, to mention just a few. Selections in this unit should provide greater familiarity with various activities of state and local governments.

Related to the provision of services by state and local governments is the distinction between the *provision* and *production* of goods and services. For example, a local government may be responsible for *providing* garbage collection for residents and might meet that responsibility by paying a private firm or a neighboring unit of local government to *produce* the service. Similarly, a state government may be responsible for providing penal institutions to house certain kinds of criminal offenders, but might meet that responsibility by paying a private concern or another state government to produce (plan, build, organize, and operate) a prison where inmates will be confined. In recent years, the concept of privatization has figured prominently in discussions about the best ways for state and local governments to deliver services.

Policies and policymaking processes treated in this unit of the book can be viewed as the consequences of topics treated in earlier units. Intergovernmental relations, finances, elections, parties, interest groups, and governmental institutions all shape state and local government responses to policy challenges and opportunities. In turn, policies that are adopted then interact with other components of state and local politics and modify them accordingly.

Article   Prepared by: Bruce Stinebrickner, *DePauw University*

Raising Children: It Takes State and Local Governments, Too

BRUCE STINEBRICKNER

Learning Outcomes

After reading this article, you will be able to:

- Assess the relative importance of parents, other family members, friends and peers, and state and local governments in shaping American children's lives.

- Evaluate how well state and local governments are performing in each of the five clusters of children-related public policy identified in this article.

Speaking in Cleveland in 1991, then-Governor of Arkansas Bill Clinton declared that

There is an idea abroad in the land that if you abandon your children, the government will raise them. I will let you in on a secret. Governments do not raise children—people do. And it's time they were asked to assume their responsibilities and forced to do so if they refuse. (1)

Clinton was right, of course: governments in the United States do not generally "raise" children. But they are hardly idle bystanders either.

Some people, perhaps many people, may object to the significant roles that national, state, and local governments play in American children's lives and prefer that governments were less involved; others may wish that governments did more and did it better. But whatever one's assessment of governments' performance in what I shall call "children-related public policy," the involvement of governments in children's lives in the United States is certainly extensive and worth exploring.

This article surveys the significant involvement of state and local governments in the lives of American children today. What do American state and local governments do that affects the raising of children? How can we begin to make sense of the variety of children-related activities in which state and local governments engage? What can be said about the structures through which government shapes the lives of children? What are the different emphases in state government activities and local government activities aimed at children?

Before beginning this exploration of the roles of state and local governments in the lives of children, let me clarify what I mean by "children-related public policy." While it can be argued that *everything* American governments do affects children directly or indirectly, "children-related public policy" refers to government policies or activities in which children are explicitly and intentionally distinguished from adults and treated differently. The precise age that divides "children" from "adults" can vary from issue to issue and from jurisdiction to jurisdiction. The principle, however, of treating people younger than a certain age differently from those who are older remains the essence of "children-related public policy."

In this article I shall elaborate on five "clusters" of children-related public policy that can help capture the contours of how state and local governments affect the lives of children in the United States: (1) *custody* and related matters, (2) *schooling and education,* (3) *restricted access* to specified activities and objects, (4) the *juvenile justice* system, and (5) provision of *material resources.*

(1) *Custody* and Related Matters

My treating *custody* as the first of the five clusters is not accidental or random, for I think that *custody* is *the most central* children-related policy in which state and local governments engage. For many people, "custody" calls to mind custody disputes or arrangements ensuing from a break-up, especially divorce, of parents of minor children (that is, children under the age of 18). But such disputes or arrangements are just the tip of an iceberg. Adoptions and adoption arrangements, procedures, and so forth are another element of the *custody* cluster that periodically receives prominent attention in news media and the like, usually because of tragic and heart-rending circumstances. Foster care and particularly instances of foster parents' abuse and neglect of foster children are still another custody matter that periodically makes headlines.

Two other significant components of state and local policies and practices relating to *custody,* however, get far less visibility and attention than they deserve: (i) initial grants of custody to biological parents as a matter of course, and (ii) legally mandated relinquishment (also known as "court-ordered termination") of parental rights/obligations. These two components of custody arrangements are less visible than they ought to be, and the first of them—initial grants of custody to biological parents as a matter of course—is so taken for granted that I would not be surprised if most Americans do not even *recognize* it as a government policy.

When a woman gives birth to a baby, American state governments record the birth and *automatically* assign custody to the parents or the single mother in virtually every case. Few people, including government officials, give any thought to this routine policy followed in all fifty American states. Perhaps routine assignment of legal responsibility ("custody") to birth parents or the birth mother is the best way for state governments to proceed. Some have said that even if a couple had been convicted of horrendous abuse or neglect of a previous child, that that misconduct would not bar them from automatically receiving custody of a subsequent child. Whether that observation is—or ever was—entirely accurate is not the point here; it almost certainly contains at least a kernel of truth and can serve to pique our interest.

What are the alternatives to automatic assignment of custody of a newborn to the biological parent(s)? Let me set forth a few conceivable—even if unconventional and, in most cases, unappealing—options that governments might, at least in theory, adopt: (1) Require prospective biological parents to obtain licenses to raise a child before s/he is born. Biological parents of a newborn child without the proper license would not be granted custody of the child. (2) Put newborns up for adoption, with birth parents free to join the pool of prospective custodial parents and compete, in effect, for custody of their biological child. (3) Assign custody of all newborns to collectively operated child-raising institutions similar to those that exist or have existed in the United States and elsewhere (orphanages, "boys (or girls) schools," Israel's *kibbutzim*).

I readily concede that the three possibilities described are neither plausible nor politically feasible options in the contemporary United States. Indeed, any of them being put into effect by even a single state government is about as likely as my being elected president the day after I return from a one-week round-trip to Mars on a spaceship that I built in my backyard. Nor am I suggesting that they are good or desirable options. But I have presented them to reinforce the point that a legally binding custody decision is made in the case of each and every baby whose birth is recorded in the United States. That that decision is automatic, largely unnoticed, and taken-for-granted does not make it any less consequential for children, not to mention the adults to whom legal custody is granted.

The unquestioned assignment of custody of newborns to birth parents is accompanied by another noteworthy phenomenon, the infrequency with which such initial custodial assignments are terminated. Two routes to termination of parental status over a child can be distinguished. *Voluntary* relinquishment occurs when a custodial parent or parents voluntarily give up legal custody of a child, handing the child over to a government (typically a state government) that assumes custody until or unless it re-assigns custody to someone else, typically through adoption. *Involuntary* relinquishment (or court-ordered termination) occurs when an appropriate state or local court with the proper jurisdiction (often a juvenile or family court) orders that a parent's custody of a child be terminated, whether the parent likes it or not.

State and local government judges are generally very reluctant to order the termination of parents' custody of their biological children, and some or even many observers would say *notoriously* so. One only needs to talk to a few social workers or child welfare workers employed by state or local governments to hear the strongly held view that too many children remain in the custody of unfit parents whose custody should have been terminated. Reports of children coming to some grievous harm, including death, at the hands of custodial parents whose parenting deficiencies had previously come to the attention of authorities (that is, state and local government personnel such as child welfare workers, police officers, public school teachers, and/or judges) are, alas, all too frequent. Even when such parenting shortcomings come to authorities' attention more than once, parents are usually allowed to retain custody. Typically, it is only after grievous harm to the relevant child or children becomes known that the performance and oversight by relevant government authorities are judged to have been inadequate.

The *custody* cluster of children-related public policy is anchored by the bedrock principle that some specifically identified adult or adults are to have legal custody of *every* child. As already noted, for all but a small minority of children, the custodial adult(s) include(s) one or both biological parents. Adoptive parents have custody of the big majority of those children for whom neither biological parent holds custody. Indeed, adoption can be defined as the process wherein governments re-assign—typically, from one or both birth parents, but sometimes after a brief transitional period of custody by the state—legal custody of children to one or more adults who are not the birth parents. The adoptive parents thereafter have all the rights and obligations that birth parents routinely get for the vast majority of American children.

Another portion of the small minority of children for whom neither biological parent holds custody are declared "wards of the state," which means that a state government is the custodial entity legally responsible for the child's well-being. Orphanages were traditionally the residences of children who were wards of the state. Sometimes wards of the state are placed in the care of foster parents, who do not have legal custody of their foster children. Such foster parents serve, in effect, as paid child-care workers in their homes, with responsibilities for and jurisdiction over their foster children far exceeding that of any ordinary child-care worker, but falling significantly short of having the rights and responsibilities invested in biological or adoptive parents. All custodial arrangements—birth parents' custody over their biological children, adoptive parents' custody over their adoptive children, state governments' custody over wards of the state—are subject to change, but, as already noted, termination of birth parents' custody over their biological children (or of adoptive parents' custody over their adopted children) is rare.

That custodial arrangements can and do change when divorces occur need only be mentioned in passing. In the context of divorce, notions such as "joint custody" and "custodial parent" (that is, the one parent in a divorced couple who has primary responsibility for the children of the previous marriage and with whom the children legally reside) are generally familiar and such divorce-related arrangements are what typically come to mind when the word "custody" is heard.

The emphasis in this overview of the *custody* cluster of children-related public policy has been the "elephant in the room": state governments' automatic and almost-never-terminated assignment of custody to birth parents, an assignment of custody that is rarely, if ever, questioned and that, statistically speaking, dwarfs the sum total of all the other state and local government policies and activities in the *custody* sphere.

(2) *Schooling and Education*

"Schooling and education" is a second and particularly prominent cluster of state and local governments' children-related public policy. This cluster consumes more tax dollars, receives more sustained attention (today mostly in the form of hand-wringing and consternation—but perhaps that has always been so), and is probably considered by most people to be more important than any other.

The foundations of this public policy cluster are state laws that require children between approximately six and seventeen years of age to attend school or be guilty of truancy, i.e., unexcused failure to attend school while one is subject to compulsory attendance laws. Truancy regulations and laws can affix responsibility on both truant students and their parents. But legal responsibility mostly attaches to parents, who are subject to fines, temporary over-riding of custody, and, only very rarely and in the most extreme of circumstances, incarceration and involuntary termination of custody.

Besides mandating that children attend school or receive an alternative form of education (such as home schooling), state and local governments establish and maintain public schools beginning with kindergarten (attended by children aged approximately five) and running through grade 12 (attended by students who are typically 17 or 18). These public schools are free of charge to those who attend, enroll more than 80% of all American children aged five to 18, and are financed by tax revenues. The remaining children mostly attend private schools, about 80% of which have some religious affiliation, and a growing number—though still less than 1%—are educated through what has come to be known as "home schooling," wherein parents assume responsibility for educating their children and are subject to state regulations and testing regimes that vary widely among the states. State governments' oversight of home schooling can range from the simple requirement that a parent declare the intention to home school his or her child to the provision of required curricula and tests by state education authorities.

The operation of public schools costs taxpayers more than $600 billion a year, a sum greater than that spent on almost any other U.S. government function. Control and funding of public schools are shared among local, state, and national governments. The autonomy and funding roles of school districts, the special-purpose units of local government that every state except Hawaii uses to govern and administer public schools, vary from state to state. But the unmistakable trend in the past half-century has been toward greater state control and state financing of public schools, less autonomy and less funding responsibility for school districts, and an increasing curricular and funding role for the national government. "No Child Left Behind," important and controversial national legislation enacted in 2001 with the backing of President George W. Bush, has contributed to more standardized testing of K-12 children and growing use of those test results in evaluations of teachers, principals, and schools; in allocation of funding; and sometimes in decisions to close particular schools.

This children-related policy cluster of *schools and education* includes both provision of early childhood education and training (e.g., Head Start) and after-school care and, as already mentioned, schooling or education provided in private schools and home-schooling. It also includes so-called charter schools, which are schools that have received a "charter" from a specified government authority to operate and, in turn, receive public funds. Relevant procedures and authorizing agencies for charter schools vary from state to state. Big city mayors, specified colleges and universities, state government charter school commissions, and even existing school districts are among the authorizing government agents for charter schools in different states. Typically charter schools have relatively small enrollments and they often purport to have a particular focus that distinguishes them from regular public schooling. That focus or angle might be a particular emphasis on character or moral training; immersion in a foreign language; a curricular specialty such as art, music, math, science, or drama; or an innovative or experimental approach to teaching and learning. The charter school movement has been picking up steam and approximately 3% of all American children aged 5 to 18 attend charter schools today. Along with the increase in home schooling and voucher systems, the growing charter school movement is probably the most visible manifestation of the "school choice" phenomenon that has gained prominence and credibility in recent decades and continues to gather support from both the public and government policy-makers.

Notwithstanding private schools, charter schools, home schooling, and the growth of the school choice movement, the nation's approximately 15,000 school districts continue to be mainstays in the *schooling and education* cluster of children-related public policy. Most school districts are headed by elected school boards (or "boards of education") consisting of five to nine part-time, unpaid community members. Each of these boards is, formally speaking, the superior of a full-time professional educational administrator known as a "superintendent." In theory, superintendents run school districts on a day-to-day basis according to the policies of the governing school board. In practice, however, superintendents are almost always far more autonomous from their nominal school board superiors than the formal organizational chart would suggest.

The power and authority of superintendents vis-à-vis their school boards stem from superintendents' full-time professional status (the majority of superintendents hold doctorates in education); the deference paid to them by school board members, organizational subordinates, and parents because of their experience—they have typically worked their way up through the ranks of teacher, principal, and the like, and are assumed to have considerable professional expertise about schooling and education; and their having been licensed by their state department of education to be a superintendent (often as a result of their earning a doctorate in education). In the majority of school districts across the country, there is a noteworthy status gap between the superintendent and most of his or her board members. Board members, on average, have less formal education and earn lower incomes, and they almost always have far less expertise in curricula, testing, and other educational matters. It is the unusual school district in which a superintendent is unable to parlay these advantages into a position of power and authority that belies his or her formal status as a subordinate to the *de jure* governing entity, the school board.

Two features of the way governments in the United States provide and govern public schooling are particularly noteworthy. First, "local control" of public education through school districts remains an article of faith among most Americans. The growing roles of state and national governments continue to reduce and limit the reality of local control, but national, state, and local government officials and the public at large continue to pay lip service to this historic ideal. Second, the separation of local public school governance from governance of other local functions provided by general-purpose local governments such as cities, towns, townships, and villages is striking. In the language of organizational theory and public administration, this structural separation of local public school governance from general-purpose local government significantly inhibits rational "cross-functional" resource allocation. In other words, prevailing local government structures in the United States typically prevent local government officials from shifting resources from policing, sewerage and water provision, mass transit, road maintenance, and the like to public schooling, or vice versa.

Americans, including state and local government officials, seem mostly to accept these structural arrangements as if they were the only way to proceed. The role of school districts in governing public education is essentially unique to the United States, even if, as already noted, appointed superintendents typically dominate local public school governance and the autonomy of school districts from state and even national government educational and financial mandates or incentives is declining. Moreover, the powerful role of the fifty state governments in providing public education—instead of having, in essence, a national public school system—is also worthy of note. The, until recently, minimal role of the national government in public education may well stem from the country's having a federal system of government in which the fifty states play important governing roles. Canada and Australia are two other geographically large, English-speaking, industrialized countries with federal structures similar to that of the United States, although they have much smaller national populations. In both of those nations, provincial (Canada) and state (Australia) governments play central roles in school governance.

(3) *Restricted Access* by Children to Specified Activities and Objects

This cluster refers to state and local government restrictions on children's access to particular material substances and images and on their participation in specified activities. The relevant public policies discriminate between children and adults in that governments restrict children's access to specific items and activities while allowing adults either unfettered—or at least significantly less restricted—access to the same items and activities. State and local government policies make a clear distinction between children and adults with respect to these matters, which, of course, is the very essence of children-related public policy.

Alcohol and tobacco are two familiar substances to which children are mostly denied legal access, even as adults are mostly free to buy, possess, and consume them in the United States. Some qualifications are necessary, however. In 46 states, 18-year-olds are legally entitled to tobacco access, while four states restrict access to those nineteen and over. As a result of national legislation enacted in 1984 that mandated that highway funds be withheld from states with a legal alcohol age of less than 21, all 50 states restrict purchase of alcohol by those under 21, although a good number of states allow those under 21 to consume alcohol in specified circumstances (e.g., in their family homes in the company of their parents).

Children's access to pornographic and sexually explicit materials and performances—books, magazines, movies, videos, strip clubs, and the like—are another element in this policy cluster. The "adult bookstore" billboards that one sees on Interstate highways reflect state laws that forbid such establishments from allowing children access to the sexually explicit materials for sale. Typically, anyone under the age of 18 is forbidden to enter such premises, with owners or sellers punishable by law if they do not bar children.

In what sorts of *activities* are adults legally free to engage while children are not? The most noteworthy and important answer is probably sexual activities. "Statutory rape" is a crime wherein an adult engages in sexual intercourse with a child (variously defined as someone under 18, someone under 16, etc.), whether consensual or not. Other sexual contact by adults with children is also criminal for the adult involved—fondling, touching, etc. For sexual intercourse between adults to be rape, one party to the intercourse must not have given consent. When sexual intercourse or other sexual activities occur between adult and child, however, the consent of the child is irrelevant in the eyes of the law.

In the context of contemporary American society, eligibility to acquire a driver's license is another conspicuous and, in the lives of many teenagers, highly significant children-related public policy in this *restricted access* cluster. In most of the United States children who have reached the age of 16 or thereabouts are eligible to acquire driver's licenses, which means that *older* children (i.e., those aged 16 and 17) can legally drive while *younger* children cannot. In recent decades, systems of graduated driver's licenses have come into effect in most states—systems whereby newly licensed drivers under the age of 18 face restrictions on *when* they can drive (driving after dark is typically restricted), *with whom* they can drive (in some states only parents or family members may ride with a newly licensed driver and in some states only a limited number of children may ride with a newly licensed driver), and even *where* they can drive (New York City is off-limits to licensed drivers under 18 unless they have acquired what New York State calls a "senior driver's license," for which 17-year-olds are eligible only under certain circumstances).

Another activity in which children may not legally engage is "running away from home" or some variant thereof. In this context, the difference in reaction of police officers to reports of missing children and missing adults is worth noting. A report of a missing *child* brings almost immediate and energetic police response (consider AMBER Alerts); a missing *adult* report, unless there is good reason to believe that the missing adult has been abducted, has been injured or become sick, or in some other respect is thought to be in harm's way, typically brings a much less immediate and proactive police response.

This policy cluster is called "*restricted access* by children to specified activities and objects," and local government curfews for children fit under this heading. Except at times of civil unrest (e.g., after urban race riots and protests broke out in particular cities in the tumultuous 1960s), adults are free to walk the streets or sidewalks, ride public transportation, and engage in similar activities at any time of day or night. In contrast, some local government jurisdictions establish and enforce curfews for children, that is, restrict the times at which children can be on the streets or sidewalks or even outside their homes. Such curfews might extend from 11 p.m. to 7 a.m. on the five nights a week that precede school days. Fitting curfews under this policy cluster involves framing them as restrictions of children's access to streets, sidewalks and the like during specified hours.

A minor, even trivial, variant of—or perhaps distant cousin to—local government curfews is the practice of local governments specifying appropriate times for door-to-door trick-or-treating on Halloween. It seems inconceivable, of course, that any local government would apprehend children (or their parents) who engaged in trick-or-treating outside the stipulated hours. In Greencastle, Indiana, the small city where I live and where I have observed this practice for years, the officially prescribed hours have seemed to control and channel almost all trick-or-treat soliciting by children. Moreover, when it rained heavily on October 31, 2013, the city of Greencastle and many other Indiana local governments alertly postponed, so to speak, Halloween for 24 hours, delaying children's trick-or-treating until the evening of November 1.

(4) The *Juvenile Justice* System

The state and local government criminal justice system includes courts in which adults are formally processed and tried as well as prisons and jails wherein convicted criminal offenders are incarcerated. Paralleling the criminal justice system is the *juvenile justice* system, whose differences from the adult criminal justice system vary from state-to-state, but whose essential function is to process children who engage in behaviors that breach the criminal law. In its landmark decision *In re Gault* (1966), the U.S. Supreme Court ruled that basic constitutional safeguards—so-called due process protections—that shape and constrain the (adult) criminal justice system also apply to the juvenile justice system. Lying at the heart of the *juvenile justice* cluster of children-related public policy is the practice of treating accused juvenile offenders differently and separately from adult defendants. Both the institutions and procedures for processing juveniles *and* the institutions and objectives that come into play for juvenile offenders differ from those that apply to adults; moreover, many behaviors that are specified to be juvenile offenses are different from the criminal behaviors relevant to adults.

Notwithstanding the *Gault* decision and subsequent rulings, juvenile justice systems process children under somewhat different rules (e.g., "closed" courtroom proceedings are the norm) and sometimes in "juvenile courts" that specialize in processing children accused of criminal behavior. Moreover, "juveniles" (i.e., children) are usually not sent to the same prisons as adults. Children judged to be "juvenile delinquents" and in need of detention are sent to "reform schools" and other such institutions in which only youthful offenders live.

At least in theory, the juvenile justice system is intended to isolate and rehabilitate delinquent children, not to punish them. Different states use different ages to distinguish between those eligible for processing in the juvenile justice system and in the adult criminal justice system, and almost all states allow for transfer of "older" juveniles (sometimes as young as ten or twelve) to the adult criminal justice system for particular crimes and in particular circumstances. The age used to distinguish juvenile and adult offenders varies from jurisdiction to jurisdiction and according to offense.

(5) Provision of *material resources*

While under American state laws children generally do not and cannot own things in the way that adults do, this cluster of children-related public policy includes those government programs in which the adults with custody of children receive material benefits targeted for their children.

Temporary Assistance to Needy Families (TANF) is the national government's signature "welfare" program that in 1997 replaced the Aid to Families with Dependent Children (AFDC) program enacted as part of the New Deal. TANF operates through bloc grants to state governments, which are responsible, within national government guidelines, for determining the specifics of eligibility, amounts of assistance, and so forth. TANF belongs in the *material resources* cluster of children-related public policy because, with a few exceptions, only families with children under 18 are eligible for assistance. In other words, poor families with children receive welfare benefits and the intended beneficiaries are the dependent children living in the household. TANF is a hybrid state-national government program, whose state government component warrants its inclusion in this overview of state and local government children-related public policy.

Tax breaks (that is, tax deductions, exemptions, or credits) for "dependent children" are another policy mechanism intended to provide material benefits for children. Consistent with the rationale of TANF, income earners who have children pay less income tax, with the intended objective of making additional funds available to help parents provide for their children. While tax exemptions or tax credits for dependent children are most significant in federal income tax, they apply in many state income tax schemes as well.

As these two examples suggest, the roles of state and local governments in providing material benefits to children play out in the context of administering or implementing programs of the national government or in stand-alone state and local government programs. To be sure, state governments can and do add funds to increase the material benefits afforded to families of children eligible for welfare assistance and, within limits, they can and do shape eligibility requirements. Even so, in this particular cluster of children-related policy, state and local governments play somewhat secondary, even though still significant, roles.

Conclusion

I began this article with a quotation from then-Governor of Arkansas Bill Clinton telling an audience in 1991 that "Governments do not raise children—people do." Five years later, Hillary Rodham Clinton, when she was First Lady, published a book on children and child-rearing entitled *It Takes a Village*. (2) The title came from a traditional African proverb, "It takes a village to raise a child," and the book emphasized the idea that more than parents are necessary in raising children. In 2005, Rick Santorum—then a U.S. senator and in 2012 a contender for the Republican presidential nomination—countered Hillary Clinton's book with one of his own, tellingly entitled *It Takes a Family*. (3)

The differences between the two books are important. Clinton's "village" includes a "host" of grown-ups, in addition to parents, who play a role in children's lives: "grandparents, neighbors, teachers, ministers, employees, political leaders, and untold others who touch . . . [children's] lives directly and indirectly." (4) In Clinton's view, governments are only part of the village mix, and she makes clear that "parents bear the first and primary responsibility for their sons and daughters." (5) Santorum, however, suggests that Clinton sees her metaphorical village as "society as a whole—influenced by, directed by, supported by the supposed goodness of the Bigs in general and big government in particular." (6) Taking pains to distinguish his perspective from what he considers Clinton's "top-down" approach to raising children, he anchors his analyses and prescriptions in the family, which he considers the fundamental unit in society, and repeatedly mentions the negative and "liberal" influence of "village elders" in American child-raising today.

Despite their differences, Hillary Clinton and Santorum agree on the primary responsibility of parents in raising children. Moreover, despite Clinton's reliance on the concept of "village" throughout her analysis and the primacy that Santorum accords the family, both authors repeatedly address the significant roles of *governments* in raising children.

Policies relating to and shaping the "next generation" of Americans—that is, today's children—lie at the forefront of what state and local governments do. While state and local governments perform a number of functions—they operate criminal justice systems; provide or regulate the provision of water, power, sewerage, and trash removal services; provide roads and public transport; and so forth—no state and local government function seems more important and consequential than the five clusters of children-related public policy identified in this article.

For all the new concerns and responsibilities that the three levels of American governments—and especially the national government—have embraced over the course of more than two centuries of American history, children-related public policy seems destined to remain critically important. In this policy sphere, the national government seems likely, by and large, to continue to play second fiddle to state and local governments.

Notes

I want to thank Kelsey Kauffman, who teaches at Martin University in Indianapolis, for her careful reading of a draft of this article and for her valuable suggestions about how to improve it.

1. As quoted in Matt Bai, "The Clinton Referendum," *The New York Times Magazine,* 23 December 2007, p. 45.
2. Hillary Rodham Clinton, *It Takes a Village* (New York: Simon & Schuster, 1996).
3. Rick Santorum, *It Takes a Family: Conservatism and the Common Good* (Wilmington, Delaware: ISI Books, 2005)
4. Clinton, p. 5.
5. Clinton, p. 4.
6. Santorum, p. 66.

Critical Thinking

1. Which of the five clusters of children-related public policy do you think is most important in affecting the lives of children?
2. Which one of Hillary Rodham Clinton's "village" or Rick Santorum's "family" do you think is more important in American children's lives today?
3. How important a role do governments, especially state and local governments, play in American children's lives today?

Create Central

www.mhhe.com/createcentral

Internet References

Children's Defense Fund
www.childrensdefense.org
First Focus
www.firstfocus.net
Focus on the Family: Parenting
www.focusonthefamily.com/parenting.aspx

Article

Prepared by: Bruce Stinebrickner, *DePauw University*

One Size Doesn't Fit All

Rick Hess's big new school reform idea is that no big new school reform idea works everywhere.

STEVEN M. TELES

Learning Outcomes

After reading this article, you will be able to:

- Evaluate Rick Hess's theory about what makes schools succeed or fail and what is needed for successful education.

- Assess the validity of Rick Hess's view that two ways have been used to address the diversity and conflict that are inherent in public education in the United States, "democracy" for the less well-off and "freedom" for the well-to-do.

Since arriving at the American Enterprise Institute in 2002, Rick Hess has become the de facto education spokesman for respectable, reality-based conservatives. His new book, *The Same Thing Over and Over Again: How School Reformers Get Stuck in Yesterday's Ideas,* is as close as the feverishly productive Hess is ever likely to get to a genuine magnum opus. No one will be shocked that a scholar at AEI has a lot to say that will infuriate liberal defenders of the educational status quo. The book's real surprise is that he is perfectly willing to take on the sacred doctrines of conservative education reformers, arguing that some of them may actually be hampering the process of educational innovation.

Much of what we now accept as fundamental, almost definitional, aspects of schools—that a school must be a wholly geographically based institution, for example—was a "makeshift response to the exigencies of an earlier era," says Hess. Standard "chalk and talk" schooling made sense for a basically agrarian, small-town nation in which communications and transportation were slow and expensive and schools could rely on an army of talented, underpaid women who had few job opportunities outside of teaching, nursing, and secretarial work. The length of the school day is another relic of a time when relatively few women worked outside the house. Today it makes little sense that most schoolchildren are let loose at three P.M. when their parents often don't get home from work until the dinner hour. Our current model is increasingly obsolete in a society where demand for high-skilled labor has accelerated, the population has become urbanized, and young people are as comfortable

communicating virtually with people around the world as they are with someone at the front of the class.

Almost all efforts at major education reform over the last few decades have been compromised by the failure to recognize this obsolescence. School districts have accepted (if sometimes reluctantly) demands for higher teacher preparation standards, additional Advanced Placement classes, and a greater focus on the "core" subjects of math, science, English, and history. But more radical changes—such as replacing teachers with technology, using a global labor pool, or hiring a lower-paid staff—face much fiercer opposition. This has led reformers, for all their good intentions, to simply add more rules and regulations over existing ones. The result is an accumulation of claims on institutional time and resources which makes for an increasingly resentful bureaucracy and schools that have become unmanageable.

It isn't just the school districts and teacher's unions that resist systemic change. Interests as varied as school construction firms, textbook publishers, summer camps, and amusement-park owners (whose survival depends in part on America's relatively long summer vacations) have a powerful stake in the maintenance of outdated educational practices.

All this because most of us have difficulty imagining schooling occurring outside of a single, physical place led by a full-time, salaried professional who teaches students organized by age-appropriate grades. Even more prosaic are the physical constraints of our existing schools, in which the practices of the past are often quite literally bolted in place. Challenging these deeply embedded practices would require the kind of institutional and physical creative destruction—comprehensive, systemic change from the inside out—for which even the most enthusiastic of reformers may lack the stomach.

As a result, advocates for better education have repeatedly latched on to a depressing litany of fads as the panacea for what ails American education. Believing that they have only a short window of opportunity for change, these reformers push for their ideas to be applied uniformly across the board. "New math," standardized testing, centralization, merit pay, small schools, community control, mayoral control, and dozens of other ideas have ripped through schools, often with disappointment and disillusion not far behind.

Many of these ideas actually did have some merit, says Hess, in the sense that they could help some specific students in some specific circumstances. For example, a rigorous focus on a narrow set of tested subjects may be reasonable for schools in chaotic, urban contexts where simply focusing on *anything* counts as success. But that treatment, like chemotherapy, has powerful side effects that should not be risked on the (relatively) healthy "patients" in more advantaged school districts.

The same can be said about the often-furious conflict over pedagogical practices. From the start, there should have been more discussion about what style of teaching or curriculum fits the needs of particular students, rather than the establishment of a one-size-fits-all model. Instead, we have seen wave after wave of disappointment, as some promising changes have been overapplied and not worked as advertised. Which, in turn, paves the way for the next overapplied fad, creating another cycle of failure and disillusionment.

Hess is a refreshing change from many other analysts who hold forth on the subject of education. He is unafraid to take on flaws even in policies he largely supports—such as merit pay, school choice, and greater competition, which, he says, were at once oversold and misunderstood.

But the most critical lesson from the book is Hess's powerful theory about what makes schools succeed or fail. That theory, simply put, is that the basic components of schooling—parents, children, school leaders, and teachers—are irreducibly diverse. Parents have different ideas about what a "well-educated" child is, and children differ quite significantly in temperament, aptitude, habits, and interests. School leaders vary as to how they think schools should be run, while teachers have different skill levels, enthusiasm for different tasks, and ideas about what children should learn and know.

Successful education requires alignment between these four groups. Educators will always be less effective if they are made to teach in a way that they believe is wrongheaded or that they haven't bought into. Students will have difficulty learning if they are forced to work at a pace that is too fast or too slow, or if they are taught in a manner that doesn't match their individual learning styles. Parents can be disengaged or hostile if the pedagogy, discipline, or school culture differ fundamentally from what they think is right for their child. And schools as a whole will be incoherent and disorganized if they cannot count on some baseline of agreement as to what—and who—the school is for.

The implications of this simple set of assumptions are profound. If you take them seriously, almost every aspect of schooling—how students are assigned to schools, who teaches and how they are trained, where and when teaching and learning occurs, who provides education and who regulates it, and, most radically, how disagreements are settled—must be called into question.

For almost the entire span of America's experiment with universal education, we have had two ways of dealing with the diversity and conflict that are inherent in public education. For those without substantial mobility or means, that approach has been democracy: parents and other interested community members argue about what schools should do, and then the majority determines what plans will be put into place. Parents and their children can either accept what they are given or organize through the political system for change.

Persons with means and mobility, however, have a different set of educational options: they can try to match their preferences and attributes to a public jurisdiction they think is appropriate; they can supplement public schools with other educational experiences in order to bring their children's education closer to their preferences; or they can opt out of public schools entirely and place their children in private schools. The preferences of the well-to-do thus are aggregated through the classically liberal mechanisms of choice and markets, while those without such means must content themselves with majoritarian, democratic mechanisms.

One takeaway of Hess's argument is that, where education is concerned, democracy is distinctly inferior to liberty. The basic issues we fight over in education, he suggests, are not susceptible to definitive settlement. We will never agree on the question of what it means to be truly educated, because this is a matter of principle and preference rather than science. We will never be able to come up with a single model of schooling that works for everyone, because the needs and habits of students differ so dramatically. The reforms most likely to creative vibrant, creative organizations are those that are most freely consented to—those in which students, parents, teachers, and school leaders are all on the same page, because they have agreed in advance on the fundamentals.

The basic issues we fight over in education are not susceptible to definitive settlement. We will never agree on the question of what it means to be truly educated, because this is a matter of principle and preference rather than science.

Rather than aggressively imposing a single set of best practices on all schools, then, Hess argues for narrowing the scope of choices that are made by majorities, and increasing those made by smaller, self-chosen groups of common sentiment. Policy changes that insist on one way of compensating, training, and recruiting teachers, one way to use the school day or year, one way of organizing classrooms or defining what should go on in them—regardless of how they try to establish this uniformity—are steps in the wrong direction. "The frustrating truth," Hess tells us, "is that there are no permanent solutions in schooling, only solutions that make sense in a given time and place.

"Rather than education reform again being, as in the 1980s, a matter of prescriptive state policies on teacher ladders and additional course requirements, or as in the 2000s, a matter of accountability systems and mandated interventions in low-performing schools," he continues, "perhaps it is time for an agenda that creates room for problem solvers rather than prescribing solutions." Much the same thing could be said about other reform favorites, such as the adoption of Common Core State Standards (a set of standards now approved, as of this writing, by forty-three states and the District of Columbia), a greater use of standardized tests, and "value-added" metrics of teacher effectiveness and merit pay. These may be great ideas in particular places and with certain groups of students. But we cannot be presumptuous enough to assume that they will work in all the nation's schools.

The key to effective reform, Hess concludes, is ridding ourselves of the pipe dream that dramatically improved schools are just one silver bullet away. Instead of doubling down on a particular set of supposedly research-driven "best practices," we should hedge our bets by allowing radical new models of schooling and eccentric and unproven ideas to gain entry into the system—while resisting any force, be it public, private, or philanthropic, that would foist a new orthodoxy on a system which has already seen far too many of them.

Critical Thinking

1. What is Rick Hess's fundamental theory about "what makes schools succeed or fail"?

2. What, according to Hess, is needed for successful education?

3. What are the two ways that have been used to deal with the diversity and conflict related to education since the early days of public schools in the United States? Which, for Hess, is the better of the two ways?

4. What is, for Hess, the key to effective educational reform?

Create Central

www.mhhe.com/createcentral

Internet References

The Common Core Kool-Aid (Rick Hess, "Straight Up," *Education Week*, November 23, 2013)
http://blogs.edweek.org/edweek/rick_hess_straight_up/2012/11/the_common_core_kool-aid.html?utm_source=twitterfeed&utm_medium=twitter&utm_campaign=Walt+Gardner+Reality+Check
Frederick M. "Rick" Hess profile (American Enterprise Institute)
www.aei.org/scholar/frederick-m-hess

STEVEN M. TELES is associate professor of political science at the Johns Hopkins University and the author most recently of *The Rise of the Conservative Legal Movement.*

From *Washington Monthly*, March/April 2011, pp. 43–45. Copyright © 2011 by Washington Monthly Publishing, LLC, 1319 F St. NW, Suite 710, Washington DC 20004. (202)393-5155. Reprinted by permission. www.washingtonmonthly.com

Article   Prepared by: Bruce Stinebrickner, *DePauw University*

License to Kill

Immunity for Stand Your Ground shooters. Packing heat in bars. Gun permits for wife beaters. How radical gun laws spawned by a band of NRA lobbyists and Florida politicians have spread nationwide.

ADAM WEINSTEIN

Learning Outcomes

After reading this article, you will be able to:

- Assess the pros and cons of Stand Your Ground laws.

- Put the controversial and much-discussed shooting of Trayvon Martin by George Zimmerman in 2012 into broader perspective.

- Determine whether you are inclined to support or oppose NRA and American Legislative Exchange Council positions on gun control and related issues.

The Florida law made infamous this spring by the killing of unarmed teenager Trayvon Martin was conceived during the epic hurricane season of 2004. That November, 77-year-old James Workman moved his family into an RV outside Pensacola after Hurricane Ivan peeled back the roof of their house. One night a stranger tried to force his way into the trailer, and Workman killed him with two shots from a .38 revolver. The stranger turned out to be a disoriented temporary worker for the Federal Emergency Management Agency who was checking for looters and distressed homeowners. Workman was never arrested, but three months went by before authorities cleared him of wrongdoing.

That was three months too long for Dennis Baxley, a veteran Republican representative in Florida's state Legislature. Four hurricanes had hit the state that year, and there was fear about widespread looting (though little took place). In Baxley's view, Floridians who defended themselves or their property with lethal force shouldn't have had to worry about legal repercussions. Baxley, a National Rifle Association (NRA) member and owner of a prosperous funeral business, teamed up with then-GOP state Sen. Durell Peaden to propose what would become known as Stand Your Ground, the self-defense doctrine essentially permitting anyone feeling threatened in a confrontation to shoot their way out.

Or at least that's the popular version of how the law was born. In fact, its genesis traces back to powerful NRA lobbyists and the American Legislative Exchange Council (ALEC), a right-wing policy group. And the law's rapid spread—it now exists in various forms in 25 states—reflects the success of a coordinated strategy, cultivated in Florida, to roll back gun control laws everywhere.

Baxley says he and Peaden lifted the law's language from a proposal crafted by Marion Hammer, a former NRA president and founder of the Unified Sportsmen of Florida, a local NRA affiliate. A 73-year-old dynamo who tops off her 4-foot-11 frame with a brown pageboy, Hammer has been a force in the state capital for more than three decades. "There is no more tenacious presence in Tallahassee," Gov. Jeb Bush's former chief of staff told CNN in April. "You want her on your side in a fight."

Ever since neighborhood watch volunteer George Zimmerman shot Trayvon Martin point-blank in the chest, the term Stand Your Ground has been widely discussed, but what does it really mean? A *Mother Jones* review of dozens of state laws shows that the concept is built on three planks from the pioneering Florida legislation: A person claiming self-defense is not required to retreat from a threat before opening fire; the burden is almost always on prosecutors to prove that a self-defense claim is *not* credible; and finally, the shooter has immunity from civil suits relating to the use of deadly force. While the so-called Castle Doctrine (as in "a man's home is his") has for centuries generally immunized people from homicide convictions if they resorted to deadly force while defending their home, Florida's law was the first to extend such protection to those firing weapons in public spaces—parking lots, parks, city streets.

Stand Your Ground was shepherded through the Legislature with help from then-state Rep. Marco Rubio and signed into law by Bush on April 26, 2005. It was the "first step of a multi-state strategy," Wayne LaPierre, a long-standing NRA official who is now the group's CEO, told the *Washington Post*. "There's a big tailwind we have, moving from state legislature to state legislature. The South, the Midwest, everything they call 'flyover land.'" The measure was adopted as model legislation by ALEC, a corporate-sponsored national consortium of lawmakers—which is how it ended up passing in states from Mississippi to Wisconsin. "We are not a rogue state," says Baxley, who was bestowed with the NRA's Defender of Freedom Award shortly before his bill passed. "But we may be a leader."

Supporters of such laws cite the slippery-slope argument: Seemingly reasonable regulations—waiting periods, licenses, limits on assault weapons and high-capacity magazines—inevitably lead to ever-stricter measures, they argue, until citizens' constitutional right to defend themselves against government tyranny has vanished. Hammer suggests that an assault on gun rights motivated her move to Tallahassee from her native South Carolina in 1974: "Florida was seeing what I would call a burst of gun control measures being filed by Northerners who had moved to South Florida," she told a radio interviewer in 2005. "There was so much gun control being filed that it was very difficult for the NRA to deal with it from over 1,000 miles away."

After leaving work late one night in the mid-1980s, Hammer claims, a group of men in a car threatened her, only to be scared off when she pulled a gun on them. No police report was ever filed, but Hammer maintains that shortly after this incident a local police chief told her that she could have been arrested had she shot them. It was a convenient tale. She soon became a driving force behind Florida's "shall issue" legislation, passed in 1987, which stripped authorities of the ability to deny a concealed-weapons permit to someone they consider potentially dangerous. The law would allow thousands of ex-convicts and spouse beaters to pack heat; a Florida state attorney called it "one of the dumbest laws I have ever seen." A 1988 investigation by the *St. Petersburg Times* found permits had been given to two fugitives with outstanding arrest warrants, a disgraced cop who'd been convicted of a DUI and turned down for a county gun license, a man charged with fondling an eight-year-old girl, and a dead man. Florida has since issued more than 2 million concealed-weapons permits.

That same year Hammer called a panel of Florida legislators "a modern-day Gestapo" for considering legislation to keep guns away from violent criminals and the mentally ill. ("This is the lowest standard of integrity I have ever seen for a lobbyist in Tallahassee," one pro-gun Republican responded at the time.)

But Hammer's efforts really picked up steam when she served as the NRA's first female president from 1995 to 1998—by the end of which time Bush had been elected governor and the GOP had taken firm control of the Statehouse. Hammer and her allies have since barred city and county governments from banning guns in public buildings; forced businesses to let employees keep guns in cars parked in company lots; made it illegal for doctors to warn patients about the hazards of gun ownership (this controversial "Docs versus Glocks" law was overturned by a George W. Bush-appointed federal judge); and secured an exemption to Florida's celebrated open-records laws in order to keep gun permit holders' names a secret. (Baxley had cosponsored a similar bill, explaining in its original text that such lists had been used "to confiscate firearms and render the disarmed population helpless in the face of Nazi atrocities" and Fidel Castro's "tyranny.")

As Florida became known to some as the "Gunshine State," it began exporting its laws, with ALEC's help, to other statehouses. This effort was no doubt aided by the fact that the vice president of Hammer's Unified Sportsmen of Florida is John Patronis, cousin to Republican state Rep. Jimmy Patronis—sponsor of the aforementioned bill that kept names of concealed-weapons license holders secret and ALEC's current Florida chairman. The organization would also be instrumental to spreading Stand Your Ground nationwide. "We definitely brought that bill forward to ALEC," said Baxley, a member of the group. "It's a place where you can share ideas. I don't see anything nefarious about sharing good ideas." The NRA has served as "corporate co-chair" of ALEC's Public Safety and Elections task force, which pushed Stand Your Ground and other gun laws. Since 2005, the year Florida's law was passed, gun manufacturers like Beretta, Remington, and Glock have poured as much as $39 million into the NRA's lobbying coffers.

Baxley defends the NRA's involvement: "They have lots of members who want this statute. They're people who live in my district. They're concerned about turning back this lawless chaos and anarchy in our society." Records show that the NRA's Political Victory Fund has long supported Baxley—from a $500 contribution in 2000 (the state's maximum allowable donation) to $35,000 spent on radio ads in support of his state Senate bid in 2007. Peaden received at least $2,500 from the NRA and allied groups over the years. The NRA also maxed out on direct contributions to Jeb Bush's gubernatorial campaigns in 1998 and 2002, and it gave $125,000 to the Florida GOP between 2004 and 2010—more than it gave to any other state party. According to the Center for Media and Democracy, the NRA spent $729,863 to influence Florida politics in the 2010 election cycle alone.

Once fairly open to speaking with the media, Hammer has proved elusive since the Trayvon Martin killing. When I approached her for this story, explaining that I was a third-generation gun collector with a Florida carry permit, she declined to comment on the record. "Unfortunately," she wrote in an email, "if you did a truly honest article on the law, it would either never be printed in *Mother Jones,* or if they did publish it, it would not be believed by the mag's audience!"

A climate of fear helped spread Stand Your Ground, according to the National District Attorneys Association. In 2007, it conducted the first in-depth study on the expansion of the Castle Doctrine and found that it took root in part because "there was a change in perceptions of public safety after the terrorist attacks of 9/11. Many citizens . . . became concerned that government agencies could not protect every citizen in the event of subsequent terror attacks." Indeed, the NRA used 9/11 to promote its legislative agenda, most notably in its unsuccessful push to let all commercial airline pilots pack heat. "What would have made 9/11 impossible?" LaPierre asked a crowd at the 2002 NRA convention in Reno, Nevada. "If those pilots on those four airplanes had the right to be armed."

Steven Jansen, vice president and CEO of the Association of Prosecuting Attorneys and a former prosecutor in Detroit, was one of the study's authors. He first noticed the Stand Your Ground movement in early 2006 when it spread from Florida to Michigan, sponsored there by Republican state Sen. Rick Jones, an ALEC member. The law was "troublesome to me," Jansen told me. "We didn't really see a public safety need for it, and it could only muddy the legal waters."

With a confrontation like the one between Trayvon Martin and George Zimmerman, cops and prosecutors would now be forced to make judgment calls about which participant felt like he was in more peril. That raised serious questions about whether real-world situations would ever be as clear-cut as the lawmakers assumed. Jansen pointed to scenarios ranging from road rage to scuffles between rival fraternities: "To presume from the outset, as Florida's law arguably does, that a deadly response in these situations is justified would be at best irresponsible; at worst, that assumption could create a new protected set of behaviors that might otherwise be considered hate crimes or vigilantism."

But legislators across the country nevertheless ignored objections from law enforcement. Indeed, Stand Your Ground gives armed civilians rights that even cops don't enjoy: "Society hesitates to grant blanket immunity to police officers, who are well-trained in the use of deadly force and require yearly testing of their qualifications to carry a firearm," Jansen has written. "Yet the expansion of the Castle Doctrine has given such immunity to citizens."

Back when Florida passed Stand Your Ground, a few legislators did raise concerns. "This could be two gangs, deciding to have a fight in the street in Miami," said then-Rep. Jack Seiler, a Democrat from South Florida. "They both have a right to be standing on Biscayne Boulevard." It was a prescient warning. In 2006, a Miami man avoided prosecution after spraying a car filled with gang members with 14 bullets. In 2008, a 15-year-old Tallahassee boy was killed in a shoot-out between rival gangs; two of the gang members successfully took refuge behind Stand Your Ground.

The cumulative effect of those cases has been staggering: Two years after Stand Your Ground passed in Florida, the number of "justifiable homicides" by civilians more than doubled, and it nearly tripled by 2011. FBI statistics show a similar national trend: Justifiable homicides doubled in states with Florida-style laws, while they remained flat or fell in states that lacked them. (**Update, 6/11/12:** A new study from Texas A&M University shows that SYG laws result in no crime deterrence—while adding 500 to 700 homicides per year nationally across the 25 states with the laws.) Jansen also notes that research has shown that, when it came to domestic-abuse cases, "the only thing Stand Your Ground did was blur the lines between who was the batterer and who was the victim."

He says the laws have been passed without legislators asking basic questions: What, exactly, makes a fear of imminent harm reasonable? Do the laws have a disparate negative effect on minorities or juveniles? And, perhaps the simplest question: "Is it worth losing a life over a car radio?"

That's happened, too. In Miami, a man was granted immunity in March for chasing down a burglar and stabbing him after the thief swung a bag of stolen car radios at him. He "was well within his rights to pursue the victim and demand the return of his property," the judge ruled. A state attorney for Miami-Dade County disagreed: "She, in effect, is saying that it's appropriate to chase someone down with a knife to get property back."

For now, Florida has deemed that it is indeed appropriate, and polls taken after the Martin killing show that half of voters agree. But outrage over that case (as well as ALEC's push for voter ID laws;) has cost ALEC prime corporate sponsors—including McDonald's, Coca-Cola, Pepsi, Kraft, and Procter & Gamble—and its tax-exempt status has been challenged by Common Cause. In April, ALEC disbanded the panel that pushed Stand Your Ground and redirected funds to "task forces that focus on the economy."

But Hammer and her allies are still pressing for laxer gun laws. This spring, Hammer got Florida to drop the cost of gun permits and lower the age restriction to 17 for military members, and she's still fighting to allow residents to carry their guns openly. And the NRA is pumping millions into the November elections nationally. "America needs us now more than ever as we gather together as one in the most dangerous times in American history," LaPierre told the NRA's annual convention in St. Louis in April. "By the time I finish this speech, two Americans will be slain, six women will be raped, 27 of us will be robbed, and 50 more will be beaten. That is the harsh reality we

---

Safety Off

Since 2005, Florida lawmakers have taken aim at gun control with a barrage of deregulation measures:

- Requiring employers to let employees keep guns in their cars while at work
- Requiring city and county governments to allow guns in public buildings and parks
- Lifting a long-standing ban on guns in national forests and state parks
- Allowing military personnel as young as 17 to get concealed-weapons licenses. (Age limit remains 21 for everyone else.)
- Withholding the names of concealed-carry licensees in public records
- Permitting concealed-carry licensees "to briefly and openly display the firearm to the ordinary sight of another person." (The original bill would have allowed guns on college campuses, but it was amended after a GOP lawmaker's friend's daughter was accidentally killed with an AK-47 at a frat party.)
- Prohibiting doctors from asking patients if they keep guns or ammo in the house unless it's "relevant" to their care or safety. (Overturned by a federal judge.)
- Allowing legislators, school board members, and county commissioners to carry concealed weapons at official meetings. (Didn't pass; another bill to let judges pack heat "at any time and in any place" died in 2009.)
- Designating a day for tax-free gun purchases. (Didn't pass.)
- Exempting guns manufactured in Florida from any federal regulations. (Didn't pass.)

face every day." With an unabashed reference to the shooting that brought Stand Your Ground to national attention, LaPierre drove home his point. "But the media, they don't care. Every-day victims aren't celebrities. They don't draw ratings and sponsors, but sensational reporting from Florida does."

Critical Thinking

1. What is a "Stand Your Ground" law and what roles did the NRA and the American Legislative Exchange Council play in such laws being enacted in 25 states between 2005 and 2011?

2. What do FBI statistics show, according to Adam Weinstein, about the incidence of justifiable homicides in states with "Stand Your Ground" laws and those without them?

3. What measures related to deregulating gun control in Florida were enacted or proposed by Florida legislators since 2005?

Create Central

www.mhhe.com/createcentral

Internet References

American Legislative Exchange Council (ALEC)
www.alec.org
Brady Campaign to Prevent Gun Violence
www.bradycampaign.org
National Rifle Association (NRA)
www.home.nra.org

Weinstein, Adam. From *Mother Jones,* July/August 2012, pp. 45–47, 65. Copyright © 2012 by Mother Jones. Reprinted by permission of the Foundation for National Progress.

Article   Prepared by: Bruce Stinebrickner, *DePauw University*

The Conservative War on Prisons

Right-wing operatives have decided that prisons are a lot like schools: hugely expensive, inefficient, and in need of root-and-branch reform. Is this how progress will happen in a hyper-polarized world?

DAVID DAGAN AND STEVEN M. TELES

Learning Outcomes

After reading this article, you will be able to:

- Assess the reasons why prison reform is occurring and determine whether you support the reform efforts.

- Evaluate the suggestion that the prison reform story holds lessons applicable to other policy areas.

American streets are much safer today than they were thirty years ago, and until recently most conservatives had a simple explanation: more prison beds equal less crime. This argument was a fulcrum of Republican politics for decades, boosting candidates from Richard Nixon to George H. W. Bush and scores more in the states. Once elected, these Republicans (and their Democratic imitators) built prisons on a scale that now exceeds such formidable police states as Russia and Iran, with 3 percent of the American population behind bars or on parole and probation.

Now that crime and the fear of victimization are down, we might expect Republicans to take a victory lap, casting safer streets as a vindication of their hard line. Instead, more and more conservatives are clambering down from the prison ramparts. Take Newt Gingrich, who made a promise of more incarceration an item of his 1994 Contract with America. Seventeen years later, he had changed his tune. "There is an urgent need to address the astronomical growth in the prison population, with its huge costs in dollars and lost human potential," Gingrich wrote in 2011. "The criminal-justice system is broken, and conservatives must lead the way in fixing it."

None of Gingrich's rivals in the vicious Republican presidential primary exploited these statements. If anything, his position is approaching party orthodoxy. The 2012 Republican platform declares, "Prisons should do more than punish; they should attempt to rehabilitate and institute proven prisoner reentry systems to reduce recidivism and future victimization." What's more, a rogue's gallery of conservative crime warriors have joined Gingrich's call for Americans to rethink their incarceration reflex. They include Ed Meese, Asa Hutchinson,

William Bennett—even the now-infamous American Legislative Exchange Council. Most importantly, more than a dozen states have launched serious criminal justice reform efforts in recent years, with conservatives often in the lead.

Skeptics might conclude that conservatives are only rethinking criminal justice because lockups have become too expensive. But whether prison costs too much depends on what you think of incarceration's benefits. Change is coming to criminal justice because an alliance of evangelicals and libertarians have put those benefits on trial. Discovering that the nation's prison growth is morally objectionable by their own, conservative standards, they are beginning to attack it—and may succeed where liberals, working the issue on their own, have, so far, failed.

This will do more than simply put the nation on a path to a more rational and humane correctional system. It will also provide an example of how bipartisan policy breakthroughs are still possible in our polarized age. The expert-driven, center-out model of policy change that think-tank moderates and foundation check-writers hold dear is on the brink of extinction. If it is to be replaced by anything, it will be through efforts to persuade strong partisans to rethink the meaning of their ideological commitments, and thus to become open to information they would otherwise ignore. Bipartisan agreement will result from the intersection of separate ideological tracks—not an appeal to cross them. This approach will not work for all issues. But in an environment in which the center has almost completely evaporated, and in which voters seem unwilling to grant either party a decisive political majority, it may be the only way in which our policy gridlock can be broken.

Republicans' rhetorical campaign against lawlessness took off in earnest during the 1960s, when Richard Nixon artfully conflated black rioting, student protest, and common crime to warn that the "criminal forces" were gaining the upper hand in America. As an electoral strategy, it was a brilliant success. But as an ideological claim, the argument that America needed more police and prisons was in deep tension with the conservative cause of rolling back state power.

The paradox flared up occasionally, as during the National Rifle Association's long-running feud with the Bureau of Alcohol, Tobacco and Firearms during the 1990s. But for the most part, conservatives lived with the contradiction for forty years. Why?

For one, it worked political magic by tapping into a key liberal weakness. Urban violent crime was rising sharply during the 1960s and liberals had no persuasive response beyond vague promises that economic uplift and social programs would curb delinquency. The conservatives' strategy also provided an outlet for racial anxieties that could not be voiced explicitly in the wake of the civil rights movement. Sometimes, the racial appeals were impossible to miss, as when Ronald Reagan warned that "city streets are jungle paths after dark" in his 1966 California gubernatorial campaign. More often, anti-criminal chest-thumping played into the division of society between the earners and the moochers, with subtle racial cues making clear who belonged on which side.

Meanwhile, the more threatened ordinary Americans came to feel, the angrier they became at elites who appeared to side with the criminals, and the more they revered the people designated as society's protectors. As a result, conservatives came to view law enforcement the same way they had long seen the military: as a distinctive institution whose mission somehow exempted it from the bureaucratic failures and overreach that beset school districts, environmental agencies, and the welfare office. Yet the two surging wings of the conservative movement—libertarians and religious conservatives—have since each found their own reasons to challenge long-standing orthodoxy about crime.

Antitax activist Grover Norquist appeared last year at a Washington confab on criminal justice billed as the "Last Sacred Cow" briefing. For years, Norquist said, conservatives were too busy rolling back government extravagances to worry about the workings of essential operations like crime control. But conservatives can no longer afford to direct their critique of government only at their traditional targets, he told his audience. "Spending more on education doesn't necessarily get you more education. We know that—that's obvious. Well, that's also true about national defense. That's also true about criminal justice and fighting crime."

Once you believe that prisons are like any other agency, then it is natural to suspect that wardens and prison guards, like other suppliers of government services, might submit to the temptations of monopoly, inflating costs and providing shoddy service. And, of course, conservatives have long made such arguments to justify their pet project of bidding out incarceration to for-profit businesses. But the prisons-as-government critique has acquired a new force that makes the privatization debate almost irrelevant. Far from shilling for corporate jailers, conservatives now want to shrink the market. "We certainly don't need to be building new prisons, whether they're public or private," said Marc Levin, an analyst at the conservative Texas Public Policy Foundation. The American Legislative Exchange Council, long a proponent of privatizing prisons, no longer has an official position on that issue (nor does it have any prison corporations left as members). Instead, it is pushing bills that would reduce prison populations. For fiscal hawks, the point

now is not to incarcerate more efficiently or profitably, but to incarcerate less. They are making that leap with a boost from two other camps: evangelicals and experts.

Over the last two decades, religious conservatives have increasingly come to see prisoners as people worthy of compassion and capable of redemption. "These people have committed crimes, but they're still human beings, created in the image of God. Can we help them restore what's left of their lives?" asks Tony Perkins, president of the Washington, D.C.-based Family Research Council. Perkins has doubted the efficacy of incarceration since serving as a guard in a Louisiana lockup as a young man. Though that experience also made him skeptical of jailhouse conversions, Perkins said, religious outreach behind bars has the benefit of making prisoners seem like real people—much as the pro-life movement has done with unborn children. "As more and more churches are involved in prison ministries, they begin the process of rehumanizing the criminal."

Meanwhile, the tide of professional opinion is turning away from what had been a depressing consensus that warehousing prisoners was the best society could do. For many years, the hope that "rehabilitation" could change people's behavior was dismissed as a liberal fantasy. The role of prisons was much simpler: to incapacitate reprobates and deter opportunists. The dean of this school of thought, former Harvard and University of California, Los Angeles, professor James Q. Wilson (who died this year), put it like this: "Many people, neither wicked nor innocent, but watchful, dissembling, and calculating of their chances, ponder our reaction to wickedness as a clue to what they might profitably do." Social service approaches to criminal "wickedness" not only did not work, but they symbolized a society unwilling to stand up against violations of the law. Increase incarceration, conservatives argued, and potential criminals will get the message.

But in recent years, experts in criminal justice have become more optimistic about alternatives to prison. A promising example is Hawaii's Opportunity Probation with Enforcement (the HOPE program, now hopscotching to other states; see Mark A. R. Kleiman, "Jail Break," *Washington Monthly*, July/August 2009). HOPE has been shown to significantly cut drug offending by hitting users who are on parole or probation with swift, certain, and moderated sanctions, such as a few days of jail time, rather than arbitrary and draconian parole revocations. New technologies from rapid-result drug tests to GPS monitoring have also bred optimism, and professionals are even beginning to feel better about their ability to predict an offender's risk of recidivism. Because these approaches emphasize control more than therapy, they don't seem squishy or soft on crime, even as they make it easier to let criminals out of prison.

The world has also changed in ways that favor fresh thinking. In the 1990s, Democrats diluted the Republican electoral advantage on crime by pushing their own set of tough measures. Then Arkansas Governor Bill Clinton oversaw the execution of a brain-damaged convict during his 1992 presidential campaign, and once elected president he pushed through a cast-iron crime bill that combined longer sentences, restrictions on gun purchases, and more cops on the street. While the subsequent drop in crime gave the GOP fodder to argue that punitive poli-cies work, it has also drawn the venom out of the issue. And since the 1990s, terrorism has displaced crime as the nation's top security preoccupation and honeypot for law-and-order zealots. If you consider all these issues together, it makes sense that conservatives have more space to rethink their positions on crime. And so, with jailers newly suspect, inmates ripe for redemption, and alternative discipline ascendant, conservatives have decided prisons are a lot like schools: hugely expensive, inefficient, and in need of root-and-branch reform.

Such second thoughts are creating the first significant open-ing in years for a criminal justice overhaul. Neither Repub-licans nor Democrats can reform the system alone given the continuing fear of being tarred with the "soft on crime" label, said Gene Guerrero, a policy analyst at the Washington office of George Soros's Open Society Foundations. It can only hap-pen, he said, "if there is real leadership from both sides and if the reforms are developed and move forward on a bipartisan basis."

Still, it's conservatives who bring the most muscle to the job. A handful of liberal organizations have valiantly kept alive the argument for reform even through the dark days of the 1980s and '90s—places like the American Civil Liberties Union, Open Society Foundations, and the Public Welfare Foundation. By and large, however, it is conservative institutions who now pay the most attention to criminal justice, Guerrero said. In rare cases, Democratic politicians have proved willing to take up the cause, as when Michigan Governor Jennifer Granholm directed an overhaul of that state's parole system during her first term—though her second-term push for broader reform legislation fizzled (see Luke Mogelson, "Prison Break," *Washington Monthly*, November/December 2010). But most Democrats are still terrified of appearing timid before voters and are therefore loath to lead the way. At best, they can be persuaded to go along if the right gives them cover.

The right's belated awakening to America's incarceration crisis may seem little more than an obvious extension of liber-tarian and socially conservative philosophies. But logic rarely determines how movements put together their various ideo-logical commitments. Making and changing positions is tough, entrepreneurial political work, especially when long-held, elec-torally successful ideas are being called into question.

Few people have done as much to subvert the conservative orthodoxy on crime as Pat Nolan, a former California state legislator who now works at the jailhouse ministry Prison Fellowship. Called "the most important person to make any of this happen" by Julie Stewart of Families Against Man-datory Minimums, Nolan has been so effective as a revisionist precisely because he was weaned on the traditional politics of law and order.

Nolan grew up in LA's Crenshaw Boulevard neighborhood during the 1950s. "Everyone in my family and all of our neigh-bors had been victims of crime," says Nolan. "I came from a family that was pretty pro-police, feeling as [though] they were kind of beleaguered." When his family moved to nearby Bur-bank, Nolan signed up for the Police Explorers, a group for kids interested in law enforcement careers. He also joined Young Americans for Freedom, the conservative activist group that ral-lied behind Barry Goldwater in 1964. As a Republican Califor-nia state assemblyman in the 1970s, '80s, and '90s, Nolan helped push through some of the nation's most draconian sentencing laws. While he did visit prisons to investigate conditions there, he recalls, "I was very much the 'We need more prisons' type."

That changed after Nolan got to see prison from the other side of the bars. In 1993, Nolan was indicted on seven counts of cor-ruption—including accusations that he took campaign money to help a phony shrimp-processing business the FBI dreamed up as part of a sting. He ultimately accepted a plea deal and was sentenced to thirty-three months in prison for racketeer-ing. Nolan maintained his innocence, but said he would take the plea to avoid the risk of longer separation from his family. Before he left, Nolan recalls, a friend told him, "View this time as your monastic experience"—a chance to follow generations of Christians who have retreated from daily life to work on their faith. Nolan, who is Catholic, resolved to follow that advice.

While Nolan was locked up, a mutual acquaintance put him in touch with Chuck Colson, the biggest name in prison min-istry. Colson, a former Nixon aide, had gone to the clink for Watergate-related crimes and experienced what he described as a religious transformation behind bars. After his release in 1975, Colson founded Prison Fellowship, which provides reli-gious services and counseling to inmates and their families. By the time Colson died this past April, he had become a star in the evangelical community, rubbing shoulders with the likes of Billy Graham, Rick Warren, and James Dobson.

Nolan enrolled his kids in a Prison Fellowship program for children of inmates and began corresponding with Colson. Even before Nolan got out, he had an offer to run the group's policy arm, which had been languishing.

"I'd really been praying about, 'Okay, Lord, what's the next chapter in my life?'" Nolan recalls. "I'd seen so much injustice while I was inside that I felt I really wanted to address that. My eyes had been opened." Nolan is devoting the rest of his life to opening the eyes of his fellow conservatives, getting them to see the tragic cost of putting so many Americans under lock and key.

When Nolan first arrived in Washington, the only real foothold reformers had in the conservative move-ment was with a small band of libertarians at places like the Cato Institute and *Reason* magazine, who objected to the prohibitionist overreach of the drug war but were treated as wildly eccentric by mainstream conservatives. To find allies with unquestioned right-wing credentials, Nolan prospected among two groups with whom he had credibility: evangeli-cals who admired Prison Fellowship, and his old friends from Young Americans for Freedom, some of them longtime crime warriors themselves.

Colson had already persuaded evangelicals that prisoners were appropriate objects of personal compassion, but had yet to find an angle that would convince the faithful that the criminal justice system was fundamentally flawed. Nolan hit upon two perfect issues in short order.

The Supreme Court opened the first window in 1997 by striking down most of a federal law intended to expand the religious freedoms of prisoners. The specter of wardens putting bars between inmates and God energized social conservatives. Prison Fellowship threw itself into the fight, and a revised law was passed in 2000.

Around the same time, Reagan administration veteran Michael Horowitz was casting about for a cause to show that conservatives have a heart. Previously known for his advocacy on issues like human trafficking and peace in Sudan, Horowitz decided to make protecting the victims of prison rape the next step in what he called his "Wilberforce agenda," after the famous British evangelical abolitionist.

Prison rape was a natural issue to express conservatives' humanitarian impulses. Evangelicals who think homosexuality is immoral can easily be persuaded that homosexual rape under the eyes of the state is an official abomination. More importantly, Horowitz had put his finger on a nightmare of massive proportions. Human Rights Watch had gathered evidence suggesting an epidemic of torture to which many wardens were turning a blind eye. Last May, the U.S. Justice Department estimated that more than 209,000 prisoners suffered sexual abuse in 2008 alone.

Horowitz proposed a bill designed to have cross-partisan appeal, with provisions for penalizing lagging states and shaming recalcitrant wardens. Evangelicals were sold right away. "Everyone has basic human rights, even if they are being dealt with and sanctioned for inappropriate social behavior, and prison should not take those away," the Southern Baptist Ethics and Religious Liberty Commission's Shannon Royce would explain to the *Washington Post*.

Horowitz focused on negotiations with a skeptical Justice Department and state corrections officials, while Nolan worked the corridors of the Capitol. The Prison Rape Elimination Act passed both houses of Congress unanimously in 2003.

Nolan then used this big win as a springboard to an issue where the moral lines were more blurred: helping released prisoners adjust to life back home and stay out of trouble by pumping money into "reentry" programs. Republican Congressman (and now Senator) Rob Portman agreed to champion legislation that would become known as the Second Chance Act. President George W. Bush endorsed the idea in his 2004 State of the Union Address, after lobbying by Prison Fellowship and Portman's office, according to Nolan. Hammering out the bill took several more years, but the Second Chance Act was finally passed with solid conservative backing in 2007.

These measures all had bipartisan support, but they were not the product of centrists: the top Senate backers of the Prison Rape Elimination Act were Ted Kennedy and Alabama's Jeff Sessions, who spent a dozen years as a tough-as-nails U.S. attorney and is ranked the Senate's twelfth most conservative member by the *National Journal*. Liberal reformers did bargain with conservatives behind the scenes—the biggest example was an agreement that the Second Chance Act remain silent on funding faith-based reentry programs. But Nolan's conservative allies were confident that bipartisan reform efforts brokered by Prison Fellowship would remain consistent with conservative principles, thanks to groundwork laid by the previous religious freedom and prison rape efforts.

Even as the Second Chance Act edged forward, Nolan was tapping old friendships to pull together more conservative dissenters. David Keene—then head of the American Conservative Union, now president of the National Rifle Association—was tracking post-9/11 encroachments on civil liberties and turning a wary eye to criminal justice. Richard Viguerie, a direct mail pioneer in the conservative movement, was a longtime death penalty opponent. Nolan began calling them for advice. Soon, antitax activist Norquist was being looped into the conversations, as was Brian Walsh, a Heritage Foundation analyst who studied the rapid expansion of federal criminal law. The group started holding regular meetings to brainstorm ideas. They toyed with proposing a federal criminal law retrenchment commission similar to the base-closure commission of the 1990s, or pushing congressional judiciary committees to demand jurisdiction over any bills that created new crimes.

Despite all of Nolan's progress, it soon became obvious that the juice on criminal justice reform would not come from Washington. The real potential lay in the states, where a combination of fiscal conservatism and budget pressure was beginning to crack the status quo. The opportunity to turn those tremors into a full-blown earthquake would come from a very unlikely place.

"Don't Mess with Texas" bumper stickers have long found their most extreme confirmation in the state's criminal justice system. Over the last two decades, Texas has been one of the most avid jailers in the nation. It was home to the largest prison-conditions lawsuit in American history, a thirty-year ordeal that infuriated conservatives and led them to plaster the state with posters calling for the impeachment of Judge William Wayne Justice. And of course, no prison cooks have taken as many last-meal orders as those in the Lone Star State—until officials recently did away with that perk for the condemned. But even as Texas continues to buff its toughest-on-crime reputation, it is also becoming, unexpectedly, a poster child for criminal justice reform.

It started in 2005, when Tom Craddick, the first Republican speaker of the state legislature in more than a century, appointed Jerry Madden, a conservative from Plano, to run the House Committee on Corrections. As Madden recalls, the speaker's charge to him was clear: "Don't build new prisons. They cost too much."

Madden was a corrections novice with a disarming, aw-shucks manner; his Senate counterpart, Democrat John Whitmire, was an old hand whose resume included being robbed at gunpoint in his garage. The greenhorn and the veteran soon agreed on what ailed the Texas criminal justice system: it was feeding on itself. Too many people flunked probation and went into prison. And too many prisoners committed new offenses shortly after being released, landing them back behind bars. To tackle the first problem, Madden and Whitmire suggested cutting loose veteran probationers who had proved reliable, thus allowing officers to focus their time on people at higher risk of screwing up. The legislature signed off, but Governor Rick Perry vetoed the bill.

At the start of the 2007 legislative session, legislative analysts predicted that Texas was on track to be short 17,700 prison beds by 2012 because of its growing inmate population. The Texas Department of Criminal Justice's response was to ask legislators to build three new prisons, but Madden and Whitmire had other ideas. Not only did they bring back a revamped version of their probation proposal—they also took aim at the revolving-door problem by cranking up funding for programs such as in-prison addiction treatment and halfway houses. This time, Perry relented (persuaded at least in part, the duo contends, by a high-stakes meeting they held with him shortly before the opening of the legislative session). Since then, the prison population has not increased, and last year, the TDCJ closed a prison for the first time in decades.

Budget shortfalls do not explain this shift. In 2007 Texas was basking in a huge projected surplus, and the Great Recession was still a year away. Instead, Madden and Whitmire had different winds at their backs. For one thing, the policy context favored reform. One legacy of the state's prison litigation trauma is that Texas has strict restrictions on overcrowding (unlike, say, California). Under Texas law, when the system approaches capacity, corrections staff must seek certification from the attorney general and the governor to incarcerate more prisoners. The approval process forces state leaders to confront the choice between more prisons and more diversion programming. The political environment had also changed since the GOP completed its takeover of state politics in 2003. As a longtime observer of the state's criminal justice notes, "Now . . . all the tough guys are Republicans. They don't want to be outdoing each other on this stuff."

Texas was not the first state to experiment with common sense. Several others had begun tinkering with their criminal justice systems in the wake of the 2001 recession. When the fiscal belt tightened on a swelling inmate population in New York, for example, corrections officials prevailed upon then Governor George Pataki to take steps leading to earlier releases. But none of these initiatives reverberated like the Texas reforms.

The Texas turnaround created a golden opportunity to rebrand prison reform nationally. "People think if Texas does something, by definition it's not going to be soft," said Adam Gelb, director of a criminal justice initiative at the Pew Charitable Trusts. "There's just this instant, deep credibility on the crime issue for Texas." In 2005, the Texas Public Policy Foundation (TPPF)—the state's premier conservative think tank—hired Marc Levin to become its first-ever crime wonk. The position was financed by Tim Dunn—a deeply conservative oilman, Republican donor, and Colson-inspired critic of the criminal justice system. Levin promptly threw himself into the Texas debates of 2005 and 2007, but his biggest contribution came later in building momentum for prison reform among conservatives across the country.

The TPPF is one of the most prominent members of the State Policy Network, which connects free-market think tanks in every state. Founded in 1992, the Arlington-based SPN zaps ideas—like Wisconsin-style restrictions on public employee pensions—from one member organization to another. Levin was and remains the only full-time crime analyst at any SPN member organization. As a result, he quickly became the go-to guy on the issue among state-level conservatives, fielding calls from curious colleagues, cowriting editorials and policy briefs, and making presentations at conservative conferences. Eventually, he decided to convert the effort into a formal campaign he called Right on Crime.

When Nolan heard about Right on Crime, he contacted Levin to offer his support—and his Rolodex. Nolan rounded up the members of his informal working group and other conservative luminaries to endorse a revised approach to crime control. Among the signatories: Keene, Viguerie, Gingrich, former Attorney General Ed Meese, and former drug czars Asa Hutchinson and Bill Bennett. Political scientist and long-time prison proponent John DiIulio is there, too, as is Grover Norquist. The Family Research Council's Tony Perkins and other social conservatives also signed on. Right on Crime backers say explicitly that their goal was to lend their reputations to the effort and give conservatives political cover to launch reforms. "We wanted to create an atmosphere in which, amongst conservatives, there would be total legitimacy," Nolan said.

Perhaps the surest sign that conservatives were embracing the new model came from the American Legislative Exchange Council—the conservative network of state legislators. In the 1990s, ALEC had peddled mandatory minimums, prison privatization, and the like to its members in statehouses across the country. But in 2007, ALEC hired Nolan's friend Michael Hough to run its criminal justice task force, and Nolan soon persuaded ALEC to endorse the Second Chance Act. Within a few years, the trio of Hough, Nolan, and Madden had brought ALEC to the point of pushing out model bills based on proposals borrowed from Gelb's criminal justice project at Pew, which has been dispatching teams of sentencing wonks to state capitals around the country to help reformers develop specific plans. All this work was done through the same ALEC committee whose advocacy for "stand-your-ground" laws prompted a backlash in the wake of the Trayvon Martin killing. ALEC announced in April that it would disband the committee, but, in fact, it ended up giving the panel a new mandate. The committee now focuses exclusively on sentencing reform and has dropped all of its unrelated model bills, from mandatory minimums to prison privatization, Hough said.

With conservatives less willing to defend the lock-'em-up status quo, prison reform now seems to have the momentum of an issue whose time has come. States from Kentucky to Pennsylvania to North Carolina have passed bipartisan criminal justice overhauls, preventing thousands of prison commitments. And the wave continues. In May, Georgia Governor Nathan Deal was on the verge of tears at a signing ceremony for legislation designed to keep nonviolent offenders out of prison. When his Ohio counterpart, John Kasich, signed a similar bill in June, he said it would "result in the saving of many, many lives."

To be sure, the new conservative critique has so far largely overlooked the most glaring problem in American criminal justice—its profound racial skew. African Americans account for some 40 percent of the U.S. prison population, three times their proportion of the general population. The liberal legal scholar Michelle Alexander, whose 2010 book compares mass incarceration with Jim Crow, argues that the system will only be dismantled with a return to 1960s-style movement politics.

But it is also important not to underestimate how much the emerging conservative reform movement can do. For starters, conservatives did step into the terrain of racial justice when they took the lead in 2010 to reduce the disparity in federal sentences for crack and cocaine offenses. And reframing criminal justice in terms of efficacy and cost has already prevented many thousands of unnecessary prison terms.

Moreover, this line of argument can also open the door to more radical critiques. Just listen to Tim Dunn. The conservative Texas oilman declaims that the "purpose of the criminal justice system should be to secure liberty and promote justice between people rather than to enforce the power of the state over the lives of its citizens." Or take Mark Meckler, co-founder of the Tea Party Patriots. "We're destroying a significant portion of our own population, especially in the inner cities," Meckler has written. Meckler and Dunn have appeared on MSNBC to endorse the work of David Kennedy, a liberal criminologist who has criticized the failure of the drug war in inner-city communities. And Meckler vows on his blog, "I'm all in on the fight for criminal justice reform here in the U.S."

The story of how conservatives began to change their positions on incarceration holds lessons far from the world of prisons. Advocates of policy change, their funders, and well-meaning pundits regularly bemoan the ideological stiffening that bedevils efforts at bipartisan cooperation. The usual answer to hyper-polarization is to somehow rebuild the center. But the power of party activists (especially on the right) to control primary elections and discipline politicians who step out of line is not going to go away anytime soon. The center, it seems, will not hold—in fact, it barely even exists anymore.

The lesson of the slowly changing politics of crime on the right is that policy breakthroughs in our current environment will happen not through "middle-path" coalitions of moderates, but as a result of changes in what strong, ideologically defined partisan activists and politicians come to believe is their own, authentically conservative or liberal position. Conservatives over the last few years haven't gone "soft." They've changed their minds about what prisons mean. Prisons increasingly stand for big-government waste, and prison guards look more and more like public school teachers.

This shift in meaning on the right happened mainly because of creative, persuasive, long-term work by conservatives themselves. Only advocates with unquestioned ideological bona fides, embedded in organizations known to be core parts of conservative infrastructure, could perform this kind of ideological alchemy. As Yale law professor Dan Kahan has argued, studies and randomized trials are useless in persuading the ideologically committed until such people are convinced that new information is not a threat to their identity. Until then, it

goes in one ear and out the other. Only rock-ribbed partisans, not squishy moderates, can successfully engage in this sort of "identity vouching" for previously disregarded facts. Of course, there are limits to how far ideological reinvention can go. As political scientist David Karol has argued, it is unlikely to work when it requires crossing a major, organized member of a party coalition. That's something environmentalists learned when they tried to encourage evangelicals to break ranks on global warming through the idea of "creation care." They got their heads handed to them by the main conservative evangelical leaders, who saw the split this would create with energy-producing businesses upon whom Republican depend for support.

But that still leaves plenty of issues on which bipartisanship will be possible—as long as it doesn't feel like compromise for its own sake. Defense spending, for example, is already being slowly transformed by the newly energized libertarian spirit in the Republican Party. On these matters, liberals are in a bind—while they may dearly long for partners on the right, they can't call them into being, and getting too close to conservative mavericks may tarnish their vital ideological credentials. In this confusing world where those on the extremes can make change that those in the center cannot, liberals will have to learn that they sometimes gain more when they say less.

Critical Thinking

1. How have the views on prisons of many influential conservatives, especially religious conservatives, changed over the past few decades?

2. Why have conservatives' views changed?

3. Why have conservatives' efforts at prison reform been more successful than earlier reform attempts by liberals?

Create Central

www.mhhe.com/createcentral

Internet References

The Chuck Colson Center for Christian Worldview
www.colsoncenter.org/wfp-home

Friend of HOPE (Hawaii's Opportunity Probation with Enforcement program)
http://hopehawaii.net/index.html

Right on Crime (a project of the Texas Public Policy Foundation in cooperation with Justice Fellowship)
www.rightoncrime.com

The Sentencing Project
www.sentencingproject.org/template/index.cfm

Smart on Crime
www.besmartoncrime.org/index.php

DAVID DAGAN is a doctoral student in political science at the Johns Hopkins University and a freelance journalist. **STEVEN M. TELES** is associate professor of political science at the Johns Hopkins and author of *The Rise of the Conservative Legal Movement*.

Dagan, David, and Teles, Steven M. From *Washington Monthly*, November/December 2012, pp. 25–31. Copyright © 2012 by Washington Monthly Publishing, LLC, 1319 F St. NW, Suite 710, Washington, DC 20004. (202) 393-5155. Reprinted by permission. www.washingtonmonthly.com

Article   Prepared by: Bruce Stinebrickner, *DePauw University*

Fixing the Rotten Corporate Barrel

States grant corporate charters; they should start taking some of them away.

JOHN CAVANAGH AND JERRY MANDER

Learning Outcomes

After reading this article, you will be able to:

- Assess the notion that contemporary global corporations are the dominant institutions of human activity.

- Evaluate whether state governments could and should make corporations that they charter more accountable.

The global corporations of today stand as the dominant institutional force at the center of human activity. Through their market power, billions of dollars in campaign contributions, public relations and advertising, and the sheer scale of their operations, corporations create the visions and institutions we live by and exert enormous influence over most of the political processes that rule us.

It is certainly fair to say, as David Korten and others have, that "global corporate rule" has effectively been achieved. This leaves society in the daunting position of serving a hierarchy of primary corporate values—expanding profit, hypergrowth, environmental exploitation, self-interest, disconnection from communities and workers—that are diametrically opposed to the principles of equity, democracy, transparency and the common good, the core values that can bring social and environmental sustainability to the planet. It is a basic task of any democracy and justice movement to confront the powers of this new global royalty, just as previous generations set out to eliminate the control of monarchies.

The first step in the process is to recognize the systemic nature of the problem. We are used to hearing powers that be—when faced with an Enron or WorldCom scandal—explain them away as simple problems of greedy individuals; the proverbial few rotten apples in the barrel; the exception, not the rule. In reality, the nature of the corporate structure, and the rules by which corporations routinely operate, make socially and environmentally beneficial outcomes the exception, not the norm.

Public corporations today—and their top executives—live or die based on certain imperatives, notably whether they are able to continuously attract investment capital by demonstrating increasing short-term profits, exponential growth, expanded territories and markets, and successful control of the domestic and international regulatory, investment and political climates. Questions of community welfare, worker rights and environmental impacts are nowhere in the equation. Given such a setup, Enron's performance, like most other corporate behavior—especially among publicly held companies—was entirely predictable, indeed, almost inevitable. Enron executives were only doing what the system suggested they had to do. Corporations that can successfully defy these rules are the rare good apples in an otherwise rotting barrel.

That such structural imperatives should dominate the global economic system and the lives of billions of people is clearly a central problem of our time; any citizens' agenda for achieving sustainability must be rooted in plans for fundamental structural change and the reversal of corporate rule.

New Citizen Movement

Around the world, the spectrum of anticorporate activity is broad, with strategies ranging from reformist to transformational to abolitionist. Reformist strategies include attempts to force increased corporate responsibility, accountability and transparency, and to strengthen the role of social and environmental values in corporate decision-making. Such strategies implicitly accept global corporations as here to stay in their current form and as having the potential to function as responsible citizens.

A growing number of activists reject the idea that corporations have any intrinsic right to exist. They do not believe that corporations should be considered permanent fixtures in our society; if the structural rules that govern them cannot be fixed, then we should seek alternative modes for organizing economic activity, ones that suit sustainability. These activists seek the death penalty for corporations with a habitual record of criminal activity. They also demand comprehensive rethinking and redesign of the laws and rules by which corporations operate, to eliminate those characteristics that make publicly traded, limited-liability corporations a threat to the well-being of people and planet.

Possibly the most visible and growing arm of this anticorporate movement is the one that focuses on the corporate charter, the basic instrument that defines and creates corporations in the United States. Corporations in this country gain their existence via charters granted through state governments. As the landmark research of Richard Grossman and Frank Adams of the Program on Corporations, Law and Democracy (POCLAD) has revealed, most of these charters originally included stringent rules requiring a high degree of corporate accountability and service to the community. Over the centuries corporations have managed to water down charter rules. And even when they violate the few remaining restrictions, their permanent existence is rarely threatened. Governing bodies today, beholden to corporations for campaign finance support, are loath to enforce any sanctions except in cases of extreme political embarrassment, such as has occurred with Enron, Arthur Andersen and a few others. Even then, effective sanctions may be few and small.

At the same time, corporations have obtained many rights similar to those granted human beings. American courts have ruled that corporations are "fictitious persons," with the right to buy and sell property, to sue in court for injuries and to express "corporate speech." But they have not been required, for the most part, to abide by normal human responsibilities. They are strongly protected by limited liability rules, so shareholder-owners of a corporation cannot be prosecuted for acts of the institution. Nor, in any meaningful sense, is the corporation itself vulnerable to prosecution. Corporations are sometimes fined for their acts or ordered to alter their practices, but the life of the corporation, its virtual existence, is very rarely threatened, even for great crimes that, if carried out by people in many states of the United States, might invoke the death penalty.

Of course, it is a key problem that these "fictitious persons" we call corporations do not actually embody human characteristics such as altruism or, on the other hand, shame—leaving the corporate entity literally incapable of the social, environmental or community ideals that we keep hoping it will pursue. Its entire structural design is to advance only its own self-interest. While executives of corporations might occasionally wish to behave in a community-friendly manner, if profits are sacrificed, the executive might find that he or she is thrown off the wheel and replaced with someone who understands the rules.

State charter changes could alter this. State corporate charter rules could set any conditions that popular will might dictate—from who should be on the boards, to the values corporations must operate by, to whether they may buy up other enterprises, move to other cities and countries, or anything else that affects the public interest. In Pennsylvania, for example, citizen groups have initiated an amendment to the state's corporation code that calls for, among other things, corporate charters to be limited to thirty years. A charter could be renewed, but only after successful completion of a review process during which it would have to prove it is operating in the public interest. In California a coalition of citizen organizations (including the National Organization for Women, the Rainforest Action Network and the National Lawyers Guild) petitioned the attorney general to revoke Unocal's charter. Citing California's own corporate code, which authorizes revocation procedures, the coalition offered evidence documenting Unocal's responsibility for environmental devastation, exploitation of workers and gross violation of human rights. While this action has not yet succeeded, others are under way.

Revoking a charter—the corporate equivalent of a death sentence—begins to put some teeth into the idea of accountability. Eliot Spitzer, Attorney General of New York, declared in 1998: "When a corporation is convicted of repeated felonies that harm or endanger the lives of human beings or destroy our environment, the corporation should be put to death, its corporate existence ended, and its assets taken and sold at public auction." Although Spitzer has not won a death sentence against a habitual corporate criminal, he has taken up battle with several giants, including General Electric.

Even if corporations were to be more tightly supervised, that would not be enough to change society. Such actions must be supported by parallel efforts to restore the integrity of democratic institutions and reclaim the resources that corporations have co-opted. But tough charters and tougher enforcement would be a start.

Alternatives

Names like Exxon, Ford, Honda, McDonald's, Microsoft and Citigroup are now so ubiquitous, and such an intimate part of everyday life, that it is difficult for many people in the industrial world to imagine how we might live without them. But there are hundreds of other forms of economic and business activity. And by whose logic do we need transnational corporations to run hamburger stands, produce clothing, grow food, publish books or provide the things that contribute to a satisfying existence?

Transition to more economically democratic forms becomes easier to visualize once we recognize that many human-scale, locally owned enterprises already exist. They include virtually all of the millions of local independent businesses now organized as sole proprietorships, partnerships, collectives and cooperatives of all types, and worker-owned businesses. They include family-owned businesses, small farms, artisanal producers, independent retail stores, small factories, farmers' markets, community banks and so on. In fact, though these kinds of businesses get very little government support, they are the primary source of livelihood for most of the world's people. And in many parts of the world—notably among agricultural and indigenous societies—they are built into the culture and effectively serve the common interest rather than the favored few. In the context of industrial society, the rechartering movement and the parallel efforts to eliminate "corporate personhood" and exemptions from investor liabilities are important steps in a similar direction, seeking to alleviate the dominance of institutions whose structural imperatives make it nearly impossible for them to place public interest over self-interest.

Critical Thinking

1. What, according to some political observers and activists, is the "dominant institutional force" at the center of contemporary human activity?

2. What is a corporate charter and who grants corporate charters?

3. What rights have courts granted to corporations, and what requirements or responsibilities have *not* been imposed?

4. What could state governments do to shape corporations' behavior more than they currently do?

Create Central

www.mhhe.com/createcentral

Internet References

Corporations (Legal Information Institute, Cornell University Law School)

www.law.cornell.edu/wex/corporations

Our Hidden History of Corporations in the United States (Reclaim Democracy!)

http://reclaimdemocracy.org/corporate-accountability-history-corporations-us

SumOfUs: Fighting for People Over Profits

www.sumofus.org

JOHN CAVANAGH, director of the Institute for Policy Studies, and JERRY MANDER, president of the International Forum on Globalization, are authors, along with seventeen others from around the world, of *Alternatives to Economic Globalization: A Better World Is Possible* (Berrett-Koehler), from which this article is adapted.

Article   Prepared by: Bruce Stinebrickner, *DePauw University*

Gagging on the Ag-Gag Laws

Jim Hightower

Learning Outcomes

After reading this article, you will be able to:

- Assess the pros and cons of ag-gag laws, whose interests they serve, and whose interests they undermine.

- Evaluate ag-gag laws in the context of the U.S. professed commitment to freedom of speech, property rights, and free enterprise.

In most state legislatures today, "bizarre" is not unusual. Still, it seems especially strange that legislators in so many states have simultaneously been pushing "ag-gag" bills that are not merely outrageous, but downright un-American. Each is intended to prevent journalists, whistleblowers, workers, and other citizens from exposing illegal, abusive, or unethical corporate treatment of animals confined in factory feeding operations.

Our nation's founders mounted a revolution to establish our constitutional right to a free press and free speech. Yet here come a mess of so-called conservatives using state governments to outlaw messengers who shine a light on corporate wrongdoing. Even kookier, these repressive laws declare that truth-tellers who so much as annoy or embarrass the corporate owner of the animal factory are guilty of "an act of terrorism."

Oddly, each of these state proposals is practically identical, even including much of the same wording. That's because, unbeknownst to the public and other legislators, the bills don't originate from the state lawmakers who introduce them, but instead come from the corporate front group named ALEC (the American Legislative Exchange Council). Lobbyists from the companies that fund ALEC periodically convene with rightwing state legislators to write "model" bills. The secretive ALEC network produced the ag-gag model in 2002, titling it the "Animal and Ecological Terrorism Act."

But the only terrorists in this fight are the soulless profiteers in the corporate suites and the cynical lawmakers who serve them.

Factory farms are not farms at all. They are corporate-run concentration camps for pigs, cows, chickens, turkeys, and other food animals.

Held in confinement, these creatures of nature are denied any contact with the great outdoors. Instead, they are crammed by the thousands into concrete-and-metal buildings where they are locked in torturously tiny cages for the duration of their so-called life, which is nasty, brutish, and short.

This is all so food giants like Tyson, Smithfield, and Borden can grab fatter and quicker profits. It's so disgusting that America's consumers would gag at the sight of it.

That's why the profiteers are desperate to keep you from knowing what goes on inside their factories. Nonetheless, word has been getting out as animal rights advocates, consumer groups, unions, and others have exposed some of the disgusting realities of animal confinement to the public.

Rather than cleaning up their act, however, the industrial food powers have simply doubled down on disgusting. Their lobbyists have been swarming state legislatures to demand passage of laws that would prosecute anyone who would reveal the industry's ugly secrets.

Six states have passed ag-gag laws, and six more are moving toward passage. (To see what's happening in your state, go to www.humanesociety.org.)

It's enough to make you gag.

Critical Thinking

1. What is an "ag-gag" law and whose interests do such laws serve? Whose interests do they not protect?

2. What has been the role of the American Legislative Exchange Council in enacting ag-gag laws in a number of states?

3. What are author Jim Hightower's perspectives on ag-gag laws?

Create Central

www.mhhe.com/createcentral

Internet References

American Legislative Exchange Council (ALEC)
www.alec.org

Anti-Whistleblower Laws Hide Factory-Farm Abuses from the Public (Humane Society of the United States)
www.humanesociety.org/issues/campaigns/factory_farming/fact-sheets/ag_gag.html#id=album-185&num=content-3312

The Hightower Lowdown
www.hightowerlowdown.org

Jim Hightower produces The Hightower Lowdown newsletter and is the author, with Susan DeMarco, of *Swim Against the Current: Even a Dead Fish Can Go with the Flow*.

Hightower, Jim. Reprinted by permission from *The Progressive*, June 2013, p. 46. Copyright © 2013 by The Progressive, 409 E Main St, Madison, WI 53703. www.progressive.org